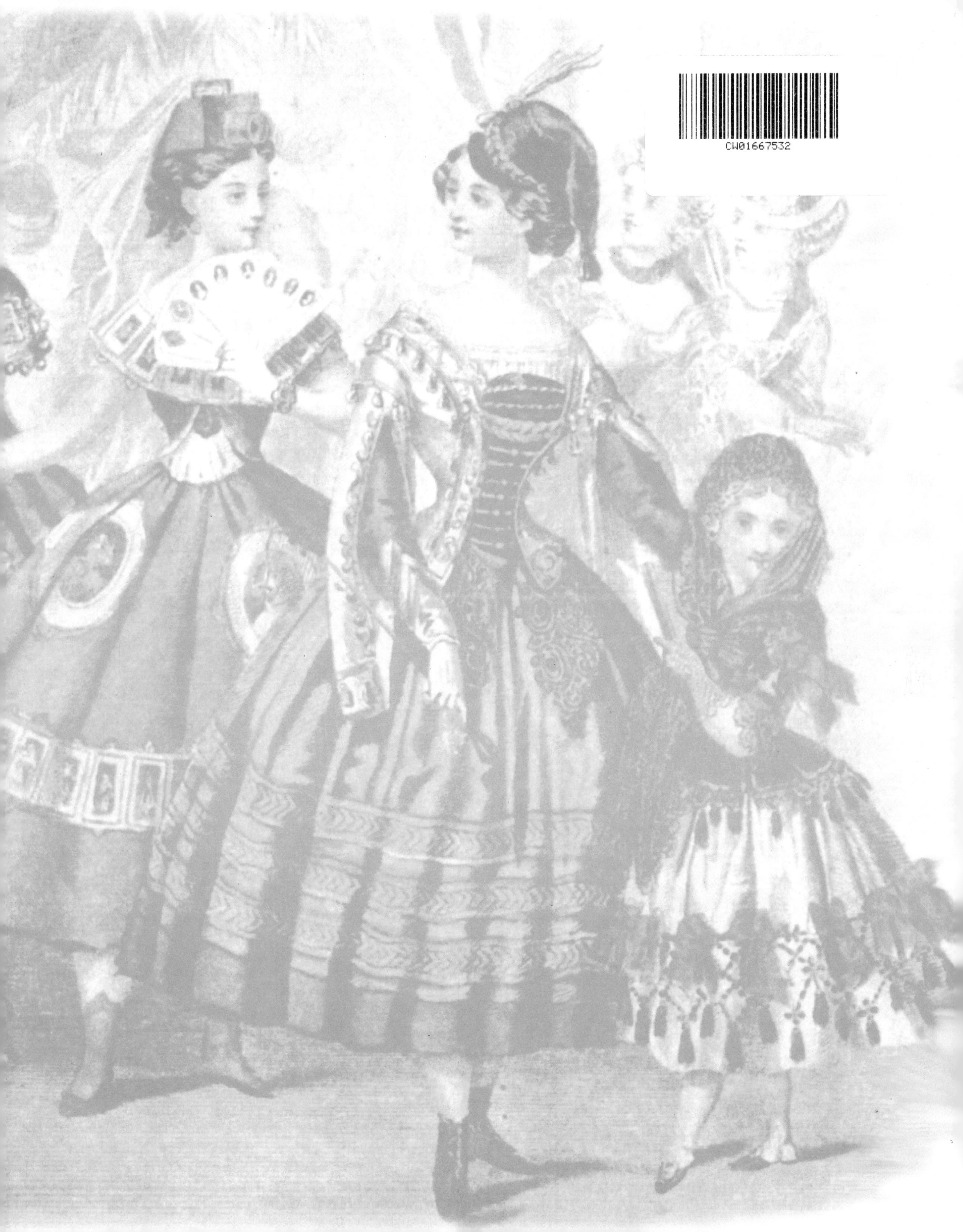

Magnificent Entertainments

Magnificent Entertainments

Fancy Dress Balls *of* Canada's Governors General
1876-1898

CYNTHIA COOPER

GOOSE LANE EDITIONS
and
CANADIAN MUSEUM OF CIVILIZATION

Published by Goose Lane Editions and the Canadian Museum of Civilization with the assistance of the Canada Council, the Department of Canadian Heritage, and the New Brunswick Department of Municipalities, Culture and Housing, 1997.

Edited by Laurel Boone.
Cover illustration: Mr. and Mrs. George Marler as "Francis I" and "Marguerite de Valois," 1898. NPA/MMCH/II-123159
Cover and book design by Julie Scriver.
Printed in Canada by Tri-Graphic Printing.
10 9 8 7 6 5 4 3 2

Canadian Cataloguing in Publication Data

Cooper, Cynthia, 1963-
Magnificent entertainments.
Co-published by the Canadian Museum of Civilization.
Includes bibliographical references.
ISBN 0-86492-187-X

1. Balls (Parties) – Canada – History – 19th century.
2. Canada – Social life and customs – 19th century.*
3. Costume. I. Canadian Museum of Civilization. II. Title.

FC88.C67 1997 793.3'8'097109034 C97-950159-8
F1021.C67 1997

Goose Lane Editions
469 King Street
Fredericton, New Brunswick
CANADA E3B 1E5

Canadian Museum of Civilization
100 Laurier Street
PO Box 3100, Station B
Hull, Quebec
CANADA J8X 4H2

For my father
Robert Edwin Henley Cooper
(1936-1995)

Contents

Foreword

Magnificent Entertainments: Fancy Dress Balls of Canada's Governors General, 1876-1898, Cynthia Cooper's fascinating glimpse into the lives of the rich and famous in *fin-de siècle* Canada, is, on one level, a good story about those most glamorous and important social events of the day: the vice-regal costume balls. Late nineteenth-century Canada was still in many ways a rough and ready society, but the vice-regal court represents the closest we would ever come to a gilded age. The guest lists for these quintessentially Canadian events included all the movers and shakers in political, commercial and social life. Each ball ignited great anticipation and anxiety, and the reader can feel the excitement mounting as the guests prepared for the big day: frenzied rehearsals, last-minute fittings and assembling of costumes, hair coiffed and wigs adjusted, carriages made ready. After the ball, everyone commemorated the occasion by having photographic portraits taken, and we meet the elite of Canadian society face to face throughout *Magnificent Entertainments*, their serious expressions an amusing contrast to their fanciful garb.

On another level, *Magnificent Entertainments* explores some of the most enduring themes in Canadian history, particularly French and English Canadian relations. This topic has preoccupied historiography, but here it is rendered in a new way: the political agenda was played out in the social arena, indeed, on the ballroom floor. The great majority of guests at the historical fancy dress balls in Ottawa and Montreal were costumed as characters from the *ancien régime*, with a sprinkling of British generals and United Empire Loyalists. At a time when the polarization of Canada along ethnic and language lines was most acute, we witness Wolfe and Montcalm dancing a farandole side by side at the Aberdeens' Ottawa ball. This was an ingenious way for the vice-regal court to pay tribute to French Canada, while at the same time following their primary mandate of encouraging patriotism and British imperial sentiment. The balls celebrated a romantic and glorious past peopled by noble savages, French explorers and aristocratic seigneurs, now happily faded into memory.

Although history books have mentioned the story of the vice-regal costume balls – usually in connection with the role of the Governor General – *Magnificent Entertainments* presents the topic in detail for the first time. By studying reams of newspaper accounts and advertisements, period photographs and personal anecdotes, Cynthia Cooper has uncovered the explicit and implicit motivations for the balls, the elaborate planning and execution of the costumes and theatrical presentations, and the impact of the balls on the Canadian public.

Magnificent Entertainments also gives us insights into the often contradictory aspects of Victorian culture. By the end of the nineteenth century, and despite a recession, many upper-middle-class Canadians enjoyed a financial stability that allowed them time and money for leisure pursuits. They took particular delight in social events, and the costume ball was the apex of the social season. But all was not frivolity. As Cynthia Cooper ably shows, the elite recognized the relationship between participation in social events and economic and political success. Moreover, the class that defined itself by a leisured lifestyle nevertheless had to guard against the stigma of triviality or extravagance, a fear which cast a pall over the planning for the balls. Imbuing these events with educational and uplifting aims allowed the Victorians to engage in fun with impunity.

In many ways, the activities and behaviours at the balls followed what we popularly think of as Victorian decorum, but the fancy costume element so intrinsic to these balls gave scope for the other side of nineteenth-century conventionalism. Dressing up allowed a restricted but nevertheless outwardly expressed sexuality. Parts of the body were revealed, such as women's ankles and long hair, which otherwise would be hidden or restrained. Men, particularly, could flaunt their sexuality in sartorial splendour. Many men chose to costume themselves in the eighteenth-century garb of knee breeches, tight stockings, flowing wigs and fine silks that provided a complete contrast to their customary drab suits. Likewise, the war-whooping, leaping Indians gave a freedom of masculine expression usually subdued.

The stated educational and patriotic aspirations of the ball organizers epitomized the seriousness and earnestness that we often associate with the Victorians. But I think a sense of playfulness runs through the accounts of the balls and escapes from the often serious photographs. The Victorians, perhaps because of a rigid conventionality, took great joy in incongruity. The visions of a Chinese mandarin escorting an Indian princess had a hilarious streak which we can appreciate today.

Lastly, *Magnificent Entertainments* is about clothing, that most immediate and complex of our cultural expressions. As a costume historian, Cynthia Cooper presents a detailed study of fancy dress – an overlooked but very revealing aspect of the history of apparel. There has been active interest and scholarship in the history of Canadian dress over the last twenty-five years. The subject has been treated by various disciplines; folk culture has contributed to the documentation of ethnic dress, and anthropology has contributed to our understanding of the relationship between the environment and aesthetics in Native clothing and to cross-cultural exchange.

Historian have occasionally chosen topics in economic history that relate to clothing or textiles, but they tend to rely on documentary materials for evidence, to the exclusion of the actual clothing itself. Students in graduate clothing and textile science departments and in college design programmes have produced papers on western fashion which include object analysis. Museum curators have contributed the results of detailed examinations of costume collections. These visual studies often chart changes in fashion over time, with some contextualizing of the political, economic and social realities of the period. Occasionally, costume research provides critical insights into the relationship between dress and society. Cynthia Cooper's book falls into this last category, and she has taken an important step further by siting her analysis of costume within a very distinct historical context. *Magnificent Entertainments* does not just describe costume, but analyzes its meaning at a particular time and place.

The study of fancy dress may appear to be an incidental adjunct to conventional fashion scholarship, but it is actually a very powerful tool for understanding the significance of clothing. Fancy dress makes possible a heightened sense of personal identity and communication. In making conscious decisions about what type of costume to wear for the balls, the guests revealed much about the roles and images they wished to project. Some individuals appear to have been acting out personal fantasies, as in the photographic costume portraits of Agar Adamson as the brooding "Napoléon" and Eugénie Duhamel as a vivacious "Vivandière." Many people, including the Dufferins and the Aberdeens, wisely and safely chose to identify with the nobility of a more stately and majestic era. Even political statements were embedded in costumes, as in the "Our Lady of the Snows" outfit worn by the daughter of Lieutenant Governor Sir Oliver Mowat at the Toronto ball. Many of the costumes reveal imperialist attitudes of the day, exemplified in the "Africa" group at the Victorian Era Ball, the women dressed as ancient Egyptians of the upper classes and the men in the khaki uniforms of British soldiers. An age captivated by technology was evident in wonderfully imaginative costumes representing the telephone, electricity and photography.

The great delight of *Magnificent Entertainments* is, of course, the pictures, selected from hundreds of photographs mainly from the studios of W.J. Topley and William Notman, now in public archives. Everyone who was anyone had his or her costumed portrait taken by these photographers, who carefully recorded the date and name of each sitter. To really understand this visual evidence, Cynthia Cooper had to develop an extensive knowledge of late-nineteenth-century fashion. Fancy dress was often built on the foundation of conventional styles, and an understanding of contemporary fashion is necessary to distinguish the clothing from the costume. The author also had to be familiar with clothing styles of earlier eras, since many guests chose to represent historical characters from past centuries, and some wore vintage clothing that had belonged to their ancestors.

Dressing Up Canada: Late Victorian Fancy Dress Balls, the Canadian Museum of Civilization exhibition based on the research for this book and curated by Cynthia Cooper, brings a third dimension to the visual record of the vice-regal fancy dress balls by displaying several of the costumes that were actually worn to the balls. In a brilliant piece of detective work, the curator discovered these vintage garments in various museums and private collections. Often the owners did not know that they possessed fancy dress costumes. For example, the "Indian" costume worn by Hayter Reed to the Ottawa historical ball languished in the McCord Museum's ethnology collection until Cynthia Cooper cleared up the origin of this motley group of garments and accessories: Reed had collected them when Superintendent of Indian Affairs and assembled them into his fancy dress outfit. Similarly, several museums did not know that some of their eighteenth- and early-nineteenth-century costumes had been worn as fancy dress.

Dressing Up Canada introduces the Victorian passion for costumed events such as fancy dress balls, skating carnivals, historical pageants and private theatricals. Focusing on the three costume balls that the Earl of Aberdeen and his wife, the irrepressible Lady Aberdeen, sponsored in Ottawa, Toronto and Montreal, the exhibit points out the achievements of Lady Aberdeen in organizing these ambitious events as well as her work as a social reformer in Canada. She was instrumental in founding the Victorian Order of Nurses and the National Council of Women. The rich combination of costumed mannequins, related artefacts, photographs and paintings gives a flavour of the vice-regal balls and will kindle public appreciation of the costume history and costume research so evident in this book.

CHRISTINA BATES
Ontario Historian
Canadian Museum of Civilization
October 1997

Acknowledgements

I am grateful to all those who have helped me in a great many ways throughout my study of Victorian fancy dress, which has culminated in the writing of this book. My greatest thanks go to my mentor and friend, Dr. Linda Welters of the University of Rhode Island, who initially helped me to shape and direct my ideas on the subject of Victorian fancy dress, and who gave me unflagging support throughout this project. I also extend special thanks to Christina Bates, Curator of Ontario History at the Canadian Museum of Civilization, whose dedication and commitment to this topic have been instrumental in making the museum exhibition a reality, which in turn allowed me to push my research still further.

At Goose Lane Editions, I owe particular thanks to Laurel Boone, Senior Editor, for her rigorous and judicious editing of my manuscript, and to Julie Scriver, Art Director, for seeing the interest in this project and for making this a beautiful book.

A great many other people have helped me with my research along the way. For their enthusiastic assistance and inspiring exchanges of ideas, I thank Jacqueline Beaudoin-Ross, Curator of Costume and Textiles, and Moira McCaffrey, Curator, Archeology and Ethnology, both at the McCord Museum of Canadian History, and Mary Williamson, formerly Fine Arts Bibliographer at York University Libraries. At the University of Rhode Island, Dr. Margaret Ordoñez provided invaluable encouragement all through my graduate studies, and both she and Dr. Sharon Strohm gave comments and editing suggestions on my master's thesis, for which this research was originally begun.

Many organizations and individuals provided assistance in locating and providing access to materials. At the McCord Museum, Elizabeth Sifton, Nora Hague, Annette McConnell, and Pamela Miller all assisted me in locating useful material. At the National Archives of Canada, Kate O'Rourke and numerous other staff members provided valuable suggestions and assistance. André Delisle, Curator of the Château Ramezay Museum, and Gabrielle Faucher of the Women's Branch generously gave me access to their collections and archives. At the Royal Ontario Museum, Alexandra Palmer, Anu Liivandi, Adrienne Hood, Heather Meiklejohn, and Arni Brownstone assisted me with my search for extant costume. At the Canadian Parks Service, Ruth Mills directed me to much invaluable nineteenth-century advice literature, and Phil Dunning helped me locate extant military costume. Leslie Latta-Guthrie, Museums and Collections Services, University of Alberta, searched that collection for extant costume. For advice and opinions, I also thank John Vollmer.

Several people graciously provided assistance with locating and reproducing photographs. I owe particular thanks to Heinz K. Henisch, Gail and Ed Moorehead, Stephen Otto, Linda Welters, and Patrick Shield of the Royal Canadian Yacht Club Archives, as well as to the staff of the McCord Museum of Canadian History, the National Archives of Canada, the Baldwin Room at the Metropolitan Toronto Reference Library, and the Department of Rare Books and Special Collections, McLennan Library, McGill University.

Other colleagues and friends have been invaluable for their comments on portions of this book or for the inspiration they have given me. I extend heartfelt thanks to Jana Bara, Jennifer Fisher, Kristina Huneault, Diane Joyce, Jennifer Salahub, and Gabrielle and Josef Schmidt. I also thank my husband, Luc Paquette; I was always able to count on him for his willingness to share my enthusiasm about fancy dress and my new discoveries, and for his unfailing support and encouragement throughout the writing of this book.

I am grateful for permission to quote from the James Mavor papers at the Fisher Library, University of Toronto, granted by J. Mavor Moore. The illustration on page 34 is reproduced by permission of the Chatsworth Settlement Trustees. The illustration on page 120 appears here courtesy of the Royal Canadian Yacht Club Archives. I am grateful for permission to reproduce photos in the Notman Photographic Archives of the McCord Museum of Canadian History (which will be abbreviated in the photo credits as NPA/MMCH) and the National Archives of Canada (NAC), including the W.J. Topley (WJT/NAC) and other named collections. Illustrations reproduced from *Book of the Victorian Era Ball Given at Toronto On the Twenty Eighth of December MDCCCXCVII* (Toronto: Rowsell and Hutchins, 1898) are designated BB.

Despite the large volume of material I have unearthed over the course of my research on these fancy dress balls, I realize that there is no doubt a great deal more which I have not yet found, especially that which is in private or family collections. I would be most interested in learning of any further photographs, costumes, documents, or stories pertaining to these events.

The challenges of writing about fancy dress balls were captured in a nutshell by a frustrated journalist before dashing off his report of the Earl of Dufferin's Grand Fancy Ball to the *Toronto Daily Mail* over the telegraph wires on the night of 23 February 1876: "It is requisite that the reporter of such a scene should be at once an excellent historian, an artist, a poet, a reader of novels, and a milliner graduated under Worth." While I know of no living apprentices of the illustrious nineteenth-century couturier, I have the good fortune to count among my friends many others who together surpass all the other requisite qualifications.

Introduction

The highest point of what may be termed "Society" in the Dominion is of course reached in the Vice-regal entertainments which are constantly given by the Governor General and his wife.[1]

Four times in the last quarter of the nineteenth century – twice in Ottawa, once each in Toronto and Montreal – high society donned finery from other eras to promenade in glittering ballrooms. While the Governor General and his lady presided over these magnificent fancy dress balls, the reigning deity was in fact Britannia, supported by Clio, muse of history.

In 1876, the Earl of Dufferin held a fancy dress ball at Rideau Hall, an entertainment on a scale which had never been seen before in Canada. Newspapers throughout the country chronicled the preparations, the ball, and its aftermath, and it was even reported in the society press of the United States and Great Britain. Then, twenty years later, the Earl and Countess of Aberdeen took the fancy dress genre to new heights and catered to a new taste. At their 1896 Historical Fancy Dress Ball in Ottawa, guests paraded as prominent characters from Canadian history. The next year, in Toronto, their Victorian Era Ball feted Queen Victoria's diamond jubilee by celebrating in costume the glorious progress of her reign. In Montreal in 1898, the Aberdeens hosted another historical ball at which guests again incarnated personages from Canada's past.

Over several decades, Victorians of many walks of life had generated a veritable passion for dressing up. Not only balls and parties but amateur theatricals and *tableaux vivants* or living pictures had become exceedingly popular, not just in Britain, but throughout Europe and North America, and Canadians added a winter round of fancy dress skating carnivals. A carefully orchestrated, well-attended, lavish fancy dress ball, however, was the ultimate costumed event. It could leave a lasting impression that no other entertainment could match. But it was more than their magnificence which made the four Canadian fancy dress balls memorable; they rose above frivolous amusements because each had a political and educational agenda. While the Earl of Dufferin simply aimed to draw attention to Ottawa as a worthy capital city, the ambitious Aberdeens attempted to feed Canada's growing nationalism by raising the nation's awareness of its history and the benefits of its relationship with Great Britain. These fancy dress balls were a powerful means for shaping and reinforcing Canadian identity.

Lavish entertaining was in fact an ex-officio duty of the Governor General, who thereby furthered his political mandate: to foster a nationalism among Canadians that would be compatible with Britain's interests, that would build on Canadians' growing faith in the glory and consequence of Empire and their importance within it. As the Queen's representative in Canada, the Governor General carried out a ceremonial role on occasions like the opening of Parliament, represented the British Government in relations between Canada and Britain, assented to parliamentary acts, and would be responsible for ensuring the orderly succession of government if a Prime Minister resigned or died. But only part of the Governor General's power lay in his official duties. The very aura around the office and his person made his and his family's every action noteworthy. As a member of the British aristocracy, he made some of the pomp of the Court of St. James accessible to Canadians. His philanthropy and active social life set a high moral tone for the young nation and increased the popularity of the monarch and her empire. John Buchan (who served as Governor General from 1935 to 1940) described this unofficial role:

> A Governor General lives an intricate and crowded life in the public eye, and he is fortunate if from the whirl of minor duties he can snatch time for study and reflection. His mind may be absorbed in some grave discussion with his Ministers or the home Government, but he must present himself smiling at a dozen functions, and let no one guess his preoccupation. He must perpetually entertain and be entertained; he must show interest in every form of public activity, from a charity bazaar to a university celebration; he must be accessible to all men that he may learn of them and they of him; he must visit every corner of his domain and become, for the time being, not only one of its citizens, but by adoption a perfervid son of each town and province. These things are the *imponderabilia* of governorship, not less important than a cool head and a sound judgement in the greater matters of policy, and many a man who is well fitted for the latter duties fails singly in the other.[2]

Of the nineteenth-century Governors General, none understood the key to success quite like Dufferin and Aberdeen – and their wives.

The Governor General's wife channeled her energies into this second role; she served as hostess at Rideau Hall, organized entertainments, was a figurehead for charities, visited institutions, and perhaps even founded and financially supported service organizations. Like other Victorian women of her class, she was extremely careful about dress and demeanour, believing these to be outward expressions of her moral fibre. She became a favourite of the press, which eagerly latched onto her appearance and deportment, her weekly tobogganing and skating parties, and her visits to prisons, hospitals, and orphanages. In the golden age of society reporting, the vice-regal couple could rely on extensive newspaper coverage of all their activities to further their ends. While society reports of the comings and goings of the Governor General and his sparkling entourage were secondary to real news, they were nevertheless of great import to Canadians, because the entire country looked to the denizens of Government House for social and moral leadership.

Vice-regal entertainments followed an established pattern. The "season" began with the opening of Parliament in the fall, a formal and glittering affair in which the speeches were followed by a State Drawing Room, one of the most important and ceremonious entertainments on the Governor General's calendar. This was modelled on Queen Victoria's official functions, at which subjects of sufficient rank, dressed in regulation court dress, were individually presented to Her Majesty. For a Canadian State Drawing Room, official Ottawa mustered as much of this decorum as it could: the Governor General and his consort stood on a dais in the Senate Chamber while citizens, begrudgingly ranked according to a strict order of precedence, paraded past in single file and bowed or curtseyed once.

A large, very formal State Ball followed soon after a Drawing Room, and lesser balls would continue throughout the season; some Governors General held two in a row, with different guests at each, to accommodate more people. They gave dinners for Members of Parliament, often "men only" affairs, and large crowded receptions (known as "kettledrums") might follow for their families, where everyone would get a chance to shake hands with Their Excellencies. At Rideau Hall, New Year's Day was celebrated with a levee, where men would drop in to greet the Governor General and have a drink. The Earl of Dufferin began the Rideau Hall winter sports traditions of skating, tobogganing and curling. Vice-regal couples with a dramatic bent staged private theatricals in which family members and a few select friends would rehearse and perform a play, perhaps written by a member of the group, for a larger group of guests.

When Lent arrived, the major entertainments ceased for the year. Theatricals might continue, but balls were out of the question. "I never was in any place where Lent was so well observed as here," wrote Lady Monck. Then, with the arrival of spring, the vice-regal household often packed up to travel, perhaps to meet citizens in small towns and villages across the country, and then perhaps to rusticate in a cooler spot for the summer. The Governor General, often with his wife, might also take trips to centres of business and culture such as Montreal and Toronto at other times of the year, where they would hold balls and other entertainments and visit charities and institutions.[3]

Taking the panoply of the vice-regal household on the road made it accessible and all the more popular to Canadians, but regardless of their ostensible reasons for travelling, most vice-regal couples were glad to put Ottawa behind them for a few months. The newly appointed capital of Canada overlaid a town built on the lumber industry, with notoriously rough working class sections. Virtually overnight it had become a city of contrasts, muddy and dirty and lacking drains and sewers but with elegant new Parliament buildings and, two miles away, Rideau Hall and its aristocratic occupants. If the city was a disappointment to each successive Governor General, Government House was worse; they struggled to make it comfortable and presentable, and they devoted considerable energy to making improvements. After all, if the proconsul was Canada's social leader, Rideau Hall had to be made a suitable locus for the country's most exalted social gatherings.

Perhaps twelve or thirteen hundred people comprised Ottawa society in the last quarter of the century. Depending on the attitudes of the occupants of Rideau Hall, the guest list was lengthened or shortened, each time creating controversy. Cabinet ministers and high officials were at the top of the pecking order. Then came senators and members of Parliament, who might reside in the city during the session only. Civil servants, judges, doctors and lawyers made up a more consistently present group. "The trade," with the exception of a few entrenched families whose fortunes had been made in the lumber business, squeezed onto the list where it could, to the disgust of some of the more elite. At the beginning of each season, a prospective guest left a calling card and wrote his or her name in the guest book at Rideau Hall – the traditional way of ensuring an invitation to at least one large affair. With time the inner circle grew as a broader slice of the Ottawa citizenry took pains to drop by on the right day and sign the book. Shopkeepers, butchers and bakers found their way onto the guest list, and even grocers, one of whom had had the audacity to leave his name when delivering onions, and whose presence shocked a bluer-blooded couple attending a state ball. Etiquette and decorum could be difficult to maintain. Even the cream of Ottawa society was not known for its good manners, and the vice-regal hosts often found their guests rough around the edges. After a concert, Lady Aberdeen was appalled to notice her cloakroom procedures violated by Ottawa belles who vaulted over a table to retrieve their wraps. Crude manners notwithstanding, critics claimed that the presence of "the august representative of Majesty itself" encouraged the most vulgar kind of snobbery in Ottawa. "It is fatal to the social prospects of those whose names on 'the day after' are not found in the columns of the *Citizen* and the *Free Press*."[4]

The most sought-after of all vice-regal invitations were not to the Drawing Rooms, kettledrums, or State Balls, but to the four great fancy dress balls. The story of these balls, however, is more than just the chronicle of four magnificent entertainments. Such an exceptional reprieve from Victorian convention as a fancy dress ball gives a privileged glimpse into many cultural contradictions and tensions; the logistics behind these events show the complexities of life in that era; the characters people chose to represent and the costumes they devised reveal their perceptions and beliefs about their own identities and the identity of the country; and the patriotic intentions of the balls mirror each vice-regal couple's vision of their role and of the needs of the nascent dominion.

The most important clue to the impact of the four balls is the astounding quantity of archival material. The organizers have left their journals and papers to chronicle their anxieties and triumphs. The guests' stories come alive through the many archival photographs and glass negatives and the commemorative souvenir albums containing group portraits and sketches. After each ball, photographers braced themselves for the surge in demand. They advertised copiously, and ballgoers responded. Some eight hundred images in all, a "Who's Who" of Canadian society showing an unusually playful public face, have come to light. But the press provides by far the greatest volume of information and reveals the impact of these entertainments on the entire country. Every newspaper in Ottawa, Toronto or Montreal reported on the event on its own terrain for weeks before and after, and they also accorded space to the balls held in the other cities. The day after a ball, newspapers across Canada described the ballroom scene minute by minute and gave lengthy lists of costumes, naming all the fabrics and trimmings. Those who had never met any of Canada's urban elite could become very familiar with what it wore, what music it danced to and what it ate for supper.

One important element in the reconstruction of this story has not been easy to find. It would seem logical that fancy dress might be found in respectable quantity among the extant Victorian costume in museum and private collections, but unfortunately this is not the case. Museums have been reluctant to collect such garments, seeing them as oddities and not representative expressions of the culture that produced them, and so an initial search for fancy dress costume proved virtually fruitless. Gradually it came to light that many garments not known to have such a connection could unexpectedly reveal themselves to have been worn as fancy dress. Historic collections have yielded eighteenth- and early nineteenth-century costume which was remade or altered and worn to a fancy ball some one hundred years later. Ethnology collections have yielded aboriginal artifacts which were donned indiscriminately by their collectors when they dressed up as Indians. Though few in number and far from uniform, the items making up the small body of extant costume have each added a different and very valuable element to this story. At the same time, the information has infused each of these objects with new meaning by uncovering an important phase of its history and drawing an unforeseen connection among them all. A great deal of the individual aspirations and collective values of late-Victorian Canadians are embodied in the dress they judiciously chose and donned for these singular events.

This book is an attempt to tell the stories of these four magnificent and instructive entertainments and to recapture their moral texture and magical appeal. From the wealth of accounts and images and the few remaining costumes comes a very lively portrait of the bustle and anticipation of the preparations, the tone and texture of the events and their social impact. Canadians across the country knew that these balls were events of a lifetime. If a surprisingly intimate glimpse of their society can be obtained through only four single evenings of its amusement, it is because, true to the intentions of their organizers, these occasions were the greatest social events the country had ever seen.

CHAPTER I

Dressing Up: A Victorian Passion

Borrowed characters and borrowed plumage have ever possessed a fascination for the multitude, whether upon the stage, at carnivals or in brilliantly lighted ballrooms.[1]

When the Dufferins and, later, the Aberdeens decided that a fancy dress ball would be the entertainment of the season, they knew that public ecstasy would greet their choice. Beyond the fact that Canadians would be treated to hospitality worthy of a British peer's country house or the Vanderbilts' New York ballroom lay deeper reasons. In a society preoccupied with correct behaviour, convention and conformity, dressing up provided an outlet through which one could project oneself to a different time and place. For the space of an evening one could cast aside some of one's limitations and become Mary Queen of Scots, a dashing eighteenth-century courtier with powdered head and knee breeches, a seductive "Night" swathed in black tulle spangled with gold stars, a stern and stalwart military hero of the *ancien régime*, or a flirtatious gypsy maiden in gaudy striped skirts.

The fashion for fancy dress balls grew over the course of the nineteenth century after a shift in social mores at the end of the eighteenth century had made masquerade balls and parties seem licentious. Private costumed parties, where no masks were worn, became known as "fancy balls." The vogue picked up by the late 1830s and expanded in mid-century as Victorian morality became increasingly repressive. The fancy dress ball's heyday was in the last quarter of the century, especially in the "naughty nineties," when the greatest ambivalence was felt between entrenched ways and changing times. Costumed parties continued to be popular through the 1920s and 1930s, but by then Victorian decorum and restraint had virtually disappeared.[2]

Queen Victoria and Prince Albert had a predilection for fancy balls, and they furthered the interest in historical representations which theatre had already made fashionable. Between 1842 and 1851 they hosted three balls on historical themes. These balls set a high intellectual and moral tone for events to follow, but they also conferred the most elevated social approval on fancy dress balls in general, and historical fancy dress in particular.[3]

The young queen's first such event, the *Bal Costumé*, took place at Buckingham Palace on 12 May, 1842, and brought to life the reign of Edward III in the fourteenth century. Guests were marshalled into theme-based sets, or quadrilles, each of which performed a dance. One set included European costume from 1450 to 1600, while another featured characters from the novels of Sir Walter Scott. The royal hostess expressed a strong desire for historical accuracy in dress, which helped to justify the event as an educational opportunity and not simply a frivolous show of costume, and she commissioned historian J.R. Planché to design costumes. Prince Albert, of course,

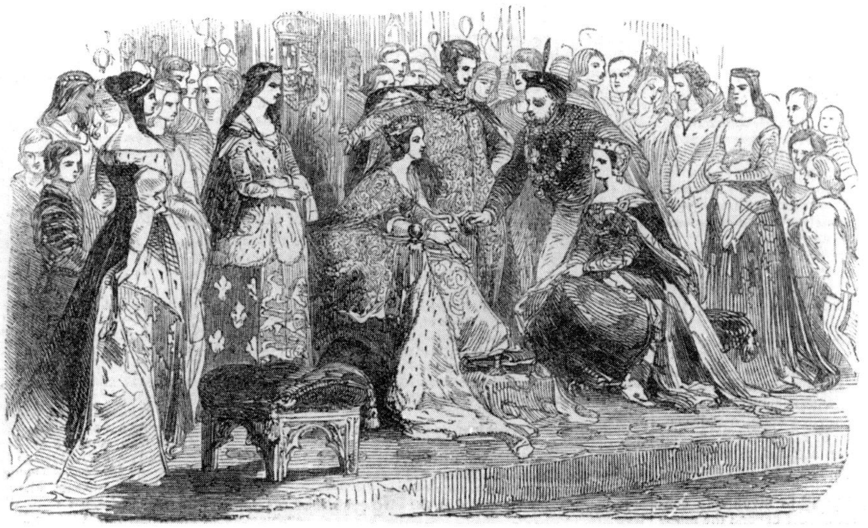

dressed as Edward III, and Victoria herself wore a cloth-of-gold and scarlet dress as "Queen Philippa of Hainault." Because the country was in considerable financial difficulty, the ball was touted as a means of assisting tradespeople, since the guests' expenditure on dress created business opportunities; to a credulous public, the Queen justified the weaving of special fabrics and the design and manufacture of accessories and jewellery as part of her commitment to fostering trade. Following the event, a souvenir book was published featuring Planché's illustrations of the most outstanding characters at the ball, headed, of course, by the Queen and her consort.

A scene from Queen Victoria and Prince Albert's *Bal Costumé*, 12 May 1842. Queen Victoria as "Queen Philippa of Hainault" is seated, flanked by Prince Albert as "Edward III" and "her royal and illustrious relatives." *ILLUSTRATED LONDON NEWS, 14 MAY 1842*

Queen Victoria held her second historical fancy dress ball three years later, in June of 1845: *Le Bal Poudré*, showcasing the costume and white-powdered hair of the mid-eighteenth century. This ball may not have had such an impact on trade as the previous one, since guests had the option of resurrecting ancestors' costumes. Victoria's third and final fancy dress event, the Restoration Ball, was held in June, 1851, when she revived the period of Charles II, the 1660s and 1670s. The men wore long curly wigs, lace collars and petticoat breeches; the women dressed their hair in ringlets and donned full-skirted beribboned gowns.

By this time, theatrical entertainment had become widespread among the middle class as well as the elite, perhaps because respecting all the unwritten codes of conduct constituted a sort of "genteel performance," or maybe because the formalities of Victorian life resembled a "status theatre." In any case, charades and private plays and theatricals were extremely popular, and a craze developed for *tableaux vivants*, in which individuals posed to represent the figures in a work of art. Sometimes a large frame was created, and often a drapery of black gauze between the actors and spectators blurred the scene to create an ethereal effect.[4]

In the last quarter of the century, the fancy dress ball became the entertainment that would enable hosts to impress society most deeply and the most worthy celebration of special occasions. The Prince and Princess of Wales held a lavish ball at Marlborough House in 1874, at which the most prominent guests were arranged into Venetian, Vandyke, Fairy Tale, Card and other quadrilles. In the first two, the costumes were found so accurate that "it was as if the originals of the old masters had come to life again." The Duke of Connaught led the Fairy Tale quadrille, trading his leopard skin headdress for a small cap after the dance to transform himself from the beast in *Beauty and the Beast* to the handsome prince. The press compared this ball with those of Queen Victoria, although the Prince and Princess had made no attempt to emphasize educational merits or to suggest any greater benefits to society; the ball was simply an entertainment commensurate with the prosperity and high social standing of the five hundred royal and noble guests.[5]

Two decades later, however, no socially responsible hostess would hold a fancy dress ball without a higher purpose. At the Devonshire House Ball of July, 1897, some seven hundred guests, nearly all with entries in *Burke's Peerage*, and a sprinkling of ultra-wealthy Americans in London for the season attended this splendid celebration of Queen Victoria's diamond jubilee – though the Queen herself was not well enough to attend. Sets and processions were designed around historical themes – the English court of Elizabeth I, the Austrian court of Maria Theresa, Queen Guinevere and the Knights of the Round Table, the courts of Louis XV and XVI, and the Russian court of Catherine the Great. The commanding Duchess herself appeared as "Zenobia, Queen of Palmyra."[6]

In the United States, the centennial celebrations of 1876 prompted a flurry of fancy dress activities through which Americans expressed their national identity and progress. Very popular were the characters "George Washington" and "Martha Washington," colonial-style garments and heirloom dress. At Boston's Centennial Ball, guests represented illustrious ancestors, many of whom had prominent roles in the forming of their nation.[7]

Later American fancy dress balls had a different function: affirmation of social status. Mrs. W.K. Vanderbilt's housewarming ball in March, 1883, in New York was described as the most magnificent and lavish fancy dress entertainment ever held, with an estimated cost of $250,000. The event marked the turning point at which the *parvenu* Vanderbilts entered society; the indomitable Caroline Astor had to pay Mrs. Vanderbilt a visit to secure an invitation. Alva Vanderbilt glowed smugly as "A Venetian Princess" in a gold-embroidered blue satin dress copied from a painting by Cabanel.[8]

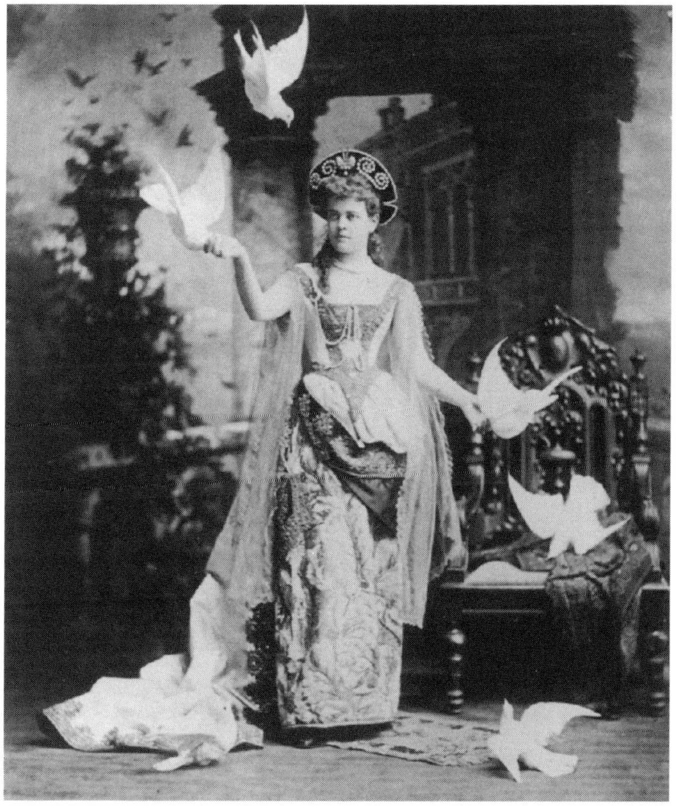

Alva Vanderbilt as "A Venetian Princess." "The underskirt was of white and yellow brocade, shading from the deepest orange to the lightest canary, only the highlights being white. The figures of flowers and leaves were outlined in gold, white, and iridescent beads; light blue satin train embroidered magnificently in gold and lined with Roman red. Almost the entire length of the train was caught up at one side, forming a large puff. The waist was of blue satin covered with gold embroidery – the dress was cut square in the neck, and the flowing sleeves were of transparent gold tissue. She wore a Venetian cap, covered with magnificent jewels, the most noticeable of these being a superb peacock in many coloured gems." The doves are of course stuffed. (*New York Times*, 27 Mar. 1883) PRESERVATION SOCIETY OF NEWPORT COUNTY

But unbridled spending did not guarantee success. In February of 1897, Mrs. Bradley-Martin held a lavish fancy dress ball at the Hotel Waldorf in New York. She had won her social entrée at about the same time as Alva Vanderbilt but republican America was getting a bit annoyed with its self-anointed aristocracy. The press still devoured the details of the ball: columns swathed in fabric with thousands of roses imprisoned in the folds; costumed detectives hired to circulate in the ballroom to foil any thieves tempted by the masses of diamond jewellery; rows of liveried servants to lead guests to the plush-draped dais where Mrs. Bradley-Martin as "Mary Queen of Scots" would receive them. In a period of economic depression, her lavish arrangements – evaluated at $370,000 – soon became the subject of noisy controversy. The vulgarity of extravagance was decried first by a single clergyman and then across the country as the ball became a lead news item. The Bradley-Martins retorted that by creating remunerative work for many tradespeople in the city, they were benevolently spreading the wealth of the upper class. The prospective guests could not ignore the criticism, however, and many backed out at the last minute or put in a brief token appearance. The Bradley-Martins left to live in England soon after the ball was proclaimed a failure, and the city of New York raised their taxes heftily.[9]

Possibly the earliest recorded fancy dress ball in Canada was held in Toronto in 1838, at Rosedale, the home of Sherriff William Botsford Jarvis. His seven-year-old daughter watched the event and lovingly recorded it in her memoirs over seventy years later. Mrs. Jarvis was "Mrs. Leo Hunter" from *Pickwick Papers* and Sherriff Jarvis a Welsh noble, "Baron Gwynnwynn." To the young child, however, the most memorable guest was a Mr. Wells as "Pocahontas," carrying a little papoose with a face made from a dried apple. In Montreal in 1865, William Notman took pictures of guests who had attended the Garrison Ball at the Theatre Royal, and he pasted prints of "Henry

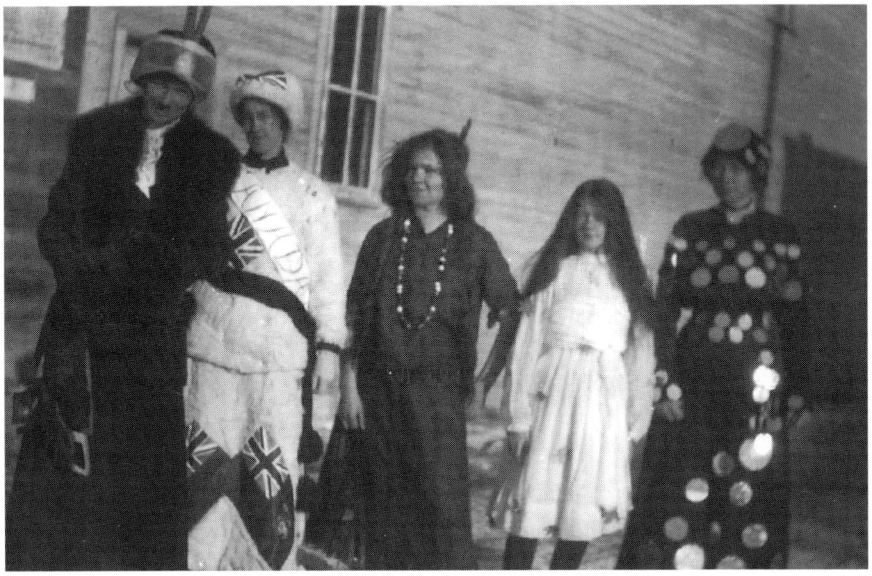

A group in costume, rural Ontario, around 1910. The penchant for fancy dress extended well beyond elite society, though few photographs exist. In this snapshot, left to right, are a skater (who appears to be a man), "Canada," "An Indian," and most probably "Morning Star" and "Moonlight," dressed in doctored-up ordinary dresses. GAIL AND ED MOOREHEAD

VIII," "Tecumseh," "Anne Boleyn," and "A Peasant Girl" into his carefully kept sitter album. Ottawa's first fancy dress ball, held in 1869 by the Desbarats family, was upstaged by a fire at the host's printing house that forced him to tear off his costume and speed away to the emergency just when the company should have sat down to dinner. "Cardinal Richelieu," "Louis XIV" and the ubiquitous Indian characters were given the signal to leave when the hostess bid the band to strike up "God Save the Queen."[10]

Although only the most privileged could afford to give and attend fancy dress balls, to have their portraits taken and to attract the attention of the press, a much broader slice of society indulged in dressing up. Fancy dress skating carnivals were immensely popular in large cities and small towns alike. Newspapers indicate that in the winter most towns and cities held one large carnival a month in the 1870s and 1880s, but that in Montreal alone there were at least two carnivals a week throughout the winters of the 1890s. Since these events were so frequent and were attended by people of many walks of life as well as by the elite, they were not fully commemorated, and there are comparatively few extant photographs and sketches. The best-known picture is the Notman studio's photograph of a carnival held at the Victoria Rink in Montreal in 1870; it was attended by Prince Arthur, who was visiting Canada. Montrealers turned out in all manner of costumes – "Morning Star," "Italian Brigand," "Highlander," and "Little Bo-Peep." Most said that Prince Arthur watched from the gallery, although a photograph and one article suggest that he joined in the fun as "A Cavalier of the time of Charles II." The Reverend Ashton Oxenden described the carnival in his memoirs: "It was one of the most beautiful sights I ever beheld. The place was hung with the gayest flags. . . . It was indeed a fairy scene to look upon. The skating was wonderful and the dresses gorgeous."[11]

A fancy dress ball brought together a profusion of characters, inspired by many different facets of Victorian culture. Newspapers often ran voluminous lists of these, sometimes with detailed descriptions of their costumes. The litany of names includes such popular figures as "George III," "Tambourine Dancing Girl," "Japanese Lady," "Sioux Chief," "Fairy Queen," "Pack of Cards," "Edgar of Ravenswood," "Marie Antoinette," and "Daughter of the Regiment." These are occasionally interspersed with cognomens such as "The Man Who Broke the Bank at Monte Carlo," "Lady Nicotine," "The Old Woman Who Swept the Sky," "Champagne Bottle," "The Bounding Ball of Babylon" and "Sabrina, Queen of the Silver Lake."

Most popular were historic characters and costumes, with names such as "Lady of the Court of Charles I," "A Pompadour" or "A Court Gentleman of the 18th Century." Of course, the most frequently chosen of all historic characters were royalty: "Louis XV," "Queen Elizabeth" and "Richard III" were favourites. The choice of a well-known or aristocratic character from history added a veneer of high-mindedness

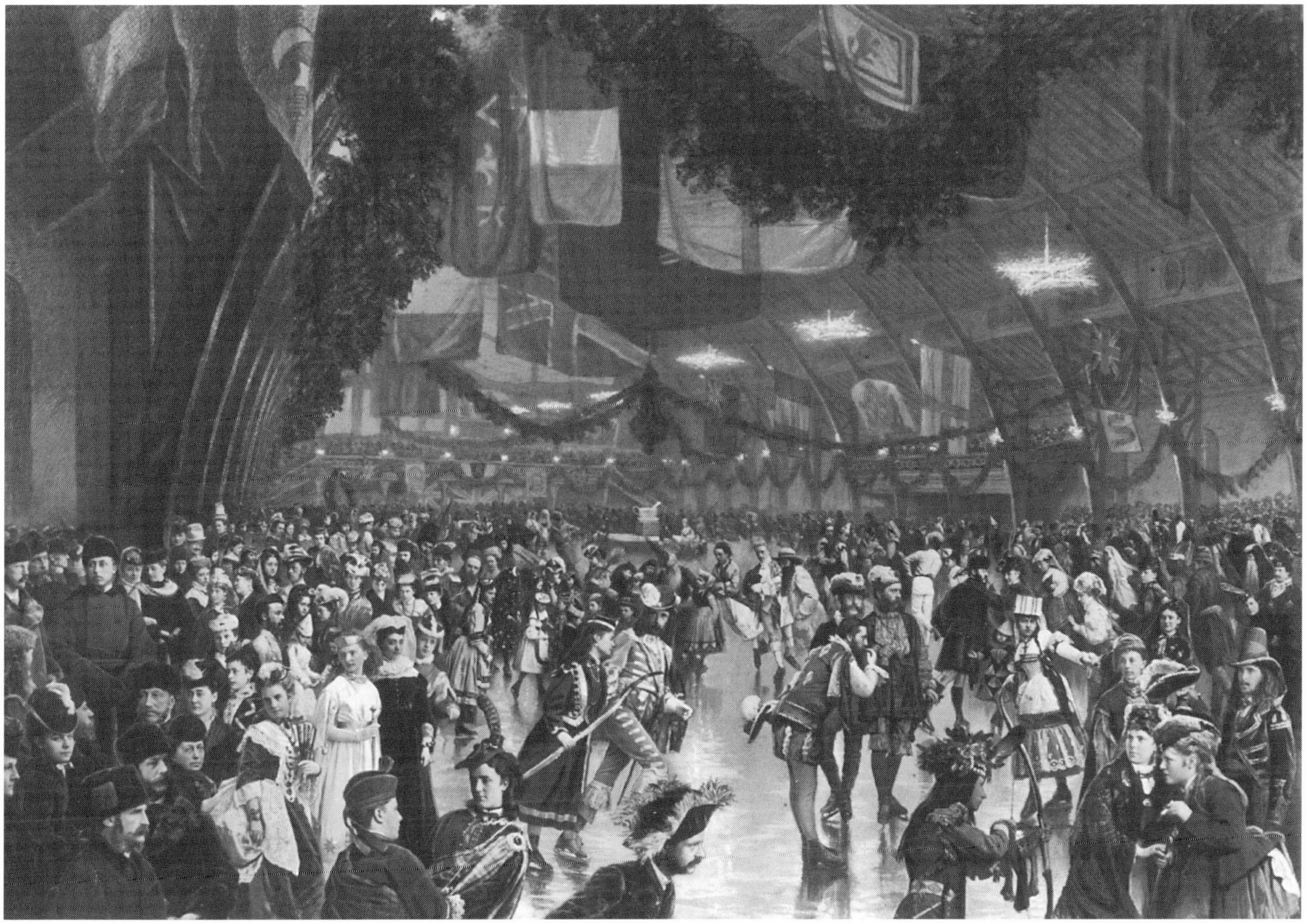

to the indulgence of vanity, and it also entailed the obligation to research the costume. Ardern Holt, the arbiter of fancy dress, pronounced, "In our day, when taste and culture are considered worthy of a thought, historical costumes should not be chosen by people of education without some little study." For *poudré* costumes, powdered hair was considered essential for authenticity; books of advice on fancy dress recommended going to considerable trouble to powder one's own hair rather than wearing a wig. A seemingly accurate costume and coiffure bespoke a cultured individual whose most gratifying compliment would be "historically correct." Those who were fortunate enough to own actual clothing from an earlier period might wear it with pride as a historical relic, though they would generally adapt or remake it in keeping with the aesthetics of their own period. Historical accuracy was always in the eye of beholders inclined to overlook elements of current fashion in a historical costume. Theatre had long taught the public that if a costume appeared tasteful and attractive, it could be assumed to be accurate. Even at Queen Victoria's fancy dress balls, costume silhouette was always far more like the fashionable dress of the period than of the time portrayed. For this reason, many extant eighteenth-century dresses show evidence of extensive alterations done in the nineteenth century, no doubt for fancy dress purposes.[12]

Characters from literature were common at fancy balls, especially those of Sir Walter Scott: "Rowena" and "Ivanhoe," "Diana Vernon," "Amy Robsart" and, most popular of all, "Mary Queen of Scots." Shakespearian characters came a close second:

Skating Carnival at the Victoria Rink, 1870. Prince Arthur (not in fancy dress) stands out prominently on the left. In the lower right corner, "An Indian" wielding bow and arrow takes aim at the emancipated cigar-smoking "Girl of the Period." With this photograph, his studio's first composite, William Notman established his leadership in Canadian photography. Individual photographs were taken of everyone in the scene. These were then cut out and pasted to a painted backdrop of the rink, and the whole rephotographed. This became a common means of recording balls and carnivals when long exposure times made group photographs impossible. NPA/MMCH

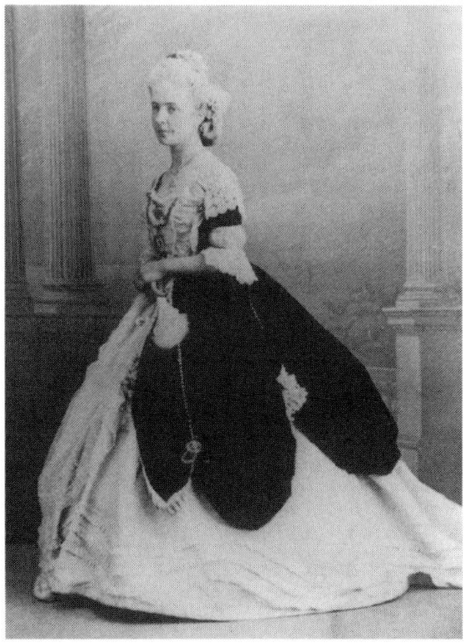

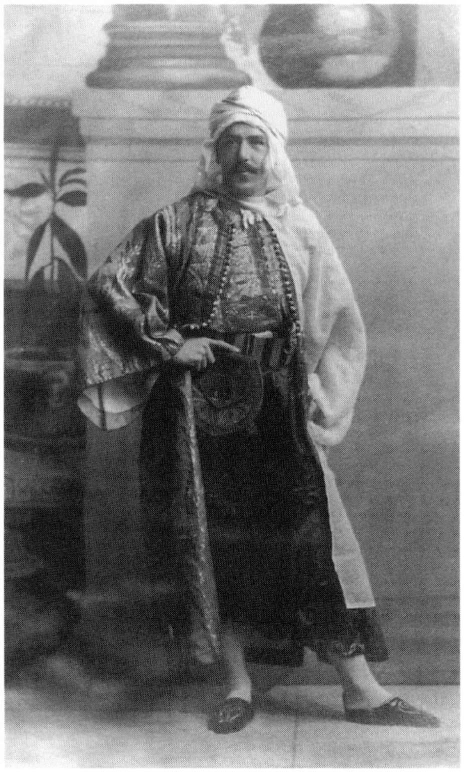

Above: Miss Starnes as "Lady Louis XV *Poudrée*" at the Garrison Ball, Montreal, 1865. Though she represents an eighteenth-century character, her skirt is not distended at the sides in the silhouette of that period; instead, her elliptical hoop crinoline has the fashionable shape of the 1860s. NPA/MMCH

Right: Mr. A. Amos as "A Turk" at the Historical Fancy Dress Ball in Montreal, 1898. His attire is "a glittering Turkish costume brought back from his travels." NPA/MMCH

"Romeo," "Hamlet," "Desdemona," and "Portia" in graduation robes. "Dolly Varden" from Dickens's novel *Barnaby Rudge*, set in the late eighteenth century, was a popular character. Mythology, legend, nursery rhymes and fairy tales were mined for ideas: "Mary Mary Quite Contrary," "Diana the Huntress," "Cinderella" and "Santa Claus" danced together at fancy balls.

Other ballgoers dressed as exotic characters, sometimes in garb collected in or acquired from other lands. Chinese and Turkish costumes were popular. Mr. A. Amos wore Turkish dress to the Historical Fancy Dress Ball in Montreal in 1898, although his attire placed him well outside the theme of Canadian historical costume. Fanciful names like "Bashi-Bazouk" enhanced less exotic or authentic dress, which usually included full trousers and an improvised turban. A newspaper reporter summed up his overall impression of such characters in verse:

> Greeks and Malays, with daggers and dirks,
> Spaniards, Jews, Chinese and Turks,
> Some like original foreign works,
> But most like bad translations.[13]

Women in particular loved peasant or pastoral dress. These costumes were highly romanticized, being based on imagery such as Dresden china shepherdesses. Italian and French peasant dress, particularly that of Normandy, had an equal attraction. With these costumes accuracy was not a particularly important aim. "No one would probably view the national costumes with more curiosity than the peasantry they are intended to portray," Holt thought.[14]

Emblematic costumes were favoured almost exclusively by women and were usually based on a dress made in a fashionable style. "Few frocks look prettier than these when well planned," wrote Mrs. Aria, another authority. An abstract concept like "Autumn" or something more concrete like "A Daffodil" would be rendered through colour, texture, trims and embellishments, and accessories. "Dawn" might wear grey tulle over pink satin, with a diadem of stars on her head and a grey veil over her shoulders. The famous "Music" dress worn by vocalist Fanny Ronalds at her New York ball in 1867 was of yellow satin embroidered with bars of music from Verdi's *Un Ballo in Maschera*; her green satin cloak was embroidered with various musical instruments, and on her head she wore a tiny lyre lit up with little gas jets. Even technological innovations and games could be represented. One book told how to devise a "Wastepaper Basket" costume consisting of a dress of beige textured fabric to simulate wicker, with scrap paper sewn "with some skill" all over the sleeves and around the hem.[15]

All these colourful characters created a rare and dazzling spectacle – newspaper accounts of these events rarely resisted the term "kaleidoscopic." The full otherworldly

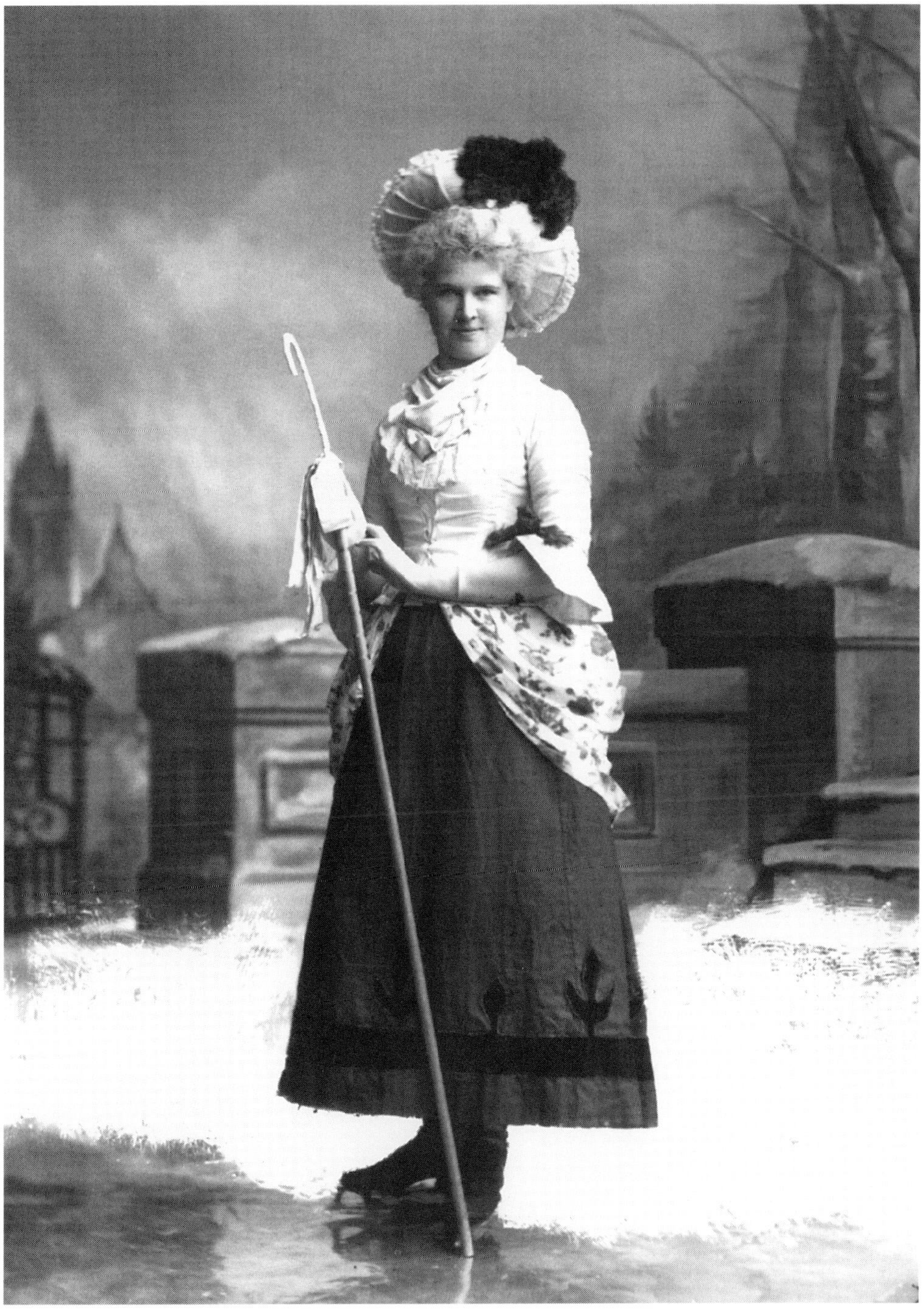

Miss Fraser as "A Shepherdess," Ottawa, 1889. Peasant-type costumes were especially popular at skating carnivals; their short skirts were a convenience for the sport. Lady Dufferin, admiring one event, wrote, "The ladies' costumes had of necessity short petticoats, so there was every variety of peasant – Dolly Vardens, Watteaus, etc., etc. – and very pretty they were!" (Dufferin, 62) WJT/NAC/PA138398

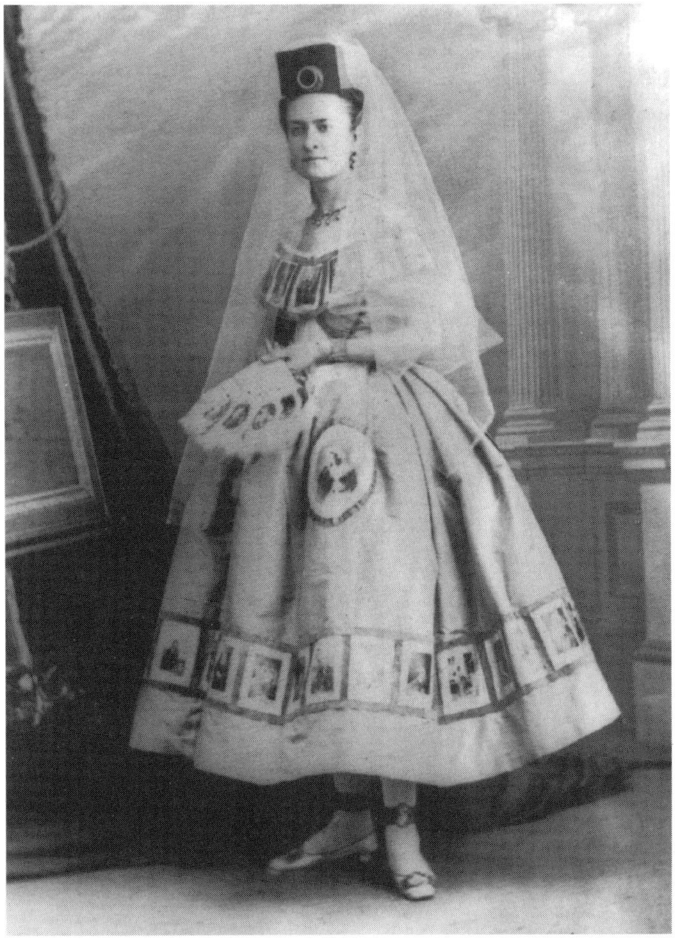

Miss Stevenson as "Photography," 1865. She wears a dress, shoes and bracelets decorated with photographs and a camera with a sheer veil draped over it on her head. She was one of three women who attended the Garrison Ball in Montreal as "Photography."
NPA/MMCH

effect of the ball could be achieved only if all cooperated by wearing fancy dress. At private affairs those who came in evening dress were liable to be turned away; Governors General magnanimously labelled such guests "spectators" and let them watch from a gallery. The sight of large numbers of guests in fancy dress contributed greatly to the sensation of escape from social conventions, and, with the requisite suspension of disbelief, the incongruities among characters elevated the experience from spectacle to fantasy. Reporters always described anachronistic scenes passionately. One said:

> The effect of the beautiful and elaborate costumes was of course very striking, while incidental absurdities and incongruities were constantly occurring. . . . Prim Puritans, casting the principles of their rigourous sect to the four winds, placed oblivious arms round seductive waists. . . . History was boldly shown to be a fraud and delusion. . . . Bluebeard was, it is true, a little shunned at first, till it was found that his sword had no edge worth speaking of. Cavaliers and Cromwellians took champagne with each other. Why even Charles I was there, and hundreds can state he wore his own head.

"The beholder . . . may no doubt get some satisfaction from the sight of Cleopatra in the arms of the Devil," wrote another.[16]

Receiving an invitation to a fancy dress ball could send potential guests into a flutter. Even though doing research, arranging costumes and practising dances were half the fun of such an event, choosing what to wear involved complex decisions. Then, obtaining costumes was a matter of some consequence: handsewing was still common, and fit often had to be exacting.

There were a number of places eager ballgoers could turn for assistance and inspiration. Those with a scholarly bent might pore over history books or study pictures of paintings or other works of art. For more direct advice, one could turn to the barrage of published information specifically on fancy dress. Women's magazines such as *Godey's Lady's Book* and *The Englishwoman's Domestic Magazine* sometimes featured fancy dress designs and articles, and enticing specialized books were available with extensive recommendations for choosing fancy dress. By far the most complete sources were the books by Ardern Holt, a prolific British authority on the subject. Holt's book for women, *Fancy Dresses Described, or What to Wear at Fancy Balls* (published in six editions between 1879 and 1896), began with the query, "But what are we to wear?" Holt's companion book, *Gentlemen's Fancy Dress: How to Choose It*, was also published in six editions from 1882 to 1905. Other prominent authorities included Mrs. Aria's *Costume: Fanciful, Historical, and Theatrical* and, in the US, the Butterick Company's *Mas-*

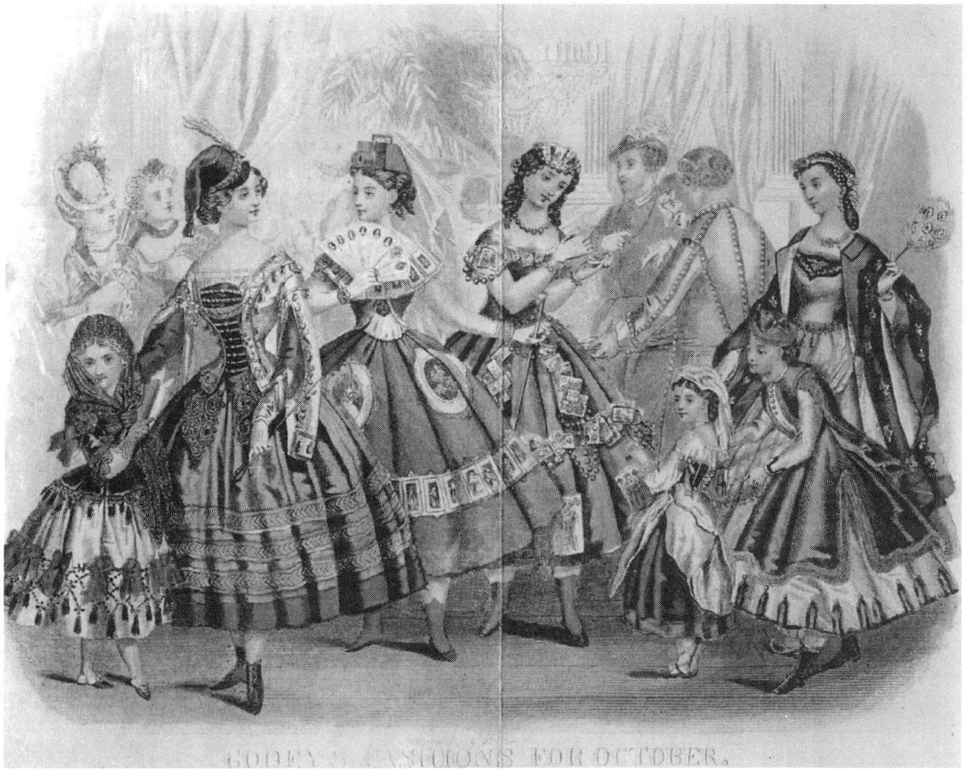

A plate from *Godey's Lady's Book*, October 1866. Left to right are costumes for "A Spanish Lady"; "A Hungarian"; "Photography," a costume almost identical to Miss Stevenson's; "Games"; "Italian Peasant"; and Polish and Turkish costumes. *Godey's* recommends that the "Photography" dress be a brilliant emerald green. This American publication often created its fashion plates by copying from European ones; a Parisian plate from 1864 illustrates the same "photography" dress. R.& H. HENISCH PHOTO-HISTORY COLLECTION, SPECIAL COLLECTIONS, RARE BOOKS ROOM, PATTEE LIBRARY, PENNSYLVANIA STATE UNIVERSITY

querade and Carnival: Their Customs and Costumes. The Butterick publication relied heavily on Holt, copying large sections of the introduction outright and paraphrasing other sections.

The advice in these sourcebooks reveals the appeal of fancy dress, especially to women. "A fancy dress ball is the plain woman's opportunity, since as a rule, everyone looks his or her best in fancy dress," says *Everywoman's Encyclopedia*. "There are few occasions when a woman has a better opportunity of showing her charms to advantage than at a Fancy Ball," Holt asserts. Fancy dress offered individuals the rare opportunity to showcase their most desirable aspects, both physical and personal. A costume could be far more flattering than current fashion, and the chosen character's qualities would be perceived, not as a transformation of the individual, but as an enhancement or amplification of his or her own fine traits.[17]

With so much at stake, selecting a costume required serious consideration. The unprecedented range of choice alone could be daunting, especially when an authority admonished: "One must be dull indeed if, with all ages and nations from which to choose, one cannot manage to devise an attractive and becoming garb which will enhance one's good points and hide one's defects." The key factor in attaining the ideal combination of a becoming fancy dress costume and an appropriate fantasy character was a judicious selection, requiring an honest assessment of one's figure and true self-knowledge – neither a matter to be taken lightly. "It is by portraying a character to whom one bears some resemblance, or that one is especially fitted by nature to assume that success 'on the night' is assured," wrote *Everywoman's Encyclopedia*. The arbiters of fancy dress intensified the pressure on those reluctant to come to terms with what they saw in their mirrors. Misguided short men must be dissuaded from portraying the statuesque Richard Coeur-de-Lion, or slender men the portly Falstaff. Blondes ought not even to consider representing Cleopatra, nor brunettes a Scandinavian Peasant. Ardern Holt must have struck fear into many a man's heart

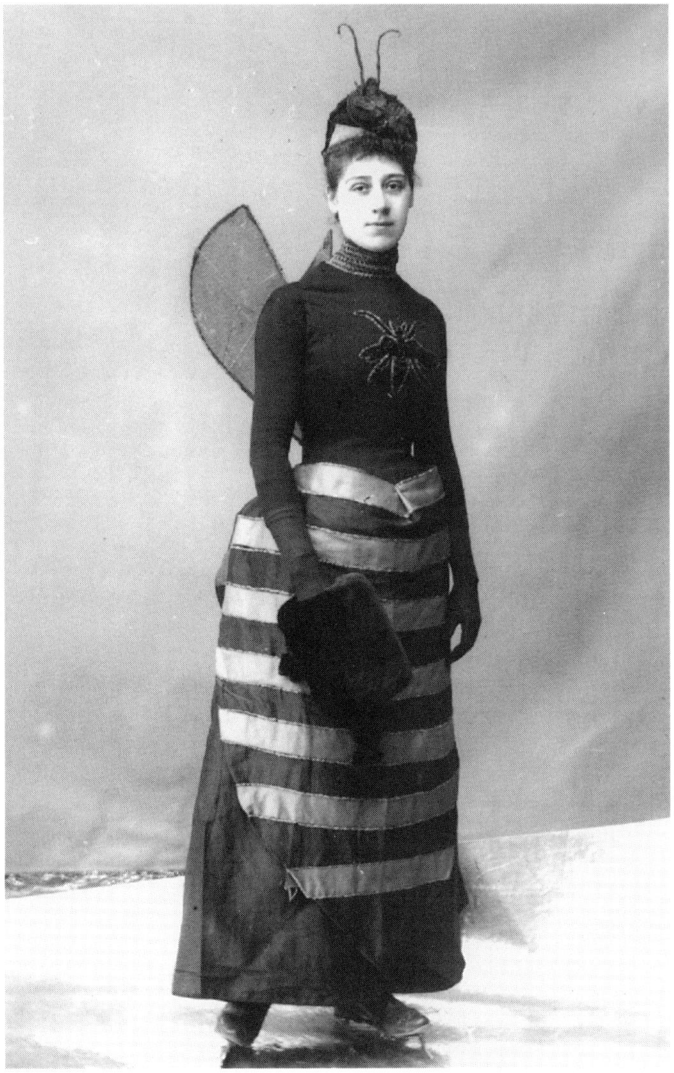

Above: Miss Laura Smith as "A Hornet," Ottawa, 1889. She has used Holt's recommendation for inspiration, apparently making over an existing dress and adding an appliquéed hornet to the front of the bodice. This photograph was taken for a composite of a skating carnival; Miss Smith did not bother to obtain matching boots for the event. WJT/NAC/PA192747

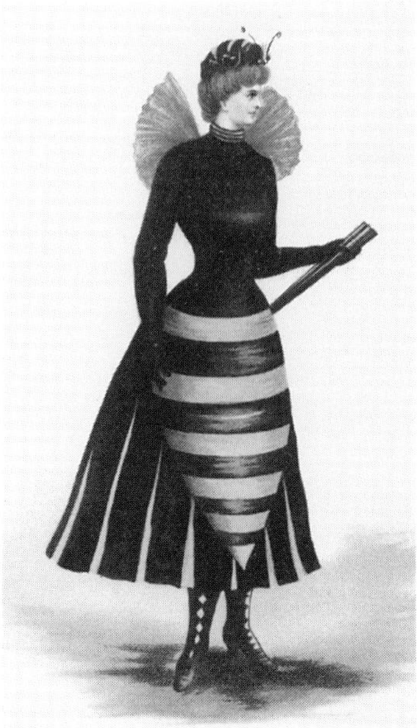

Left: "The Hornet." "Short black or brown dress of velvet or satin; boots to match; tunic pointed back and front, with gold stripes; satin bodice of black or brown with gold gauze wings; cap of velvet with eyes and antennae of insect." *FANCY DRESSES DESCRIBED* (1887), 114

when she remarked in *Gentlemen's Fancy Dress,* "People often render themselves absolutely ridiculous because they assume characters in every way opposed to their own personality." Fancy dress was not a disguise but an extension, an enhanced version, of one's true self.[18]

Guests who chose unwisely were liable to find themselves targets of journalistic derision. Most could at least take solace in the fact that society columnists were on the whole too tactful to emphasize anything other than the positive results of their anxious preparations. Compliments such as "sweet," "becoming," "handsome," "fetching" and "magnificent" pepper the pages of costume descriptions, and criticism for those whose fantasy persona was radically different from their own or whose costumes didn't suit their figures was usually very general. A *Toronto News* reporter claimed, pointedly but impersonally, that "wrinkled old ladies imagined themselves charming in costumes which were the correct thing for girls of fourteen a century ago. Fat ladies, with nothing wild or winsome about them, chose to figure as gypsy maidens. Little meek short-sighted men figured as ferocious warriors."[19]

For men, the divergence from everyday dress was greater than for women, which deepened their confusion. Given the sober uniformity of their conventional dress, a fancy dress ball was a sartorial free-for-all. Some men loved this opportunity, but others dreaded such a radical break. Worse, most people believed that expending a lot of time and effort on one's dress and feeling enjoyment in one's own appearance was a woman's prerogative. Because of this, and their supposed intuitive abilities and preoccupation with matters of dress, women were thought to find selecting a costume much easier than did men. Men readily equated the process of choosing a costume with a foray into the feminine sphere; many found it foreign and unnatural and lamented their collective lack of ability in the field. "Many are deterred from accepting invitations to Fancy Balls by the difficulties which surround appearing in appropriate guise," acknowledged Ardern Holt in the introduction to *Gentlemen's Fancy Dress,* and a newspaper reporter summed up the problem more colloquially. "The poor men.

They're not in it with women when it comes to costuming for a fancy ball."[20]

It was not only the range of choice which the "sterner sex" found especially disturbing. An impending fancy ball brought men a new consciousness of their bodies. Rotund midriffs or slender calves, obliterated by the conventional dark suit, caused agony to many, and overweight men were inclined to "go on the Banting system" for weeks or even months beforehand. Facial hair was inappropriate for many characters, so men felt goaded into shaving their beards and moustaches, a daunting sacrifice. "A Question of Moustaches – Some Problems Which Are Causing Much Tribulation," ran a headline in the *New York Times*. Inadequate legs were the worst shame, however; "silken hose would have . . . the same effect over pipe stems."[21]

Some men dismissed the preparations as frivolity and attended the balls begrudgingly or stayed home while their wives and daughters went, but others fully enjoyed their newfound freedom. An old joke had a guest in a toga sweeping into the ballroom and proclaiming with a wide gesture, "I am Appius Claudius." "Oh, are you?" came a mumbled reply. "Well, I am uncomfortable as Richard the Lion-Hearted." One fancy ball was said to be much awaited "by not a few of the masculines who pride themselves on a portly or genteel figure, or a taste in dress whose luxuriance is too much pruned by our present severe and sombre costumes." After another, it was suggested that "perhaps many present, particularly among the men, found in their minds a wish that something of the picturesqueness of the past survived in the attire of the present."[22]

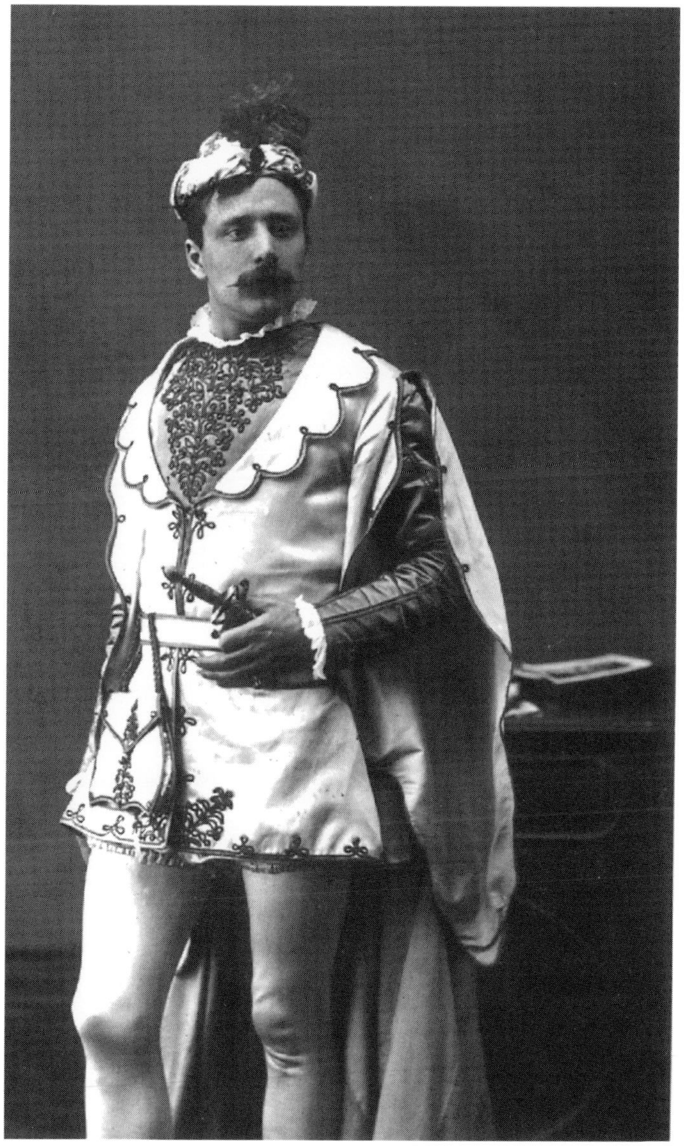

Mr. Dunlevie as "Romeo," Ottawa, 1876. When Dunlevie described his scarlet velvet and mauve satin costume for the press, he was careful to mention his "mauve tights to thigh." WJT/NAC/PA193693

Once they had come to terms with any confusion over their attire, ballgoers made every attempt to prolong their escapist experience. They stayed until the wee hours of the morning. After the Dufferins' and Aberdeens' balls, guests improvised a second, though much less formal, fancy dress event about a week later. Nevertheless, the Victorian cult of respectability tempered the degree of their escapism. The fantasy experience resided in costume as an enhancement of the individual and in the individual as a component of the spectacle. One's true identity must shine through the trappings of fancy costume; likewise, one's behaviour must be consistent, and acting out one's fantasy role had its risks. The subtle performance individuals allowed themselves is most apparent in photographic poses. A "Napoleon" slouches and scowls. Stately "Pompadours" affect haughty manners. "Gypsy Dancers" appear to jingle their beribboned tambourines. But those who embraced their roles with fervour at the fancy dress balls were exceptional and always conspicuous.

Similarly, moral conventions in dress could be cast aside only in keeping with certain tacit restrictions. There was a definite propensity for emphasizing some normally concealed parts of the body. Men enthusiastically revealed their calves or even more of their lower limbs in silk stockings, indicating that many saw their legs as an attrac-

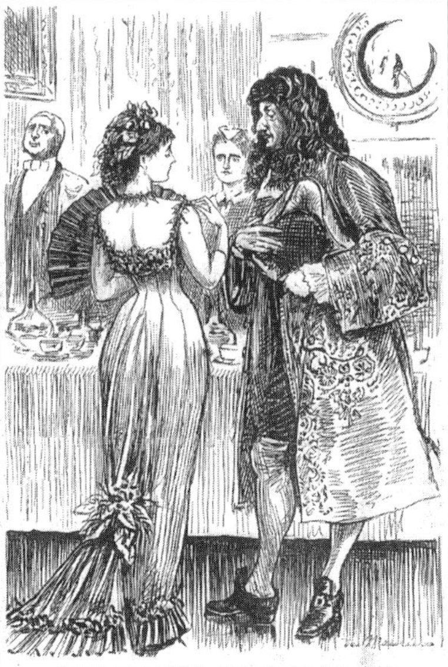

"VAPID VEGETABLE LOVES."—"*The Talking Oak.*"

Scene – Tea Room at Fancy Ball.
Uncle John (who is chaperoning his Niece). "What *are* you, my Dear?"
Pretty Niece. "Oh! I am a *Salad*, Uncle John! See, there's Endive, and Lettuce, and Spring Onions, and Radishes, and Beetroot. Nothing wanting, *is* there?"
Uncle John. "H'm! – ah! – Perhaps a little more *Dressing*, my Dear!" PUNCH, 30 MAR. 1878.

tive feature and a ball as an opportunity to show them off. Given reporters' frequent mockeries, it appears that some overestimated their charms and others yielded unwisely to their wives' entreaties. Women flouted moral convention with shortened skirts which revealed their ankles and legs; peasant costumes had this advantage. Some women donned relatively loose garments with uncorseted bodices. Greek and Roman costumes, styled much like the avant-garde "aesthetic" dress, lent themselves to this effect. Women sometimes wore their hair loose, too, no doubt choosing costumes which would allow the display of their crowning glory.

Under ordinary circumstances, disregarding any of these conventions of dress would signal sexual laxity, but a fancy dress ball was a condoned opportunity to be more overtly alluring. In fact, fancy dress could be charged with erotic power. "She who represents Cleopatra, or some other Oriental queen, blazing with jewels, will not be allowed to sit in a corner," wrote Mrs. Aria. Emblematic costumes had special potential, particularly "Night," in a seductive black dress swathed in black gauze and spangled with gold sequins in the shape of stars and crescent moons. Perhaps some women went overboard in "showing charms," like the young woman dressed as a "A Salad" whose uncle remarks on her lack of "dressing" in a Punch cartoon.[23]

A young woman dressed as "A Rainbow" at the Garrison officers' fancy ball at the Theatre Royal in Montreal on 24 February 1865 created a strongly erotic effect:

> Miss Magruder went to the fancy ball at Montreal as a rainbow. I believe her dress was composed of skirts of different colours, and flowing gauze, and scarves of the same on her head, which enveloped her partners' heads when she danced. She wore very tight blue boots, and very short petticoats.[24]

Miss Magruder's statement comes through loud and clear. Her "very short" petticoats revealed a good expanse of leg, and her "very tight" boots showed every curve of her ankle, both highly erotic zones kept well hidden under respectable dresses. Then, her boots were not the usual black, brown or white, but blue, which would draw still more attention to her lower limbs. Her multicoloured flowing skirts were a bohemian departure from the typical crisp taffeta, but it was her headdress which must have been most titillating. At a time when men were literally kept at a distance from women by their hoop crinolines, this costume's gauzy scarves reached out and wrapped themselves around a man's head. No doubt Miss Magruder, dripping with sexuality, was the first to fill her dance card with officers' names.

Reports of fancy dress balls convey the impression of a generally heightened sense of sexual excitement. At Ottawa's Historical Fancy Dress Ball, an unmarried couple was caught in an inappropriate display of affection in a corridor. At Toronto's Victorian Era Ball, a man and woman absconded together in a carriage, and when they returned to the ball they claimed that they had each believed themselves to be with their lawful spouse, and that their fancy dress, combined with fatigue, caused the mistaken identity. Worst of all, it was rumoured that at a New York ball in 1840 a couple found themselves so attracted to each other that they ran off, awakened a preacher at four a.m., and were married then and there – still in costume.[25]

The way ballgoers chose *not* to dress is equally revealing of their mores. Masks were strictly prohibited at large fancy dress balls as implying too great a degree of licence. (Masked parties were held but were generally smaller private affairs.) Even using dark makeup on the face, as some did who represented exotic characters, was quite daring. Apart from décolletage and a certain show of ankle and leg, more open display of the body did not occur. Men who appeared to be bare-chested Zulus in fact wore jersey garments (perhaps with painted "tattoo" designs), as fancy dress books recommended.

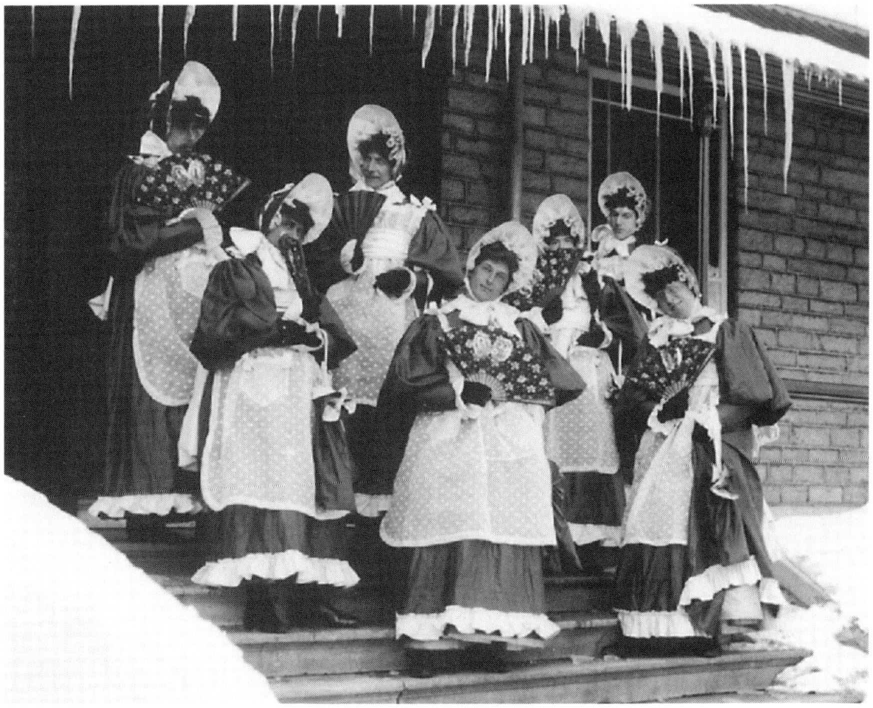

"Dame Marjorie's School," Ottawa, 1894. For a skating carnival, the male Aberdeen staff dressed as village schoolgirls. Dressing as the opposite sex was rarely tolerated and hardly ever photographed; this group, costumed and recorded with full vice-regal approval, is exceptional. WJT/NAC/PA27373

Dressing as the opposite sex was taboo in formal ballroom settings. No women wore pants to the large fancy dress events in Canada; the most masculine garb for women seems to have been the quasi-military "Vivandiere" (canteen-keeper) costumes, which were always worn with skirts. Even a plate from *Fancy Dresses Described* (1896), illustrating Rosalind from *As You Like It*, recommends a skirt for fancy dress even though this character appeared in pants on stage.

On the other hand, men were at least tempted to dress up as women. Otherwise ads for skating carnivals would not have habitually warned, "No gentlemen to appear in Female Attire," or "No gentleman will be allowed to personate a female character." At an Ottawa skating carnival where no such warning was given, a Mr. Hill came in the character of "Female Juvenility," and a Mr. Grant came as a "Delegate of the Society for Women's Rights"; neither was photographed. Lady Aberdeen evidently approved of her staff's antics at a skating party in 1894:

> All our staff . . . dressed themselves as village schoolgirls, in green Kate Greenaway dresses & poke bonnets with pink sashes & ribbons & muslin pinafores & fans. . . . The effect was comical – Dr. Shirres made a very good, huge, girl. Actually, he and Mr. Ferguson shaved off their moustaches for the occasion.

Of course, no men dressed as women at the Aberdeens' fancy balls.[26]

Norms of good taste which had to be respected at a fancy dress ball were far more subtle than the simple respect of gender boundaries. With fancy dress, as with other types of dress, society placed limits on conspicuous consumption and waste. Daily, individual integrity had to be maintained through exceedingly careful choices that would allow one to appear at one's best yet avoid semblance of frivolity or vanity. Fancy dress increased the difficulty of this balance. Balls were rare occasions for people to show themselves at their most attractive, and they wanted to invest a lot of money in their costumes. Yet a garment created for a single wearing was considered wasteful. All but the cream of international society found it difficult to reconcile frivolous spending with true gentility, and hosts, society columnists, and fancy dress authorities alike frequently warned guests to avoid the temptation to go overboard.

Of course, some elite individuals – like Alva Vanderbilt and Mrs. Bradley-Martin – did give themselves over to spending on fancy dress with complete abandon. For the Devonshire House ball in 1897, the internationally renowned Parisian couture house of Worth made a costume for the Duke of Marlborough which involved so much labour and costly materials that the couturier himself was appalled at the bill. The dandiacal Marlborough could well afford it, however, because, two years earlier, he had married the wealthy American heiress Consuelo Vanderbilt. But outside the circles where such costumes could be worn with impunity – for instance, in Canada, where middle-class values held sway – this kind of lavish expenditure and display was seen as tasteless. Following the Dufferin ball in 1876, Canadian ballgoers were reminded that the pleasure to be gained from an expensive costume was inevitably dampened by an awareness of one's excess:

> A great many go to all sumptuary entertainments with a very practical thread running through the woof of excitement and hopeful feeling. Beneath the costly headdress is the consciousness of the large price paid for it, and the heart beating under a new brocade not infrequently keeps sad time to calculations of ways and means. The ordinary headdress and brocade will be useful again; but only in exceptional society can there be recurring opportunities for wearing the costume purchased for a fancy dress ball, and neither the society nor the opportunities are within the reach of persons of moderate means. The money is as good as thrown into the lake.[27]

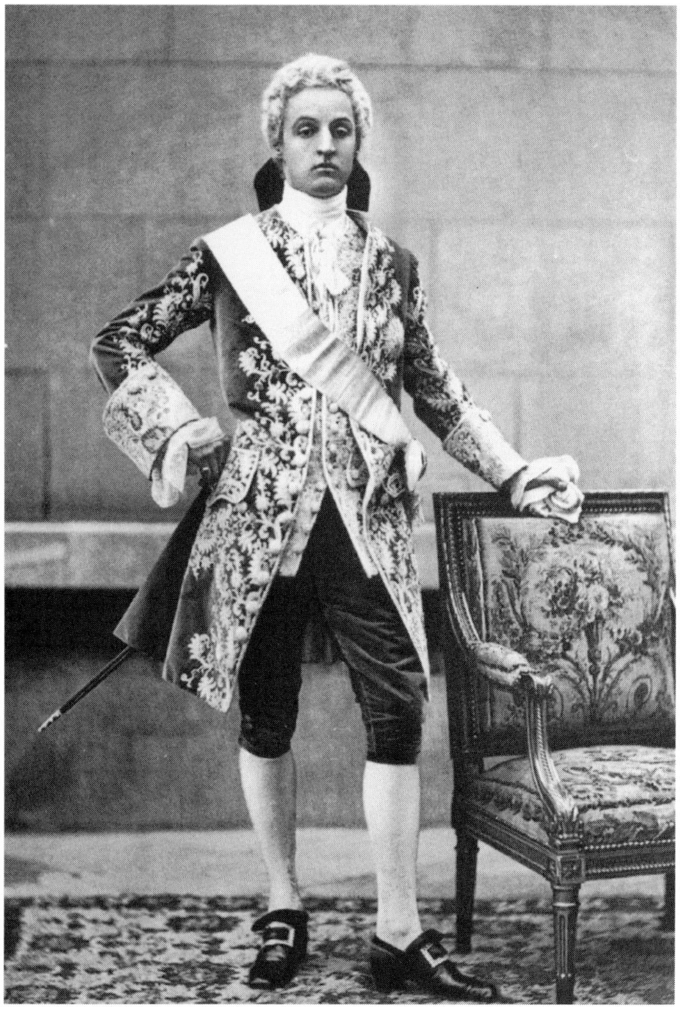

The Duke of Marlborough as "The French Ambassador at the Court of Catherine of Russia" at the Devonshire House Ball, 1897. The embroiderers at the Parisian couture house of Worth took a month to embellish the straw-coloured velvet coat with silver, pearls and diamonds, and Jean-Philippe Worth remembered it as the most splendid and costly fancy dress costume his atelier had ever turned out. DEVONSHIRE COLLECTION, CHATSWORTH.

A more appropriate means of displaying status without compromising integrity was to portray an ancestor or wear heirloom articles. A valiant forebear's military uniform or great-grandmother's jewels, pointed out in the newspaper descriptions, would add an element of dignity which no fictitious noble character or magnificent dress could equal. When numbers of upstarts were attempting to climb the social ladder, heirloom dress could set "old blood" apart from "new money" without costing a cent.

Calico balls deterred expense on a large scale. For these events fancy dress had to be made of sateen, printed cottons, muslins and other unassuming fabrics. Even then, some guests would be tempted to overdo it. "A few people are still struggling to translate the word 'cotton' into 'velveteen' but I won't have it," wrote Lady Dufferin. Any character could be represented, but in keeping with the frugal aims of the event, peasant types were most popular. "The charms of the fair dancers, set off by nothing richer than calico, are voted more captivating than when costly costumes compete with them for admiration."[28]

On the other hand, there was always one good argument for those who wanted to spend – to help poor seamstresses and give trade a boost. Having a costume made had far more prestige than renting one. "There are so many objections to wearing hired costumes that wherever at all possible men and women will prefer spending a little more upon a gown and suit of their own," a Toronto paper prodded. Costume rental was an option aimed particularly at men who wanted a minimum of trouble over garment selection. But there was a third option. Women, in particular, might wear remade or altered articles. One writer suggested that "a woman can unearth wonderful odds and ends of evening gowns and reconstruct them into a marvellous facsimile of something historic," especially if she could cast off a lifetime of education and allow herself a slipshod evening. "As the dress is worn but once or twice at most, there is not much matter about the length of stitches. Indeed, a very pretty costume has been finished with the aid of *pins* alone," admitted *Godey's Lady's Book*. Some of the extant examples of fancy dress, particularly the remade garments, do reveal haphazard construction, while others are made in the best couture tradition and show very little sign of wear, indicating that they were indeed acquired for one night's entertainment.[29]

Regardless of guests' expenditure on the costumes themselves, economic effects extended to hairdressers, cosmeticians, shoemakers and florists, not to mention dancing instructors, caterers, electricians and other tradesmen, and, in two instances, furnace companies. Nevertheless, journalists' commentary on far-reaching benefits for the trade was often offset by biting criticism of the huge expenditure. This is one reason why Lady Aberdeen emphasized the educational value of her fancy dress balls, succeeding where Mrs. Bradley-Martin failed.

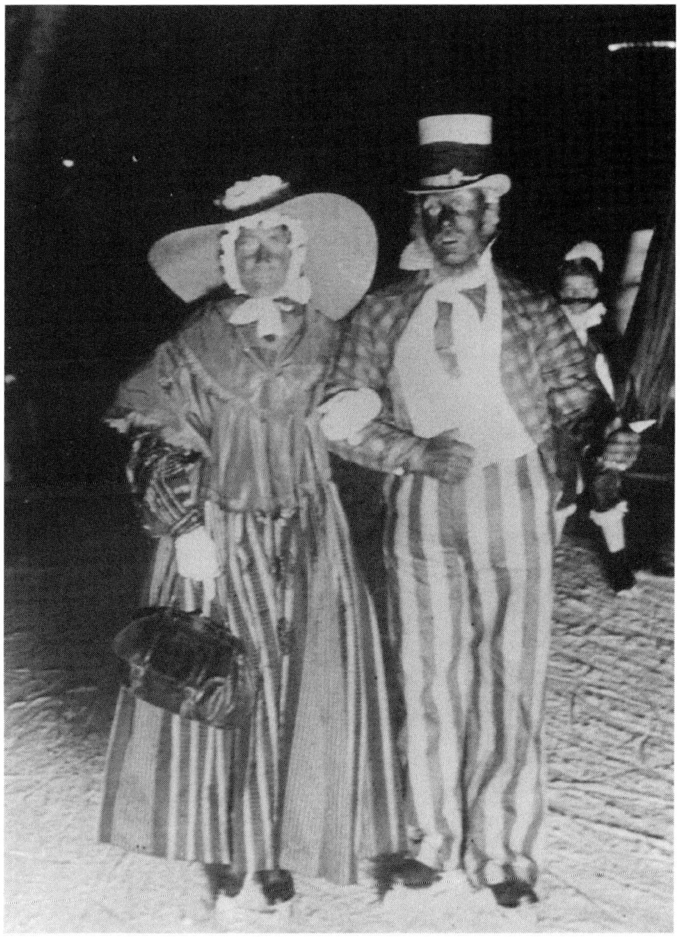

Blackface costume. Such characters appeared frequently at skating carnivals but were rarely photographed. JULES-ERNEST LIVERNOIS/NAC/PA24048

The dazzling spectacle of fancy dress balls tends to obscure the ingrained assumptions underlying conventions of fancy dress, assumptions about gender, race, social class, and even politics. Fancy dress both challenged and reinforced stereotypes and values. When late Victorians exploited a stereotype as a character for fancy dress, they showed their fascination with traits which generally carried negative connotations. More often than not, however, adoption of stereotypes reinforced widely accepted cultural ideas about "the other."

Fancy dress conformed to prevailing ethnocultural and racial stereotypes. In Canada, "Indian" characters appeared often at fancy dress events, sometimes with made-up faces and unpronounceable names such as "Quewaygoos-quequamteros." The appropriation of this image shows a certain fascination, but connotations of "savagery" lie behind its appeal. The people portraying these characters glowered fiercely for photographs, whooped wildly, and chased others with tomahawks and bows and arrows. Blackface costume was fairly commonplace at skating carnivals, especially for men. The terms used to name these portrayals were derogatory, and Holt's and other fancy dress books and newspaper reports refer to blackface characters in derisive terms. Men in blackface and the occasional female "Topsy" indulged in burlesque and comical behaviour, and therefore they were popular where a carnival-like atmosphere prevailed. For this very reason, these characters were rarely photographed, and they almost never appeared at fancy dress balls, where a measure of dignity was desirable. For women, emblematic representations of Africa often skirted the issue of skin colour altogether with gypsy-like Algerian costumes or regal ancient Egyptian dress. Nor did ballgoers feel smugly superior only on account of skin colour; one Canadian ball was attended by two men who proclaimed themselves to be "Heathen Hindoos."

Attitudes towards feminism, too, were expressed through fancy dress. At a Montreal skating carnival in 1870, there were no less than four young women who chose a character called "Girl of the Period," a name derived from the moralistic writings of Eliza Lynn Linton that lamented the morals of young women. The Girl of the Period was "fast." She was not shy, naive, or sentimental – that is, she was not feminine. She had a love of gaiety and a bold, determined manner. Her dress was sometimes mannish but more often immodest or excessively fashionable. She had dyed or artificial hair and painted her face. Worse yet, she was comfortable, not bashful, with men, and she flirted openly. She might even smoke a cigar.

No doubt the women who represented her in fancy dress were taking advantage of the opportunity to act a bit "faster" than usual, but they also reinforced the negative stereotype which had emerged from Victorian anxieties about women's sexual behaviour.

> Among the ladies who fully sustained their characters may be mentioned Miss Mathewson as "A Girl of the Period" . . . [with] 40 pounder chignon, eyeglass, cigar, walking cane, &c, &c . . . Several other ladies ticketed themselves "Girls of the Period," but Miss M. was *the* "Girl."
>
> A gentleman in his nightgown and nightcap with lighted candle in hand, in search, apparently, for his bedroom, caused considerable fright to the females at first, but their shyness wore off, and he and the Girl of the Period, true to her character, became quite confidential.[30]

By the 1890s, the "Girl of the Period" was replaced by the new challenge to femininity, the "New Woman." Set apart by her independence, she was active and athletic, a working woman. She could also be parodied through fancy dress.

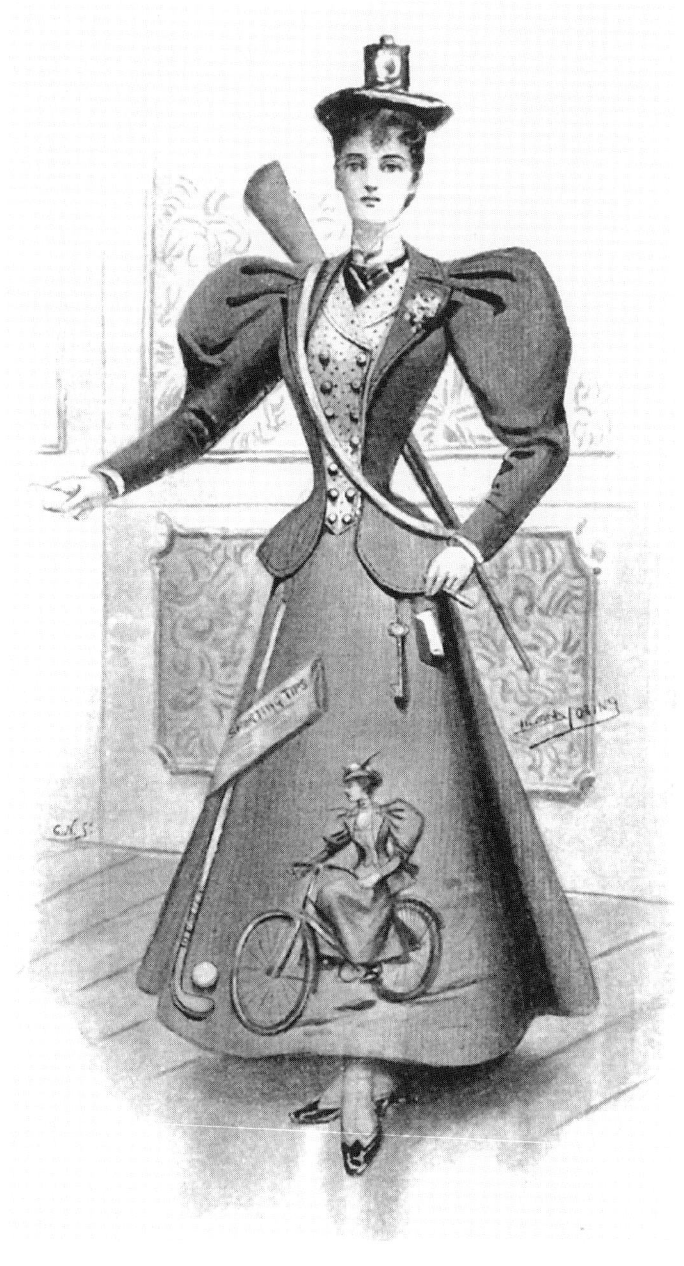

"New Woman." Like "The Girl of the Period," she holds a cigarette in her hand. FANCY DRESSES DESCRIBED (1896)

> NEW WOMAN. She wears a cloth tailor-made gown and her bicycle is portrayed in front of it, together with the *Sporting Times* and her golf club; she carries her betting book and her latch-key at her side, her gun is slung across her shoulder, and her pretty Tam o'Shanter is surmounted by a bicycle lamp. She has gaiters to her patent leather shoes and is armed at all points for conquest.

No evidence exists that the "New Woman" turned up at any ball in Canada, but at a skating carnival in New Glasgow, Nova Scotia, she was incarnated by no less than eight men, including one who called himself "The New Woman Up to Date." Perhaps she was more worrisome to both men and women than the "Girl of the Period" had been. *Everywoman's Encyclopedia* told of a slightly later experiment in emancipation with a sad result:

> An exceedingly pretty and popular girl once spent the dullest of evenings at a fancy ball, carrying a banner and attired in shirt, collar & tie, and short skirt, with spectacles, paint-wrinkled brow, and hard straw hat, as a "Militant Suffragette."

No doubt she had to sit out every dance.[31]

It was a serious matter for Victorians to cut loose for the space of an evening. Fancy dress balls fulfilled a social need by seemingly offering a reprieve from society's limitations on their identities, but ballgoers had to tread a very fine line between enjoying their ephemeral freedom and retaining their integrity. Their moral holiday in fact embodied the preoccupations of their rigidly conventional lives.

CHAPTER 2

The Earl of Dufferin's Grand Fancy Ball Ottawa, 23 February 1876

The entertainment was one of transcendent brilliancy, and will be looked on hereafter, when the Earl of Dufferin and his noble consort will no longer be amongst us . . . as the great festive event of their career in Canada.[1]

Frederick Temple Blackwood, Earl of Dufferin (1826-1902), was the perfect candidate for Governor General of Canada. His appointment in 1872 marked the end of the British government's ambivalent attitude towards Canada in the years immediately following Confederation in 1867. A grandson of the dramatist Richard Brinsley Sheridan, the Irish-born Dufferin brought the new imperial enthusiasm to the masses with his romantic temperament and charismatic presence. Accompanied by his much younger wife, Harriot Rowan Hamilton, Dufferin recreated the vice-regal role by setting a precedent for the degree of social involvement which Canadians could expect from their Governor General.

Dufferin saw himself as a unifying force, a considerable challenge considering that Canadians were strung out sparsely in small towns and rural areas across thousands of miles and that a major schism existed between the English and the French. The Dufferins travelled extensively to meet large numbers of Canadians face to face, so that, although the task of bringing Canada's disparate parts together was far too great for one six-year term, he did further the cause of Empire by bringing his brand of officialdom to the people. Dufferin also managed to maintain his popularity in the political arena despite the eruption of such difficult issues as the messy Pacific Scandal, which led to Sir John A. Macdonald's resignation and the forming of a new government under Sir Alexander Mackenzie. During Dufferin's term, too, the country suffered a severe economic depression.

In 1872, Ottawa was still a discouraging sight. On arriving in June, Lady Dufferin wrote, "The first sight of Rideau Hall did lower our spirits a little!" But the next day she observed, "The morning has brought more cheerful reflections." One of Dufferin's early letters described the city as "a very desolate place, consisting of a jumble of brand new houses and shops, built or building, and a wilderness of wooden shanties spread along either side of long broad strips of mud," but soon he declared himself "much taken with the country and the people." From then on the couple optimistically made efforts to improve Rideau Hall and its grounds and add what dignity they could to its appointments and their social life. At public expense Dufferin added a new ballroom and a tennis court which served alternately as a supper room; from his own pocket he built an indoor curling rink and a monumental toboggan slide. The Governor General's salary of £10,000 would have severely

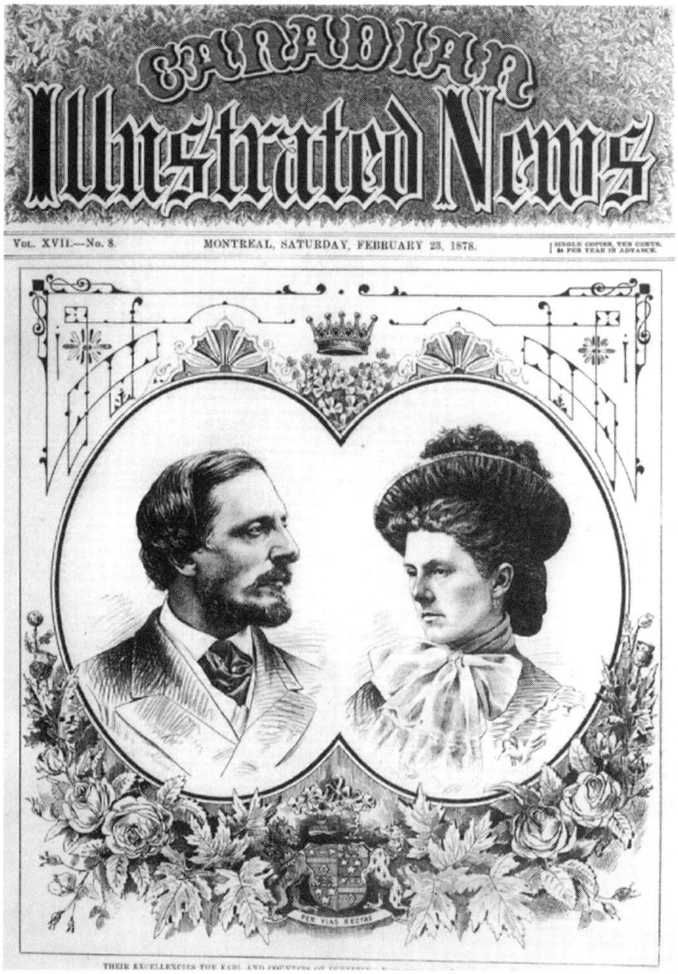

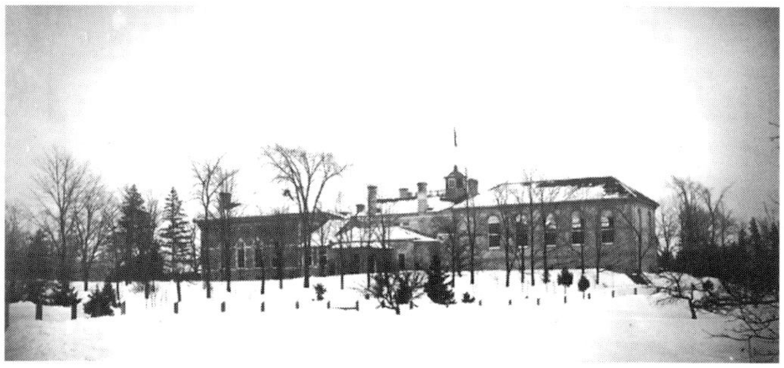

Above: Frederick Temple Blackwood, the Earl of Dufferin, Canada's third Governor General, and Harriot Rowan Hamilton, Countess of Dufferin. *CANADIAN ILLUSTRATED NEWS*, 23 FEB. 1878, COVER

Right: Rideau Hall prior to 1882. On the cold winter evening of the Grand Fancy Ball, Government House must have appeared much like this. NAC/PA8610

cramped Dufferin's prodigal style, but dipping into one's personal funds had become practically a requirement of the office anyway. The Governor General was expected to pay the cost of operating Rideau Hall (which was very expensive to heat) and the salaries of his domestic staff, as well as providing all his own household items such as furniture, linen and dishes. He also had to cover his own expenses for entertaining and for travelling throughout the country. With a strong sense of purpose, the Dufferins engaged wholeheartedly in these activities, and they spent copiously.[2]

Their life in the capital included frequent short trips to Montreal and Toronto, the two main commercial centres of the country, where they attended and gave entertainments. In 1872 they held a ball in the Parliament buildings in Toronto, and in 1873 they were honoured at a memorable Citizens' Ball in Montreal. On one trip to Montreal, Notman included the entire vice-regal party in his composite photograph "Curling in Canada."

In Ottawa, the Earl and Countess created a social whirl befitting a capital city, and Lady Dufferin chronicled the never-ending round of events in her journal. Shortly after they arrived, she wrote, "Society is at present my business in life, and this is how my week is laid out: Monday I remain at home to receive visitors. Tuesday, Wednesday, Thursday, we have large dinners. Friday we keep for sightseeing, and Saturday we have small dinners. On the big nights we have a 'drum.'" They also held large balls, and Dufferin, who loved to dance, had to be torn away from balls and parties. He remained "dancing with dowagers until four o'clock in the morning," wrote his wife after one event. For this propensity, some young ladies of Montreal pronounced him "a brick."[3]

Lady Dufferin, considerably more reserved than her husband, embodied the Victorian ideal of True Womanhood. Like the Earl, she had the ability to maintain an air of urbane sophistication without seeming affected or condescending. Her Irish background gave her a down-to-earth side which Ottawa loved. She was thrilled when a local paper described how she dressed plainly and sensibly, wearing thick boots which took her through the muddiest crossings, and she was avid about salmon fishing. Yet evenings would find her presiding at dinner in a gown from the House of Worth, of which she was a devoted client; her nephew, Harold Nicolson, found her downright "bigoted" about haute couture. "There was no lady in Europe who could enter a room like Lady Dufferin," the King of Greece remarked, and her perfect court curtseys later became famous throughout India. But beneath the surface, Lady Dufferin was in fact quite shy and diffident, uncomfortable when she had to receive large crowds of guests on her own and hard pressed to think of ninety different ways to talk about the weather. On a trip to Halifax, when Dufferin was called away suddenly, she was most ill at ease "doing Governor General" alone.[4]

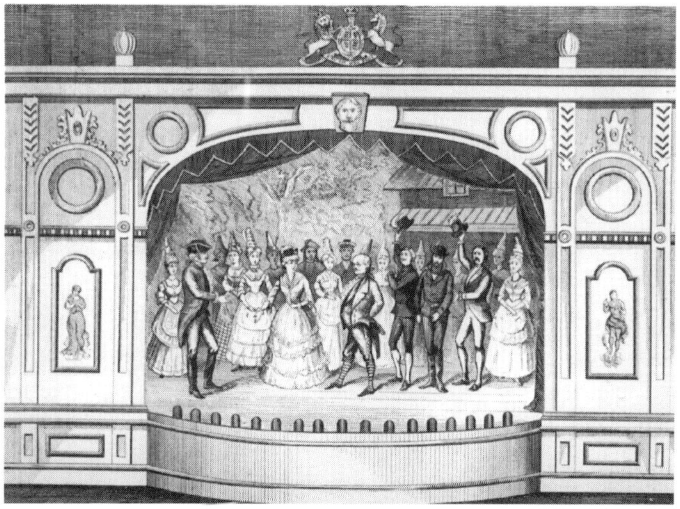

Scene from *The Mayor of St. Brieux* on the stage of the Rideau Hall ballroom, 31 March 1875. CANADIAN ILLUSTRATED NEWS, 24 APR. 1875, 264

Lady Dufferin did have a theatrical bent, however, and loved nothing better than dressing up and acting. "She adds histrionic talents of a high order to her many other accomplishments," wrote a spectator of the parlour theatricals at Rideau Hall, and Nicolson recalled "certain moments when she would discard her stateliness and appear wholly different. . . . Such moments were always connected with some form of travesty, whether charades, dumb-crambo, practical jokes even, or merely dressing up." She was delighted once when she could not guess the identity of an "Arab" at a fancy dress ball, only to be told that it was His Excellency.[5]

Both Lord and Lady Dufferin set out to make their favourite activities social rituals in Ottawa. Among the amateur theatricals and *tableaux vivants* were the play *To Oblige Benson* in 1873, and, on New Year's Day, 1874, children's *tableaux* including "Sleeping Beauty in the Woods." One of the most outstanding original productions was *The Mayor of St. Brieux*, written by the children's tutor, Frederick Dixon, and the church organist, F.W. Mills, and performed in March 1875. After the play, the Countess "asked the actors to keep on their costumes during the evening, and they made the party look very gay and pretty." She herself played lead roles in no less than three plays in 1877.[6]

The Earl, with his sporting turn of mind, embraced the gamut of Canadian winter sports: skating, hockey, curling, tobogganing and snowshoeing. His Excellency was already an experienced skater, and although Lady Dufferin found skating in front of a group of experts intimidating at first, with practice she could soon "go more than a mile as fast as possible on the outside edge." Not surprisingly, Lord and Lady Dufferin both relished fancy dress skating parties. After a carnival in Montreal, she wrote, "The fancy dress skating ball . . . was a most beautiful sight, besides being great fun. . . . It was like a fairy pantomime of gigantic size, and was most striking." The Earl could be persuaded to leave only after the final strains of "God Save the Queen," and this time she too was loathe for the party to end.[7]

The most memorable social event of the Dufferins' term elevated their love of theatricals and parties to a height previously unknown in Canada. Their Grand Fancy Ball, held in their own Rideau Hall ballroom on 23 February 1876, was chronicled all over North America and in Europe, and it stood as a benchmark for Ottawa entertainments for a full generation. Like the Marlborough ball in London two years earlier, the lavish event was in a sense its own end; Ottawa could now be seen to have a social life and a select society to rival that of any other major city in the eyes of the rest of Canada, Great Britain and the United States. "It could not have been surpassed by the Court of the French Empire in its palmiest hour," wrote an observer.[8]

Getting to Government House, inconveniently located two miles from Ottawa, was never easy, but on the long-awaited evening of the ball, woe betide the guest who had not made arrangements well in advance. By seven o'clock traffic was backed up along the avenue leading to the vice-regal residence. Guests who rode in their own vehicles

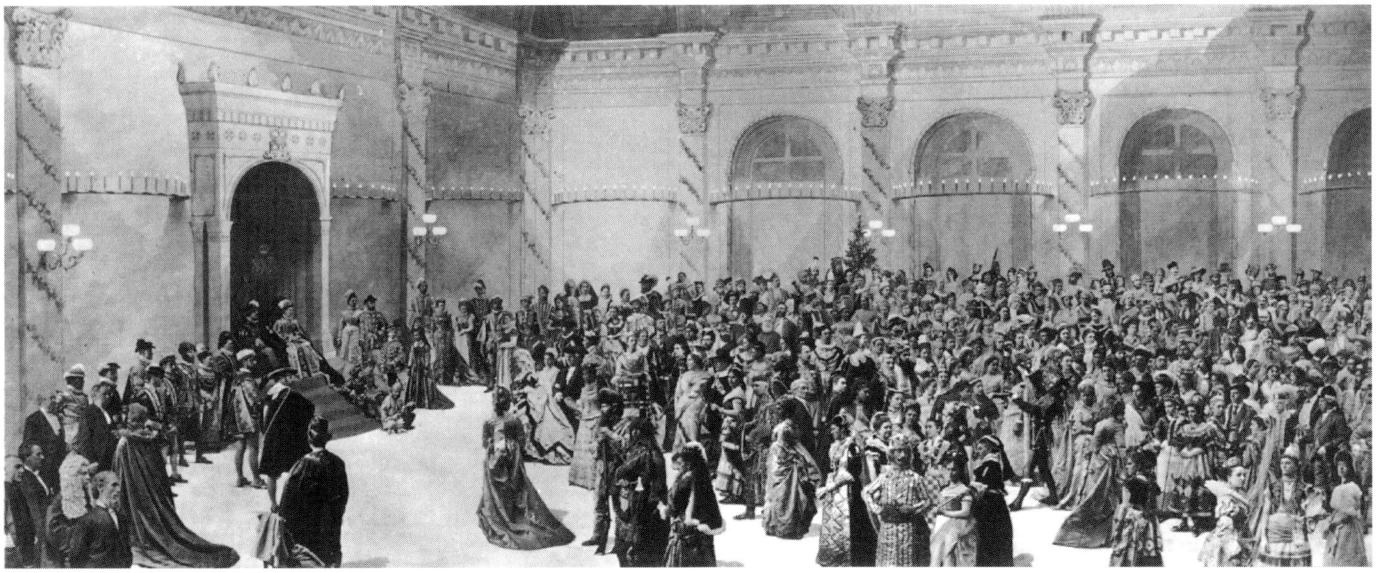

The Grand Fancy Ball at Rideau Hall, 1876. Ottawa photographer William James Topley created this composite photograph by taking some three hundred individual portraits over the months following the ball, pasting them onto a painting of the ballroom to create the crowd scene, and rephotographing the whole scene. On the left, the Dufferins are seated in their throne chairs, with their entourage surrounding them and William Campbell, the jester, seated at the foot of the dais.
WJT/NAC/C6865

hardly dared to feel smug; in the muddy new capital serviceability still outweighed appearance, and on this evening, when glitter and sparkle were *de rigueur*, the shabbiness of the carriages, some "amusingly novel" and others "judged by the most liberal interpretation to be presentable," stood out even more than usual. Those who hired a cab went at their own risk, for cab drivers were known to extort as much as $20 for a trip outside the city where there was no control over their fares. For guests who could neither use their own conveyance or hire a cab, the Governor General had made special arrangements: the new streetcar system, the Ottawa City Passenger Railway Company, went from house to house to pick up guests who reserved beforehand. Never mind that arriving this way meant a less elegant entrance and clearly marked passengers as among the less fortunate; the colour and hilarity which prevailed in the horse-drawn vehicles was the stuff of lifelong memories. For Fanny Meredith, "The drive out to the fancy ball was most amusing. The carriage was crowded with costumes from many parts of the world and many ages. Oh, what a merry company we were."[9]

Guests stepped out of their carriages into the bitter cold only to get caught in a crush at the door. Despite these inconveniences, everywhere "cheeks were flushing with the fanciful pleasure of growing anticipation." As the elite of Ottawa were not easily recognizable in the garb of many ages and nations, rigorous security was in place; invitations had to be presented before guests could enter Rideau Hall. But on this night it was not only the confusion occasioned by Tudor queens and Spanish bandits which necessitated these precautions. Newspaper hype had spread across the country, and the entire Dominion was thought to be "mentally journeying" to the event. Certainly the uninvited of Ottawa were. "Went downtown in the afternoon," Janet Hall wrote in her diary from her modest dwelling over a hardware store. "Great excitement over the Fancy Ball which is taking place now." No doubt a few would actually attempt disguise and entry.[10]

As police officers approved invitations and directed carriage drivers away from the crowded entrance, the excited guests entered Rideau Hall. Blasts of warm air came from the two furnaces installed for the occasion. From the vestibule a broad flight of stairs led to the supper room on one side and to the ballroom on the other. The Dufferins had arranged royal treatment for their guests. A guard of honour from the ranks of the Governor General's Foot Guards flanked both side of the entrance hall, and a military band played marches. Liveried servants conducted women up the staircase, whereupon ladies' maids whisked them off to dressing rooms to remove their fur wraps and don the gloves and slippers which they had brought with them.

Despite the hubbub throughout the crowded lower floor of the house, the vice-regal party in their quarters was calm – perhaps for the first time in months. As early as the formal announcement of their ball in mid-November, 1875, Lady Dufferin was "already deep in millinery talk." Throughout the next three months, the Governor General's entourage plotted and planned an entertainment which only a full-fledged capital city could merit. The Dufferins hired orchestras and had a new tennis court built to serve as a supper room. Lady Dufferin wrote out programmes and oversaw dance rehearsals. Over a week before the event, she had the ballroom decked with artificial flowers, and the supper room decorated. The day of the ball, however, the Dufferins turned their minds to other pursuits, taking in a furious curling match and then lunching with the players. Unlike their eager guests, who dressed and were on their way early in the evening, the Dufferins and their friends relaxed as they imagined the hustle and bustle below and only began to don their finery at nine o'clock.

In fact, almost everyone had arrived by the time His Excellency rang for Mr. Nowell, his valet, to dress him, and Mrs. Dent began lacing and hooking her ladyship into her splendid costume. Dent may have felt the slightest twinge of envy at not being part of this evening's proceedings, but she knew that in two days she, too, would have her chance to whirl around the ballroom and partake of choice viands in the new supper room. Of course the cut flowers would by then be rather wilted, not unlike her ball gown – perhaps a cast-off from her mistress – but the Dufferins would magnanimously open their "servants' ball" themselves. From the comfort of the boudoir, Dent and the Dufferins could only imagine expectant guests "anxious to see and be seen" mingling in the corridors, the library and the dining room, which for this evening had become a tea room piled high with sandwiches and refreshments.

In the hallways some guests busied themselves "criticizing the costumes of their acquaintances." Men who recognized their belles in the stately guise of "Amy Robsart" or found a plain woman unusually alluring as "Night" busily wrote their names in dance cards, while parents and chaperons periodically swooped down on their charges to ensure that the same name appeared no more than twice. The crowd slowly drifted into the thirty-by-sixty-foot ballroom, a "well proportioned apartment, of the Corinthian order, with pilasters set in the wall at regular intervals, surmounted by a highly ornamented entablature, and supporting an arched ceiling." At the first ball the Dufferins had held in this room three years earlier, the walls were still bare plaster streaked with a first coat of paint – a far cry from the current "French grey" decorated with a few touches of gold and pink. Pink, white and pale blue flowers festooned the eighteen pilasters in the brilliantly lit room.

Finally, at nearly ten o'clock, a footman swung open the Rideau Hall ballroom doors

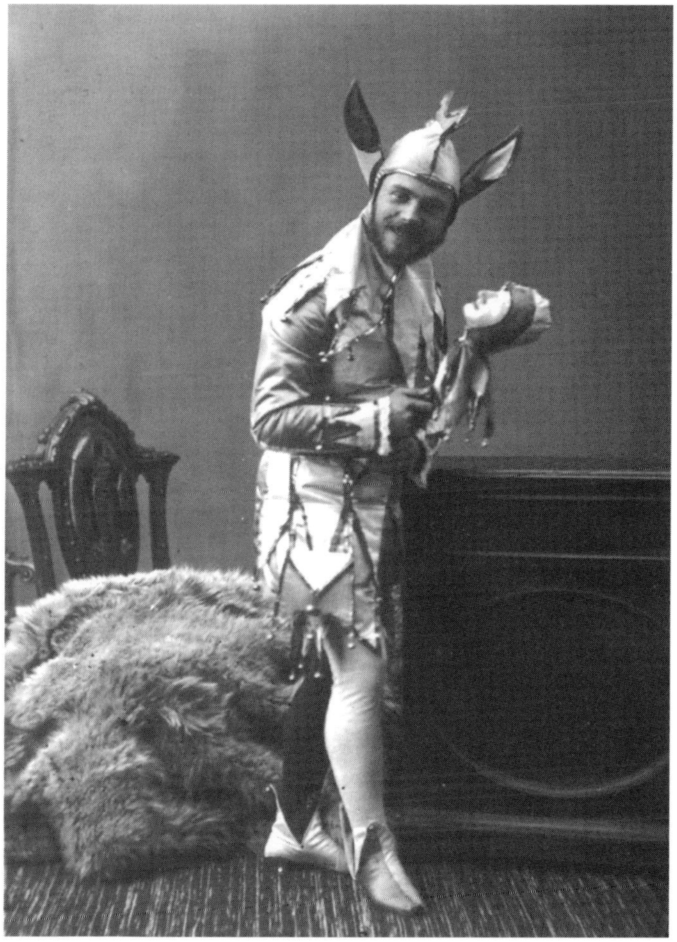

Above: William Campbell, private secretary to Lord Dufferin, as "The Court Jester." WJT/NAC/PA138393

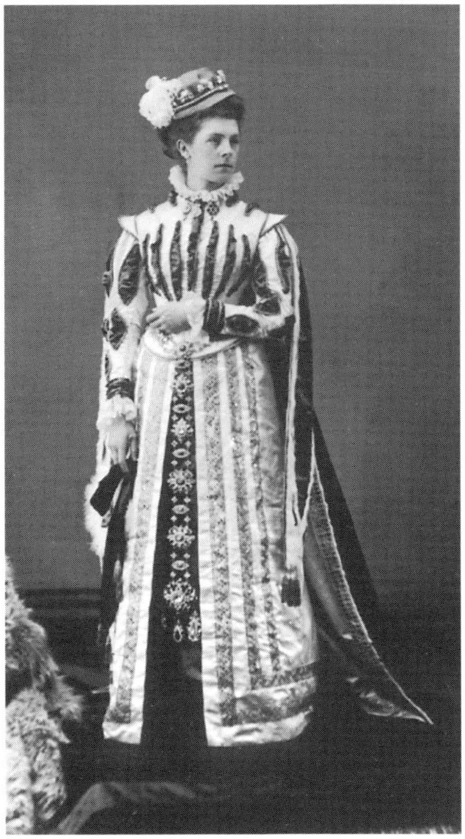

The Countess of Dufferin as "Mary of Guise" in a "petticoat of crimson satin under a white satin train with two rows of gold embroidery; high white satin bodice with closed sleeves. The waist and sleeves were trimmed with small puffings of crimson satin, each puff edged with gold cord; long hanging sleeves of crimson lined with white. A small toque of the period, made of crimson velvet, most bewitchingly shaped, and ornamented with a handsome river and coronal of shamrocks in diamonds. Round her waist she wore a jewelled belt and girdle, the latter almost reaching the skirt of the petticoat. From her shoulders hung a beautiful robe of rich crimson velvet, lined with white satin and bordered with ermine; round the throat Her Excellency wore a magnificent set of diamond stars, from which depended three handsome gold lockets set with rubies, turquoise, pearls and gold." (*Toronto Globe*, 24 Feb. 1876) WJT/NAC/PA26462

connecting with the Dufferins' apartments, and eight hundred guests surged forward and craned their necks to view the vice-regal procession. Those in front pressed against the silk cord creating a pathway between the open doors and the crimson-draped dais, with its richly carved chairs. Hearts beat faster as the band of the Governor General's Foot Guards struck up a march. "Short people are on tiptoe, tall people's noses are tickled by short peoples' feathers, and there is a general squeeze; but no matter, the Court jester leads the way, and one feels able to endure anything and everything until the procession is over."[11]

The jester was none other than the diminutive William Campbell, the Earl of Dufferin's private secretary and a favourite staff member. A natural ham, Mr. Campbell was in his element in his particoloured costume decked with bells and carrying a puppet on a stick. In he pranced, stopping to bow with mock solemnity to those lined up along the cord and to gesture comically with his arms and puppet. He stole the show when he skipped forward and took the Earl's place on the throne. No doubt Lady Dufferin, still out of view, was inclined to giggle, because "Little Campbell," as she called him, always made her laugh, but she kept her composure to emerge from the doorway beside her spouse with her usual stately poise and presence.

"A most brilliant *coup d'oeil*," gushed one of the many reporters on the scene: the twenty-one members of the vice-regal procession were decked out as "The Court of James V of Scotland," with the proconsul as the sovereign himself. Even the three oldest Dufferin children were fitted out for the occasion. Lady Dufferin, as "Mary of Guise," looked especially regal in her white satin dress with crimson puffs on the sleeves and bodice. Her crimson velvet train trimmed with ermine was borne by two pages, one of them her third child, seven year-old Terence Blackwood. His sister, Lady Helen Blackwood, barely into her teens, was a young "Mary Queen of Scots," and his brother, Viscount Clandeboye, was "Lord Darnley as a Child."

At first glance, the costume worn by the Earl appeared rather ordinary; nevertheless, Dufferin's charismatic and dignified presence quickly turned surprise to praise. What the guests did not know, in spite of weeks of discussion about who would go as what and the numerous stories circulating about the Earl's character, was that Dufferin did not dress as he had planned. He had returned his first costume, ordered from London. Two days before the ball, his second choice arrived from a New York costumier, but he discovered that it had "inexcusable defects" which rendered it unwearable. With forty-eight hours left, and nothing to wear to the most magnificent event the capital had yet seen, Dufferin was in a bind. Obviously he had felt that Ottawa tradespeople were incapable of creating something worthy of His Excellency, but now he had no choice but to turn to them. His regular tailor, G. M. Holbrook,

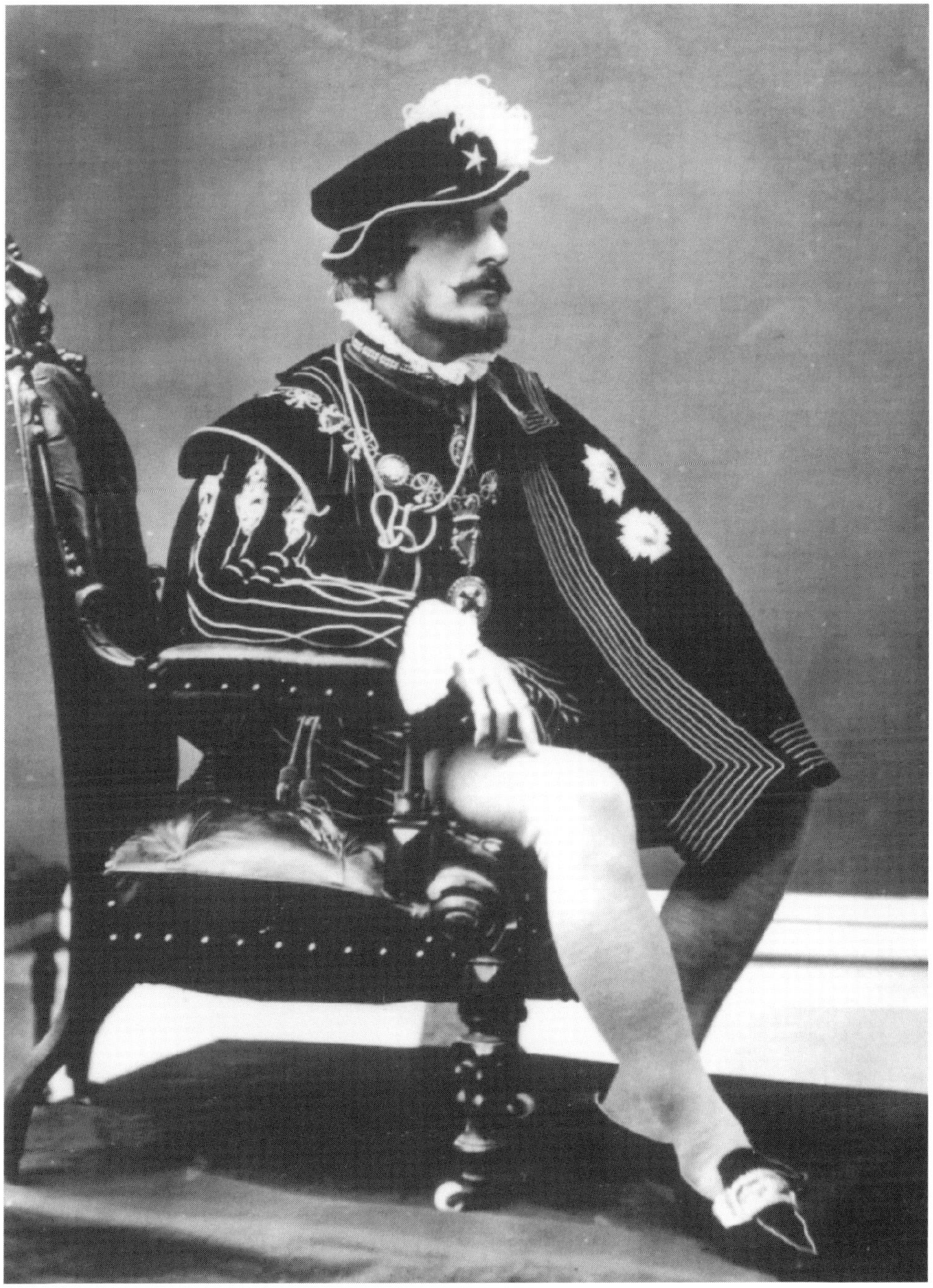

The Earl of Dufferin as "James V of Scotland." "The costume as worn by His Excellency was generally admired, on account of its elegance and richness, and its adaptation to the 'style' of the wearer. It was of rich black silk velvet, doublet, trunk hose, and short cloak gracefully trimmed with gold braid, and ornamented with puffings of slate coloured satin. The stars and collars of his orders showed in pretty relief upon the exceedingly rich material composing the dress; a cap of black velvet with white feather fastened by a diamond *aigrette* completed a costume by all odds the handsomest of the hundreds of brilliant and elegant costumes which thronged the room." (*Ottawa Free Press*, 25 Feb. 1876) WJT/NAC/C2109

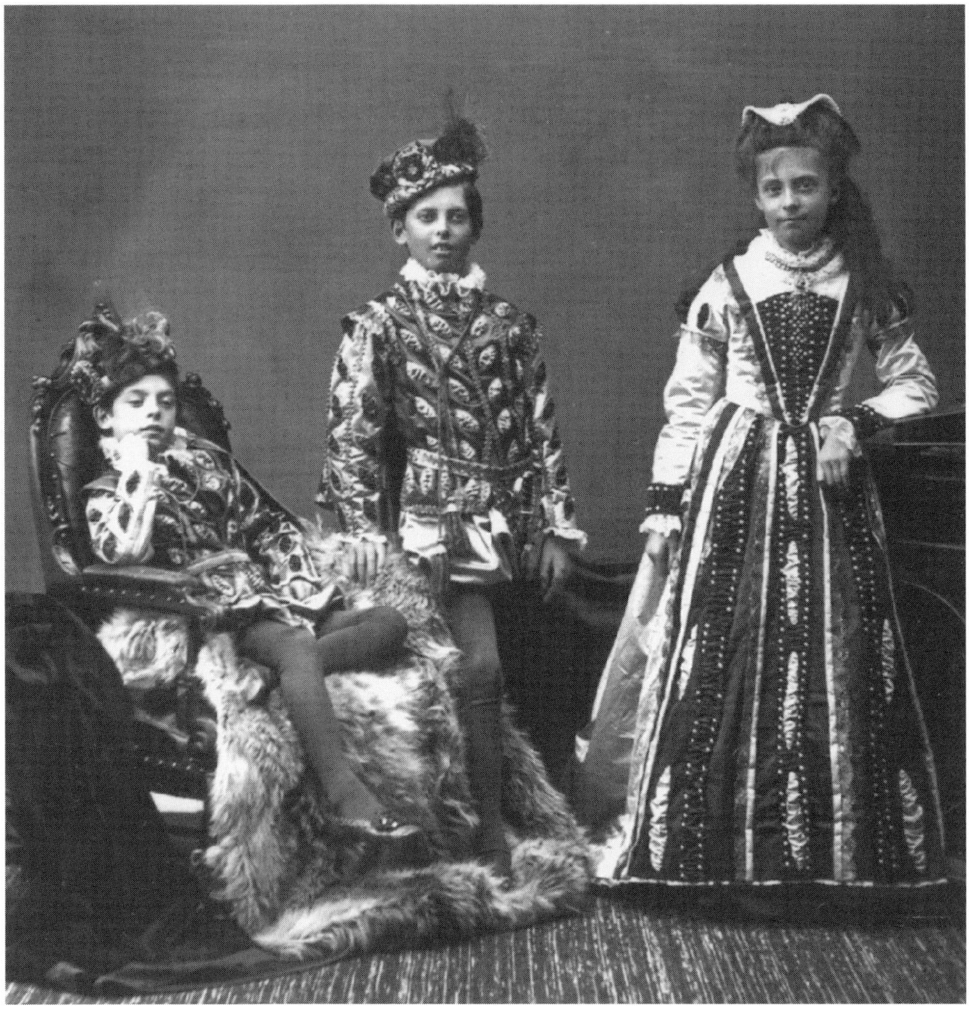

The Dufferins' three oldest children, Terence, Archie (Viscount Clandeboye) and Nellie (Lady Helen Blackwood). All three children's costumes are in blue satin with orange satin trim. Nellie represented "Mary Queen of Scots" as a child. "Her hair was raised over a cushion and allowed to flow down the back, thus forming a golden veil to this beautiful costume." (*Toronto Globe*, 24 Feb. 1876) WJT/NAC/PA193687

had no previous experience whatsoever with fancy dress, but all the same he managed to turn out a satisfactory costume in time.

The Earl's garments created an effect on the expectant audience a bit like that caused by the fabled emperor's new clothes: "His Excellency's costume, though very rich, was perhaps the plainest in the room; but the good taste that marked its selection made his plain black-and-gold-clad figure more distinctively *the* figure there." No doubt a few other guests gazed disappointedly at their own satin and sequins; wishing to appear worthy of their hosts, perhaps, colonials that they were, they had overdone it. But no matter, Her Excellency had only positive comments on their efforts. "The dresses of our guests were beautiful and there was great variety in them."[12]

And indeed, Ottawa was exceptionally well turned out. The men of the Dufferin entourage were not the only ones clad in the short breeches and tights of "the period of English society life in which doublet and trunk hose gave scope for artistic treatment." From the sixteenth century were two "Sir Walter Raleighs," two "Earls of Leicester," and two "Henrys of Navarre." Those wishing to reveal less of their limbs opted for seventeenth- or eighteenth-century characters in knee breeches – courtiers and cavaliers of Charles I and Charles II, Louis XIV and XV, and George II and III. Accompanying them were regal dames from the pages of history – three versions of "Mary, Queen of Scots," a "Queen Elizabeth," many "Ladies of the Time of Charles II," and a couple of incarnations each of "The Princesse de Lamballe" and "Marie

Miss Alice Lee as "Amy Robsart," from Sir Walter Scott's *Kenilworth*. *Fancy Dresses Described* recommends "an Elizabethan dress of the richest materials. . . . Any rare lace and jewels may be worn." Miss Lee makes a striking Elizabethan heroine in a "handsome court train of white satin, with puffed sleeves to match; a ruffle of white lace coming down heart shaped in front; stomacher embroidered in fine pearls. The hair was rolled over a cushion in front, and hung down the back far below the waist, and on this she wore a coronet." While long loose hair was not prescribed for the character, Miss Lee took the opportunity to show off her splendid dark mane. (Holt, 1896, 7; *Toronto Globe*, 24 Feb. 1876) WJT/NAC/PA193682

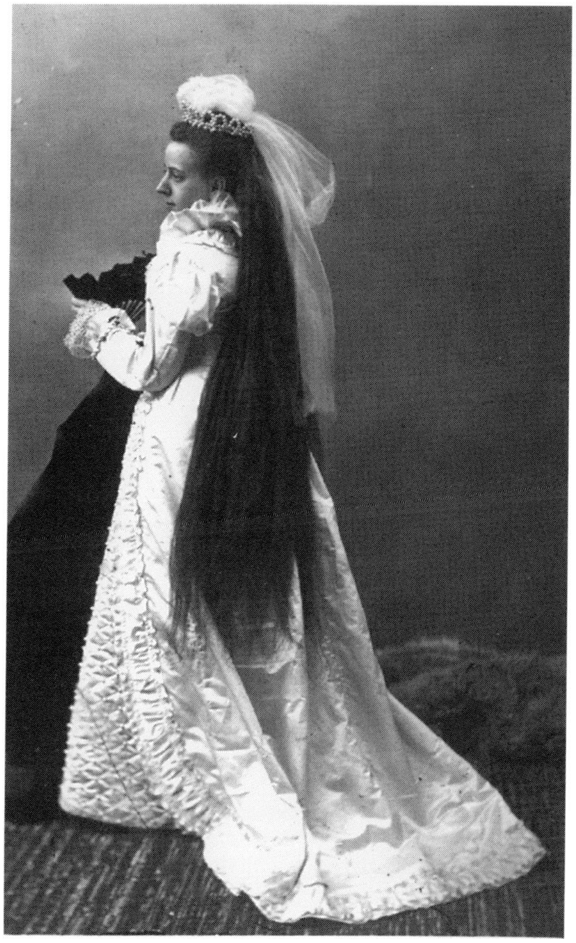

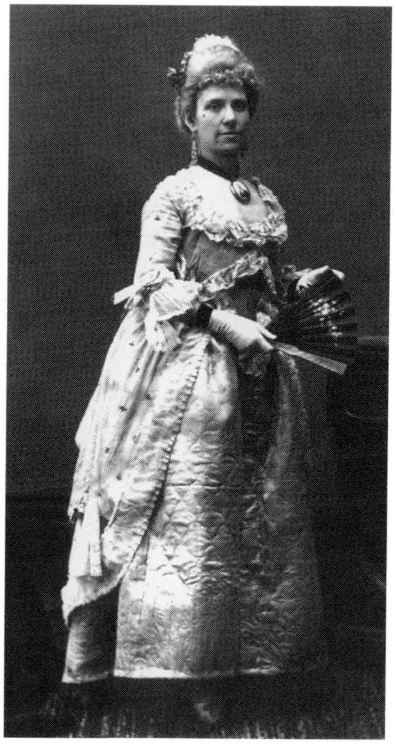

Mrs. John Courtney (a daughter of Fennings Taylor, Deputy Clerk of the Senate) as "Lady Esmond Warrington" in heirloom garments: "Petticoat pink satin, quilted by hand; dress muslin covered with flowers worked by hand and lined with pink silk; white satin shoes, silver buckles, hair *poudré*. Dress, petticoat, and shoes 120 years old." In keeping with the eighteenth-century style, she wore black "patches" or beauty spots on her face. The bodice of her dress has been considerably altered, but like others who donned heirloom garments, Mrs. Courtney was able to express her status very thriftily. (*Toronto Globe*, 25 Feb. 1876) WJT/NAC/PA193689

Antoinette." Some took the opportunity to showcase family heirlooms. Buckles worn at the court of Louis XIV by the Marquis of Lotbinière ornamented the black velvet shoes of financier R.E. O'Connor. Mrs. James Patterson, the "Pompadour" wife of a civil service clerk, wore family jewels one hundred and fifty years old (which included shoe buckles on velvet ribbons for bracelets), and Miss Taylor as "Princess Amelia, daughter of George II" showed off a handpainted silk court train which had been in her family for a hundred and fifty years. Mrs. John Courtney as "Lady Esmond Warrington" wore heirloom garments from the third quarter of the eighteenth century.

Literary figures included several "Anne Pages" from *The Merry Wives of Windsor*, three "Portias" from *The Merchant of Venice*, a "Hamlet," a "Romeo," and a "Mercutio." Sir Walter Scott rivalled the bard in popularity with four "Amy Robsarts" from *Kenilworth*, a "Rowena" from *Ivanhoe*, and the ever-popular fancy dress heroine "Di Vernon" from *Rob Roy*. Very conspicuous were three couples as "Lady and Sir Peter Teazle" – a compliment to the distinguished host, as *A School for Scandal* was written by his grandfather, Sir Richard Brinsley Sheridan. Mythology provided "Diana" and "Hebe, Cupbearer to the Gods" in Grecian draperies, and fairy tales contributed "Mary, Mary, Quite Contrary," "Mother Hubbard" and "Little Bo-Peep." Senator Henry Kaulbach, a Nova Scotian barrister and ship owner, made a ferocious "Bluebeard" carrying a large knife with a pearl handle. Dr. Hamnett Hill, an Ottawa physician, inspired awe as a gruff "Santa Claus," with pockets brimming over with toys and a Christmas tree in his hand.

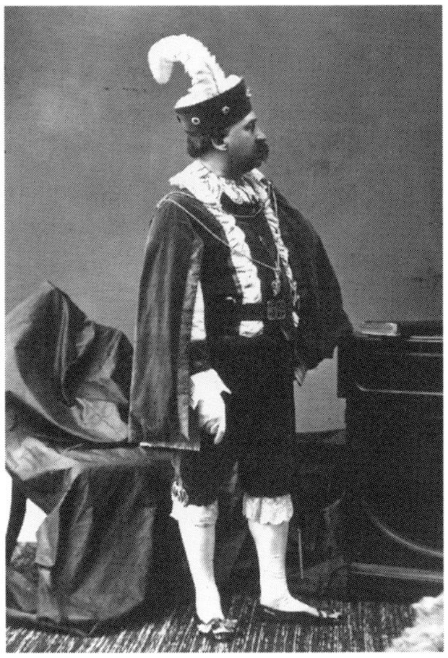

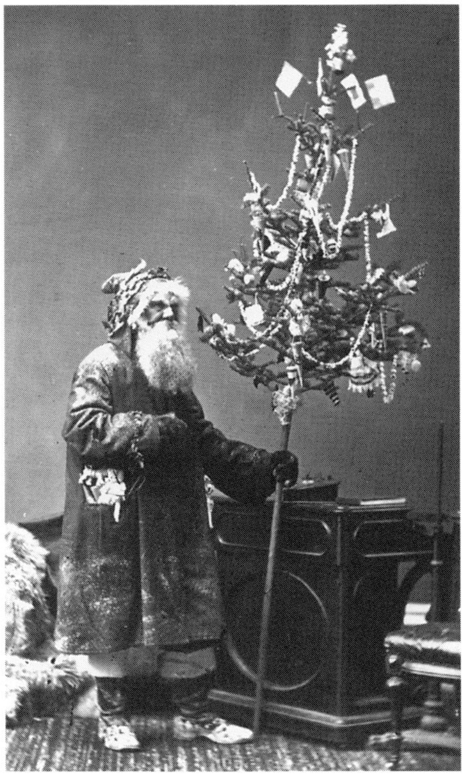

Above: The Honorable Hector Langevin as "A Spanish Prince of the 16th Century." Many of the political figures present at the ball did not attempt to dress up, but Langevin, leader of the Quebec wing of the Conservative party, got into the spirit of the event in a costume of dark blue velvet and white satin. His blue velvet cap is topped off with an *aigrette* held in place with a diamond pin. WJT/NAC/PA25571

Right: Dr. Hamnett Hill wearing a "loose dark brown blouse a la Santa Claus, with capuchin trimmed with holly leaves and scarlet berries; usual accompaniments of flowing white beard, whiskers and moustache; side pockets of coat filled with toys, &c., long boots turned down shewing pink linings; the whole snowed over, carrying in hand a time-honoured Christmas tree elegantly decorated with toys, flags, candles, &c." (*Ottawa Daily Citizen*, 24 Feb. 1876) WJT/NAC/PA189666

Spanish dress was by far the most popular; the assembly included numerous bullfighters, tambourine girls, and no less than sixteen "Spanish Ladies" and twelve "Matadors." Spanish and Italian bandits abounded, among them six swashbuckling "Fra Diavolos" and four "Don Cesar de Bazans," all with ostrich plumes waving in their hats. A few women called themselves "Brigand's Bride" or "Bandit Queen." Miss Emma Lemoine, as "A Brigand Queen," draped herself in scarves trimmed with coins. "This dress was a decided success," said the *Ottawa Times*.

Several women made a stunning turnout in emblematic dress. Most popular was "Night," with five incarnations, all swathed in black gauze spangled with star-shaped sequins and bearing crescent moons on their heads. Two "Winters" appeared in white fur-trimmed gowns decked with holly berries and glass icicles; one was embellished with a few real stuffed robins and snowbirds. But, most fetching of all, Miss Fennel came as "Twilight Star," in two shades of royal blue with silver stars on her wand and even embroidered on the toes of her boots.

Two amusing dresses represented games. Grace Ritchie, the wife of Supreme Court Judge William Ritchie, embodied "Chess," with red and white checkerboard inserts on her black velvet dress and a coronet and necklace of chessmen, while Miss Edith Macpherson wore every appurtenance of "Tric-trac" (a version of backgammon) on her dress and dice for earrings. Four versions of "Folly" sported pointed caps and dresses trimmed with bells, and two women as "The Press" danced in fashionably styled dresses made entirely out of newspapers.

Among the characters from other lands, William Allan, the owner of a mining company, stood out as a Chinese mandarin in what he claimed was "a real Chinese nobleman's costume imported from that country." In fact, it was a Cantonese theatre costume associated with female roles. The more fanciful exotics included "Ali Buck of the Dhurrumtollah Bazaar, Calcutta" and "Nourshadene, a Cabul Woman"; Mr. Cowper Cox of the Department of the Interior as "A Mohammedan Zemindar" accompanied his wife, "A Madrassee Ayah"; and Mrs. R.E. O'Connor was garbed in an exquisite costume as "A Turkish Lady," with "a magnificent switch of hair four feet long falling down her back." Mr. Waddell and another man disported themselves in makeshift costumes as "Heathen Hindoos," not yet aware that the friend who had painted their faces brown had used iodine, which left a stain that stayed for days. Peasantry was represented by a couple of "Dolly Vardens," two "Bonnie Fishwives of New Haven" with nets full of *papier maché* fish, and several Neapolitan and Italian peasants in striped skirts and flat headdresses.

Despite the wild variety, decorum reigned. As the invitation specified, "fancy dresses imitating the costume of any religious order" were off limits. There were but few short hemlines, no masks, and absolutely no one dressed as the opposite sex; the

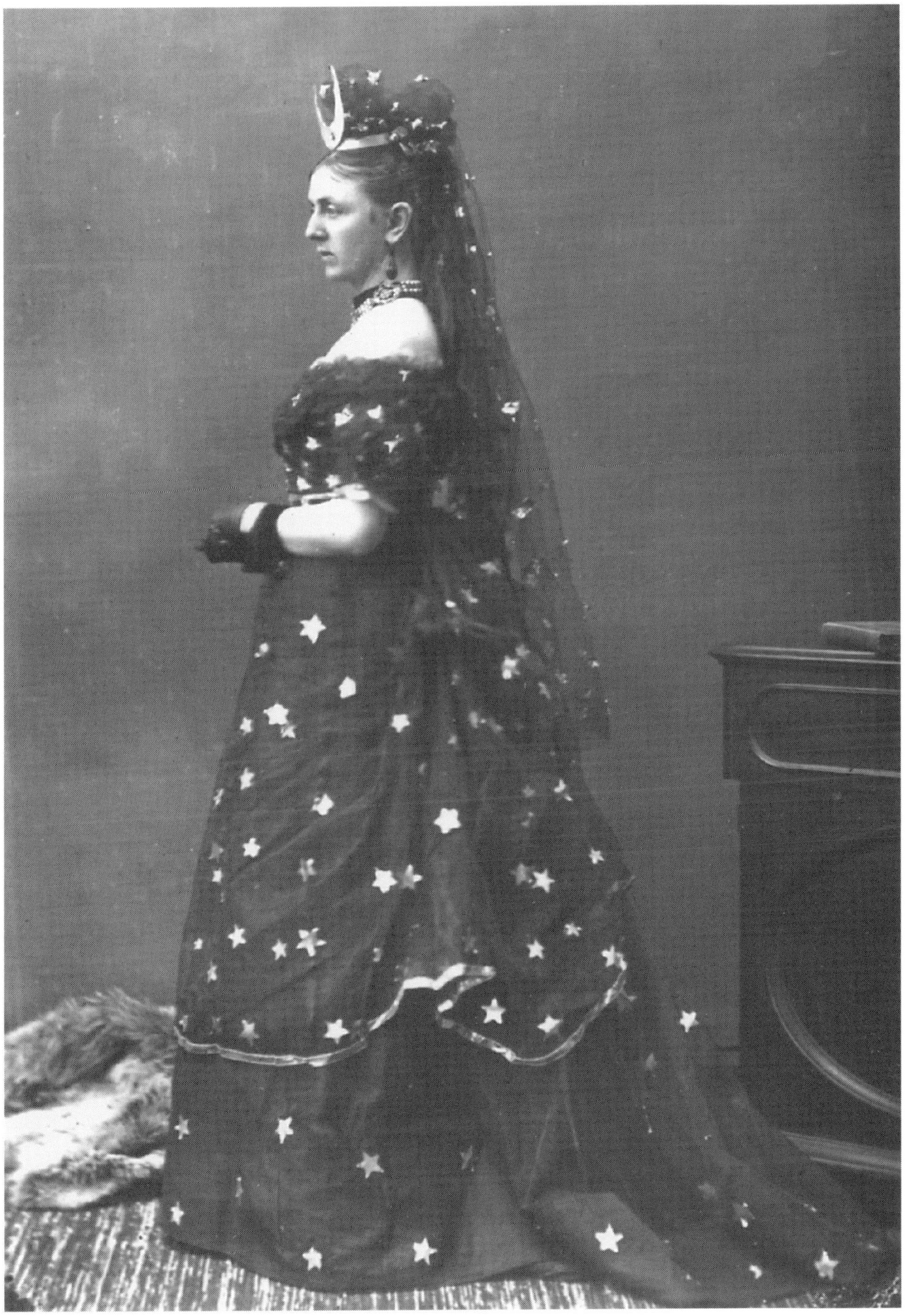

Miss Agnes Yielding as "Night," in "black tarletan with silver stars over black moiré overskirt, handsomely trimmed with silver bands; Brussels net veil, silver stars and crescent and silver ornaments." (*Toronto Daily Mail*, 24 Feb. 1876) WJT/NAC/PA192351

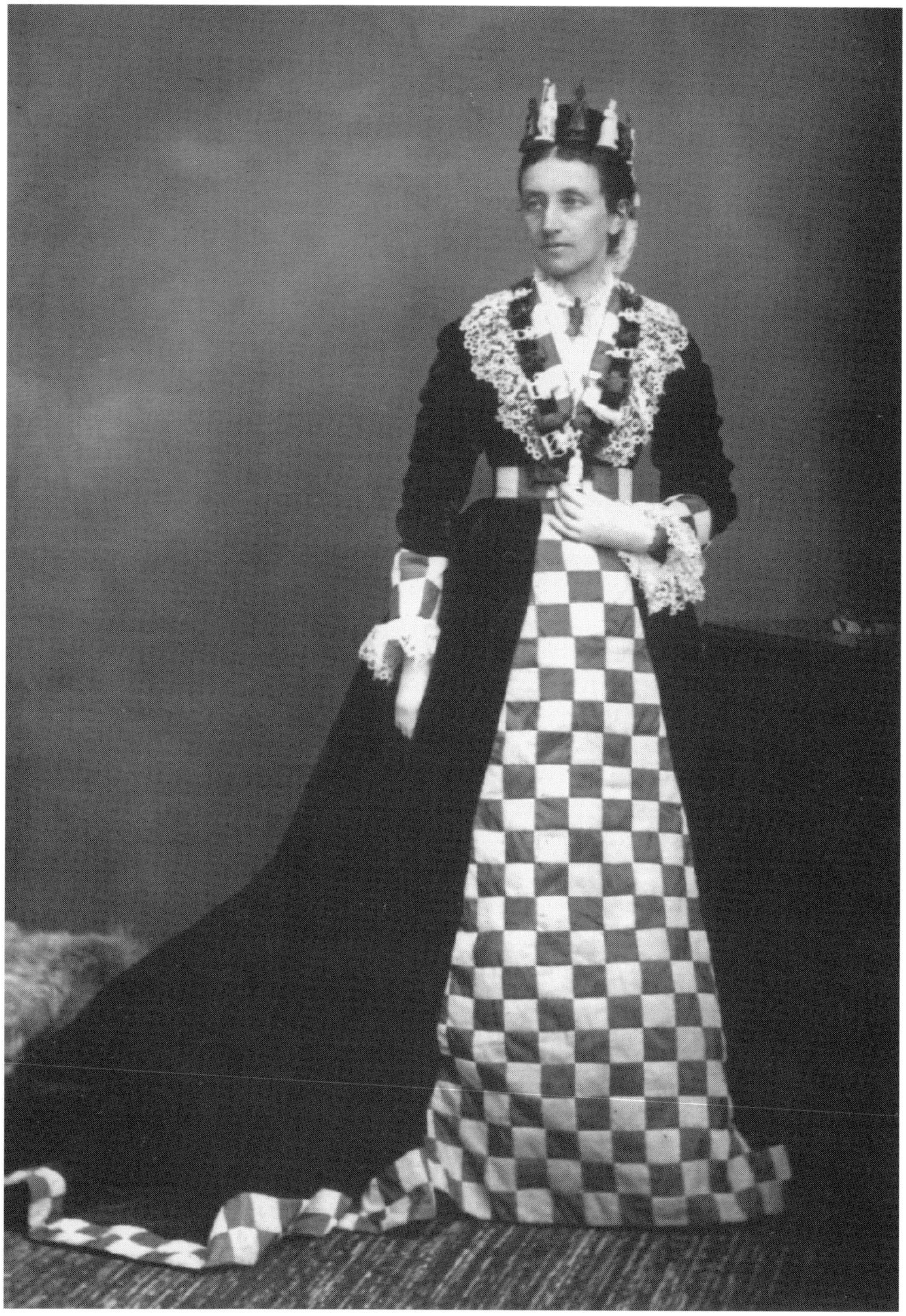

Grace Ritchie as "Chess." Her dress, made by the Saint John costumier Louis Hammondi, has a black velvet bodice and train, with a skirt front of white velvet and red silk squares to represent a chessboard. Most outstanding are her coronet and necklace of "carved eastern chessmen."
WJT/NAC/PA 138390

closest to crossing gender boundaries was Miss White, dressed in a uniform as "Daughter of the Regiment." Her costume included scarlet trousers – well hidden under her skirt. Yet an escapist sensation pervaded the ball, which Edmund Allen Meredith, Deputy Minister of the Interior, accounted for in his diary: "The sight was magnificent, there being hardly any dresses not 'fancy.' It was dazzling and as perplexing as a kaleidoscope."[13]

Once the glittering vice-regal procession had reached its place on the dais, most of the elbowing subsided, and the throng stood at attention while the Gruenwald's Quadrille Band, imported from Montreal for the occasion, played "God Save the Queen." Then the members of the procession stepped back down onto the floor to officially open the ball with the vice-regal quadrille. Ottawa had been eagerly anticipating this moment for months. The Governor General's secretary, Colonel Littleton, who lived on the premises at Rideau Cottage, danced with Lady Dufferin's sister, Mrs. Russell Stephenson, while his wife was paired off with an aide-de-camp, Major General Selby Smith. Another aide-de-camp, Major Hamilton, danced with Mrs. William Hingston, the wife of the mayor of Montreal. Lady Dufferin's brother, aide-de-camp Frederick Rowan Hamilton, danced with Miss Macdonald, the daughter of the Lieutenant Governor of Ontario, and Captain Frederick Ward with Miss Morris, daughter of the Lieutenant Governor of Manitoba. (So many members of the household, including His Excellency, shared the same first name that they had formed a hockey team called "The Freds.")

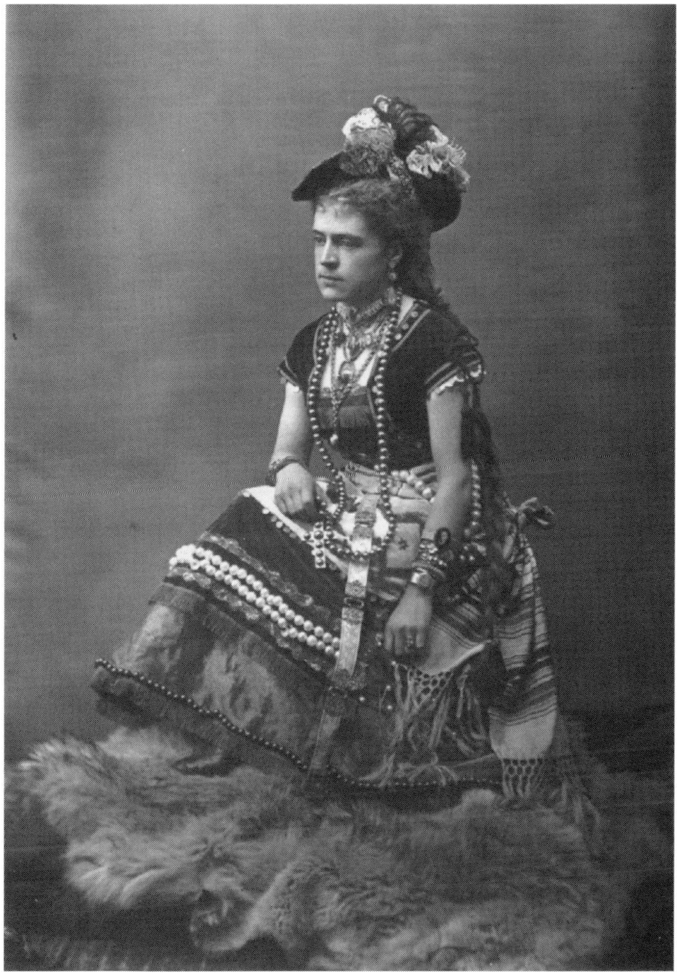

Miss Emma Lemoine as "A Brigand Queen." "Underskirt gold cloth trimmed with gold fringe; second skirt scarlet velvet trimmed with gold lace and pearls; overskirt trimmed with gold stars and fringe gold coins, maroon scarf tied around waist, black velvet bodice, worked with gold, armlets, necklets worked with coins, peaked hat, hair braided with feathers, gold coins, bronze shoes, red heels and rosettes, diamonds and jewelled dagger." (*Ottawa Free Press*, 24 Feb. 1876) WJT/NAC/PA193685

Even Nellie and Archie, as the Dufferins fondly called their titled offspring, showed their tutoring as they danced to "*La Fille de Mme Angot*." Neither Lord nor Lady Dufferin lost concentration as the only members of their party left out of the quadrille, their son Terence and his fellow page Teddy Littleton, lolled about on the steps of the dais. They may have winced if they noticed when the two boys commenced an enthusiastic and potentially dangerous swordfight; the clashing of metal was almost, but not quite, drowned out by the music.

After the requisite bows and curtsies (at which point the swordfight also concluded abruptly), Dufferin made the rounds of the country's most important political figures, shaking hands with the prime minister, cabinet members, and supreme court judges. Prime Minister Alexander MacKenzie stood out in the court dress he wore to be presented to Queen Victoria the year before. Several senators entered heartily into the spirit of the event: David Macpherson appeared as "A Highland Chief," Mr. Botsford as "A Mexican Gentleman" in cherry satin and gold lace, Mr. G.N. Haviland as "Oliver Cromwell," and Mr. Girard as "Falstaff" in blue velvet and white satin. Others in official positions, such as the judges of the Supreme Court, felt dressing up to be beneath their dignity. Edward Blake, the Minister of Justice, and Sir William Buell Richards, Chief Justice of the Supreme Court, wore legal robes or court dress. Member of Parliament A.P. Cockburn attracted snide notice as "A Gentleman of 1806": "It was exceedingly striking because there is such a vast difference between the clothes of 1806 and those of 1805 and 1807 that a man on horseback could not

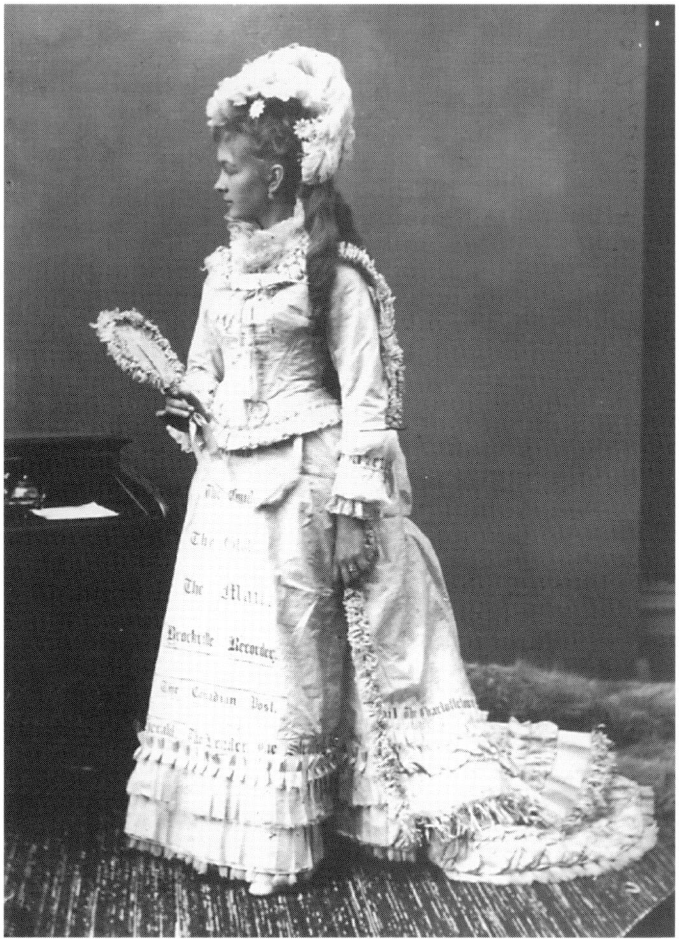

Miss Richards as "Spirit of the Press," a costume which, Ardern Holt promised, "has a much better effect than would appear, and has been a favourite dress at Fancy Balls." The mastheads of major Canadian papers are pasted across the front of her skirt, and the fine print elsewhere shows that her dress is covered entirely in newspaper. (1887, 187) WJT/NAC/PA139847

fail to notice it," the *Free Press* reporter wrote. Isaac Burpee, Minister of Customs, and Richard William Scott, Secretary of State, dressed very plainly as Puritans "John Alden" and "Miles Standish," perhaps in protest against some of the extravagance.

Sir John A. Macdonald was conspicuous by his absence. His wife did not approve of balls, or perhaps his nose was out of joint and he did not wish to see Prime Minister Alexander MacKenzie in the spotlight. But Lucius Seth Huntingdon, who had blown the whistle on Macdonald in 1873 in what became known as the Pacific Scandal, was present, dressed as "A German Prince of the 16th Century," while Hector Langevin, in the midst of a five-year hiatus in his federal political career for his involvement in that scandal, was resplendent as "A Spanish Prince of the 16th Century."

The American painter Albert Bierstadt and his wife, who were the Dufferins' friends, added an international touch. The wealthy playboy James Gordon Bennet, editor of the *New York Herald*, was to confer further prestige, but misfortune struck him and his fiancée, Miss May, when their train derailed and they were held up in Montreal for a day. Despite Bennet's insistence to the contrary, the *New York Daily Graphic* maintained that they had arrived late at the ball only to be refused admission by a footman, and for the following week the paper had a field day criticizing Dufferin and personalizing the British aristocrat's supposed rejection of an elite American. (Indeed, trouble dogged Bennet; a scant year later, a scandal having something to do with mistaking a fireplace for a toilet facility at Miss May's New Year's Day levée made him *persona non grata* in New York, and he spent the rest of his days in Paris.)

But the Grand Fancy Ball could not be clouded by the absences, despite some journalists' claims that out of fifteen hundred invitations issued, only eight hundred people came to Rideau Hall that evening. If the claim about the number invited was true, the Dufferins must have expected that half would not attend, for Rideau Hall was filled to the bursting point. The ballroom was so crowded that dancing was difficult. While Lord Dufferin whirled through the first waltz, Strauss's "Approach of Spring," with Mrs. William Hingston, some danced in the antechambers, where there was more space. Those who chose not to dance roamed at will throughout the house, with the conservatory being the preferred place for "sitting out." The light of Chinese lanterns set off the camellias, azaleas and other exotic blooms arranged to provide a maximum of nooks and crannies for "the quiet chats which go so far to make up a good ball."

The reporters in attendance remained in the ballroom to avoid the risk of losing their seats and scribbled down every detail. One took time to count the sources of the blaze of light: two gas chandeliers containing a total of thirty-six lights, an additional forty-two gas lights on the walls, and another 228 wax candles in candelabra around the room. Another noted how it set off Miss Carruthers of Kingston to advantage. Her pale green gown, sprinkled with pearly shells, seaweed, and dragonflies, "when viewed by gas light, looked so watery that the goddess Undine herself might have been

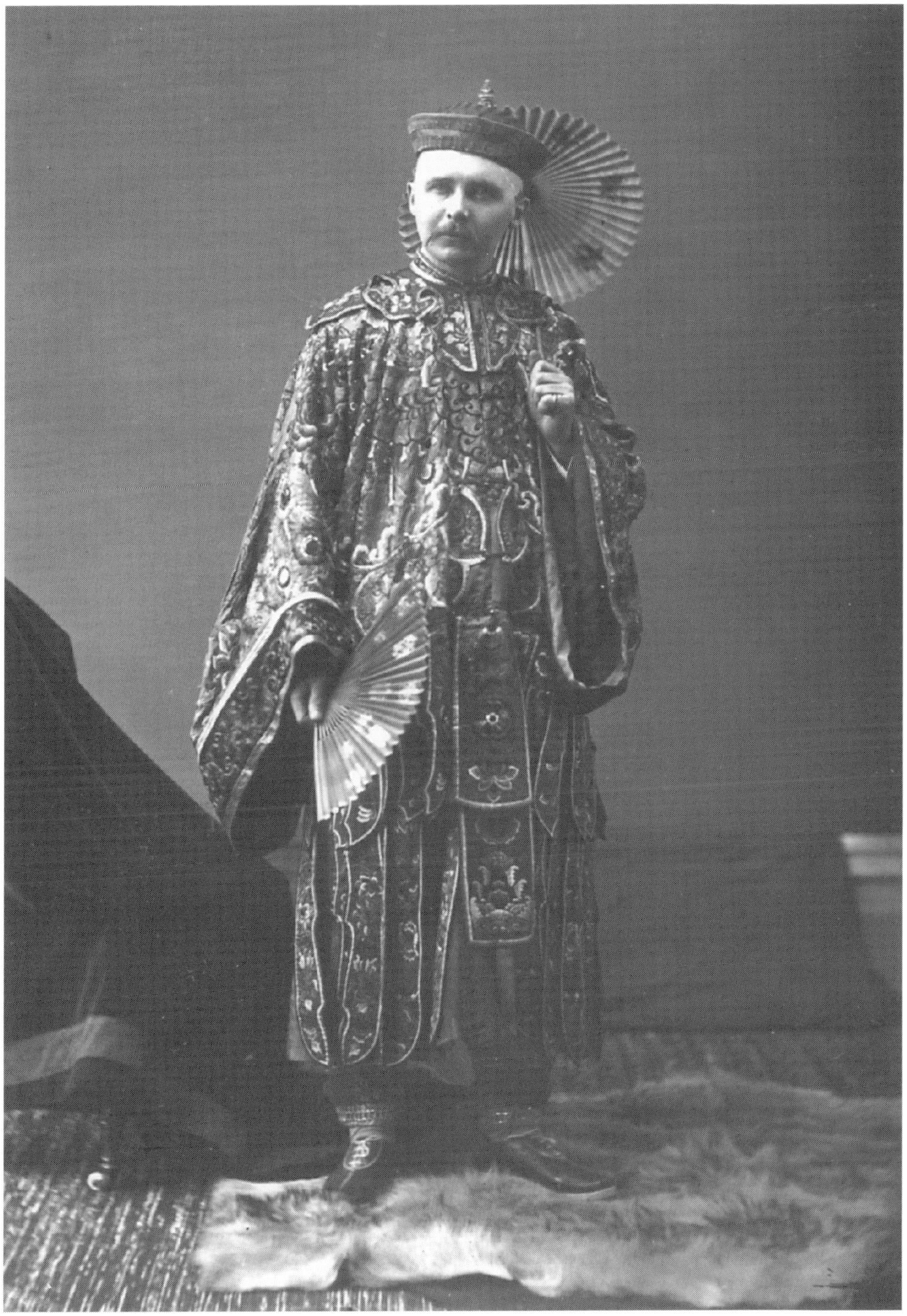

William A. Allan as "A Chinese Mandarin." "The robe was of pale green satin embossed in the finest embroidery of flowers beautifully bewildering in variety and hue. Among them were scattered tiny round mirrors no larger than a cent piece, and very dazzling. The sleeves were long and peculiar in shape, richly embroidered, and bordered with a black band with mountings of gold. Several inches below the waistline the robe was slashed into embroidered bands falling over a flowered yellow brocade skirt reaching the feet. Except for the cut of the dress there was nothing grotesque, the ornamentation being naturally beautiful. The hat had a round crown and basin-like brim, from which the pig-tail depended. The shoes, slightly curving upward, were of red morocco, bound with white." (*New York Daily Graphic*, 24 Feb. 1876) WJT/NAC/PA189667

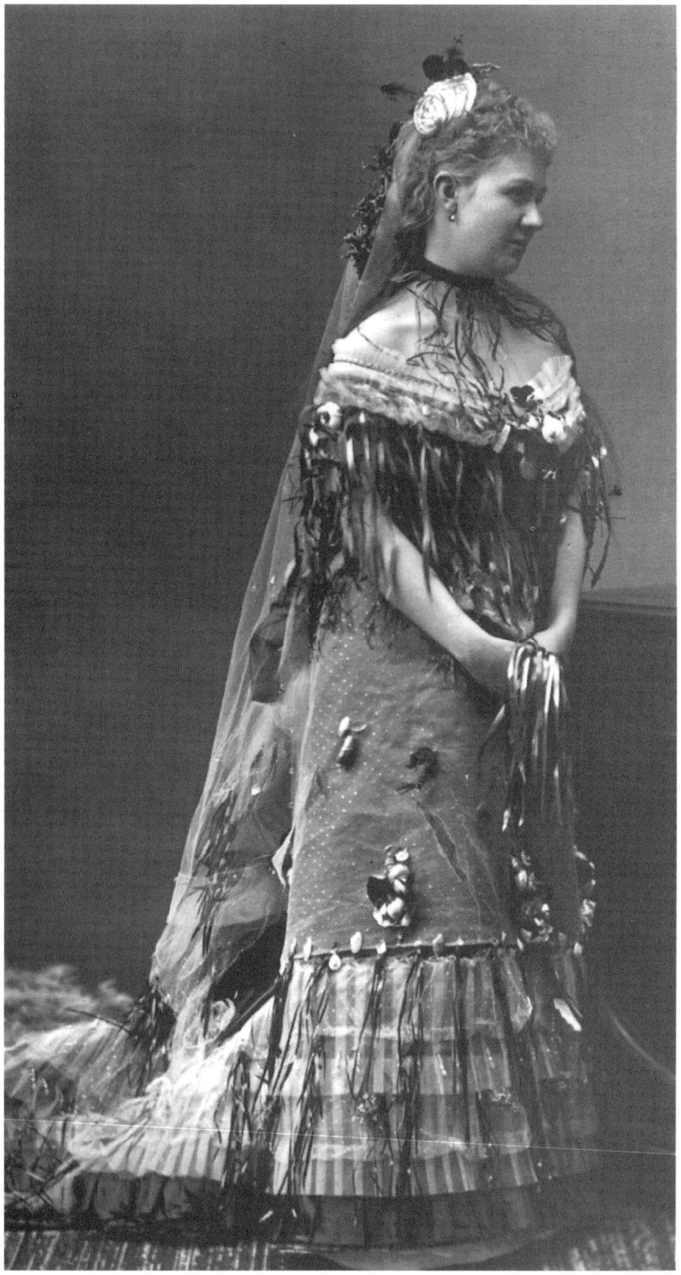

jealous of her correct representation" – that is, until the end of the waltz, when a large tear could be seen in her tulle overskirt. The *Free Press* reporter, who was the most attentive to the fine points of dress, surveyed the damage. A few gentlemen beat a hasty retreat to the most private corner they could find after making some hurried inquiries about pins. Poor Miss Ritchie, who at sixteen was not yet into long skirts and was attending her first ball that evening, had the silver tissue wings of her "Fairy" costume torn; they bobbed feebly from side to side.[14]

Then followed the most eagerly awaited part of the evening's proceedings, the Singing Quadrille, in which a select group performed a series of dances to the tune of their own singing. It had been the rage of the English aristocracy in the previous season, and Lady Dufferin herself masterminded the plan. She spent a few days "over a most troublesome business," she reported in late January, copying out 150 singing parts, thirty for each of five figures. "You can imagine the confusion and difficulty of arranging all these separate bits of paper," she wrote. Her aide-de-camp in fact did most of the work, but Lady Dufferin tossed and turned over it at night, copying and compiling sheaves of paper in her dreams. The thirty participants, Government House favourites and members of the Ottawa Choral Union, began rehearsing the four-part harmonies and intricate steps in mid-January. By early February they had perfected the lancers and waltz, while the two quadrilles and the finale were still a bit unpolished.[15]

The seriousness of the challenge stood out in sharp contrast to the lyrics, nursery rhymes such as "Old King Cole" and "Humpty Dumpty." From time to time, men and women alternated singing lines or verses to lessen the exertion of simultaneous singing and dancing. The total effect was hard to describe. One reporter found it rather ridiculous: thirty men and women "lustily singing 'Baa! Baa! Black sheep, have you any wool?' skipping here and there in lively time," with expressions of extreme concentration on their faces. "A wavering or break in the time throws the whole ballroom into confusion," remarked a second. To a third it sounded "graceful and sweet," yet all the while, "within reason, ludicrously comic," and he noted that the stiff upper lip had even disappeared from the dais; Their Excellencies "could not refrain from smiling."[16]

No doubt the incongruous mix of costumes heightened the comical effect. "Beatrice, an Italian Lady of Rank," in twelfth-century costume and with flowing hair, was partnered by "Fra Diavolo" in a mountaineer hat. "A Japanese Lady" and "A Turkish Gentleman" sang "Pussy Cat, Pussy Cat, Where have you been?" "The Goddess of Liberty" in stars and stripes with the American eagle emblazoned on her head-dress promenaded with a man in the uniform of the British Artillery of 1775 – a defender of Quebec against American attack. "Romeo" danced not with Juliet but with "Diana," her bow and quiver full of arrows at the ready.

The finale concluded with a grand chain to the sounds of the women jingling bells on their wrists and a cacaphonic blend of all the nursery rhymes sung at once. The musical aspects of the performance and the piano accompaniment were the efforts of F.W. Mills, the Christ's Church organist, conductor of the Choral Union, and composer of *The Mayor of St. Brieux*, the operetta performed at Government House the previous year. The lancers and waltz, scored for voice and piano, went to press a few days after the event.

Dancing continued as Gruenwald's Quadrille Band played more waltzes, several by Strauss and some of the conductor's own composition. Between selections, they changed the blue silk bannerets flanking the stage to announce the number of the next piece as listed on the dance card and the type of each dance, a "most novel procedure." Typically, Lady Dufferin sat out all but her dances with her husband, her regal figure framed by the crimson-draped niche, its backdrop of bannerets and shields bearing heraldic devices, and its crowning monogram VR and coat of arms of the Dominion. She watched the expert dancers glide through the "Boston" to the envy of their less co-ordinated friends, who stuck with the older, more traditional steps. The Earl spent the whole evening dancing, each partner aware that not only was she the cynosure of all eyes, but at least a dozen reporters were busily querying footmen and scribbling her name into their notebooks for the next day's paper. The Earl was not the only one to spend the whole evening on the floor. Major Chapleau of the Department of Public Works as "A Spaniard" must have been a favourite dance partner; though married, he was said to be "the finest-looking gentleman in Ottawa." Miss Featherston, the sister of the Mayor of Ottawa, as "Kate" from *The Taming of the Shrew,* had no doubt filled her dance card early, for she was reportedly "the most beautiful of Ottawa belles." Yet another popular maiden must have been Isabel Macpherson as "Queen of the Gypsies"; "there was no more complete and becoming array in all the bright dream of fair women" than Miss Macpherson's coin-trimmed dress. Her beauty and charm later served her well in the marriage market; she wed Sir George Kirkpatrick, who became Lieutenant Governor of Ontario.

Befitting his vice-regal status, Dufferin's dance partners were not only prominent members of society, but were almost all "royalty." The Prime Minister's wife, Mrs. Alexander MacKenzie, was "The Countess of Buchan in the Days of Robert the Bruce" in dark crimson velvet richly embroidered with gold. Mrs. Edward Blake was "Katherine of Aragon" in black velvet trimmed with sable fur, a character particularly well suited to her. Mrs. Edwin Vail, the wife of the Minister of Militia and Defence, was "Marguerite de Navarre" in a dress studded with pearls, and Mrs. Isaac Burpee incarnated "The Princesse de Lamballe." All but two of Dufferin's other partners were members of his own procession, suitably attired as ladies of the court of James V. Mrs. Richard William Scott was "Mrs Page, *The Merry Wives of Windsor*," and Miss Bethune was "A Neapolitan Fish Girl."

The "Fish Girls" at the ball seemed to attract as much notice as the "royalty." Miss Zaidee Cockburn and Miss Maggie Jones, each dressed as "A Bonnie Fishwife of New Haven," made a hit, with "both ladies acting the character to the life." Miss Jones was "bewitching," no doubt because her short skirt skimmed her knees. Other comical characters and attire were the source of much amusement. Mr. Fortier as "A Spaniard" and Mr. Duffy as "Don Enriquez" unintentionally appeared in identical rented costumes. Two men dressed very differently found themselves both representing "Don Cesar de Bazan." Miss Bate, the daughter of a wholesale grocer (and one of the few of her class to squeeze into the Rideau Hall set), as "Queen of Folly," was covered in bells – on every scallop of her four layers of skirts, on her yellow satin boots, and on her gold pointed hood – which created a clamour as she moved. Mr. Griffin, a post

Opposite: Miss Carruthers of Kingston as "Undine," the water spirit, in a costume created by Louis Hammondi of Saint John, New Brunswick. "Skirt made of watered green French satin with full train, trimmed with puffs of pale green tulle and alternate rows of water grass fringe and lilies, tunic of pale green tulle, looped on each side with large pearley shells and finished round the bottom with sea weed and fringe made of small shells and corals, with clusters of dew drops. Here and there in the dress could be seen large dragon flies; bodice of green satin, trimmed to match the skirt. The most conspicuous part of this costume was the headdress. A large shell rested on top of the head with a wreath of water lilies. The whole costume was almost enveloped in a pale green tulle, dotted with small shells and dew drops." (*St. John Daily News*, 24 Feb. 1876) WJT/NAC/PA193690

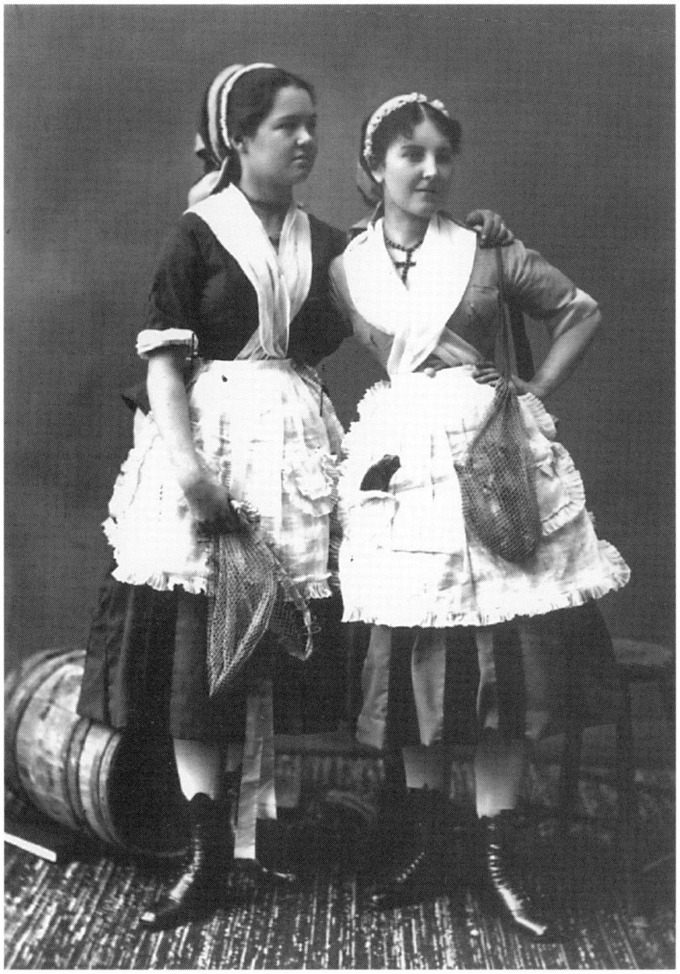

Miss Zaidee Cockburn and Miss Maggie Jones as "Bonnie Fishwives of New Haven." Miss Cockburn's costume "was a most becoming one, consisting of a scarlet [petticoat] striped with black; a pale blue skirt turned up, scarlet jacket, white apron and kerchief, white cap with scarlet handkerchief tied under the hair, blue stockings, shoes and buckles, creel with fishes strapped on the back." Miss Jones's costume was identical but for a yellow and black striped petticoat. The base of the posing stand can be seen behind Miss Jones's feet. (*Ottawa Daily Citizen*, 24 Feb. 1876) WJT/NAC/PA193681

office clerk, creaked around clumsily with his "lower extremities encased in armour." Gustavus Wicksteed, who at the age of seventy-seven was a law clerk in the House of Commons (an office he would hold for several more years) described himself with a wink as "Geoffrey Trefoil, an Ancient Counsellor-at-law." Someone in trunk hose had padded out his calves with towels, but his calves kept slipping around to the front of his legs.

Some of the more conspicuously dressed guests may have had a slight feeling of anticlimax once the first dances were over; the interminable preoccupation with dress had grown a little tiresome. After all, raiment had supplanted politics and the depressed economy as the main subjects of discussion in Ottawa for two solid months. The Parliamentary Library had become a gathering place for those in search of inspiration; costume books were left out on the tables to avoid the inconvenience of constant reshelving. Dry goods merchants, such as J.W. Ryan's, Faulkner's, and Robert Forgie had been besieged with orders, and dressmakers had been kept occupied right up to the last minute. The venerable Mrs. Cawest in the dry goods store of Hunton and Larmonth was as usual the choice of the elite, but even anonymous sewing girls which the less monied had summoned to their houses for a few days were sworn to secrecy as "all dressdom talked of what it would wear."

Four days before the event, the Russell House hotel swarmed with visitors. A few out-of-town fashionables and hundreds of Ottawa citizens wended their way frantically to rooms 99, 100 and 101, where Curtis and Weld, a Boston costume rental firm, displayed costumes and plates, including the garb of Sir Walter Raleigh, Hamlet, Richard the Third, and Charles I. The enterprising Mr. Baird of Ottawa, acting as agent for the firm, had been collecting orders for the past two months. Baird had not fared so well with another Bostonian, Jennie Kimball, billed as "one of the greatest costumiers of this Continent," whom he had brought to the city to provide costumes "perfectly free of a stagy appearance." He and Miss Kimball had spent a few days in late January at the Russell House taking orders, with the promise that she would come back prior to the ball to personally superintend and advise her clients. This never in fact occurred. A letter to the *Ottawa Free Press* a few days later by a former Boston resident revealed that the ageing actress-cum-costumier was known for her appearances in very scanty attire, and she had taken up her latest trade when her assets had lost some of their appeal. Mr. Lanouette, a New York costumier, also lodged at the Russell House, one floor below Curtis and Weld.[17]

At the Clarendon Hotel, Mr. Folston, a costumier from Saint John, New Brunswick, took two rooms and managed to rent nearly all the costumes he brought. Mr. Danielle, formerly of New York but now also based in Saint John, brought a brand new supply to garb those who had sent him their height, weight, and desired character beforehand. Mr. Hammondi, a Saint John costumier and "designer of fashions" who until recently had been plain Louis Hammond, supplied many beautiful gowns including those of the city's own Burpee family.

The bulk of the rental business went to Americans, however. Critics were quick to note that these outside rental agents were faring well, accounting for "a large aggregate amount sent outside the country for profitless luxury." Even the renowned London costumier, J. Nathan and Sons, "Costumers to His Royal Highness the Prince of Wales and Court," had advertised that it would fill orders placed by mail or telegraph. Fortunately for Nathan's local competitors, the intercontinental trade suffered from the fact that he had inadroitly advertised in Montreal rather than in Ottawa.

In fact, Ottawa business people were painfully aware of outside competition. Preston's advertised that orders for boots and shoes would be sent for making up to a shop in New York. In reaction, Ottawa's R.J. Bird promoted himself vigorously, filling his windows with the shoes and boots he had already turned out for ballgoers, perhaps including those studded with tiny As and Bs to be worn by Mrs. Horace Lee as "The Alphabet." "A glance at them will immediately disabuse the mind of the absurd idea that boots and shoes of fancy styles could not be made in Ottawa. In making any sort of feet ware, Mr. Bird cannot be excelled in any city on the continent." This and another ad gushing about skilful workmanship and styles of the most *recherché* kind brought Mr. Bird almost more business than he could handle, with orders to supply more than four hundred guests with "feet ware." Edmund Miles, the hairdresser by appointment to Their Excellencies, extolled the appearance and quality of his locally produced hair pieces. "Wigs from Boston, New York, etc. cannot compare with them in any way."[18]

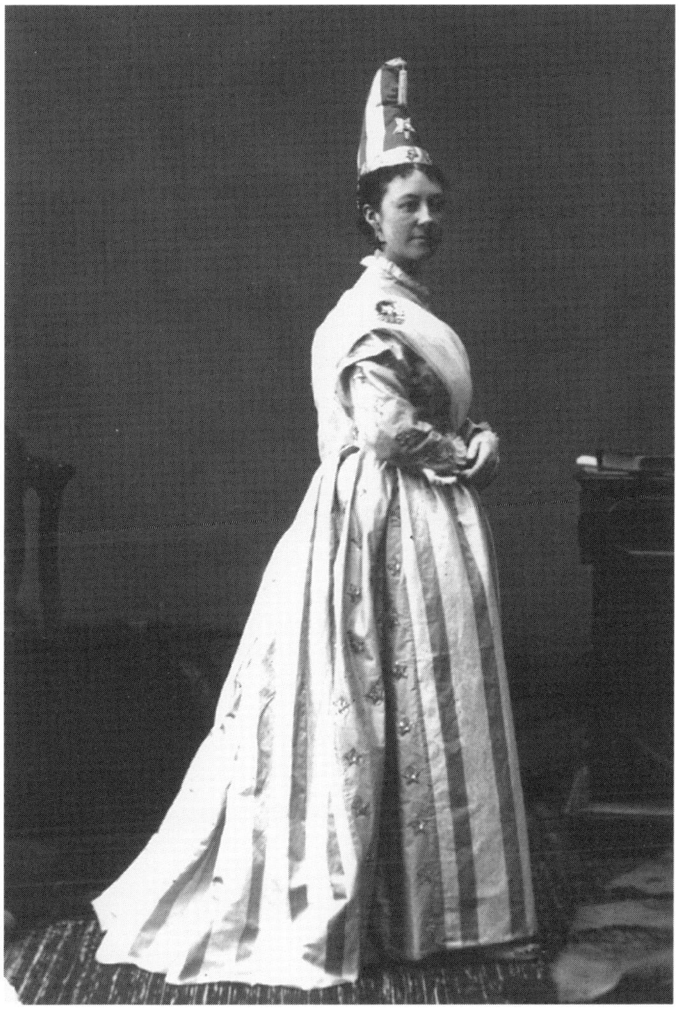

Mrs. W.G. Perley as "The Stars and Stripes" or "Goddess of Liberty," wearing a "red and white striped silk skirt, with side widths of blue silk, covered with silver stars; 'Goddess of Liberty' cap, made of red and white, the blue band ornamented with silver stars; blue bodice, silver stars." (*Ottawa Daily Citizen*, 24 Feb. 1876) WJT/NAC/PA193688

In the end, the most eloquent testimonial to the abilities of Ottawa tradespeople was the hastily made costume worn by His Excellency. If wearing locally produced attire instead of that from England and New York increased Dufferin's pride of place at all, perhaps as he tripped the light fantastic he noticed that a few guests' costumes were in fact inspired by Canadian experience. Their numbers paled in comparison to those in American patriotic costume, however, worn by a group known as "the American Colony" who had taken up residence in Ottawa for the lumber trade. The ball fell on the day after Washington's birthday in the centennial year, and fittingly "Martha Washington" and "George Washington" were portrayed, along with "Ladies and Gentlemen of 1776," the women all wearing "Martha Washington fichus." The US Consul General and his wife represented "Miles Standish" and "Rebecca of the Friends," and two "Goddesses of Liberty" wore red, white and blue stripes spangled with silver stars. But, with Confederation not quite a decade old, slowly rising Canadian nationalism found only moderate expression in fancy dress.

Mrs. St. Denis-Lemoine, in allegorical costume as "The Dominion of Canada," wore a costume of her own invention, a pastiche of symbols including a coat of arms on the front of her dress, a Union Jack draped across her back, and a gold beaver on her shoulder. Two men portrayed "Jacques Cartier," one of them Mr. St. Denis-Lemoine, the husband of "The Dominion" and Sergeant-at-Arms of the Senate. Were it not for the character name, he might have been any other sixteenth-century courtier represented at the ball, in his white satin costume with crimson puffs and gold lace trim.

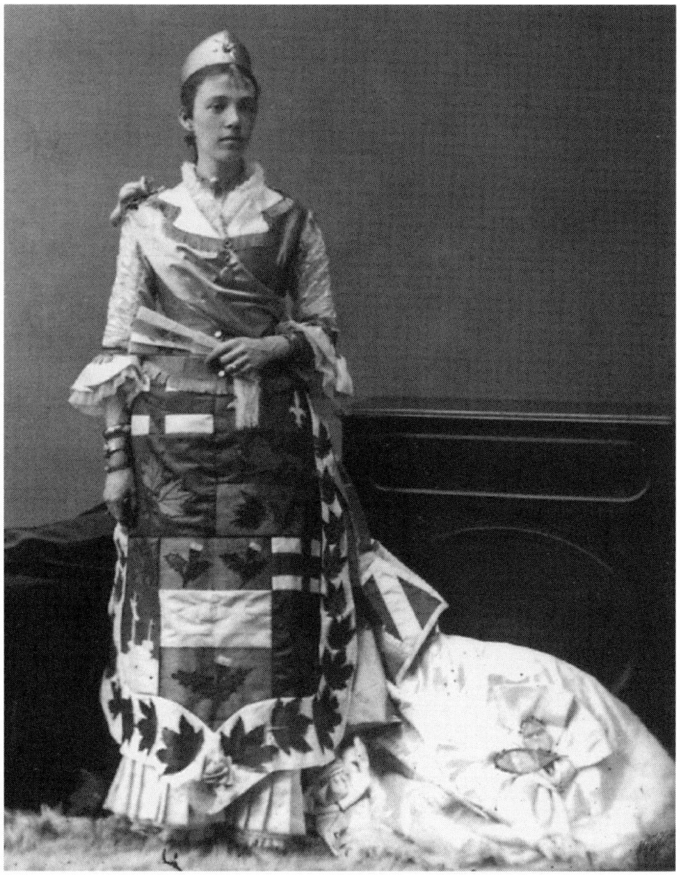

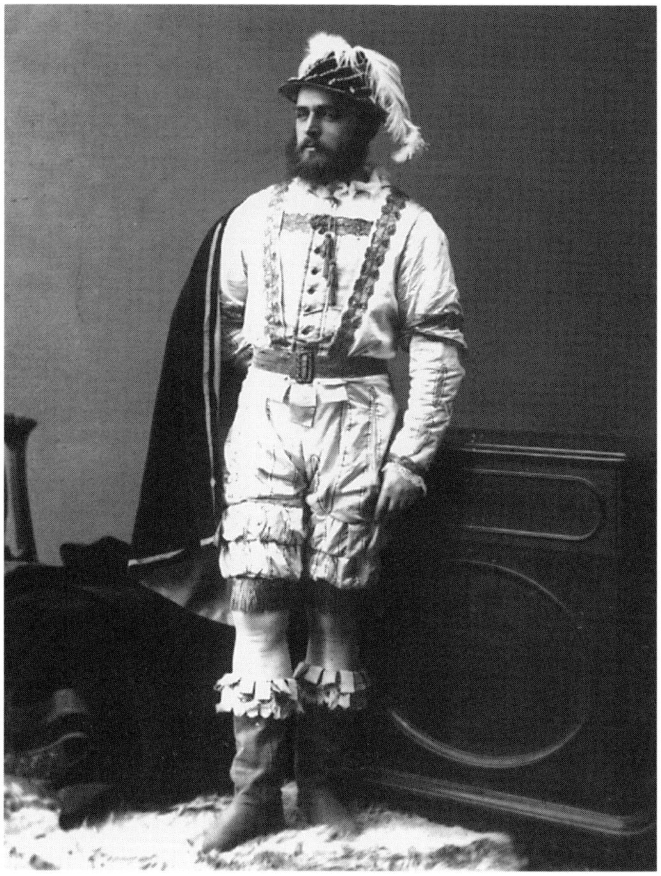

Above: Mrs. Juschereau St.Denis-Lemoine as "The Dominion of Canada." Over her gold bodice and white skirt she wears the coat of arms of the Dominion as an apron. A Union Jack hangs down her back, anchored on her shoulder with a gold beaver. Miniature snowshoes adorn her train, and her gold coronet bears a maple leaf in front. WJT/NAC/PA139848

Right: Juschereau St. Denis-Lemoine as "Jacques Cartier," sporting "jacket and knee breeches of white satin, with puffings of crimson silk, trimmings of gold lace and braid; black velvet cloak, lined with crimson; buckskin boots trimmed with lace and ribbons; black velvet cap with ostrich feathers; gold belt and dagger." (*Ottawa Daily Citizen*, 24 Feb. 1876) WJT/NAC/PA192346

The second "Jacques Cartier" was Edmund Meredith, in a brown silk tunic with slashed sleeves and a three-cornered black velvet hat. "My Jacques Cartier dress was not at all bad," he confided to his journal, "but the artificial beard and moustache were *very uncomfortable*." Dr. Edward Malloch was one of only two guests to represent Indian characters; as "A North American Trapper" he wore a long black wig and a caribou skin garment of Native manufacture, and he carried a fire bag, a knife, a tomahawk, a short rifle and some pelts. Miss Archibald, daughter of the Lieutenant Governor of Nova Scotia, appeared in full Micmac regalia.[19]

Five men dressed in the scarlet uniform worn by the King's Royal Artillery in Quebec in 1775, the year of the American attack on the city. One reporter interpreted these as uniforms of 1759, the year of the British Conquest of Quebec, and stated that "memories of two dead heroes and a vision of a certain dim grey misty plain rose up and brought thoughts which were not those of ballroom nature."[20]

After his reverie of Wolfe and Montcalm ended, the reporter noted that guests had cast aside the cumbersome paraphernalia which they brought as accessories for their costumes. First to go was the Christmas tree carried by "Santa Claus," which towered a good two feet above his head. Mrs. Horace Wicksteed, the "lady of commanding presence, who by happy inspiration appeared as Britannia," dropped her shield and trident. (By this time too, she also had "a delicate odour of the Thames about her," a frequent problem in ballrooms of the period.) All manner of wands littered the corners of the room; no wonder Ardern Holt, after her "long experience of fancy balls," advised guests to avoid the "several etceteras which have to be carried in the hand," as they would inevitably be discarded early on and retrieved only with great difficulty.[21]

A break in the dancing finally occurred at about 12:45, when supper was an-

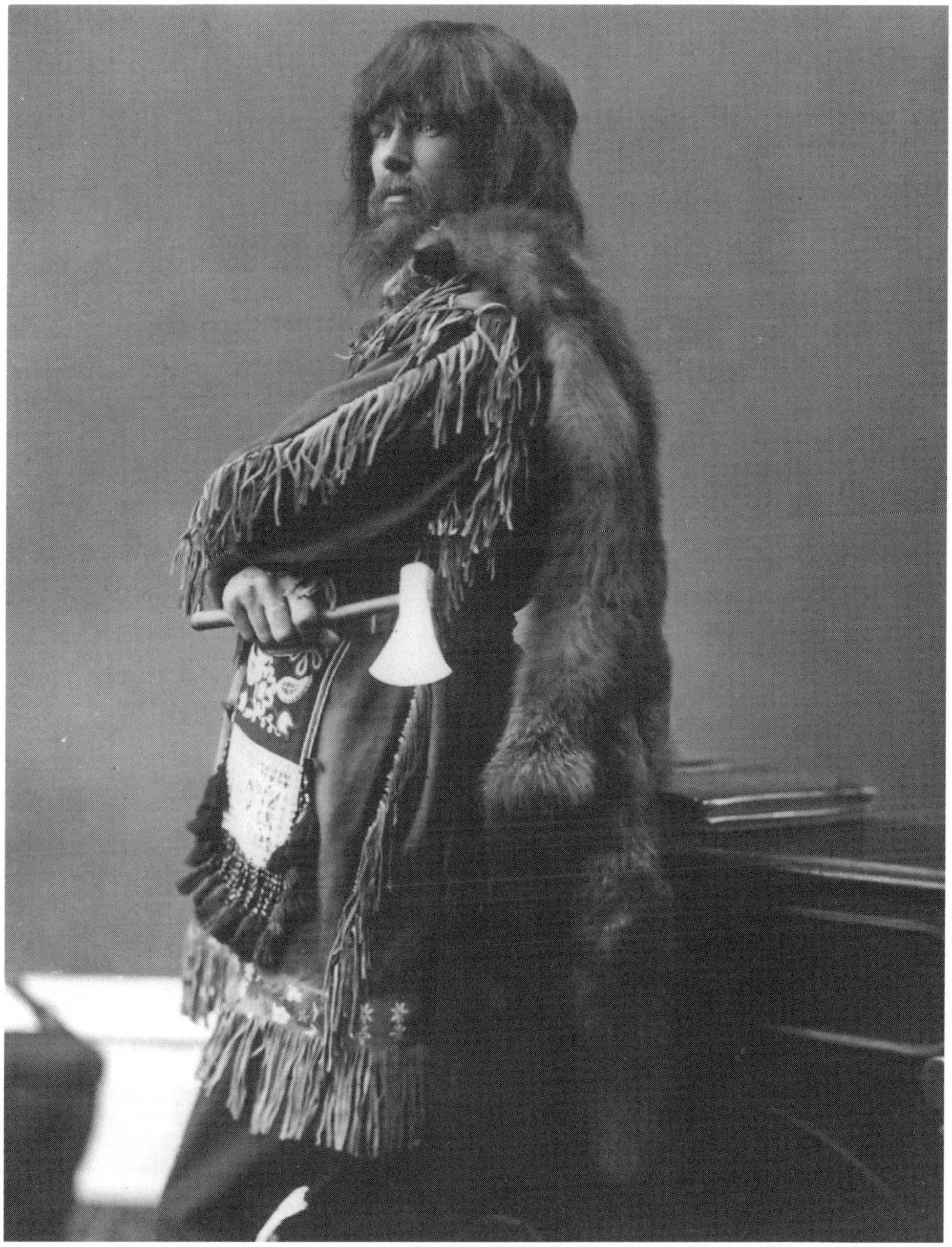

Dr. Edward Malloch as
"A North American Trapper,"
in a "long black wig; shirt of smoked cariboo skin embroidered in silk to represent flowers of the forest round the cuffs and collar; broad band of silk worn down the breast and round the bottom of the shirt, trimmed with narrow strips of ermine and mink fur; along all the seams fringe of cariboo skin; leggings, black broadcloth with bead work at the lower outside seam, gartered below the knee; scarlet silk sash containing firebag, knife, tomahawk, short rifle over the shoulder, and skins; feet gear, mocassins embroidered in silk."
(*Ottawa Free Press*, 24 Feb. 1876)
WJT/NAC/PA139846

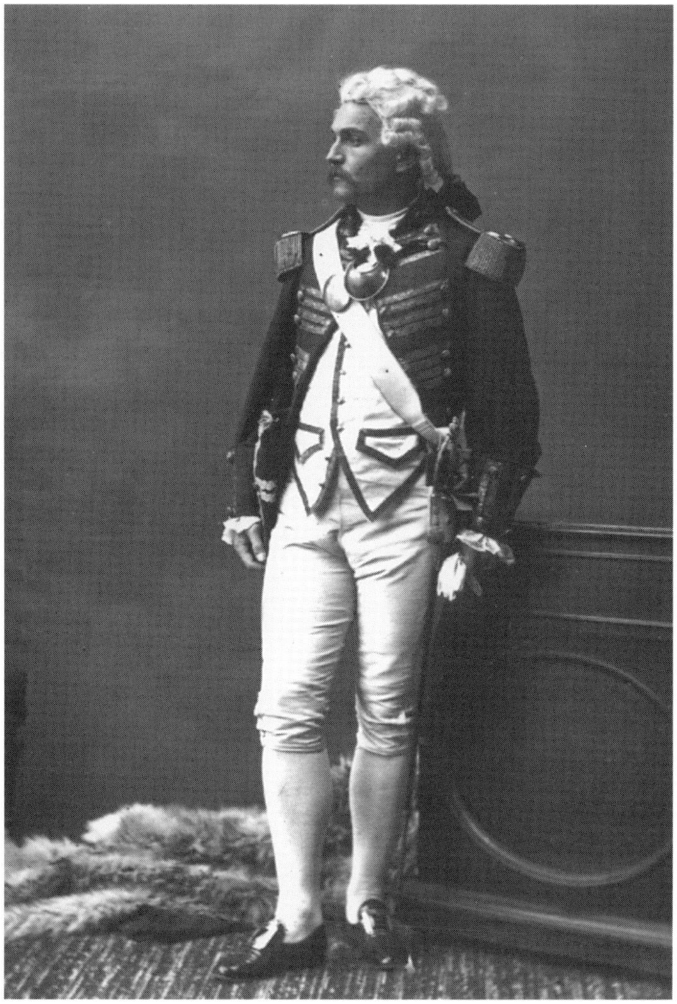

Lieutenant Fred Gauthier, one of five men dressed as "An Officer of the Royal Artillery, 1775," defenders of Quebec against American attack. He wears "scarlet cutaway coat, with black velvet slashings and gilt buttons, corners of skirts turned up and faced with white silk, high black velvet collar, trimmed with gold lace, white casimir waistcoat bound with gold braid, white lace frills filling the opening of the waistcoat, with the gorgette on the breast, white casimir knee breeches and white silk stockings, shoes with silver buckles, and powdered wig with queue." (*Toronto Globe*, 24 Feb. 1876) WJT/NAC/PA193686

nounced. The first few guests formed an orderly and decorous procession to the supper room, though not quite as orderly and decorous as their entrance. Others squeezed and elbowed their way to the fore, anxious to be part of the first of three sittings. (Official Ottawa was notorious for voracious appetites.) Some retreated to the tea room to snack on sandwiches while they waited. The orchestra continued with extra dances so that those in the now less crowded ballroom might not feel so left out in the cold.

Guests dined in new surroundings that evening, the shell contributed by the Dufferins and the special fittings paid for by the Department of Public Works. "Our new supper room, with its red and white tent, let down inside the tennis court, and the shields bearing the arms of the various provinces hung round its walls, will be very pretty," Lady Dufferin wrote. The striped and tasselled marquee with its eastern flavour had been ordered from New York, while a local craftsman, Mr. McKay, had painted the shields with the arms of the United Kingdom, Canada, and each of the provinces. Most magnificent of all was the blue shield bearing the quarterings of the Governor General, the arms of Dufferin, Blackwood, Hamilton and Temple.[22]

Ten white and gold pillars supporting gas lights ran down the centre of the room. Massive gold and silver plate and costly services of china and glass glimmered on the three long tables, which were linked by a fourth running across the top of the room. Here the Dufferins sat, flanked by the Mackenzies. The "splendid gold service which once graced the banquets of the Tuileries in the days when the Emperor sat on the throne of France" attracted almost as much attention as the vice-regal party itself. Waiters and domestics ran up and down between the kitchen and supper room, serving "the repast . . . which would please the taste of the most fastidious epicure" and francophile. *Le Souper de Bal* included *saumon en mayonnaise, pâtés de gibier, chaufroix de mauviettes*, and among the choices for dessert, *babas au cuiracas, nougats aux amandes, charlottes à la russe* and *cremes à la bavaroise*. Champagne flowed freely.

On the return of Their Excellencies to the ballroom, a second quadrille reopened the proceedings, viewed by a much less attentive audience. At two a.m., although the merriment had not yet begun to subside, the *Toronto Daily Mail* reporter dispatched his lengthy report and guest list by telegraph – a feat questioned by another paper that later begrudgingly averred it to be genuine.

On and on continued the dancing. The substitution of a Scotch reel for a waltz provided great satisfaction. At three, guests began to retrieve their wraps and the crush in the ballroom was transferred to the entrance. In spite of the orderly system for recalling carriages, the procedure could still take a full hour. Lady Dufferin began to notice her "extremely pleased" guests leaving at four. At almost five the band struck up "God Save the Queen," which signalled stragglers that they were "at liberty to depart." In other points of etiquette Ottawa residents might fall short, but the familiar melody sent them scurrying home, and the Dufferins' Grand Fancy Ball had ended.

Few enjoyed going "from the charms of the unreal world back into the daily monotony of this very real and grimly practical nineteenth century." "Very cold going home," wrote the tired "Jacques Cartier," Edmund Meredith.

Guests and uninvited alike relived the ball for the next few weeks through extensive newspaper reports. If each newspaper had had to compile its own guest list and costume descriptions, the task would have been daunting. Instead, Frederick Dixon, a Dufferin aide-de-camp and the children's tutor, prepared a press circular to request that guests send him their chosen character and costume description. One who took this task very seriously indeed was Fennings Taylor, Deputy Clerk of the Senate, who wrote several paragraphs about the symbols on the tall pointed cap and embroidered robes of his character "Quaken van Atom, a Professor of Ologies."

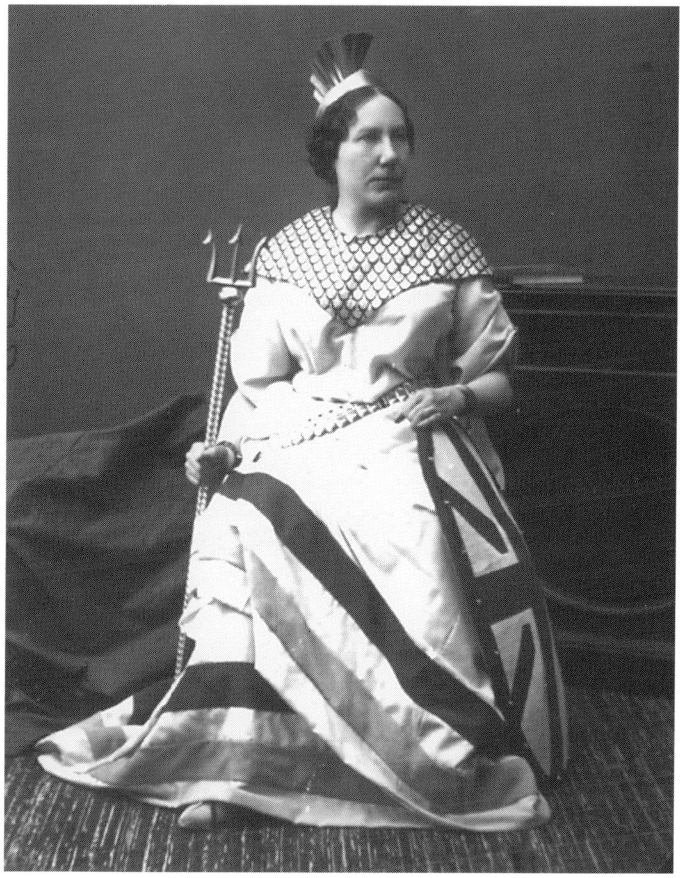

Mrs. Horace Wicksteed as "Britannia" in a "skirt of white cashmere trimmed with folds of scarlet and blue, classical bodice of cashmere with a long train of the same trimmed to match the underskirt. The train was looped up on one side with a silver chain, a gorget of scaled armor, a helmet of silver and gold, a trident to match, and a handsome shield." (*Toronto Globe*, 24 Feb. 1876) WJT/NAC/PA138395

> A conical black hat, brim turned up with red. The Pole Star on the crown, Half Moon and Planet Jupiter in front (Astrology).
>
> First – A long robe of green material like a soutane, reaching from the neck to the feet, circled with belts of red and blazoned with bosses, stars, and cabalistic devices. On either side down the front are links and rings of gold, emblematic of circles of the sciences and their linked relationships.
>
> Second – A loose cloak of claret-coloured cloth faced from the shoulders with red, whereon in gold characters are placed the signs of the zodiac. A broad band of red encircles the cloak, studded with bosses, stars, moons, and shells (Conchology). A date in silver letters is printed on the collar (Chronology). At the back a representation of the Sun (Photology). On the upper part of each sleeve, martin's heads (Zoology). On the lower part of each sleeve, small birds (Ornithology). On the red lining of each sleeve, English words in silver with their Latin derivations (Etymology, Tautology, and Phraseology). The sleeves are bordered with red, whereon are gold links and in each link pictures showing the ambition of the lower animals to rise to the higher life.
>
> Third – A chequered coloured belt of different coloured leathers made in panels. On seven panels are seven pictures, illustrative of the various types of the human race (Ethnology). On seven lower panels are seven pictures illustrative of Shakespeare's seven ages. Dependent from the belt are chains of coins, stones, metals and other things representing different branches of science.
>
> Fourth – A magician's wand of vermilion, crown with ivory head phrenologically mapped. A serpent coils around the wand and peers between a stuffed monkey and a stuffed bat, representing "missing links" that are perched on two rings near the top of the wand.

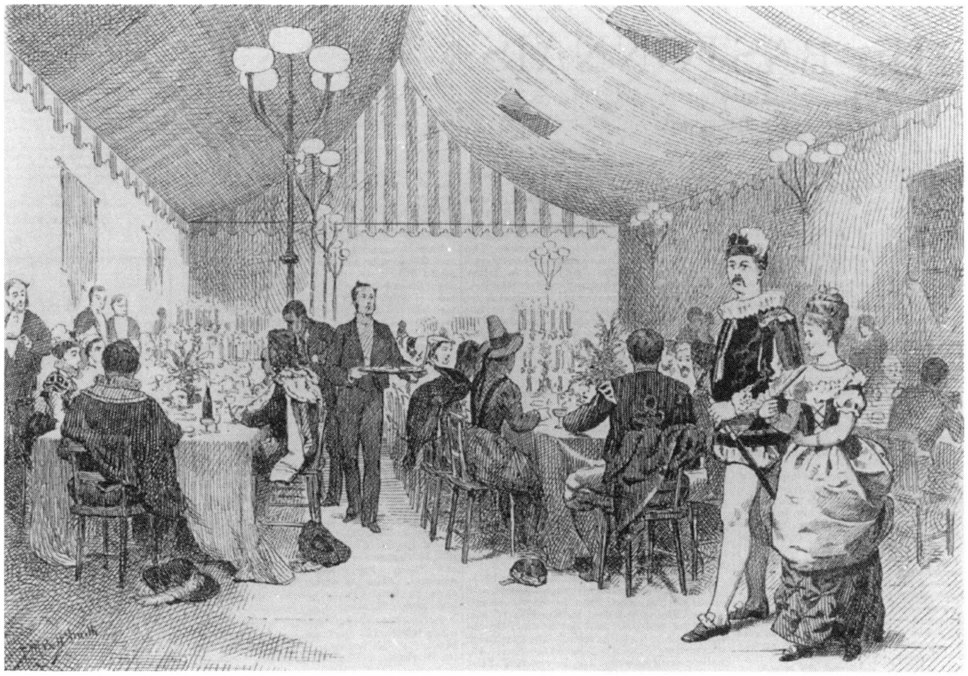

A sketch of the supper room by Toronto artist Frederic Marlett Bell-Smith. *CANADIAN ILLUSTRATED NEWS*, 18 MAR. 1876

His wife showed greater moderation in describing her costume as "Ye Queen of Hertes, Sche Made Some Tartes," but she did go so far as to mention her small heart-shaped basket containing "veritable tarts."[23]

Dixon's call for costume descriptions may have gone out a little too late. He did compile and distribute some form of circular, but the *Ottawa Free Press* requested that guests send their descriptions directly to the paper, and did so as late as the morning after the ball. They excused the incompleteness of their list by complaining that the *Citizen* had received a copy of the official list which was to be for the use of the *Free Press* also. "For some reason which we do not care to suggest we have been unable to obtain it up to the time of going to press," wrote the editor; the *Citizen* editor, Charles MacKintosh, had evident privileges, as he had attended the ball as "A Spanish Matador." Of course the lists of costumes contained inaccuracies; some guests sent in descriptions and never got to the ball, whereas others went but were not described. Even so, the ball reports covered three of the four pages in both the *Free Press* and the *Citizen*, and each paper solicited advance orders for extra copies.

The *Canadian Illustrated News* published sketches of a scene each from the ballroom and supper room by Frederic M. Bell-Smith, but many chose to relive the event by going to a photographer: William Topley, the Stiff Brothers, or Samuel Jarvis. Guests arrived at these studios with their costumes in brown paper parcels. Topley, who had just established his own studio after managing the Ottawa branch of the Montreal-based Notman studio for seven years, managed to gain the most renown from the event. He hinted at his plans on the day of the ball. "Many parties who intend going to the fancy dress ball have been photographed in costume. If all could be photographed in this manner, and the party arranged in a group, we would have something worth looking at." The Dufferins and their entourage had their portraits done by Topley two days after the ball. For the next few months about three hundred guests followed suit, most standing on a piece of fur and posing in front of the same writing desk and leather upholstered chair. Some had their heads and arms cradled in an iron posing stand to prevent them from moving during the long exposure time. Finally, Topley exhibited his large composite photograph in his studio. The glory of the evening blazed forth again, the Dufferins in their throne chairs and William Campbell the jester seated at their feet. Ballgoers purchased copies of the composite as well as their own individual portraits. That of architect Walter Chesterton as "Lyconides, an Athenian" was remembered as one of his most prized possessions when he died half a century later.[24]

If the memories of the ball could be kept alive, so could the criticism. A depressed economy made the ball controversial. "Some grumbling has been heard, reflecting upon Lord Dufferin's taste in giving such a ball during a period when there is much distress in the land; that the money spent on extravagant dresses might have been better applied to administering to the wants of the poor, and that the example is demoralizing and calculated to encourage extravagance which cannot well be afforded by most of our people," said the *Montreal Star*. "It was a mistake in both place and time," asserted an anonymous columnist in *The Nation*, whose aversion to the Dufferins' standards of entertainment betrays his probable identity. Goldwin Smith, who wrote frequently for the short-lived paper, was a harsh critic of imperialism; this was neither his first complaint about a Governor General's excesses nor his last.[25]

On the other side of the issue, "The note of preparation descended like a gleam of sunshine on that industrious and deserving class, the milliners and dressmakers, at whose earnings all philanthropic people will rejoice," wrote one reporter. "Poll the seamstresses of our Canadian cities and the advocates of the fancy ball from a single class in the community will far outnumber the grumbling malcontents who see something wrong in everything," concurred another. And it was true that Ottawa stores had been laid bare. Those wishing to have a pair of tights made at the last minute were out of luck – the fabric for that purpose was gone from the city. Even the massive sales of accessories such as gloves and buttons made a significant difference to tradespeople.[26]

Whether beneficial or detrimental, a great deal of money changed hands; busybodies speculated that the Dufferins themselves spent close to their yearly salary on the ball. "I hear terrible things about your expenditure," the Duke of Argyll once admonished Dufferin in a letter from London. "People say that you will be entirely ruinated." Renting a costume cost anywhere from $10 to $20; having one made could easily cost ten times as much, though reports of cost tended to stress the magnitude of the event rather than tell the truth. "It certainly seems a large sum to give $400, or even $200 for a dress that can only be worn once," wrote one reporter. Another, unaware that the Earl of Dufferin had actually ordered three costumes, claimed that he had spent $800 on his attire. Rumours ran wild about an American who appeared in $32,000 worth of finery.[27]

The *Montreal Gazette* reporter recognized that, because of the cost, there must have been a few "prosy paterfamiliases with an abundance of marriageable daughters" who did not entirely welcome their invitations. Edmund Meredith, whom the description fit, cast an approving eye over the garments of his daughters and Fanny, his wife: "Mary's Greek dress – a Maid of Athens – was very beautiful and very becoming. Alice as Queen of the Butterflies was also very pretty. . . . Fanny as a lady of the last century was very elegantly dressed." Meredith had rented his Jacques Cartier costume with its prickly facial hair, and had not even bothered to go to the photographer. The women in his family went to the studio, however, leaving a clue to the family's outlay. Seventeen year-old Alice's costume probably had not required any great expense, for she had transformed her best dress with yards of tulle and swarms of cardboard butterflies. Mary's exotic assemblage of a "brilliantly striped dress of many colours . . . short crimson jacket trimmed with gold lace and fringe, head-dress of crimson velvet . . . long scarf looped on side, of bright colours" could have been improvised, but not on the cheap. And Fanny's velvet and pearl-trimmed splendour could only have been specially created at the dressmakers. Even at the lowest popular estimate of $30 per person, Meredith must have spent $120, a sum that represented two weeks' pay for him. "There is no doubt that as to Ottawa itself the effect will be to run the heads of families and young civil service men heavily in debt."[28]

While the ball's detractors claimed that "no dress, no matter how costly the material, nor how elaborate the making up, can possibly be worn twice, at least in the same city, on a similar occasion," many ballgoers found a chance to wear their costumes again. Five days later, on 28 February, a ball was held for the opening of the Library of Parliament. Several who "wished to 'get the good' out of their fancy dresses they had ordered for the Governor's ball" requested to wear them again, the organizers began to encourage it, and in the end "numbers of people wore their fancy dresses." Some continued to "get the good" out of their costumes for a very long time. Mr. Newby, a court jester eclipsed at the Dufferins' ball by the antics of Mr. Campbell, donned the same costume for a skating carnival in 1881, where he took centre stage. William Allan wore his Chinese costume to a skating party thirteen years later, in 1889.[29]

Politically, the Dufferin's Grand Fancy Ball served nationalism by "bring[ing] together the social elements of the country," and it confirmed Canada's status, at least in its own eyes, as a world leader. Socially, the ball proved that life in Ottawa could be as exciting, refined, and lavish as life in any other capital city. "There never was so splendid a ball on this side of the Atlantic as that given by Their Excellencies on the 23rd ult. It has not often been excelled, even where silks and satins are more indigenous to the soil than in this young Canada of ours," pronounced the *Canadian Illustrated News*. The *New York Daily Graphic* agreed that it was "probably the most distinguished affair of the sort which has been given on this continent in a great number of years."[30]

Even by 1897, after the Vanderbilts and Bradley-Martins had completely upstaged Dufferin and Canada had just witnessed its most spectacular fancy dress ball, the benefits of the Dufferins' efforts were still recognized, and the prejudices that the ball was intended to eradicate were more directly addressed.

> It is well known enough that Lord Dufferin's ball did an immense amount of good to Canada. It was chronicled all over the continent and in Europe, and taught a great many, who previously had thought differently, that Canada is not a mere "frozen north" or a place of backwoods and eternal snow, that we do not hibernate like Esquimaux or live on seals and fish.

And, to put an end to any remaining controversy over the expense, the *Toronto World* proclaimed: "As a mere means of making the Dominion of Canada known that event was probably worth all it cost and a large amount over."[31]

The Dufferins' term ended in 1878, and none of their successors ever quite matched their *panache*. The arrival of the Marquis of Lorne with his wife the Princess Louise created considerable excitement, but socially the couple never lived up to expectations. Politically, appointing an in-law of the royal family as Governor General seemed a strong move for Empire, but the Princess could not mix freely enough with Ottawa and Canadian society. The next two Governors General, Lord Lansdowne and Lord Stanley, continued the tradition of amateur theatricals and turned out regularly for fancy dress skating carnivals, but they entertained modestly in comparison with the Dufferins. Only after the arrival of the Earl and Countess of Aberdeen did vice-regal entertainments approach the splendour of the Dufferins' Grand Fancy Ball.

CHAPTER 3

The Historical Fancy Dress Ball Ottawa, 17 February 1896

A brilliant spectacle, replete with the deepest interest for the historical and political student, as well as delightful to the eye of the lover of the dramatic and picturesque.[1]

John Campbell Gordon (1847-1934), 7th Earl of Aberdeen, was a grandson of George Hamilton Gordon, 4th Earl of Aberdeen and Prime Minister of Great Britain from 1852 to 1855; his wife was Ishbel Maria Marjoribanks (1857-1939). The balance of power in this couple was atypical for the time: Lady Aberdeen, not content to remain a figurehead, often dominated. On the surface she assumed the woman's role, lavishing attention on good causes and entertaining. Behind the scenes, she often put a bug in her husband's ear about political matters, and her more feminine employments were zealously manipulated by her drive for influence in the male sphere. "She might well be graced with the title of Governess General," says John T. Saywell in the introduction to the published version of her journal, which is among the most important records of Canadian social and political life in the 1890s.[2]

The Aberdeens were familiar with Canada because of a long trip they had made in 1890, when they purchased a ranch in the Okanagan Valley in British Columbia. In September, 1893, when Aberdeen's term as Governor General began, they returned with two of their four children and numerous household staff and moved into Rideau Hall. "It is not so much what is done or what is said," wrote Lady Aberdeen at the end of her husband's first day in office. "It will be the *tone* which will make itself felt, and in this every member of the Household, even down to the smallest child, will have a share." Though Lady Aberdeen might establish a particular tone for the household, she would find it difficult to extend it beyond Government House. The social landscape of Ottawa had not changed a great deal since the Dufferins' time, and the city itself had retained its objectionable character. "Happily, Ottawa does not mean Canada, nor does it represent Canada," Lady Aberdeen wrote on an evening when she felt particularly gloomy about returning home after a trip.[3]

Like the Dufferins, the Aberdeens worried about Canadian unity, still not achieved in the 1890s. In fact, Canadians were sharply divided along religious and racial lines, a schism deepened by the Manitoba Schools Question, the worst political crisis since the Pacific Scandal. Nationalism was on the rise but was seen differently by English and French. Imperialism, centred on Canada's freedom and prosperity within a strong British Empire, was rapidly gaining ground in English Canada, though its opponents saw Canada's history and mission as quite separate from those of England. French Canadian nationalism was based on different grounds entirely – an ancestral past which would guarantee survival of their rights in the future. The Aberdeens brought an exceptional sensitivity to these issues and conflicts, no doubt honed by their vice-

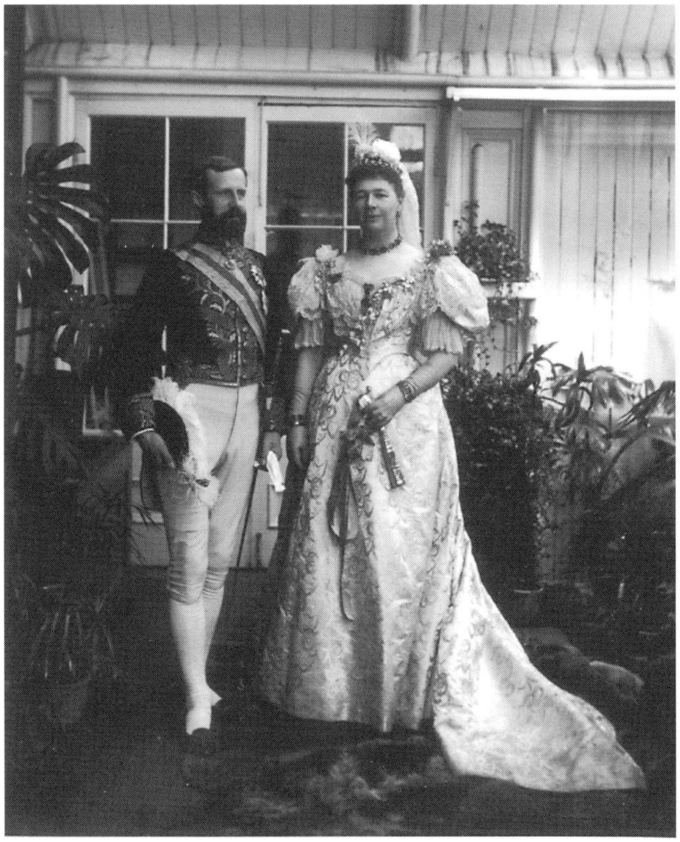

The Earl and Countess of Aberdeen, Ottawa 1896, dressed as they appeared at the Historical Fancy Dress Ball. The Earl wears his Windsor uniform, the court dress worn by peers for formal occasions, and Lady Aberdeen wears a fashionable court dress of mauve satin. WJT/NAC/PA28026

regency in Ireland in 1886; while representing the Queen, they sympathized with the Irish cause and in fact promoted Home Rule.

Such conflict of interest also characterized their Canadian vice-regency. Despite the requirement that Canada's Governor General be politically neutral, Lady Aberdeen, a fervent supporter of the British Liberal party leader, William Ewart Gladstone, had wielded considerable political influence over her husband. Nor were the Aberdeens above getting involved in Canadian politics: when the Conservative Prime Minister Sir John Thompson died in 1894, Aberdeen chose as his successor the inept Sir MacKenzie Bowell. A crisis built over dissatisfaction with Bowell's leadership, which, combined with the Manitoba Schools Question, created deep rifts within the Conservative party. The Aberdeens' involvement in the matter went well over the boundaries of their position. Some suspected that the couple's actions were guided by their desire to see the party split in order to ensure a Liberal victory for Sir Wilfrid Laurier, which did come to pass in 1896; Lady Aberdeen's journal chronicles numbers of secret meetings and messages transmitted by go- betweens.

Outside the political arena, Lady Aberdeen had a very socially responsible turn of mind. She and her husband had been ridiculed in Britain for their Household Club, an organization of family and servants that met weekly for entertainment and provided the household staff with opportunities for recreation and education; they continued this practice in Canada. Lady Aberdeen also brought along her strong desire for social reform. On her first visit in 1890, she had established the Lady Aberdeen Association for Distribution of Literature to Settlers in the West. In 1893, she helped found the National Council of Women, a thorny endeavour because of disagreements within the ranks over religion and temperance. In 1897, she overcame considerable controversy and criticism from the medical profession to found the Victorian Order of Nurses. As well, throughout her five years in Canada, she served as honorary president of dozens of organizations.

While Lady Aberdeen extended her influence to politics and other matters more than any other Governor General's wife, she knew how to make her role in the feminine sphere serve the same ends. She had a sophisticated understanding of the meaning of dress and of how her own clothing could inspire patriotic feeling in others. During her short period of vice-regency in Ireland in 1886, which she cherished dearly, she vigourously promoted Irish textile industries by wearing Irish poplin and lace at prominent social events. To please her subjects who espoused the Home Rule movement, she had considered dressing her children in green coats for a parade, but she was forced to revert to cream poplin instead. She had herself photographed at a flax wheel wearing what was described as a thirteenth-century Irish costume. Time and again in her journal she mentions Irish symbolism in her dress.[4]

In 1886, Lady Aberdeen held an Irish garden party, publishing prior to the event her recommendations for fancy dress representations of Irish peasantry. During the Aberdeens' second stint in Ireland, after they had left Canada, the Countess sponsored an Irish charity ball in which each set represented different Irish textile products. An

Irish lace ball promoted industry by requiring everyone to come dressed in a gown trimmed with it.

Lady Aberdeen embraced pageantry for its patriotic and educational value, but she also had a weakness for pageantry for its own sake, which was thought out of place in Ottawa. She had none of Lady Dufferin's delicacy; her brand of poise and stateliness was far more awe-inspiring. Official occasions found her in regulation court dress with veil, feathers, and train, but she soon recommended that Ottawa women not attempt to keep up with her. "It would be a needless expense where most ladies are not well off," she wrote. Only once was she conscious of overdoing it, admitting that "it is too ridiculous to be driving through this very colonial town dressed up in diamonds & evening dress in full daylight." All the while she continued to dress her two youngest sons as pages, with knee breeches and powdered wigs, to carry her train and stand respectfully behind her chair at official dinners, a performance which she thought made the affairs "more finished." Lady Aberdeen's daughter links her "great pleasure in ceremony and picturesque effect" with her choice of fancy dress entertainments.[5]

Like the Dufferins, the Aberdeens overspent; in fact, their expenditures in Canada were thought to be double their salary. The couple entertained incessantly, with dinners, balls, drawing rooms and skating parties. Under the Aberdeens, the list of those included in vice-regal entertainments lengthened, to the dismay of many, and their move to extend tram lines to the door of Rideau Hall met with strong opposition. In winter, sports were in full swing. Young Archie Gordon was photographed on skis; his athletic sister, Lady Marjorie Gordon, enjoyed hockey; Lord Haddo, the oldest brother, when told he could have anything he wanted on his seventeenth birthday, insisted that his fearful mother come down the toboggan slide with him. The Aberdeens held occasional amateur theatricals or musical performances, generally for the benefit of the Household Club and featuring their own children and staff members; in 1894 the group presented "David Copperfield" and "Pride and Prejudice."

Pastimes devoid of greater social benefit were of little interest to Lady Aberdeen. She tended to invest the most energy in, and derive the most enjoyment from, activities designed with some nobler intent than mere amusement. She was immensely satsified with an evening of "historical scenes," short plays and *tableaux vivants* illustrating vignettes from Canadian history, which she organized during a stay in Montreal in 1895. Of course her own children were among the performers, along with some McGill University students. The scenes included representations of Jacques Cartier meeting the Indians and planting the cross, and a conference at the court of Francis I of France; they were enlivened with real swords and weapons provided by a collector and Indian costumes lent by the chief of Kahnawahke. The entertainment was deemed a success and was repeated to raise money for charity. Even so, Lady Aberdeen regretted a lack of greater spectacle, confiding to her journal that "*tableaux vivants* must always be dull."[6]

The educational aspect of the historical scenes had been a tremendous success and served as her inspiration when she planned her next major entertainment. She always found something lacking in ordinary balls and even in fancy dress balls, as her journal reveals.

> Now a great big Ball to which all the world and his wife is asked always seems a meaningless and ponderous affair, the main features of which are simply its size and its supper. Then a Fancy Dress Ball without any central idea has too much of the Carni-

val about it and must always have a certain amount of the comical and clown element about it.

Now she had a new idea: a fancy dress ball with an edifying, morally uplifting theme.[7]

"Dufferin Outdone!" the *Toronto World* proclaimed. To the entire country's surprise, the Earl and Countess of Aberdeen had upstaged the memorable event of twenty years earlier. All the difference lay in the noble purpose of this ball: Canadian history, from the Vikings to the Loyalists, was brought to life through dressing up.

Right from the start the idea was extolled for its educational merit, which made such an elaborate entertainment more acceptable and less apt to encourage frivolity and waste in the name of amusement. Guests and uninvited alike were to benefit from lessons on their own past. Lady Aberdeen confided the need for such an approach to her journal:

> To tell the honest truth, we started this idea of having a Ball representing the outstanding periods of Canadian history with the hope that it might lead young people to reading up a bit & that it might divert Ottawa gossip at least into past times, away from all the painful & humiliating episodes of the present political situation [the leadership problems of MacKenzie Bowell] & the everlasting discussion of hockey and winter sports varied with Ottawa society scandal. It was a sort of forlorn hope, but actually it appears to be succeeding.[8]

At the outset Lady Aberdeen enlisted the aid of a scholar worthy of the endeavour: Dr. John George Bourinot. A clerk in the House of Commons and author of several books on Canadian history, Bourinot proposed a structure for the event. He suggested nine historical periods which could be enacted in a sort of tableau, a dance reflecting "the social condition of the time and people represented." His sequence began with the arrival of the Norsemen in North America, followed by six periods covering the French regime and two acknowledging the British conquest. The Countess then convened a group of collaborators, wives of eight prominent judges and members of Parliament, each of whom would make up a set of her friends and associates to represent one of the historical periods. Lady Aberdeen retained the first set for herself.[9]

On a Saturday afternoon in early January, while the rest of Government House was occupied with one of the weekly skating parties, Lady Aberdeen and the eight women closeted themselves with Dr. Bourinot, who answered their questions on historical matters. He "entered into the whole affair with enthusiasm," suggesting all the personages who might be represented in each set and their characteristics, from Leif Erikson to Wolfe and Montcalm. Since few women were included in written Canadian history, the many female characters he suggested were mainly the wives and daughters of well-known men. "Women of Canada were as fully represented as the men, and without them the scene would have been almost prosaic," he explained. Aside from its principal historic personalities, each group also included a small following of peasants, fishermen and fisher girls, and Indians. Religious figures were not part of the pageant; their absence was found to detract slightly from the event's historical integrity, but in the name of propriety this lapse was easily overlooked.[10]

Dr. Bourinot inspired everyone at the initial meeting, but the plans for the ball did not go smoothly; Lady Aberdeen found "a good deal of cold water dashed at it." To begin with, there were objections that Ottawa society did not have enough money and so would not cooperate by dressing up. (Perhaps memories of the expenditure required of guests for the Dufferin ball had endured.) Then it was said that historical dances were bound to be boring to watch. Furthermore, there were complaints that the Senate Chamber was not the right place to have a ball. It could hold more guests than the Rideau Hall ballroom, so when the Countess received permission to use it she was jubilant – she found it a "great privilege." Doubtless, too, hosting the event in the seat of government added considerably to its official and noble character. Although the Senate Chamber had been used for balls in the Dufferins' time, on this occasion it had to be given over for a full two days for preparations, which encouraged the press to complain still more. "Rideau Hall surely has accommodation enough even for an historical fancy dress ball – there has been money enough spent on it in all conscience," a reporter snarled.[11]

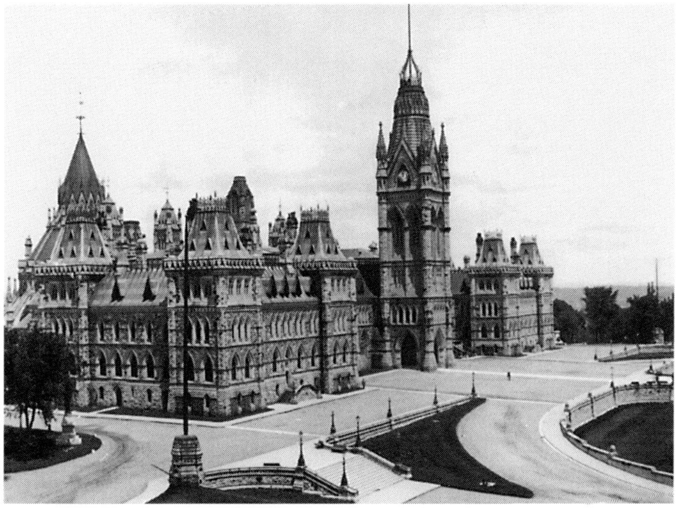

The Aberdeens held their Historical Fancy Dress Ball in the Senate Chamber of the original Parliament buildings, destroyed by fire in 1916. NAC/PA8338

Annoyed but never daunted by such critcism, the Countess forged ahead, only to encounter another setback. The death of Queen Victoria's son-in-law, Prince Henry of Battenburg, threw the court into a six-week period of official mourning, the ending of which coincided with the beginning of Lent, when no official entertainments could be held. To ignore the rules set by Buckingham Palace was a bit more risky than ignoring the local press. Lady Aberdeen justified proceeding with her plans, however, by noting that preparations were well under way and people had already started spending money. A postponement, she argued, would mean a financial loss for both guests and tradespeople counting on the business. Thus the ball was scheduled for two weeks before the expiry of the official period of mourning, not the most correct of arrangements but the most politic that Lady Aberdeen could manage.

Finally, as obstacles disappeared and complaining subsided, Lady Aberdeen's nervousness surfaced. She confided to her journal, "It ought to be pretty – but now is the anxious time when provision has to be made against hitches." The Ottawa press took up her cause. The weekend before the ball, the *Ottawa Daily Citizen* addressed the concern that the character of the event might be spoiled by too many guests choosing not to dress up:

> Their Excellencies have exerted themselves so much, and given so much time and trouble to the entertainment, that it is hoped as large a number as possible will enter heartily into the spirit of it and help to make the ball the splendid historical spectacle it is designed to be.[12]

While the Countess and the Government House staff laboured under all the threats to the ultimate success of the event, the individual historical sets set about getting ready with a strong sense of purpose. By mid-January, the ball had caused "a great deal of pleasant anticipation and planning." As the ball date neared, however, anxiety reached unnerving proportions; the responsibilities were heavy. "There is rather a demand for histories of Canada lately. . . . It is so easy to make dreadful mistakes if we do not help our memory by reading up a bit," the press urged. Ottawa ballgoers concurred that historical research for the event was tantamount to a moral obligation, regardless of whether they planned to create or rent their ball attire or have it made. A good six weeks prior to the event, costume history books were left lying on the tables of the Library of Parliament, just as they were twenty years earlier, to avoid the delay of taking them down from their places. "Ladies and gentlemen too studied them with a semi-comical, semi-tragic air of anxiety. . . . Never was the study of Canadian history so ardently pursued in our Capital City. School histories were at a discount, tossed contemptuously aside, while fair ladies pored over pages of Parkman with sighs and exclamation as the mysteries and intricacies of Canadian history were revealed."[13]

Lady Aberdeen was pleased. "Now you hear everyone anxious to trace out the lineage and deeds of General this and Admiral that and of Madame La Marquise or the others." Some thought the research was fruitful, that many costumes had been "designed in accordance with authentic documents." *The Lounger* suggested that the costumes were themselves worthy of study for the manner in which they accurately represented the periods in question, apparently oblivious to the mid-1890s leg o'mutton sleeves on sixteenth-century dresses.[14]

The official announcement of the ball occurred one month before the event, and invitation cards went out in the first week of February, only two weeks before the ball. Of course the select two hundred and fifty who were to dance in the historical sets were already involved, but the arrival – or non-arrival – of an invitation did mean surprises for some. At teas around the city that week, women who had not yet had their dresses designed, much less made, were in a state of despair. Others who were all ready could talk about nothing else. Miller and Kennedy's drugstore began advertising its "toilet preparations" with the warning: "The Historical Ball: Be Careful of Your Complexion."

Not only did ballgoers have to prepare their costumes and study their characters, they also had to rehearse their "graceful posturings" and intricate movements. Each group had to choose a dancing instructor, either Professor Frank H. Norman or Professor M.J. Sage of A. Roy McDonald's dancing academy, both of whom were well known in Ottawa, Montreal and Toronto. Norman ran a "select school for dancing and bicycle riding under vice-regal patronage," based in Montreal. McDonald's career as an instructor of Governors General had begun with Lord Elgin, and he was the dancing master Lady Aberdeen had hired on her arrival in 1893 to instruct the family in the complex Canadian steps. She described him in her *Journal* as "the great dancing master of Canada who has established branches of his Academy everywhere." He was in his seventies at the time and performed only occasional work, leaving the running of the business to his son, whom an ad in a Toronto paper described as a graduate of the Royal Schools of Ballet of Italy, Spain, and France. Despite these formidable credentials, at the ball the dances which had been choreographed by the McDonald Academy employee, Professor M.J. Sage, were generally found to be stately but "lacking liveliness," while those of Professor Norman received the highest accolades. Norman's success was attributed in part to a history of dance which he had used for inspiration.[15]

Finally, two days before the event, a full rehearsal of all the historical dances took place, "a merry informal gathering in regulation evening dress" and "a most necessary part of the performance." The Governor General first briefed all the guests on the procedure to be followed. From their station on a dais at the end of the room, Their Excellencies smiled at errors and suggested improvements, which their aides-de-camp on the floor helped to carry out. That same day, the press began requesting that guests send in costume descriptions, so that once again papers across the country could publish accounts of the event in great detail. Francis Parkman's romantic style and his blend of heroic exploits and romantic trivia permeated these descriptions.

The day of the ball, preparations were frantic. Ottawa businesses went into "a state of semi-paralyzation." There were no teas or receptions to report in the society pages. Everyone was either doing a final run-through of the dances, making a last minute rush for costumes, putting finishing touches on garments, or simply resting up. The bustle was concentrated in the city's two large hotels, the Russell House and Harmony Hall, which swarmed with excited participants trying on rental costumes. The two Montreal costumiers who had set up shop there, Raymond Beullac and Joseph Ponton, were overwhelmed with the last minute demand and claimed that in all their experience they had never seen anything like it. They had in fact been summoned to Ottawa in late January by Lady Aberdeen. Each had spent three days at the hotels to take orders, but these initial visits had not proven fruitful, at least partly because of the precarious political situation: everyone in the city had flocked to Parliament to watch the Conservative party attempt to oust Sir MacKenzie Bowell and install Sir Charles Tupper as their new leader. When the costumiers returned to Ottawa shortly before the ball, they were swamped with business (and Bowell was still the Prime Minister). Ponton, who had teamed up with Mr. Sage, the dancing instructor, had brought five hundred costumes with him. By three o'clock that afternoon, when the reporter from the *Free Press* took stock of what remained to be done, all the costumes had still not been rented out.

Nor was the Senate Chamber ready at that hour. The main entrance to the Parliament buildings and the whole Senate wing had been closed for a few days beforehand while workmen decorated the chamber. When the reporter peeked in late in the afternoon, they were still in the process of laying the temporary white pine dance floor. The journalist pronounced it "glaringly new and common," and he declared the decorations, done by the versatile Beullac, appropriate and harmonious with the ball's educational goals, if not exactly festive. Each of the sixteen marble pillars was draped with long banners of blue silk plush looped up with cords and tassels, and each was surmounted by a crown of a different colour. Along the wall to the left of the dais built to accommodate the vice-regal party were escutcheons with the arms and mottoes of the Governors of the French regime, each set off by a pair of white banners spotted with gold fleur-de-lys; to the right of the dais were the shields of the English Governors, including the Earl of Aberdeen's own, similarly backed with draped Union Jacks; most particular justice had been done to both French and English cultures. Embroidered banners bearing the British and Canadian coats of arms hung in the centre of the chamber, and banners with the arms of the Canadian provinces hung in between the escutcheons. One gallery was set aside for the orchestra, while the other galleries of the chamber were reserved for guests in costume not attached to the historical courts, the press, and senators and members of Parliament. (None of these grumbled about the seating arrangements, to Lady Aberdeen's great relief.) The great rotunda (the vestibule of the Parliament buildings), blocked off from outside, was used as a supper room, with a circular buffet table set up between two stairways.

The night of 17 February was bitterly cold, "a sparkle of frosty severity," at thirty-two degrees below zero Farenheit. Church attendance the past Sunday was low because of the cold spell, but though the weather caused guests some unpleasantness, it did not keep anyone away from the ball.

Although the ball was set to begin at nine o'clock, long before then sleighs bearing guests wrapped in furs drove through the Wellington street gateway to the Senate wing entrance. Elaborate precautions had been taken to keep out intruders. Policemen were stationed at every door, and an invitation card had to be presented by each guest. When the "motley occupants" were discharged from their vehicles, they hurried towards the doors, sped down the corridors and disappeared into dressing rooms allotted by the first initial of the last name. Then they emerged to mingle in the corridors and on the dance floor while they awaited the arrival of Their Excellencies. The Senate Chamber was brilliantly lit with every electric light available. From the gallery, the effect was most striking.

> The floor beneath resembled a mosaic, with men and women, garbed in vari-hued apparel, as the pieces that made up the whole. Every conceivable tint was in evidence. . . . Wander as the eye might, it was always met by a spectacle of colored loveliness.[16]

On the floor, spectators moved towards a suspension of disbelief as they noticed the "prettiest historic impossibilities" and the otherworldy spectacle created by the colourful costumes and characters spanning eight hundred years of history.

> Indian braves escorted countesses, United Empire Loyalists looked carefully after the comfort of French dames, and Norse Vikings might be seen attending on the wives of English generals. Feather plumes and powdered heads, moccasins and cavalier boots, pioneer jackets and embroidered cloaks soon filled the corridors with a maze of contrasting colors, while representatives of centuries far apart mingled with one another as familiarly as though they were days of the same week. It was a scene not soon to be forgotten by those who witnessed it, and formed a fascinating and instructive picture.[17]

The excitement mounted as the guests belonging to the historical sets proceeded to their assigned space, as indicated on a map of the chamber published in that day's paper, and convened around their two standard bearers. The other seven hundred fifty guests not attached to groups crowded into the galleries, where they joined spectators in ordinary evening dress.

When, at about nine-thirty, the orchestra of the Governor General's Foot Guards struck up "God Save the Queen," all hushed and turned their eyes towards the main entrance. Preceded by two heralds with trumpets, the Earl and Countess of Aberdeen entered through the main door. As hosts of a court occasion, the Earl was dressed in his Windsor uniform, while Lady Aberdeen wore court feathers and veil. She had been obliged to put aside the new dress she had acquired for the occasion to don half-mourning for Prince Henry of Battenberg, but her heliotrope satin dress trimmed with Irish point lace nevertheless received much admiration. As usual, her two youngest sons, Archie and Dudley, in powdered wigs and lace jabots, acted as pages, carrying her train.

The vice-regal party numbered fifty-nine, the women wearing court dress with requisite feathers and veil and the men wearing court dress, uniforms, robes, or gowns and hoods. In the stately procession, the Supreme Court judges and cabinet ministers and their wives followed the Aberdeens, who were perhaps almost eclipsed by two of their illustrious guests, Madame Albani, the Canadian opera diva of international renown, and Berthe Potter Palmer, the well known Chicago society leader and President of the World's Columbian Exhibition of 1893. For the evening, an aide-de-camp had paired

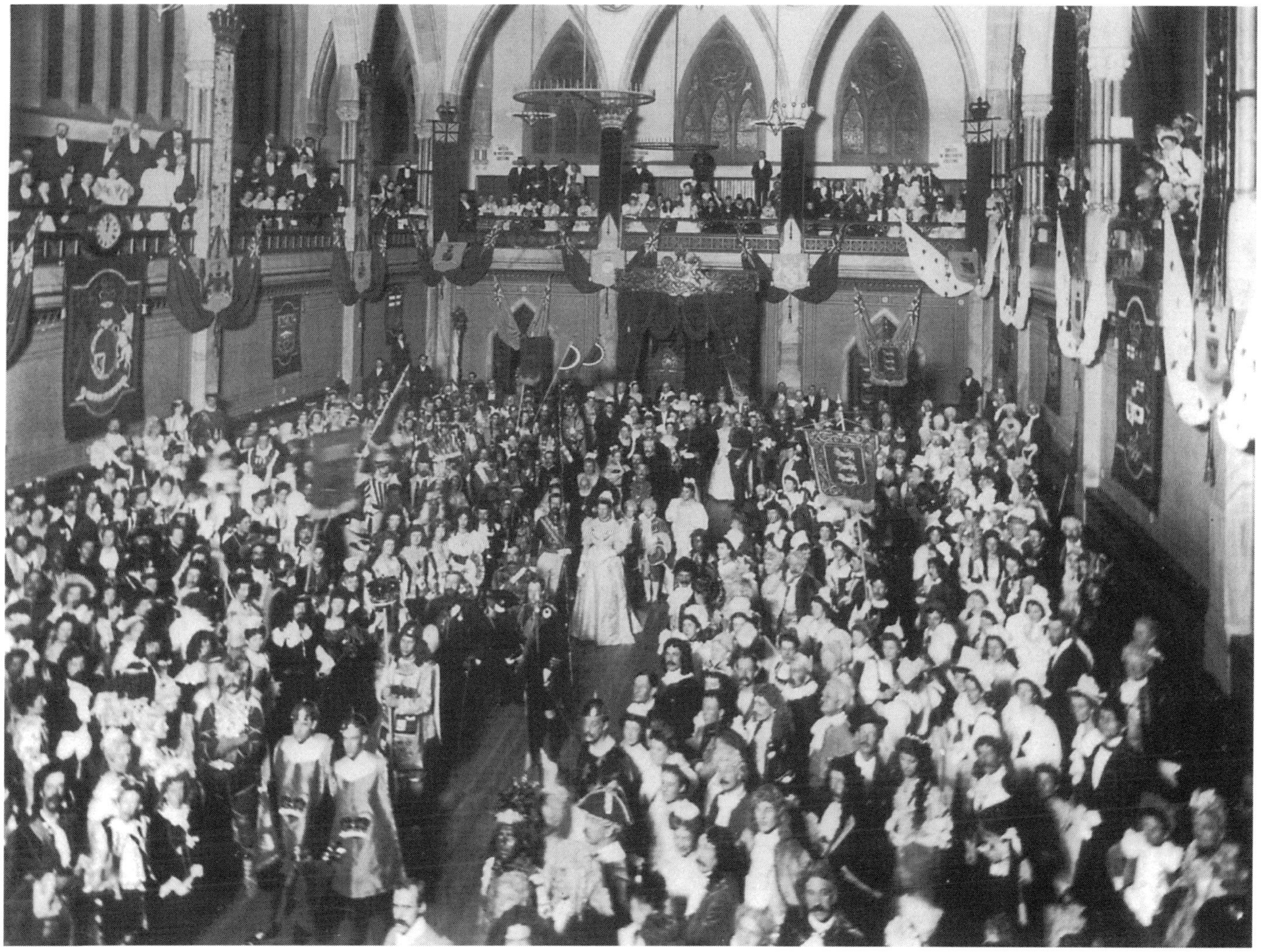

off Wilfrid Laurier, the Leader of the Opposition, with Madame Albani, "very successfully," thought Lady Aberdeen. Mrs. Potter Palmer enjoyed the ball, though her visit to Rideau Hall was not entirely satisfactory; like many others, she took offense at the servants' freedom.

Once seated on the throne chair on the dais, Lady Aberdeen gave a nod, and the trumpets of the heralds called out the first dance. "From the first moment," Lady Aberdeen wrote, "one could not help feeling that the thing was 'going.'"[18]

Amid the excitement, the Government House set assembled on the floor in some of the most colourful attire of the evening. Voyages of the Norsemen to Northeastern North America, circa 986-1015 AD, included the Aberdeens' aides-de-camp, their private secretary, and the children's governess. Their fifteen-year-old daughter, Lady Marjorie Gordon, and two of her friends, daughters of the late Prime Minister John Thompson, had been allowed to take part to make up for a shortage of women, though, not yet being "out" in society, they were properly bundled off home once the early part of the festivities was over. The group began its boisterous "polska" to the tune of a Scandinavian war song, in which all entered with the "jolly romping spirit typical of those primitive times." The men's Viking costumes in combinations of purple, red, dark green, and "snuff-colour" received much attention. Some wore winged helmets, others the heads of foxes with the back and tail hanging over their shoul-

Flash photograph of the ball, showing the Senate Chamber decorated for the evening and the kaleidoscopic blend of characters. The Aberdeens are in the centre of the photograph, with their sons Dudley and Archie Gordon just behind them, dressed as pages.
S. JARVIS/NAC/C10108

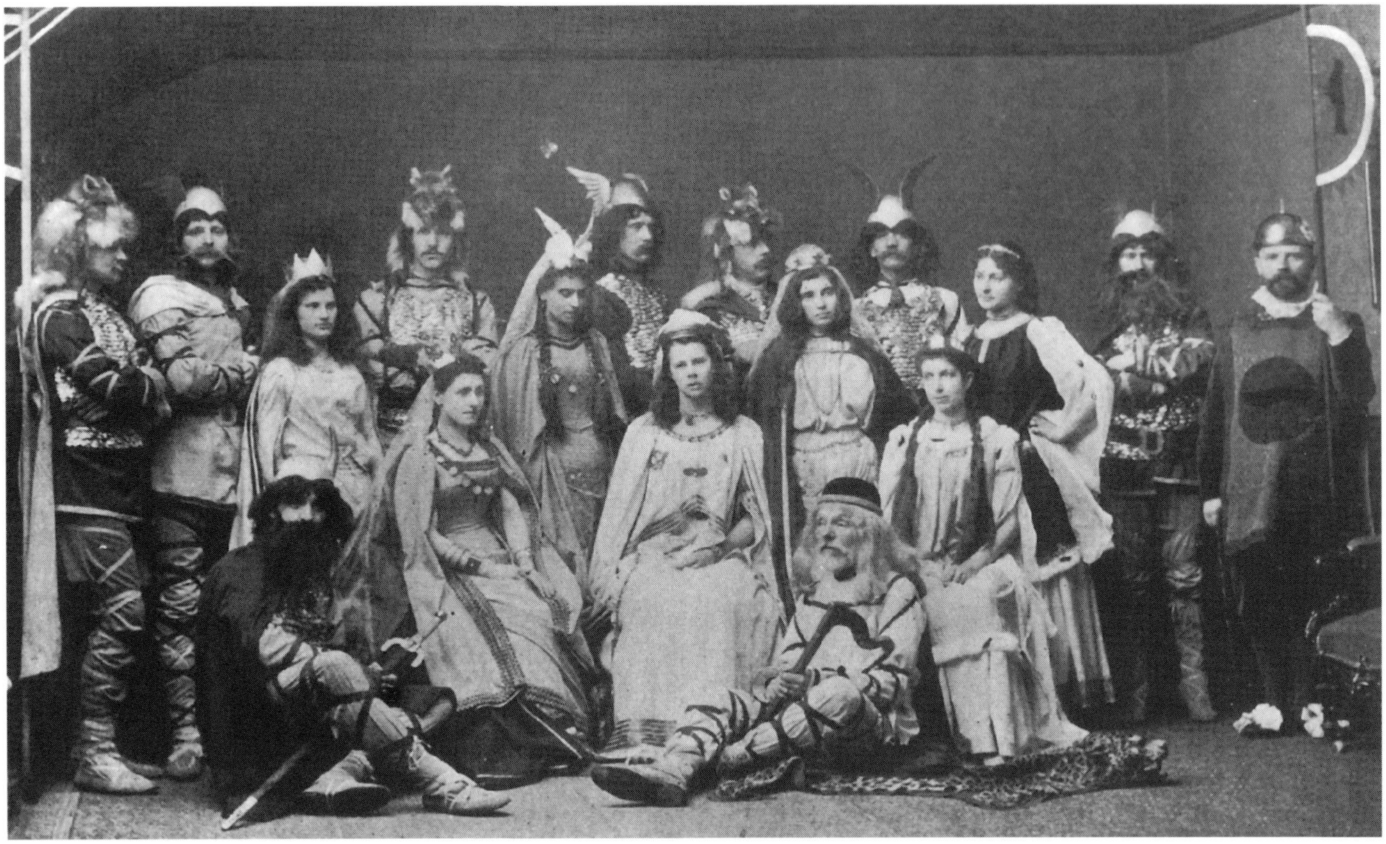

The First Historic Group: Voyages of the Norsemen to Northeastern North America. *Seated on the floor:* Dr. Gibson; Mr. Hewett as "Sigurd the Bard." *First row:* Miss Teresa Wilson; Lady Marjorie Gordon as "Freydis" in her white and gold dress and her mother's Celtic jewellery; Mrs. Strathy. *Second row:* Captain H.W. Wilberforce; Miss Aloise (Babe) Thompson; Miss Ebba Wetterman; Miss Helena Thompson; Mme Hector Prévost, with her beautiful loose hair, as "Gudrid." *Third row:* Mr. Hingston; Robert Munro Ferguson; David Erskine as "Erik the Red" in the winged helmet that fell at Lady Aberdeen's feet during the group's dance; Captain Henderson; Captain John Sinclair; Mr Thompson; Mr. Campbell.
WJT/NAC/ NL18285

ders. Lacings crossed over the sleeves of their tunics and trouser legs. A coat of mail made of several tiny disks of tin had been added to each costume at the last minute to cover up the defects Her Excellency noticed in Beullac's handiwork. Their jingling added to the noise of the "curious hippity-hop and stamping of feet."

The women in the group wore "flowing Boadicean robes" of wool, most with loose, uncorseted bodices; their ornaments were "carefully copied from those of ancient date." Lady Marjorie looked "very nice," in Lady Aberdeen's opinion, in white serge "flowing draperies" edged with bands of gold, with a white veil over her loose hair and Celtic jewellery borrowed from her mother. Ebba Wetterman, the Swedish governess, who had organized the dance with the assistance of Professor Norman, wore a dress embroidered "in true Scandinavian fashion" with rows of bright-coloured embroidery.

The "Viqueens" drew special mention for their flowing hair and headdresses. Teresa Wilson, Lady Aberdeen's private secretary, wore her hair "down the back in long braids, with gold very effectively twisted in and out of it." Mme Hector Prévost, in a red tunic trimmed with ermine over a white skirt, "look[ed] lovely with mass of pretty soft brown hair flowing," thought Lady Aberdeen.

The bold, dashing dance expressed "all the verve, the vitality and passion of the barbaric . . . the days when physical prowess and bodily conquest prevailed, the wild triumph of the drinking cup." Robert Munro Ferguson, ADC, and the eldest Miss Thompson performed particularly well. Even misfortune became festive, in Lady Aberdeen's opinion:

> One of the figures consist[ed] of the dancers going in couples under the uplifted arms of other couples. Mr. Erskine being so

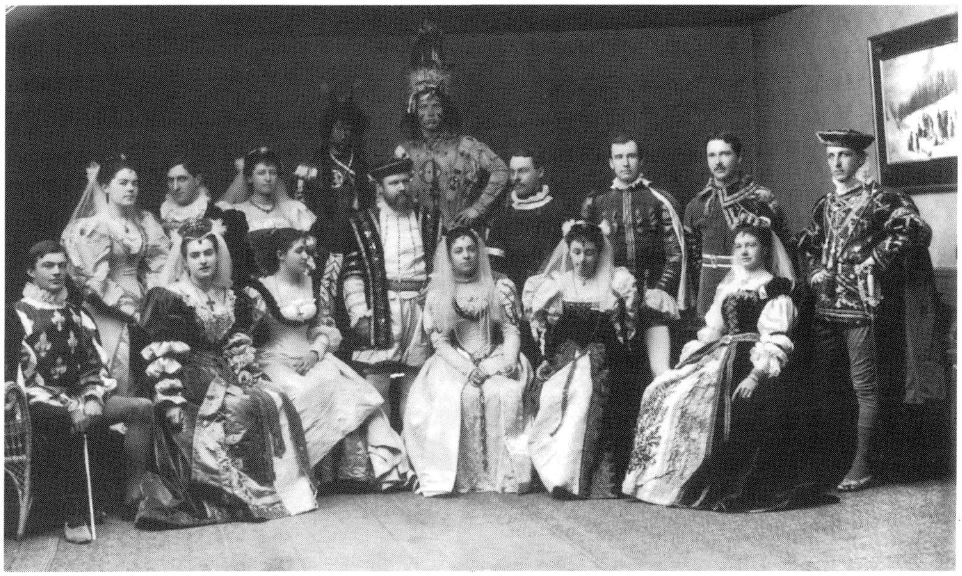

Below: The John Cabot group strikes a pose from its Pavane. Agar Adamson, in the centre with pointed toe, beckons to the seated Miss Ritchie, "Signora de Soncino," to rise. WJT/NAC/PA189688

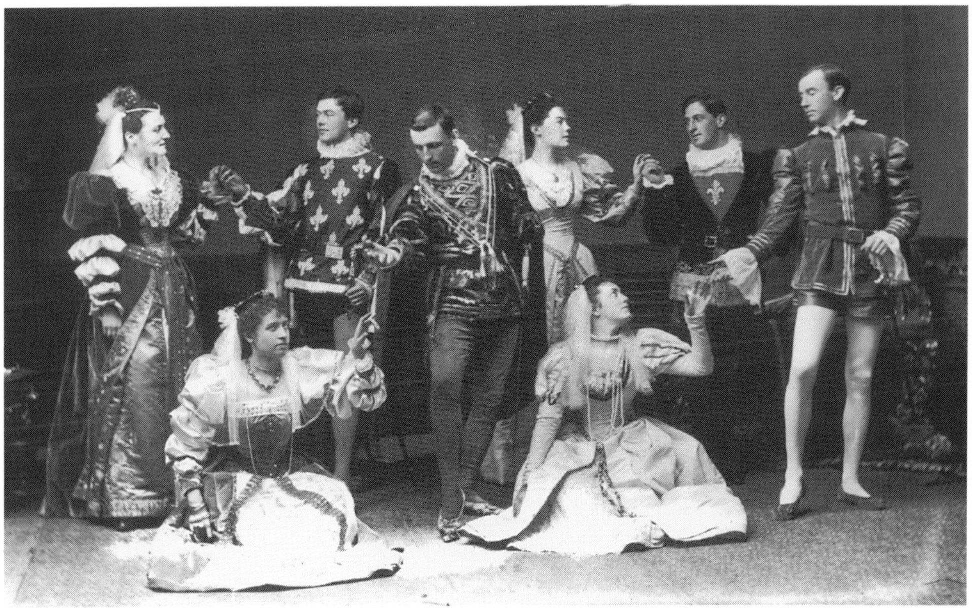

Above: The Second Historic Group: The Discovery of North America by John Cabot. *Front row:* Mr. Barwell; Miss White, in green velvet; Mrs. S.H. Fleming as "Mistress Cabot"; Miss Mackintosh, in blue moiré silk with a diamond tiara; Miss Ritchie as "Signora de Soncino"; Miss Griffin, also in green velvet. *Centre:* Alexander Burgess as "Henry VII." *Back row:* Miss Cambie; C. Mackintosh as "Sebastian Cabot"; Miss A. Ritchie; Julius Lay; Jim Smellie as "A Micmac Chief"; Mr. Haultain; J.A. Ritchie; Mr. McKay; Agar Adamson as "Signor de Soncino." WJT/NAC/PA137980

> tall managed to knock off his winged helmet and wig, amidst the cheers of the gallery. The wig was deposited at my feet and he looked very handsome without it & received quite an ovation. He made an ideal Viking.

At the end the dancers formed a circle around white-haired "Sigurd the Bard" with his miniature harp.[19]

Norsemen made way for The Discovery of North America by John Cabot, AD 1497. Mrs. Charles Mackintosh, wife of the Lieutenant Governor of the Northwest Territories, organized the set. Like all the set organizers, she was conducted to the dais and received there while her group performed and a pair of standard-bearers flanking the set stood at attention.

The characters in the Cabot set included "John Cabot" himself, impersonated by Frederick Avery of the White-Avery lumber company; "Henry VII," represented by

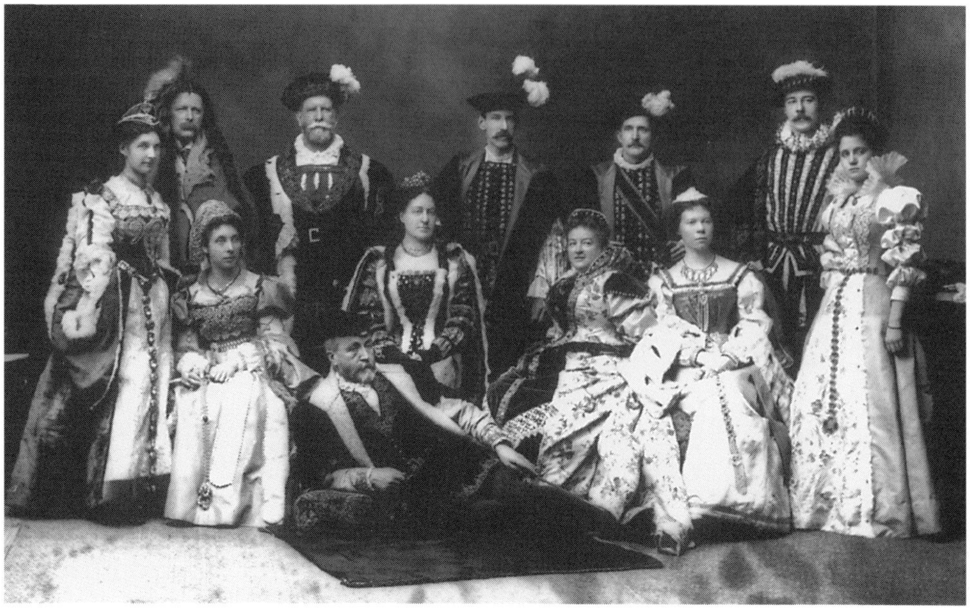

The Third Historic Group: The Discovery of Canada by Jacques Cartier. *Front, reclining on a cushion:* George Burn as "Jacques Cartier." *Seated:* Miss Hirschfelder, in purple silk and white velvet as "Anne of Cleves"; Mrs. Tringham as "Catherine of Aragon"; Mme Thomas Chase Casgrain wearing one of the most elegant costumes at the ball as "Louise de Montmorency"; Miss S. Sparks. *Standing:* Mrs. Goodeve; T. Gordon; Sherriff Sweetland, wearing black velvet trimmed with ermine, as "Henry VIII"; Lt.-Col. Jeffrey H. Burland; Mr. Goodeve as "The Earl of Surrey"; A. Powell as "Le Duc de Bourbon"; Miss Burn.
WJT/NAC/PA193692

Alexander Burgess, Deputy Minister of the Interior; "Queen Elizabeth," portrayed by a Miss Garneau; and sundry Venetian nobles. Only eight members of this set performed the "Pavane," including well-known Ottawa beau Agar Adamson, the lovely Miss Ritchie, and the Mackintosh children, young Mr. and Miss Mackintosh and Mrs. S.H. Fleming. The four ladies remained seated in chairs for the first few bars, while the gentlemen made "a series of passes with their swords," "paced to and fro," and then beckoned the women to stand. The slow, stately dance was the "very essence of rhythmic motion," though unfortunately it "lacked life above all things." The dance ended with the women making a low obeisance facing the dais, while the gentlemen did more gesturing with their jewelled swords.

The rich materials worn by this group contrasted with the humble fabrics of the previous set. "Silk and velvet were used . . . in great quantities and the style of the period was scrupulously followed." Despite this perception, Mr. Burgess, as "Henry VII," "all according to the fashion of the period," wore a lavender silk costume topped off with a cardinal plush cloak and hat in a style more like that worn in Henry VIII's time. Most of the women's costumes, too, were vaguely sixteenth-century; they included skirts open in front to reveal patterned underskirts, sleeves with tiers of puffs, and coronets with veils.

The Discovery of Canada by Jacques Cartier, AD 1534-1536 was organized by Mrs. Thomas Daly, wife of the Minister of the Interior. George Burn, Cashier of the Bank of Ottawa and a man of great musical and dramatic ability, shone as the lead character. ("Taking money to Burn" was an old joke in Ottawa.) He and the matronly Mrs. Thomas Chase Casgrain as "Louise de Montmorency" made a striking pair in the group's quadrille. Her dress, one of the most noticed at the ball, had a train and bodice of a "quaint and handsome" silk brocade with a design of morning glories. The front of the bodice and an insert in the skirt were of velvet, trimmed with *pointe de Venise* lace. The costume's "high standing collar of lace and velvet [was] edged with pearls; sleeves of pink silk, puffed from shoulder to wrist divided by bands of pearls. A ruff around the waist, a little flat velvet headdress of the period trimmed with pearls, a richly jewelled girdle completed this very handsome costume."[20]

The group also included such European royalty as "Henry VIII," "Francis I," "Marguerite de Valois," and "Catherine of Aragon." While the quadrille lacked the

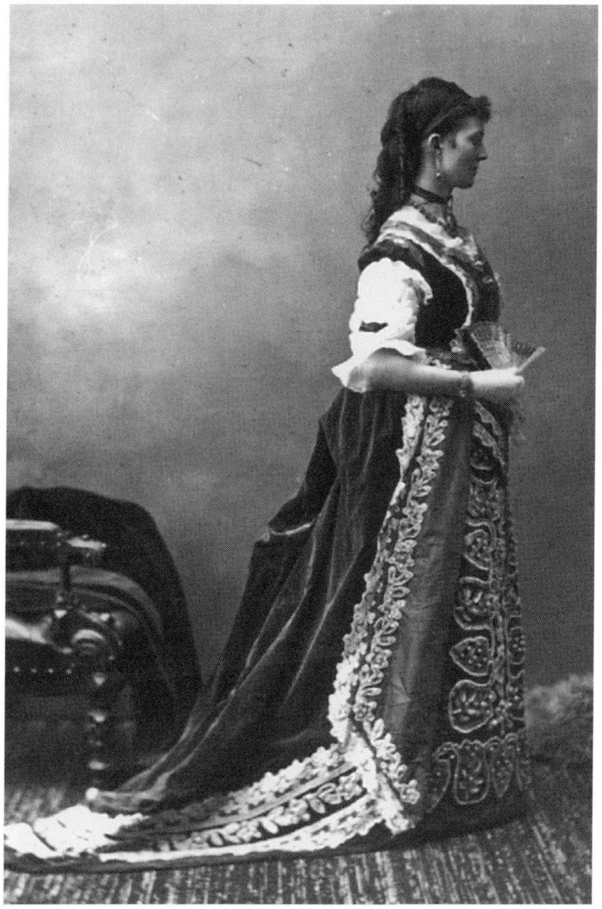

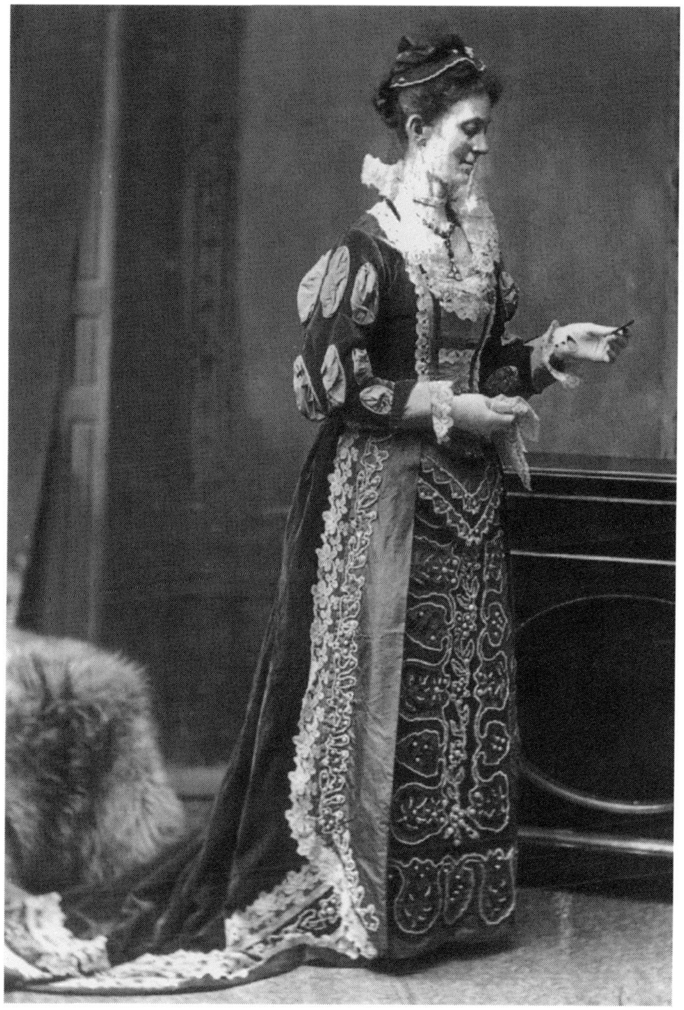

liveliness of the modern dance which it so much resembled, it was graceful and impressive, and the posing – the creation of momentary *tableaux vivants* – was carried off most acceptably. An elaborate bow before the dais was the finale.

The group's costumes were "so correct in detail that a single glance was sufficient to determine the character represented." Perhaps the elegance of the costumes contributed to this perception of authenticity. Mr. Goodeve – the "Earl of Surrey," in terra cotta velvet doublet trimmed with gold braid and very full trunks of crimson satin – explained that "costuming of that period was very rich in the use of costly fabrics and splendid decorations." E.S. Skead as "Francis I" was unfortunately not photographed, but he must have drawn much attention with "a handsome costume of rose velvet and fur. The tunic was studded with magnificent jewels of rare brilliancy" while "the mantle worn by King Francis could hardly escape notice, being of sable and pale green flowered brocade." In short, said the *Ottawa Free Press*, "The gentlemen who wore these costumes had a fine opportunity of displaying the richness of their lace and irreproachability of their garments." Most of the women's costumes in this group had long pendant sleeves, "so much worn at that time." Miss Hirschfelder's "Anne of Cleves" costume included "flowing sleeves [which] reached almost to the feet, disclosing a lining of white velvet and lace inner sleeves, puffed and confined at the wrists by bands of pink pearls."

Two individuals in this group may have been particularly striking to members of the company who remembered the Dufferin ball. Dr. John Sweetland, Sheriff of Carleton County, well known for his active role in many Ottawa charities, was "Henry

Linnie Stewart (née Powell) as "The Duchess of Suffolk" in the "Jacques Cartier" group (above). While fancy dress costumes were thought to be frivolous since they were often created for only one wearing, these photographs attest to the fact that some people got a great deal of mileage out of one garment: Mrs. Stewart has updated the dress she wore to the Dufferin ball in 1876 (above left) with a new bodice. By 1896 the skirt had lost a few beads, attesting to the effects of two decades of wear, including at least one skating carnival. WJT/NAC/PA193683; WJT/NAC/PA193694

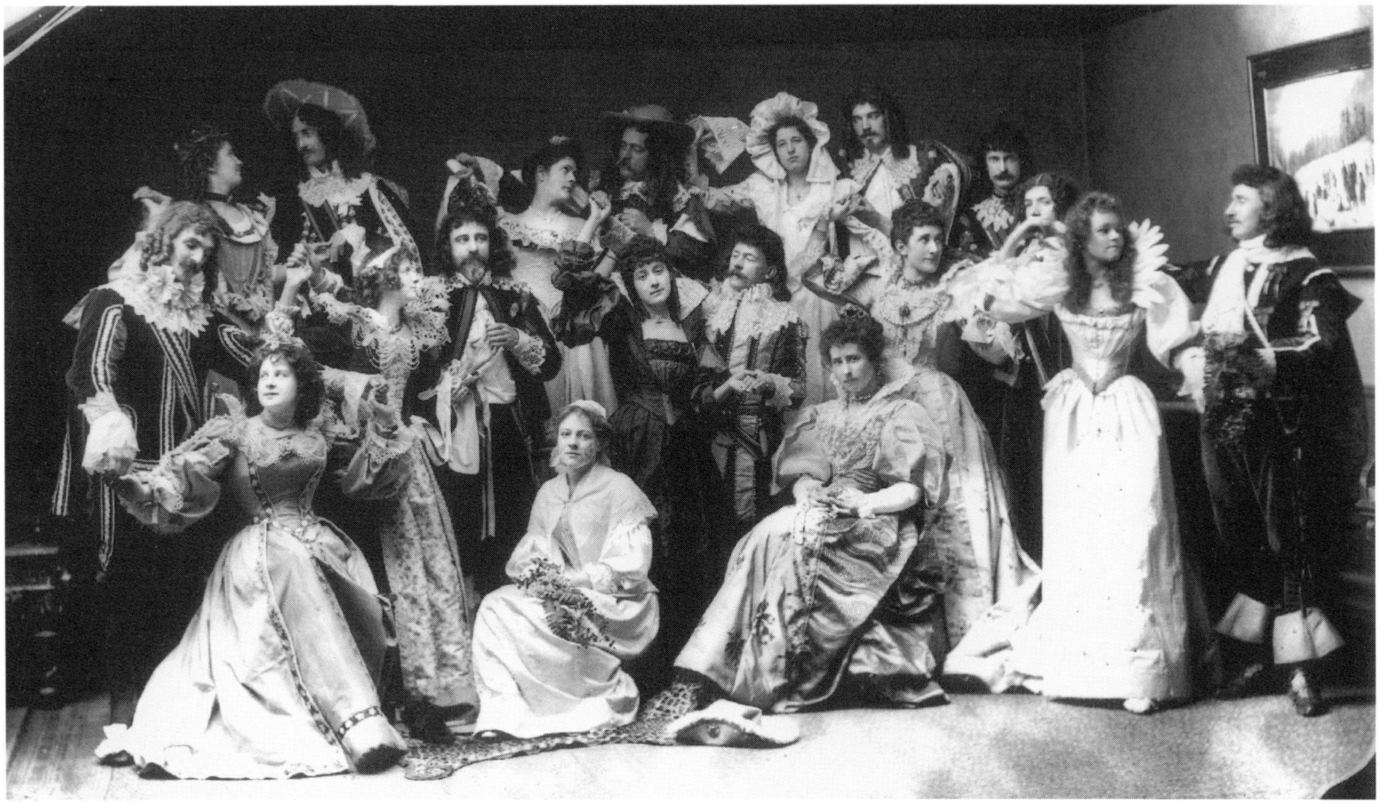

The Fourth Historic Group: The Foundation of Port Royal and Settlement of Acadia. *Seated in front:* Miss F. Wright; Miss Clarke. *Couples in front row:* Mr. Tasker as "Governor Winthrop" and Miss Cargill as "Madame de Monts"; Mrs. Stairs as "Lady Andros" and John F. Stairs as "Sir Edmund Andros"; Mrs. George Perley in black brocade and yellow silk as "Madame Denys" and Dewdney Jones in purple silk velvet as "Captain Daniel"; Miss E. Powell and Mr. Tyrwhitt; Miss Wright and Mr. Jackson. *Couples in back row:* Mrs. Spain and Mr. Lawless; Mrs. Gillies and Mr. St-Denis Lemoine; Miss Cutler and Mr. Eaton; Cameron Stanton. The group's bourrée was the most complicated dance of the evening, and this pose shows Professor Norman's careful tutoring.
WJT/NAC/PA193691

VIII," the same character he had chosen twenty years earlier. He made an imposing figure in black velvet with scarlet puffings trimmed with gold lace, a crimson plush *surtout* trimmed with ermine, and scarlet tights – a new costume. On the other hand, Linnie Stewart, the wife of former Ottawa Mayor McLeod Stewart, as "The Duchess of Suffolk," had had a new red velveteen bodice made to update the costume she had worn in 1876, which had been described as "court dress of the time of Charles II"; her red and gold skirt was the same. In fact, she wore the costume on at least one occasion between these balls. In a composite photo of an 1881 skating carnival, she wears the 1876 version with the open neckline filled in. A later, still more altered version of the costume exists today in a private collection in Ottawa.

The early French settlements in Canada were portrayed by the fourth set, entitled The Foundation of Port Royal and Settlement of Acadia, AD 1604-1677, and organized by Mrs. Arthur Dickey, wife of the Minister of Justice. "Samuel de Champlain" and "Marc L'Escarbot" were among the group, as were many of the French nobility. The group's bourrée was the most complicated dance of the evening. The dancers' initial hesitation soon wore off, and they performed the difficult movements and "intricate crossings and recrossings" flawlessly, making the dance very picturesque. At the end, after each woman made a deep court bow, her partner assisted her to her feet with such grace that the galleries applauded each couple individually.

The men's fairly uniform costumes incorporated long curly wigs and wide-brimmed hats, knee-length breeches and short capes – mostly in shades of crimson and purple velvet – and large lace collars. The women's costumes were more varied, but all included long trains which had to be "deftly handled and all in time to the music," and each woman also carried a bouquet. John Fitzwilliam Stairs, an M.P. from Halifax who belonged to a shipping company family, represented "Sir Edmond Andros," a New England Governor who declared war on Acadia in 1688. Mrs. Stairs,

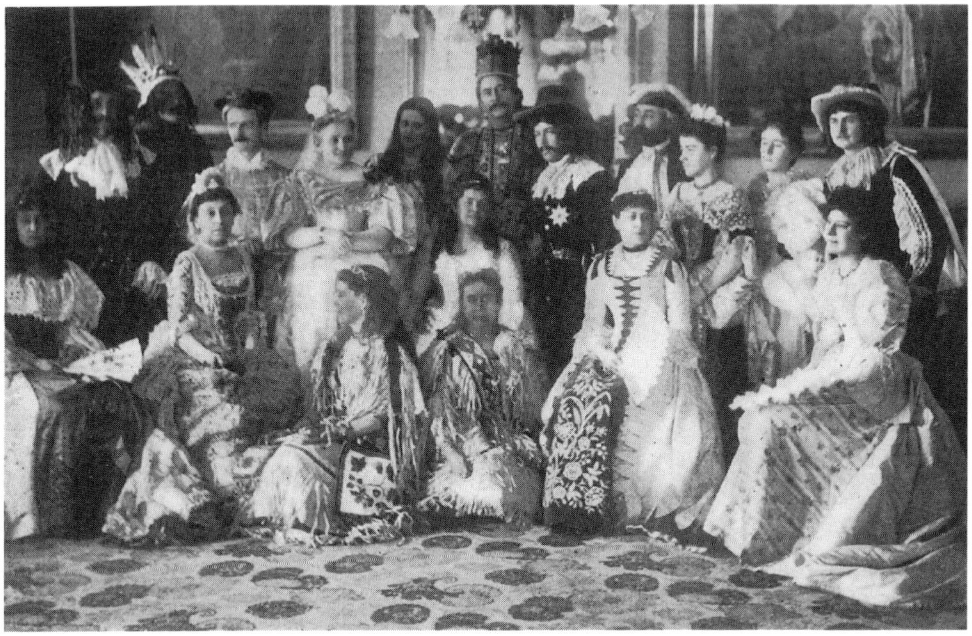

Below: John Fitzwilliam and Helen Stairs as "Sir Edmund and Lady Andros." His "court costume of green velvet" matched his wife's "court dress, white silk skirt, brocaded with pink roses; green velvet overdress and pearl trimmings." (*Ottawa Evening Journal,* 18 Feb. 1896) WJT/NAC/PA141071

Above: The Fifth Historic Group: The Foundation of Montreal and Settlement of Surrounding District. *Seated on floor:* Emily Cummings; Miss Zoe Shortt. *Seated:* Miss Gourdeau; Émilie Lavergne as "Barthes de Boulogne"; Mrs. Foster; Mrs. Wilson; Miss Panet. *Standing:* Mr. Panet; Mr. Girouard; Professor Frank H. Norman, the dancing master; Zoë Laurier; Mrs. William Wilfred Campbell; Major McGillivray; Mr. Delanaudière; J.P. Lowell; Mrs. J.P. Lowell; Miss O'Meara; W. O'Connor. This is the only group photo taken by Jarvis rather than by Topley. S. JARVIS/ NAC/ C143405.

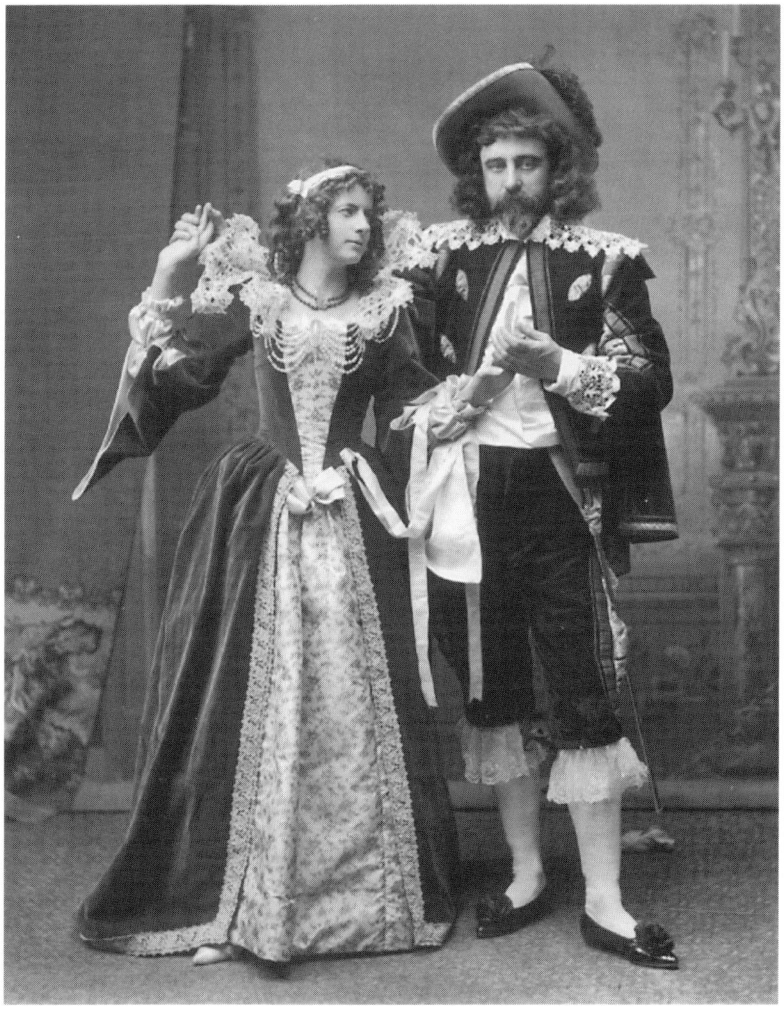

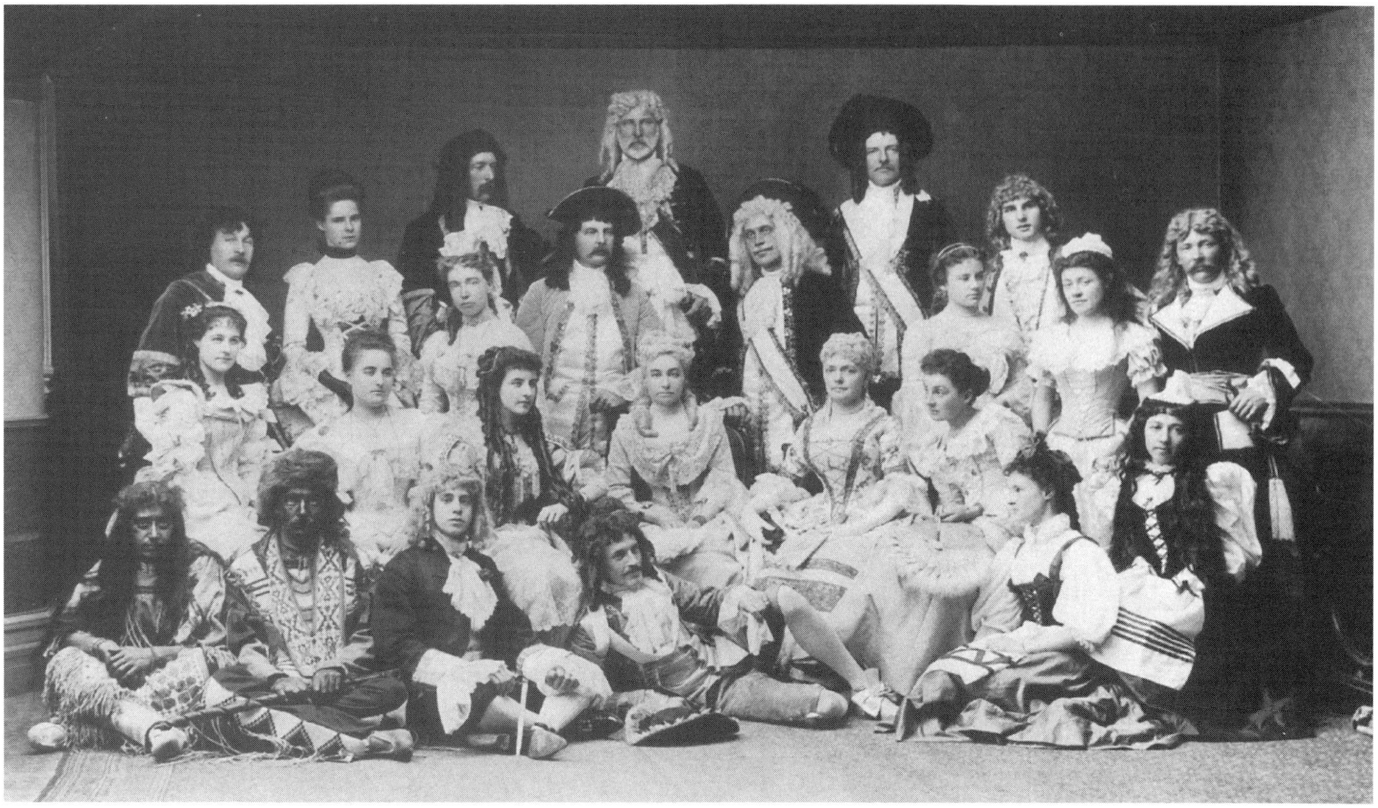

The Sixth Historic Group: Days of Settlement and Exploration from Tracy to Frontenac. *Front row, seated on the floor:* Miss Laura Smith; Mr. Critchley; V. Brown Wallis; Mr. Dumoulin; Miss Cassels. *Second row, seated:* Miss Malloch; Miss Smith; Miss Lola Powell; Mrs. Crombie; Mrs. John N. Kirchoffer as "Madame de Lotbinière"; Miss Moylan; Mrs. Morris. *Third row:* Mr. Gill; Miss Clayton; Miss Gwynne; Charles J. Jones, in pale mauve, as "Baron de Courcelles"; Charles Berkeley Powell, in red, as "Marquis de Tracy"; Miss Girouard; M. Taylor; Mrs. F. White; Mr. Middleton. *Fourth row:* E. Waldo; Waterford Lake Marler as "Count de Frontenac"; Alexander Ferguson, QC, as "Jean Talon." The costumes worn by Mr. Jones, Mr. Ferguson, and Mr. Powell, rented from Beullac, were made of velvet and trimmed with gold lace. WJT/NAC/PA138554

in a pink and white brocade skirt and sage green velvet overdress as "Lady Andros" "look[ed] charming." Mr. and Mrs. George Perley, members of a wealthy lumber family, represented "M. Leborgne" and "Mme Nicolas Denys."

The fifth group, The Foundation of Montreal and Settlement of Surrounding District, AD 1641-1670, had come under the responsibility of Zoë Laurier, wife of Wilfrid Laurier. Because of illness, she had been unable to keep her commitment. It was taken over by Émilie Lavergne, Laurier's close friend and, it was whispered, his mistress. While Mme Laurier was loved for her unaffected grace and easy manners, the cultivated and well-read Mme Lavergne, whose family had been *habitués* of the best Parisian society, had infinitely more brilliance and charisma. Of all the set organizers, only she managed to induce Professor Frank Norman, the dancing master, to dance with her group. He wore a "constantly beaming smile of satisfaction" throughout the proceedings, attesting to the group's polished performance. They danced a pavane, very similar to the previous one but with twice as many participants. Again the women sat on chairs at the outset and rose upon a salute from their partners. The dance involved a great deal of circling with hands joined and feet tapping on the floor, "like the pawing of an impatient steed."

The set included characters such as "Sieur de Maisonneuve" and "D'Ailleboust de Coulonges," with a large group of Indians. The men's costumes were similar to those of the previous group. J.P. Lowell wore a costume more akin to eighteenth-century dress than to a "Louis XIV Suit." Mme Lavergne as "Barthes de Boulogne," whose historical personage was said to be "mixed up in everything done in the country in her day," was well turned out in a gown very like contemporary evening dress, in "white silk with train and bodice of alternate stripes of brocade and white moiré, long train; front of pink and gold silk, trimmed in gold, jewelled lace and large paniers of brocade; very deep point to bodice of the pink and gold, with gold lace bows and

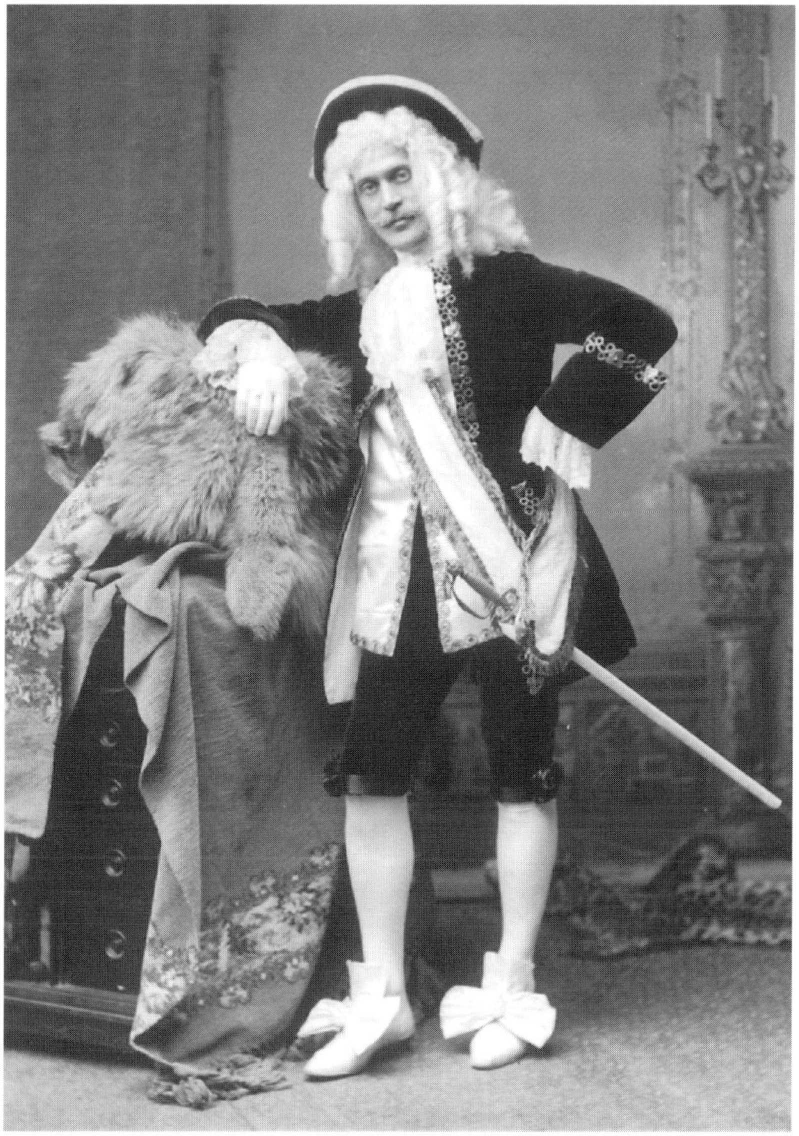

Charles Berkeley Powell as the "Marquis de Tracy." His costume, rented from Beullac, was among the most striking of the group: "period of Louis XIV; snow-white [wig], which fell in long curls about his shoulders; silk velvet frock coat of a rich ruby colour, heavily trimmed with gold lace; knee breeches of the same, with a white satin waistcoat and white satin shoes, having high red heels and very elaborate satin bows with jewelled buckles." Powell's flare for the dramatic later resulted in his appointment to the Earl Grey Musical and Dramatic Association. (*Ottawa Free Press*, 18 Feb. 1896) WJT/NAC/PA139843

pearls; pink sleeves, tight, with lace [ruffles] at the elbow; white lace mitts; red satin shoes." Her hair was dressed "exactly in keeping with the fashion of that period, with a pretty fan-shaped lace cap with tabs." Miss Laurie as "Mlle Le Gardeur de Tilly," who had "belonged to one of the greatest Canadian families," wore a white satin dress with a "long court train, made of brocaded silk, which has been in the family for generations, the whole studded with pearls and rubies."[21]

Days of Settlement and Exploration from Tracy to Frontenac, AD 1665-1698, organized by Mrs. John Gwynne, the wife of a Supreme Court judge, with the assistance of Mrs. Crombie, displayed a wealth of attractive costumes. Twenty-six characters from this striking group danced a gavotte. "Much was expected from this dance and no disappointment resulted, for it was an artistic figure given in an artistic manner." The dance was far livelier than those which had preceded it, with movements that were "the most catchy and graceful of all." Professor Norman had arranged the dance three years earlier for *Mascot*, a popular operetta that the Aberdeens had seen fit to boycott for unsuitable content.[22]

The group included Senator John Kirchoffer of Manitoba as "Sir William Phipps" and his wife as "Madame de Lotbinière." Clara Kirchoffer wore a "pink satin petticoat trimmed with bands of pink and green embroidery of Alençon lace; bodice and train of white and rose colored satin brocade; long pointed stomacher embroidered with jewels; small sleeves with lace frills at the elbow; hair dressed low, in the fashion of the period with curls, and bands of pearls; ornaments pearls and diamonds." Charles Berkeley Powell, a partner in the Perley and Pattee lumber company, in a "long snow white curling wig" and a costume rented from Beullac, made a striking figure as the "Marquis de Tracy." Similar costumes worn by Alexander Ferguson, QC, as "Jean Talon" and Charles J. Jones, chief clerk of the Governor General's secretary's office as "Baron de Courcelles," were singled out as particularly impressive. But per-

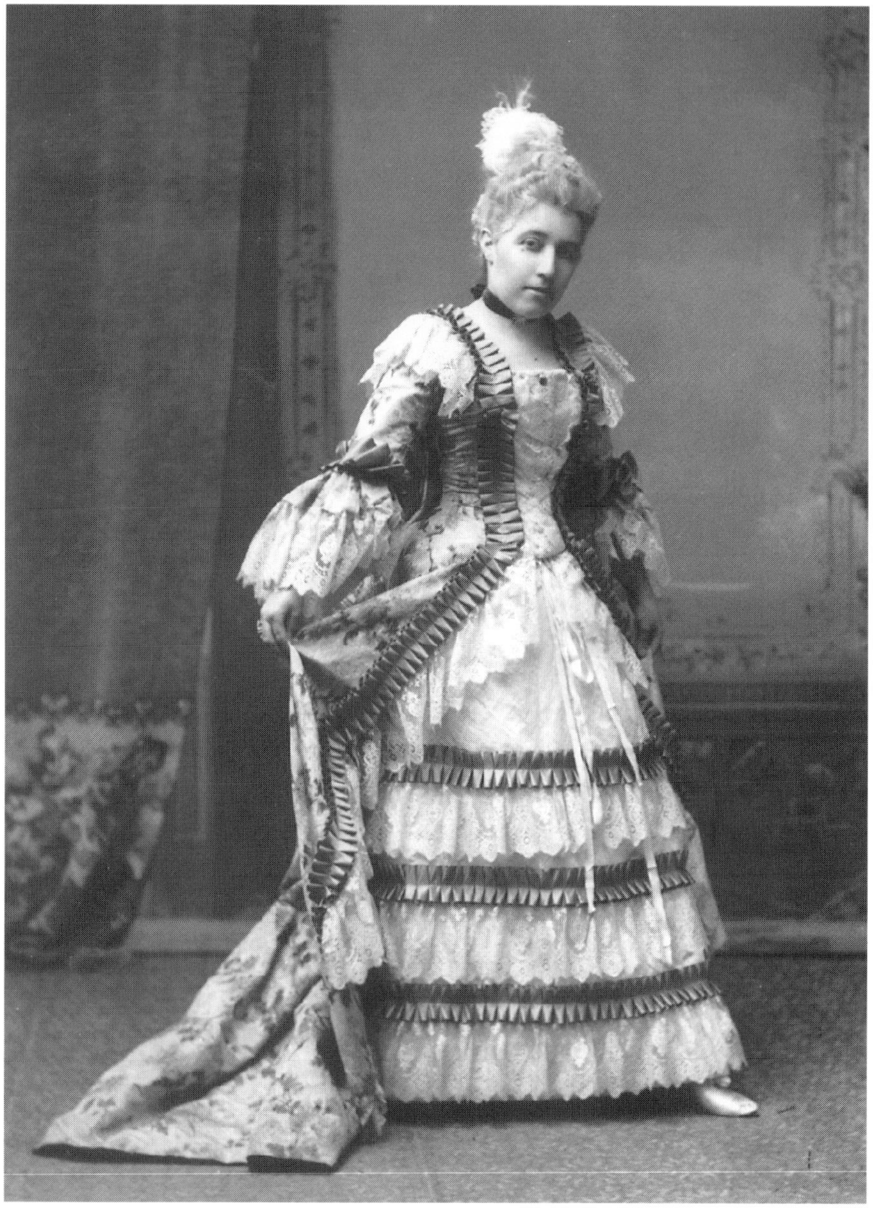

Jessie Ross Robertson (née Holland) as "Baroness of Longueuil" prepares to drop into a curtsey. Her costume "was one of the richest on the floor. . . . The petticoat was of white satin, trimmed with three flounces of point lace and old rose ribbon ruching. The gown worn over this was of the same period, with a double Watteau extending from the neck, tied with a ribbon bow. The material used was a unique brocade, a reproduction of the same period, the ground a pale yellow, with a vine of flowers of old rose and green trimmed with point lace to match. The sleeves were to the elbow with a double flounce of point lace, finished with a bow of ribbon, the gown being lined throughout with pale yellow silk. The hair was worn à la pompadour." (*Toronto Globe*, 22 Feb. 1896) WJT/NAC/PA192343

haps most striking of all was Waterford Lake Marler, manager of the Merchants' Bank of Canada: "The dress of Mr. Marler, as the Count de Frontenac, deserves special mention, and was the more noticeable inasmuch as Mr. Marler wore it with all the distinction belonging to the great historic character whom he represented."[23]

The women wore "plain skirts, large paniers, and tightly fitting pointed bodices in which the wearers looked like Dresden shepherdesses (without the crook)." Their hair was "most becomingly arranged with high coiffure from which long and short ringlets depended." Lola Powell (who would later gain notoriety as the Earl of Minto's mistress) wore such a hairstyle, as did Miss Caron, daughter of the Postmaster General, with "hair beautifully arranged" as "Madame Jean Talon." Mrs. H.C. Monk, as "Madame de St. Ours," looked "quaint and "sweet" in an overdress of pink and white silk brocade and a blue satin petticoat with pearl passementerie.

In the seventh set, Days of Montcalm and Wolfe, and the Conquest of Canada, AD 1754-1760, French and English heroes danced peacefully side by side, decked out in "the military fashion of the period." The farandole, "an exceedingly stately dance set to slow music" similar to a quadrille, ended with a march in which all eight couples saluted the Aberdeens and their court.

French governors and officers predominated, and nearly all the men wore white wigs with queues. John Christie as "Montcalm" wore a black velvet coat with a red ribbon and the order of St. Louis, and a pair of black slippers with high red heels and diamond buckles. "Wolfe," Philip D. Ross, editor and proprietor of the *Ottawa Jour-*

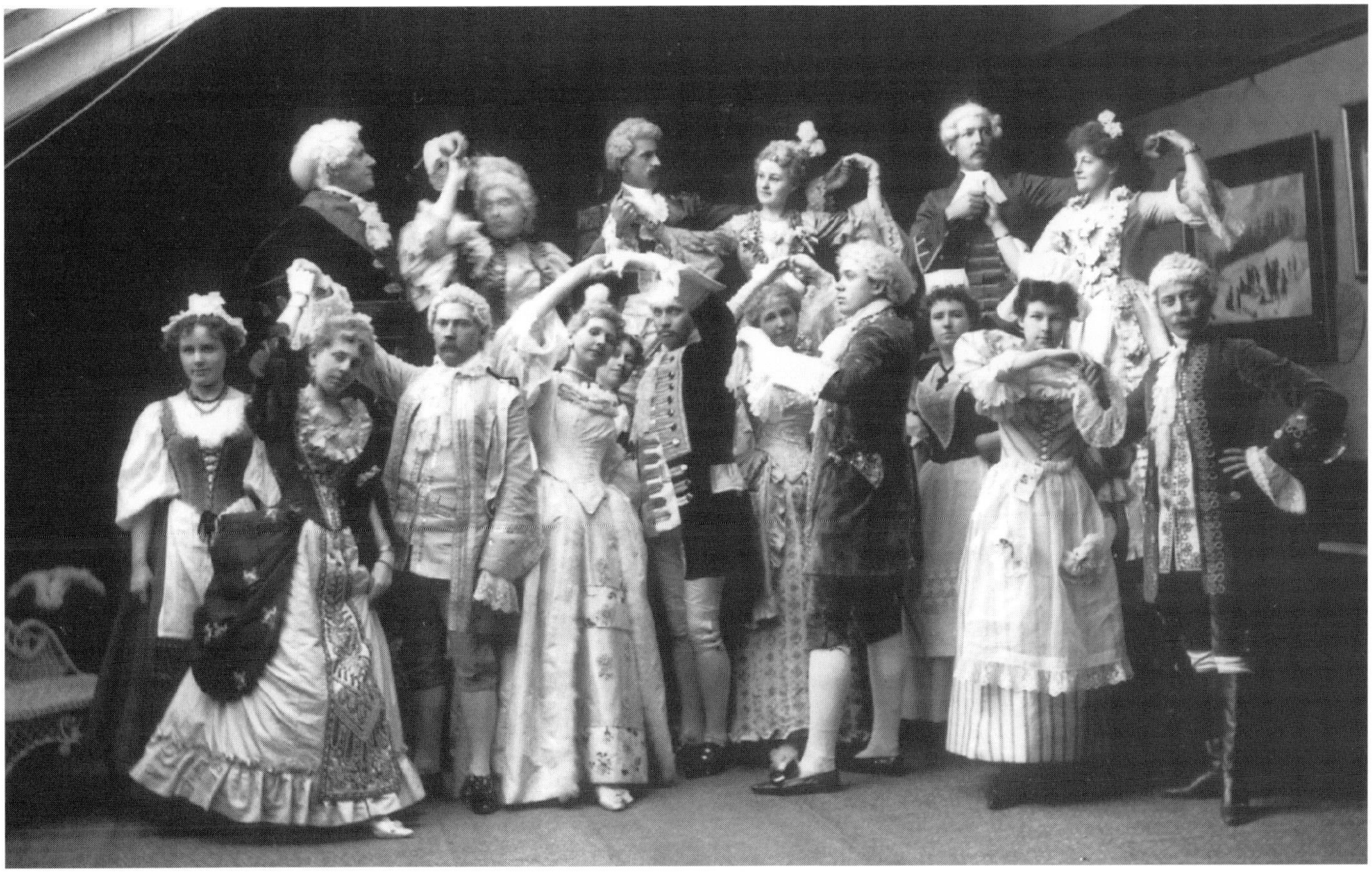

nal, opted for a scarlet uniform faced with blue and gold, with boots over his white knee breeches. Dr. Bourinot, Lady Aberdeen's advisor, as "Governor Shirley" of Massachussets, stood on the sidelines, while Mrs. Bourinot, the organizer of the set, in yellow and blue silk brocade trimmed with forget-me-nots, danced with her group as "Madame de Vaudreuil." Jessie Ross Robertson, wife of the Toronto newspaper magnate John Ross Robertson, was the special guest of the Bourinots. As the "Baroness of Longueuil," she stood out among the women in a sumptuous Louis XV costume in a reproduction fabric with elaborate trim.

The eighth set, From the Fall of Port Royal to the Second Taking of Louisbourg, Including Expatriation of the Acadians, AD 1710-1758, was one of the highlights of the evening. The Acadian peasant characters barely alluded to the grim events in the title, and the subtitle, "Acadia in the days of Evangeline," offered plenty of romantic scope. Professor Norman had choreographed an Acadian peasant dance followed by a maypole dance performed by twenty-two young women, mostly daughters of Members of Parliament. The maypole, decorated with cedar and roses, stood in the centre of the room as the peasants danced around it, colourful ribbons in hand, creating a lattice which they unwove when they reversed their steps. The ribbon lattice formed a tent over three small pages who sat in chairs against the pole. Speed made the dance still more spectacular – it was performed in "double quick time, the girls being constantly on the trot." In the midst of this group was seventeen year-old Gabrielle Lavergne, making her debut, as "Marie Landry," heroine of Napoleon Bourassa's novel, *Jacques et Marie*.

Enthusiastic applause rose from the floor and the galleries. The dance had so captured the hearts of the onlookers that, at the Governor General's request, it was

The Seventh Historic Group: Days of Montcalm and Wolfe. *Front row:* Miss Hill; Mrs. Macdonnell; H.C. Monk; Mrs. H.C. Monk as "Madame de St. Ours"; Miss J. Cameron; R. Matheson as "Chevalier de Lévis"; Miss Wilson; A.P. Campbell as "Marquis de Vaudreuil"; Miss McCuaig; Miss M. Cameron; Mr. Panet. *Back row:* John Christie as "Montcalm"; Mrs. John Ross Robertson as "Baroness of Longueuil"; Philip D. Ross as "Wolfe"; Mrs. John Bourinot as "Madame de Vaudreuil"; Mr McEvoy; Mrs. Codville. The group strikes a pose from its stately farandole. WJT/NAC/PA137982

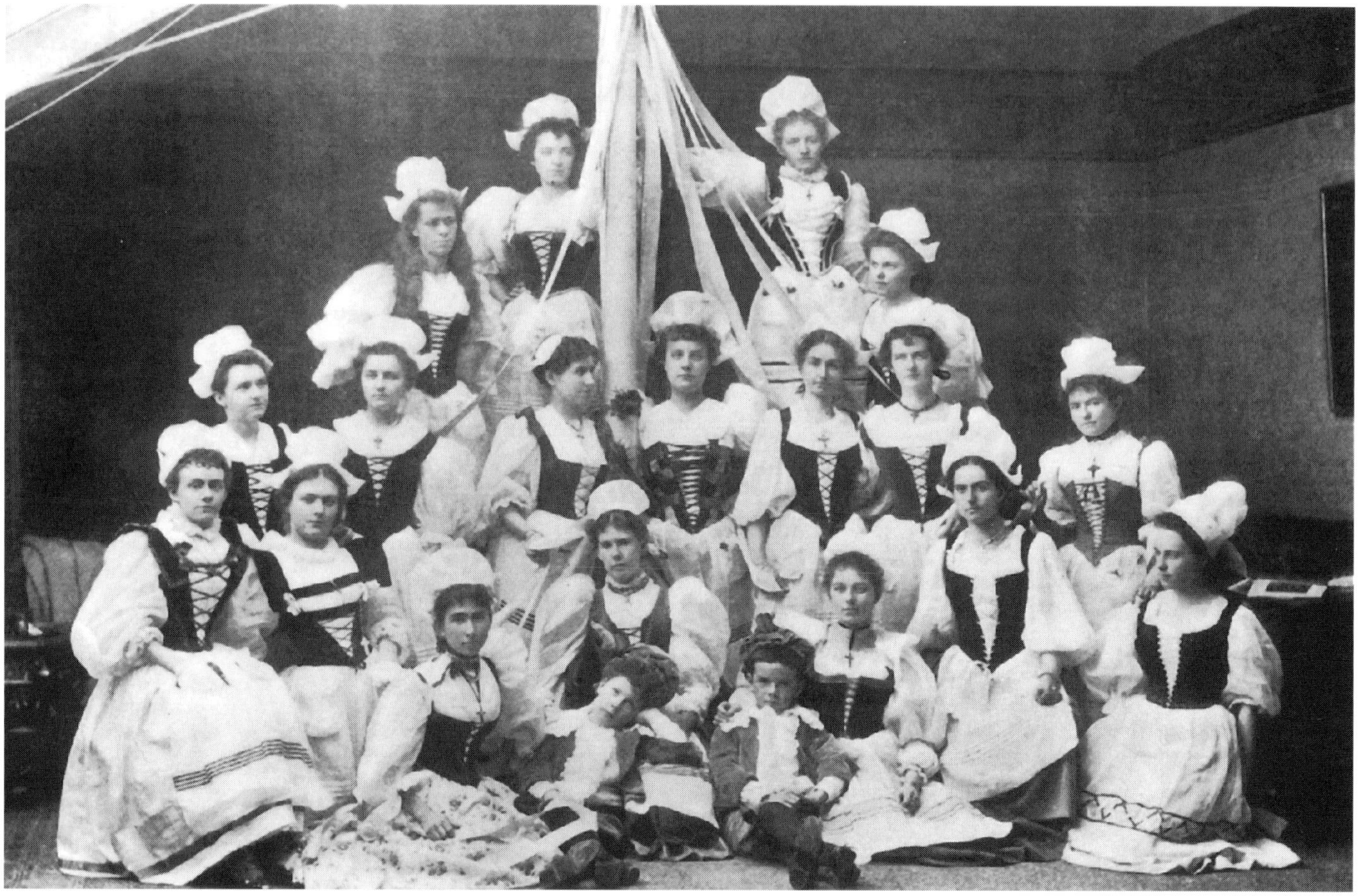

The Eighth Historic Group: From the Fall of Port Royal to the Second Taking of Louisbourg, Including Expatriation of the Acadians. *Front row:* Miss Smart; Master L. White; Master Marshall. *Second row:* Miss Gouin; Miss McKay; Miss Hunter; Mrs. McGirr; Miss E. Wilson; Miss O'Brien. *Third row:* Mrs. Cameron; Miss Beith; Miss Proctor; Miss Gabrielle Lavergne as "Marie Landry"; Miss Wilson; Miss Edwards; Miss McGee. *Fourth row:* Miss McLean; Miss Wood; Miss Cargill; Miss McRae. Any *ennui* following the other groups' pavanes and bourrées was dispelled when these daughters of MPs skipped through their sprightly maypole dance. The Aberdeens liked it so much they requested an encore. WJT/NAC/PAC143407

repeated. Later, Aberdeen personally thanked Mrs. Peter White, wife of the Speaker of the House of Commons, for her efforts in organizing this most successful set.

The requisites of the uniform costume worn by the young women were a sleeveless low-necked velvet bodice laced in front over a full white chemise, and a short, full skirt trimmed with horizontal bands at the edge, worn with a white mull apron – "short coquettish skirts, coaxing little aprons . . . and a world of airy winsomeness." Each young woman wore a "white Normandy cap, plain but very becoming, with their white flaming wings over the ears." A cross around her neck, a rosary at her waist and a basket of flowers in her hand accessorized her costume, and her thick-soled, high-heeled shoes "made a merry clatter" as she danced. Fifteen other guests, not part of the organized sets, came in a version of this popular "Normandy peasant" costume, which, as Weldon's fancy dress catalogue pointed out, "is decidedly becoming and always proves such a successful dress, and one too that is quickly made without much expense."

The final set represented The Coming of the United Empire Loyalists, AD 1775-1792. Mary Scott, wife of Senator Richard William Scott, the Secretary of State, and a doyenne of Ottawa society, organized the group. Prior to marrying she had toured Europe and North America extensively as one of the musical Heron sisters; she had been one of the Earl of Dufferin's dance partners at his fancy dress ball. The Scott family and their relatives made up a large part of the group which represented well-known Loyalist families in eighteenth-century costume, some with British military uniforms. In powdered hair and predominantly pink dresses with pointed bodices and fichus, the women looked "neat and dainty." Agnes Scott, the journalist Amaryllis (immortalized by Sandra Gwyn in *The Private Capital*) and Senator Scott's niece, represented an ancestress, "Mrs. Marjorie MacDonald," the wife of Captain Allan MacDonald; she wore pink brocade. Agnes's cousin D'Arcy Scott, barely established in his profession as a barrister and later mayor of Ottawa, impersonated "Chief Justice Haliburton" in what he described as a "Lord Chancellor wig." His brother William, also a lawyer, played "Richard Cartwright," ancestor of the Liberal MP of the same name seated on the dais. Miss Grace Ritchie represented her ancestress, "Miss Phoebe Vernon," of New Brunswick. Faith Fenton, editor-in-chief of the *Canadian Home Journal* and "at the head of lady journalists in Toronto," unlike the rest of her group, came as "Sister Martha Quincy," a "Mennonite Quakeress of the time of the coming of the United Empire Loyalists." (Her story is told by Jill Downie in *A Passionate Pen*.)

The Loyalist group danced the fashionable ending for all Canadian balls, the Sir Roger de Coverley, the fastest dance of the evening, "those engaged in it being continually on the run." After a great deal of "winding up and down, in and out, in hearty fashion," it finished with the bow before the throne.

Immediately thereafter, aides-de-camp circulated among the guests on the floor, presenting some two hundred and forty participants with silver brooches and scarf pins bearing the Aberdeen motto *Fortuna sequatur*, Let fortune follow. Each had a small pencil attached, which the guests used to fill in their dance cards, worn on their wrists. The set dances had lasted about an hour and a half, and the presentations that followed took another hour. The leader of each group introduced the others to the vice-regal court under their real and assumed names; some chose to greet Their Excellencies in character: soldiers saluted, peasants made bashful curtsies. But the leaders performed poorly, mumbling, forgetting titles, and getting stuck, to Lady Aberdeen's great embarassment. The hosts gritted their teeth and received each character with a bow and a smile, which pleased the onlookers in the galleries – including virtually all the reporters – who were oblivious to the shortcomings.

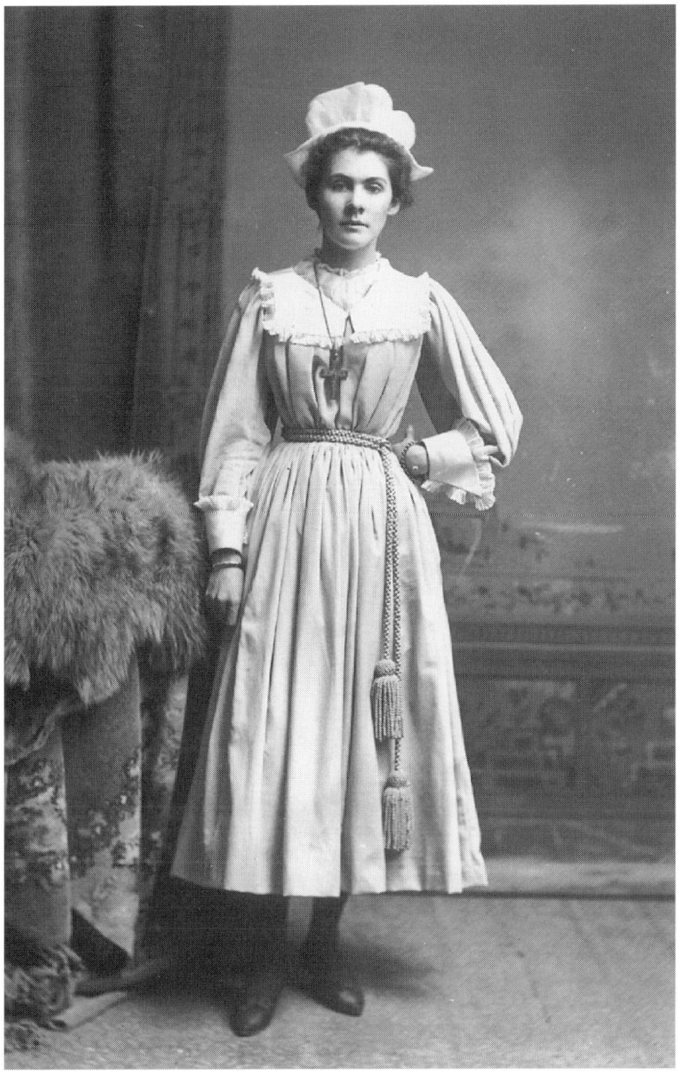

Miss Kathleen McLaren as "a quaint little Evangeline." The only one to dress differently in the eighth group, she wears "a little grey gown and golden cross" with a Normandy bonnet. (*Canadian Home Journal*, March 1896) WJT/NAC/PA193684

To begin the general dancing, eight couples from the vice-regal group, including Prime Minister Mackenzie Bowell, performed the State Lancers; to Lady Aberdeen's dismay, some of the cabinet ministers got "rather far astray." This time journalists noted the bumbling, remarking that political skill does not necessarily imply dancing ability, and that "even cabinet ministers make mistakes now and again – especially in the Lancers." Perhaps their wives had been so busy instructing their respective sets that they had forgotten to brush up on the Lancers with their husbands. Lady Aberdeen made a most imposing figure in the dance, no doubt pulling the whole thing together.

The muddle was forgotten when, to everyone's surprise, an unrehearsed, unplanned set converged from the four corners of the room. Confusion reigned as Hayter Reed, decked out in full floor-length feather headdress, led those in Indian

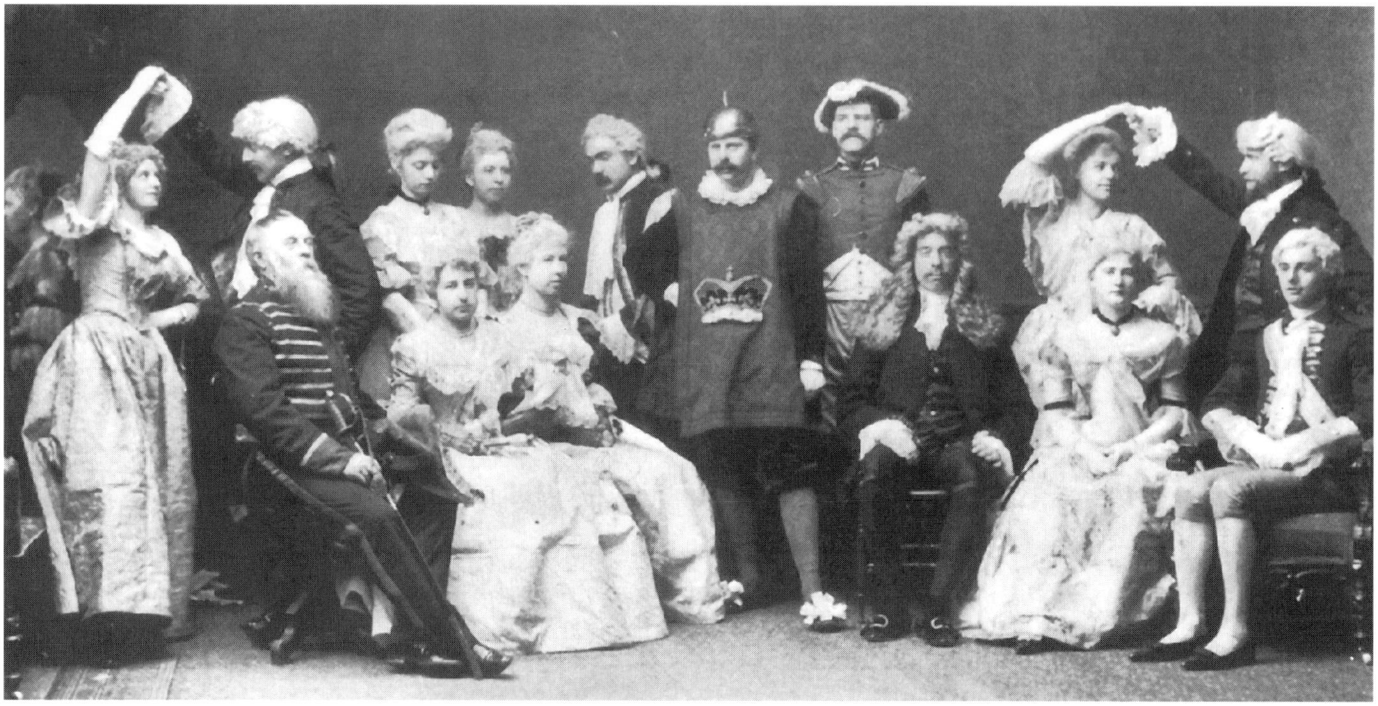

The Ninth Historic Group: The Coming of the United Empire Loyalists. *Seated:* A.C. MacDonald, MP; Miss Agnes Scott (the journalist Amaryllis) as "Mrs. Marjorie Macdonald"; Miss Scott; D'Arcy Scott as "Chief Justice Haliburton"; Miss Elmsley; Mr. Macoun. *Standing:* Miss D. Robertson; Mr. Burritt; Miss Magee; Miss Lillian Scott; Mr. Pugsley; A. Scott; Plunkett Taylor; Miss Lemoine; William Scott as "Richard Cartwright." WJT/NAC/ C143407

costume to the foot of the dais, men first, women following, all emitting melodious war-whoops. He addressed the Governor General in the Cree language, "betokening the love of his Indians for the great chief." The speech was punctuated with expressive grunts and whoops from his followers, and William Wilfred Campbell, the well-known poet, acted as interpreter. At the end the calumet was presented to the Earl.

No one questioned the stereotype this group presented of the unruly, "savage" Indian, nor the incongruity of the various elements of their dress, although several members of the group had first-hand experience with a very different reality. Hayter Reed, the instigator, was Deputy Superintendant General of Indian Affairs and had spent considerable time among Canadian aboriginal people. Duncan Campbell Scott was Accountant for the Department of Indian Affairs (though he came to be more famous as a poet). Emily Cummings, a *Toronto Globe* columnist known as "Sama" and a founding member of the National Council of Women, had made an extended tour through the Indian reserves of Manitoba, the Northwest Territories and British Columbia and had written a series entitled "Our Indian Wards" for the *Toronto Empire*. Even Lady Aberdeen repeatedly lamented not having thought of organizing a war dance.

The myth of the "noble savage" coloured European perceptions from the time of contact. By the nineteenth century, seeing how aboriginal peoples had fallen into a state of poverty and degradation, their colonizers lamented the dying of a race. Yet invoking the image of savage peoples confirmed that, ultimately, civilization and colonization had been beneficial. The "Indians" which Reed and his group imitated had nothing to do with the nature of aboriginal peoples; rather, they were part and parcel of the mythology of the Canadian past; the heroism of the other historical figures was bolstered only in the presence of this "other," in all its barbaric and savage glory.

Most of the costumes were composed of Native-produced articles, though juxtaposed in peculiar combinations. Hayter Reed's contemporary Plains headdress and Blackfoot shirt satisfied the ballgoers but had no connection with the sixteenth-

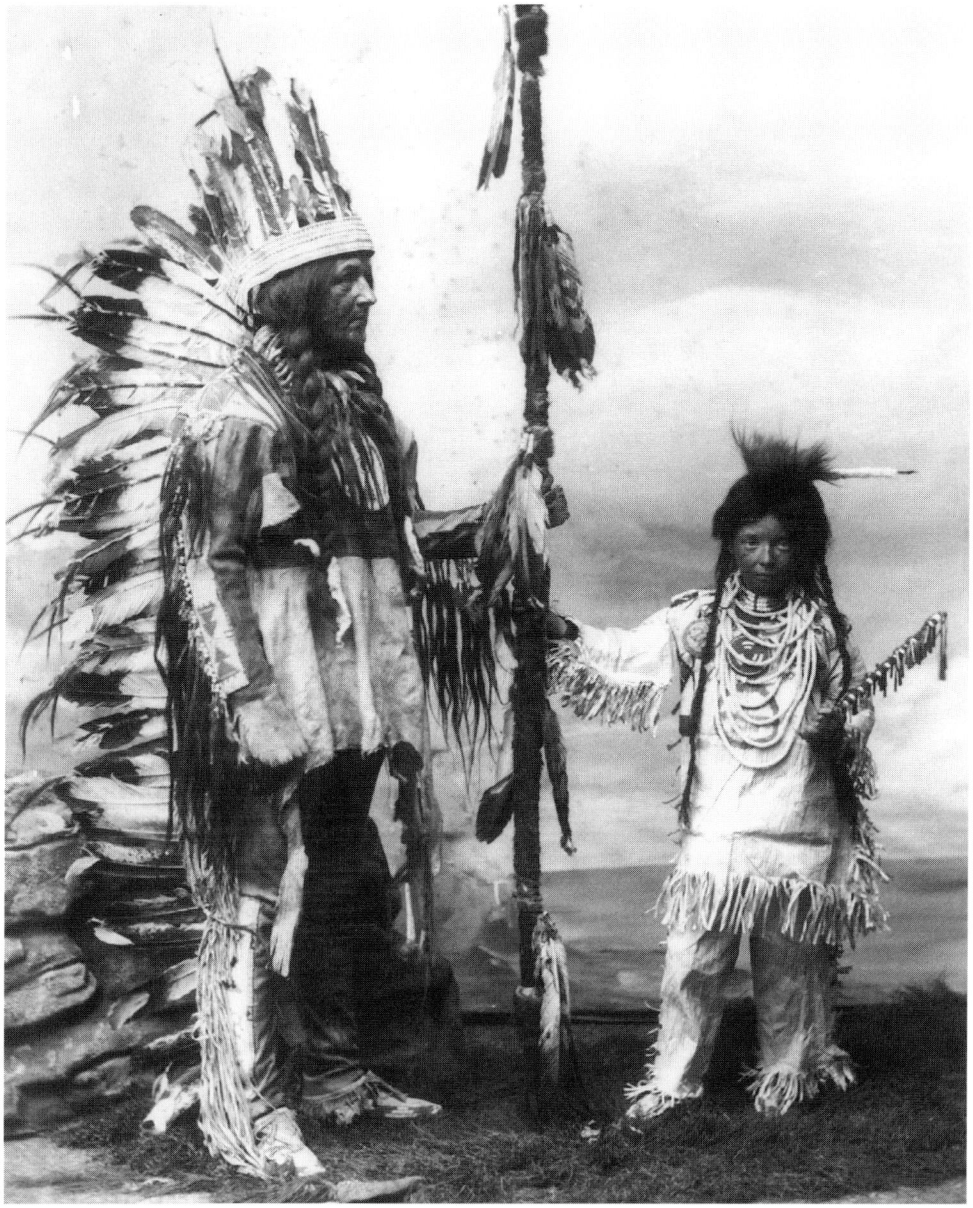

Hayter Reed as "Donnacona" and his stepson, Jack Lowery. Reed must have been aware that this Plains dress was completely unlike sixteenth-century Iroquois costume. He later donated the two shirts, the headdress, his moccasins and the staff to the McCord Museum of Canadian History. The boy's costume is made of crepe paper appliquéed with Native beadwork. WJT/NAC/PA139841

century Iroquois dress of his character, "Donnacona"; no doubt he acquired these articles during his time in the West. Miss Bloomfield and Miss Laura Smith wore dresses and accessories borrowed from Reed's collection, Miss Smith with a man's bandolier bag slung across her chest. Mr. Critchley wore garments originally belonging to the Saulteaux chief Pasquaw of the Fort Qu'Appelle Reserve in Saskatchewan, topped with a fur hat; he unwittingly had the shirt on backwards. Mrs. Cummings had a better understanding of how a beaded bag was worn, though some of her jewellery looks suspiciously like pearls, and her dress appears to be of paper. Reed's stepson's extant costume is also of paper, given a more authentic appearance with appliqués of Native beadwork stitched to it.

Makeup was essential for creating an authentic image and thus made these costumes quite daring. Butterick's *Masquerade and Carnival* suggests for those dressing as Indians that "the face be stained a reddish brown or copper color; and in addition the eyebrows must be blackened to meet at the center, and the face may be painted beneath

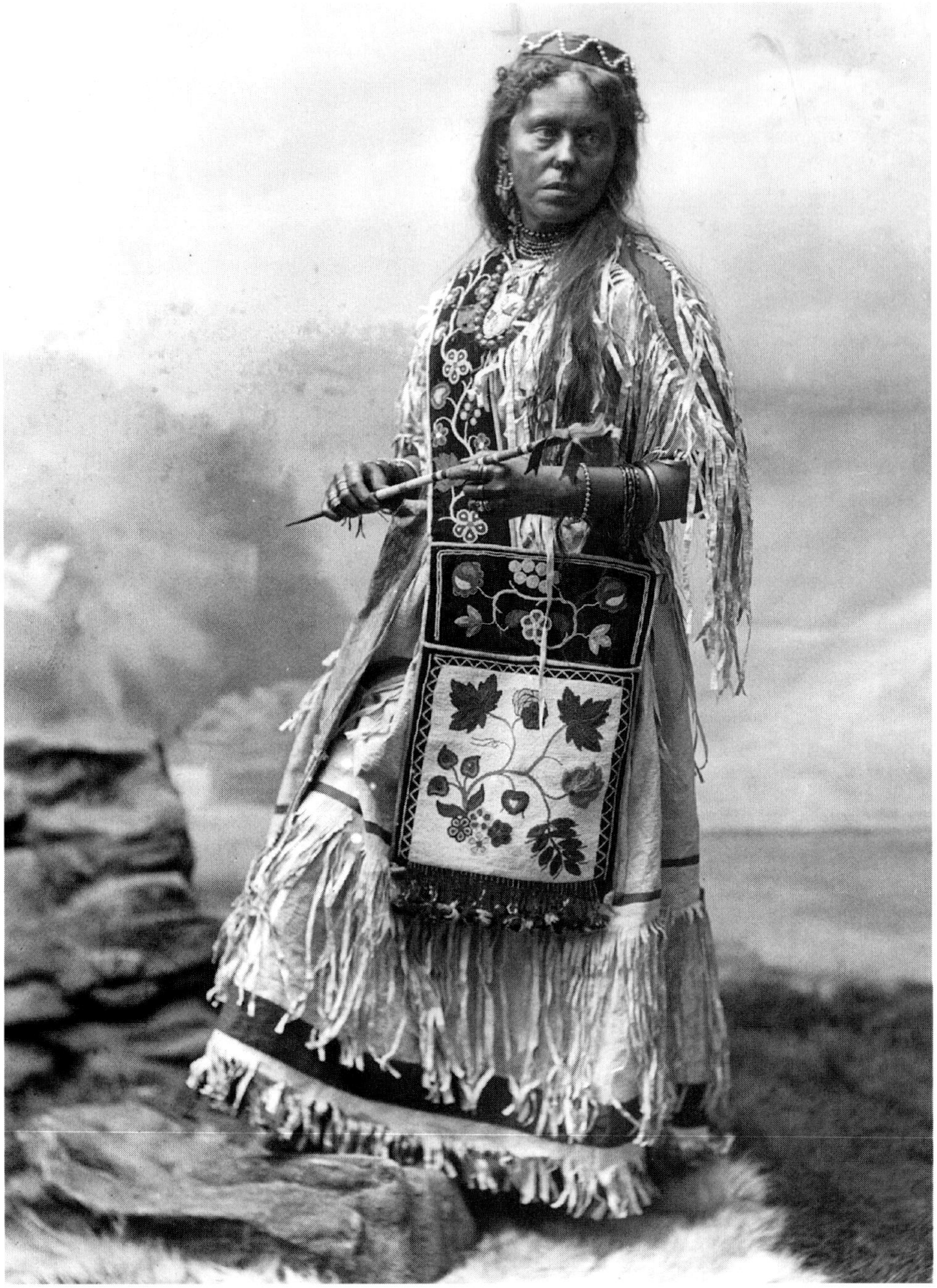

Emily Cummings (née Shortt) as "Outina." The man's beaded bandolier bag and some of her other accessories seem to be Native-made articles, but, judged by its texture, her dress appears to be paper. WJT/NAC/PA191755

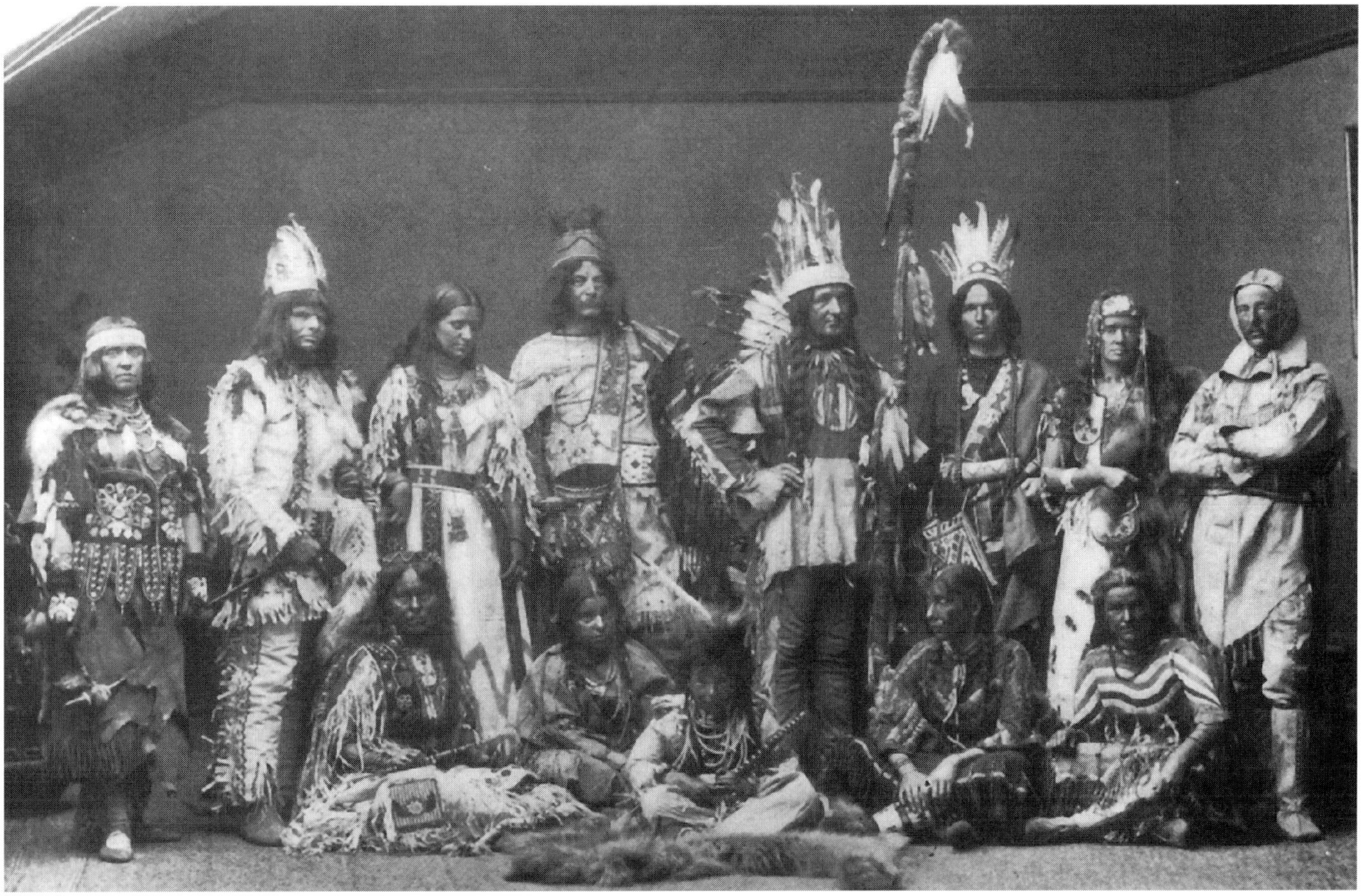

The Indian Group. *Seated on the floor:* Emily Cummings as "Outina"; Miss Grace Lowery; Master Jack Lowery; Miss Bloomfield; Mrs. Atkinson. *Standing:* Mlle de Rideau; William Wilfred Campbell as "Tessoüat"; Miss Graham; Major McGillivray; Hayter Reed as "Donnacona"; Mr. Simpson; Mrs. William Wilfred Campbell; Mr. Munn. Hayter Reed holds a staff and wears garments of Native manufacture which he aquired during his term as Deputy Superintendant of Indian Affairs. He also collected the dress and accessories worn by Miss Bloomfield. WJT/NAC/ C143408

the lower eyelids to produce a properly savage expression." The Historical Fancy Dress Ball Indians evidently followed the instructions to the letter, for the result was felt to be convincing and accurate. "They would have delighted the heart of a genuine son of the forest if he could have seen them," stated *The Lounger*. Mlle de Rideau (who wore the oddest combination of aboriginal costume and accessories) was transformed:

> She had a genuine squaw costume, effectively decorated with real fur tails; she wore her hair flowing and had a broad band across her forehead; though numerous friends could not at first recognize her, the opinion generally prevails that for the time being, she made a very typical councillor of her tribe.[24]

The total disguise which other fancy dress did not allow made these Indian costumes particularly appealing to wearers and onlookers alike. In fact, the impromptu procession shows that the individuals in Indian costume were eager to act out roles – very different from approved public behaviour. War-whooping and tomahawk-waving were part of the hammed-up violence and savagery. Julius Lay, dressed in Plains garments as "A Micmac Medicine Man," expressed these stereotypical qualities by claiming to be wearing mocassins made of human scalps and a headdress of polar bear claws, "a romantic but perhaps somewhat gory reminiscence."

As the "Indians" retreated, the entire party prepared to leave for the supper room to the tune of the national anthem in a procession ordered according to the dances.

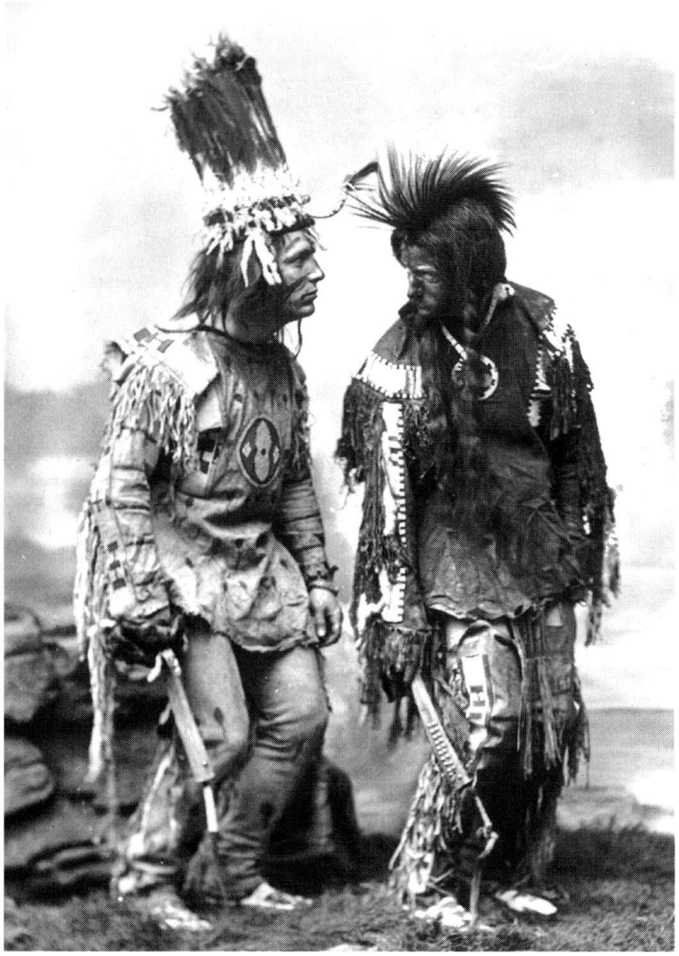

Jim Smellie and Julius Lay as "Micmac Chief" and "Micmac Medicine Man." Their Plains costume is a far cry from Micmac attire, and nothing about Mr. Lay's moccasins suggests that they are actually made of human scalps, as he claimed. The pose shows the characters' "savagery." WJT/NAC/PA189665

Samuel Jarvis, an Ottawa photographer, had stationed his camera on one of the galleries and took two flash photographs of the group as the procession began.

The buffet-style supper, organized by the Government House staff, was offered only to the guests in the historical sets. Lady Aberdeen was most pleased with her servants' efforts, and guests confirmed that the meal was a "most sumptuous affair . . . both *recherché* and delicate." Once again, official Ottawa's voracious appetite was its undoing. The rush towards the food table created a crush at the supper room door "out of which people did not emerge without their finery being sadly tumbled." "They eat very largely here, we put lots of sandwiches and jellies in the tea room as well as the supper room to keep them quiet," wrote Lady Aberdeen.[25]

With the court and historical groups out of the way in the supper room, those who had been confined to the overcrowded galleries poured down to the floor and danced waltzes and two-steps until five in the morning. These guests had been obliged to dress as some other character from any of the periods mentioned. For men, these characters ranged from Venetian noblemen to court gentlemen of a another century, with a few in military uniforms and academic robes. Among the women were a large number of Acadian and Normandy peasants, as well as Venetian and Spanish ladies. A few came simply as unnamed United Empire Loyalists. There was some duplication of characters, as some represented those already part of the historical groups, and there were two "Laura Secords."

A few chose to represent their own ancestors. Mrs. Henry Macleod played "Rosamond Smith," a United Empire Loyalist, her grandmother. Professor E. Stone Wiggins came as "Captain Thomas Wiggins, his ancestor, first Governor of New Hampshire in 1631, when New England was a British province. Governor Wiggins was the ancestor of all the United Empire Loyalists of that name who came to Canada in 1783." (In fact, he was also the ancestor of the professor's wife; "Gunhilda" Wiggins, the well-known polemic writer, had married her cousin.) Professor J.W. Robertson, representing one of his ancestors, submitted a life story, including military exploits, more detailed than any of those given for the other characters. Perhaps he did so because, although he was Dairy Commissioner at the Experimental Farm in Ottawa, he had started out at the very bottom of the cheese-making business on his arrival in Canada twenty years earlier.[26]

Roughly one thousand guests were present in the building; this made the dance floor extremely crowded, and there was continual jostling and bumping. The corridors and the Library of Parliament were open to the guests and provided welcome relief from the crowded Senate chamber, offering "every opportunity for escaping from the rabble and wandering about exchanging those confidences which to man and maid are so dear." A certain couple discovered in a compromising position – exchanging not only confidences but affectionate caresses in a secluded corner – suffered the embarassment of making the *Free Press* the next day. The tale of their misadventure, "A Story of Imprudence Which Will Go Down in History," at least gave them the solace of anonymity.

Another scandal erupted two months later. A Reverend McKay of Woodstock claimed that the Sabbath had been descrated by the workmen laying the dance floor; that the cost of $25,000 had been assumed by the federal Goverment; and that, worst of all, the ball had been the scene of vice, immorality and intemperance. These claims were indignantly refuted by the MPs in the House of Commons. Aberdeen had himself covered all expenses except for paying the workmen who laid the floor. There were no reports to substantiate the other claims. Despite the unlimited flow of champagne, "as a matter of fact, the recent fancy dress ball was a remarkable contrast to what such an affair might happen to be, and to what the last previous affair of the kind in Ottawa, the Dufferin ball, was," argued an Ottawa paper. In the 1860s, Feo Monck, sister-in-law to the then Governor General, had witnessed with disgust broken bottles on the floor and dancing on the tables at a ball. By the nineties, the temperance movement had indeed tempered ballgoers' festive spirits.[27]

But the issue of what the ball cost was no doubt a sore spot with the Aberdeens. The Countess had been adamant that guests should keep expenses low. She seemed relieved when she wrote in her journal that the guests' costumes were "really very good as a whole, in keeping with the periods without being extravagant." The Victorian double standard regarding conspicuous consumption weighed heavily on her shoulders, and a lifetime of public scrutiny had left the Countess exceptionally sensitive to this issue.[28]

Despite her warnings, guests wanted to present themselves well at the most glittering social event Ottawa had seen in years. Many must have yielded to temptation. One writer praised the Indian characters for their contribution to the success of the ball, claiming that there was altogether "too much silk, satin, velvet and gold – rather too many people wanted to look handsome." The cynical story of the "three-dollar dress" indicates the pressure individuals felt when faced with such a double standard, not to mention the disdain for those whose moral fibre buckled under the strain:

> It is said one lady, about whose costume certain rumors had reached Her Excellency's ears, assured her when questioned on the subject that the dress cost only three dollars! It arrived, however, express from New York in a box that was both large and long, and the brilliancy of whose contents was an astonishing illustration of what may be done with three dollars judiciously expended.[29]

Perhaps several guests spent excessively. Almost two years later at a society gathering in Toronto someone stated that there were Ottawa residents who had actually sold pianos to pay for costumes. While less emphasis was given to expense in reports of the ball than in those of the Dufferin ball, a comparison brings the cost into perspective:

> There was however, no regard to expense, and a scene of equal brilliance and richness of costuming was never seen in Canada. Lord Dufferin's fancy dress ball, of which people still talk, could not compare with it. Ottawa was only a small place twenty years ago and though her citizens almost outdid their means to contribute to its success, the resources were in comparison somewhat limited.[30]

In fact, controlling the expense was Lady Aberdeen's motive for summoning the rental costumiers from Montreal, who had charged between five and ten dollars for one evening's rental "according to the style of the costume required." Wigs and shoes could be rented for an additional unspecified sum. While Beullac's successes and failures have already been recorded for posterity, less information remains by which to estimate Ponton's success. Lady Aberdeen first met them both when she was organizing her historical *tableaux* in Montreal. Though Ponton had costumed a skating carnival in Ottawa in 1889, a full six years earlier, he approached her in 1895 claiming that he was a beginner trying to get into the field. He created all new costumes for the *tableaux*, which he rented for the bargain price of two dollars each. She was very impressed with his work. A barber by profession, he appears to have been still trying to establish his costuming business by the time of the Aberdeens' ball, but the company is today Montreal's foremost costume shop.

The costumiers catered to men only, however; for women they offered to supply designs and some trimmings. Some women performed a very successful "overhauling of partly-worn evening dresses"; however, *The Lounger* reported, there were many gorgeous dressmaker-made costumes. The Government House group's Viking dresses were made "most capitally," in Lady Aberdeen's opinion, by Miss Munsie, who advertised daily in one of the Ottawa papers and who had one of the larger dressmaker's ads in the city directory that year.

A few guests pointed out that their costumes, or at least certain elements of them, were family heirlooms. Professor Robertson, who gave the long-winded explanation of his ancestor's exploits, wore his Highland chief's dress of Robertson tartan, with an "ancient dirk and skean." Mrs. E. Stone Wiggins, as her ancestress, wore jewels which were "family heirlooms nearly three centuries old." C. Caron Pelletier, as "Lord Robert Prescott," wore an artillery uniform consisting of "blue tunic slashed with red, gold epaulettes, white breeches. The tunic and sword are a family heirloom and were worn by one of Mr. Pelletier's ancestors in the war of 1812." These individuals used their dress to express their status and practised thrift at the same time.[31]

Once again, guests attempted to prolong the pleasure of the ball. The Saturday following, Beullac used the same decorations for a skating carnival and offered a discount to those renting the same costumes. At least two Viking costumes made a second appearance.

During the weeks following the ball, photographs were taken of groups and individuals in their costumes. Both Jarvis and Pittaways advertised extensively, and Jarvis also advertised the flash light photograph he had taken at the ball. At a dinner for the women who had helped organize the dances, the Aberdeens gave out signed copies as souvenirs. "It is as good as flash light pictures ever are, in fact much better than the usual run of them," the *Montreal Star* said, though it was "hardly flattering to any." Unfortunately, the fluttering standards caused considerable blurring, and "one of the standard bearers towards the front held his standard so low that the people of the Maisonneuve period are doomed to obscurity."[32]

Topley, who had produced the large composite photograph after the Dufferin ball, did quite well for himself without advertising. Perhaps the other courts followed the lead taken by the Government House party, whom Topley photographed the week following the ball. Photographic technology now allowed him to take an entire group together. "Some of these groups are remarkably good," wrote one reporter. "Especially good is the picture of the Government House party in Viking dress." In early May, John Durie and Son advertised their intention of reproducing the group photographs "in an artistic manner" and publishing them with historical notes by Dr. Bourinot. All interested parties were invited to place orders to ensure that the demand would make the enterprise worthwhile, at a price of one dollar per copy. All but one of the eleven group photographs in the souvenir book were taken by Topley.[33]

The ball, Lady Aberdeen's first real social success, had "eclipsed everything of the kind ever witnessed in Canada." Lady Aberdeen was pleased yet diffident. "And in the meantime Ottawa society is enthusiastic. How to keep up the enthusiasm is another matter," she mused.[34]

Journalistic hyperbole ran rampant. The press compared the ball relentlessly with that given by the Dufferins, and guests who had attended both found themselves reminiscing throughout. Yet there was unanimous agreement that the most recent one was by far more brilliant.

> Heretofore the measure of social success in Ottawa has been measured by Lord Dufferin's grand masquerade ball 20 years ago, and which has remained unequalled until tonight, when the record was broken, and in the future the great and overpowering social triumph of Ottawa will be counted as the grand historical ball given by Lord and Lady Aberdeen.[35]

Lady Aberdeen nowhere stated her true intent in emphasizing the French regime. The growing nationalism of French Canadians in the 1890s was rooted in the belief that their ancestral past should ensure preservation of French rights in the future. Political conflict – the Manitoba Schools Question, followed by the Bowell-Tupper crisis – had deepened the schism between French and English cultures, and Lady Aberdeen's selection of historical periods may represent an innocuous means of raising consciousness in an attempt to smooth over differences. The Aberdeens were also no doubt aware that English and French would each interpret the emphasis in its own way and probably remain oblivious to the understanding of the other.

While many English Canadians could have been displeased with such conciliation on the part of the Aberdeens had they mulled it over, the romance of the French regime, fostered by the writings of Francis Parkman, easily legitimized the French emphasis for the sake of entertainment. The English press constantly gushed over the medieval, chivalrous and romantic nature of French Canadian history: "The French period lends itself to even more picturesqueness, the gallant figures that flit through its story having not yet lost the distinction and glamour of the knightly forms of the Middle Ages." With this vision of French Canadian history went the implication of its remoteness from the present, even backwardness, which made the conquest and British rule seem all the more beneficial.[36]

Montreal's *La Presse* interpreted the event as an effort to educate English Canada and its politicians as disagreement within the House of Commons flared up once again. The paper was even certain that the Aberdeens had come up with the idea after hearing certain speeches in the House of Commons. An editorial on the ball concluded:

> Our astute parliamentary correspondent assures us that in the minds of Their Excellencies, this historical spectacle was intended to remind certain English Canadians in Ontario and the West that it was the French who discovered Canada and that their descendants have retained certain rights. Heaven help us that these good Members of Parliament have understood.[37]

Whatever the intent, for the space of an evening in a highly charged political atmosphere, English Canadians eagerly identified with French Canadian history and enthusiastically claimed it as a component of their own. Educationally as well as socially, the ball seemed to be successful. One reporter claimed, "The history of our own country is too little known, and the historical pageant had the effect of bringing views of it before the society of the capital in a most striking and effective manner." Another highlighted a newfound awareness of Canadian history: "Few there were who gazed upon the spectacle from the galleries that were not troubled with the occasional thought that in the midst of all their enjoyment they, too, had been remiss in the perusal of the history of their country."[38]

CHAPTER 4

The Victorian Era Ball Toronto, 28 December 1897

All the characters in fiction, art, and music which the genius of the Victorian age has created, representatives from every land to "the last lump of coral" over which the British flag waves passed in picturesque procession, and a goodly and inspiring sight it was.[1]

In all their grumblings about Ottawa, the Aberdeens maintained that they could do a better job of exerting their influence in centres of business, education, and cultural life like Toronto and Montreal. In the 1890s, Montreal was Canada's wealthiest city and Toronto the second major centre. Yet Toronto, though the most imperialistic city in Canada, held not much more attraction than Ottawa for the Aberdeens. It "considers itself the centre of the Dominion, although in truth it is very provincial," Lady Aberdeen wrote.[2]

The Aberdeens' dislike of Toronto was mutual – "Society was dead against us," she wrote in her journal – and there were a number of reasons for this antipathy. The Aberdeens' Liberal leanings annoyed Conservative Torontonians, who held the Bowell-Tupper affair against them. The Orangemen disliked their abundance of Roman Catholic friends and their partiality to Montreal. The Temperance people were miffed that the Governor General had not supported prohibition. Furthermore, a large coterie of doctors opposed the Victorian Order of Nurses. Nasty rumours about the family and their Household Club abounded.[3]

While the Aberdeens went to Toronto from time to time, their visits to the city were perfunctory. Realizing that something more substantial was expected, they overcame their dread and took up residence in Toronto for six weeks at the end of 1897 as their term neared its close. Taking the last opportunity to counter their unpopularity, they set out to conquer the city with kindness. "Our plan of campaign was to at once begin entertaining vigorously and at the same [time] visit the Institutions and Societies of all denominations," wrote Lady Aberdeen.[4]

Their reception was not entirely cold at the outset, however. "Great crowd leaving cards on Aberdeens at Gov. House," wrote Mrs. John Cawthra in her diary on 13 November. "The struggle in the hall to get hold of the [guest] book and pens and ink was terrific," observed Lady Aberdeen. The testy relationship blossomed as once-hostile Torontonians turned out at Government House in great numbers to the weekly "at homes," the Tuesday night "Cinderella Dances," and the frequent dinners. Lady Aberdeen wanted to finish off the round of events with a splash, and another mammoth fancy dress ball seemed to be the answer; she had been "told that such an entertainment would give more solid satisfaction than anything else."[5]

Confident after the success of the Historical Fancy Dress Ball in Ottawa, she opted for a similar event. The timing of the visit determined the ball's purpose; as

Queen Victoria's diamond jubilee year neared a close, they found it appropriate to "give in the social life of Canada the same honour and distinctive stamp . . . that has been given to it in many ways in all parts of the Empire." Of course the jubilee had already been celebrated extensively that summer throughout Canada and in Toronto especially, but because of the intense imperial enthusiasm the jubilee had generated, the Queen City was still at the ready to wave its colours for Empire.[6]

The Toronto ball would also be an educational opportunity; people could "find in social recreation some incentive to thought and study, and so to surround it with a greater variety of interest." The topic of Canadian history being a bit tired after the ball in Ottawa and the *tableaux* in Montreal, Lady Aberdeen opted for nineteenth-century British history. Her scholarly consultant on the project, the historian Dr. George Parkin, Principal of Upper Canada College, suggested that such a time span would be difficult to illustrate by decades and proposed instead a division into groups based on the various areas of progress made in the Victorian era. The abundant rhetoric of the diamond jubilee emphasized the material changes of the nineteenth century, the corresponding enlightenment, and the ensuing spread of British ideals throughout the vast territory of the Empire. "Progress" was by now a very familiar concept.[7]

Dr. Parkin drew up six themes for the ball; his suggestions found unanimous acceptance with the Toronto society women recruited to organize the event. The formerly icy social leaders "threw themselves so heartily into the idea of the Ball from the outset that there was never any doubt of each period and there had to be four or five [different sets] included in each group." Again, each woman was responsible for persuading her friends and family to represent the characters in her set, devising a dance appropriate to the theme (possibly with the assistance of a dance instructor), and ensuring that her group rehearsed it to perfection.[8]

The sets were made up of the select group dubbed "Toronto's Four Hundred" and also included some members of leading families from the neighbouring cities of Hamilton and London. The Aberdeens claimed that they invited as many people as possible without spoiling the character of the event, but that they wished they could have doubled the number. "Everybody was there who was anybody, and quite a few who were nobody in particular," remarked the *Toronto Star.* Invitations were so coveted by social climbers that some individuals "devoid of gentlemanly instincts" stooped so low as to sell their tickets.[9]

Toronto's leading ladies first convened on 19 November to discuss the arrangements. Afterwards, Elizabeth Cawthra hosted dinners and minuet rehearsals with her set and continued to attend meetings at Government House. She held three dance rehearsals in close succession in early December, and three more weekly rehearsals followed.

By the first week of December, the ball was the sole topic of conversation. As the date neared, even Christmas was sidelined as people stopped their friends to ask about the ball before wishing one another Merry Christmas. The Cawthras had their last rehearsal on 23 December, but others rushed in for Christmas dinner after an afternoon of dance practice and then spent the meal discussing the long-awaited event.

Several groups learned their dances under the tutelage of instructors from A. Roy MacDonald's academy, the firm which had been involved in the Ottawa ball, and Toronto's own Professor John Freeman Davis. Davis was already well known, since he had been in business since the 1870s, when he had published *The Modern Dance Tutor, or Society Dancing.* A full rehearsal of all the sets was held the night before the ball, "when all seemed dire confusion," to Lady Aberdeen's despair.

The 2500 guests made this event much larger than the Ottawa ball, and the logistics were formidable. To accommodate such a huge group, Lady Aberdeen chose the new Militia Armouries, located on University Avenue, an "enormous gaunt building – 300 ft by 120 ft wide." Her helpers feared that it would be too vast and that they would never be able to heat it. Four large furnaces had to be brought in to run full blast for forty-eight hours before the event to make the building comfortable.

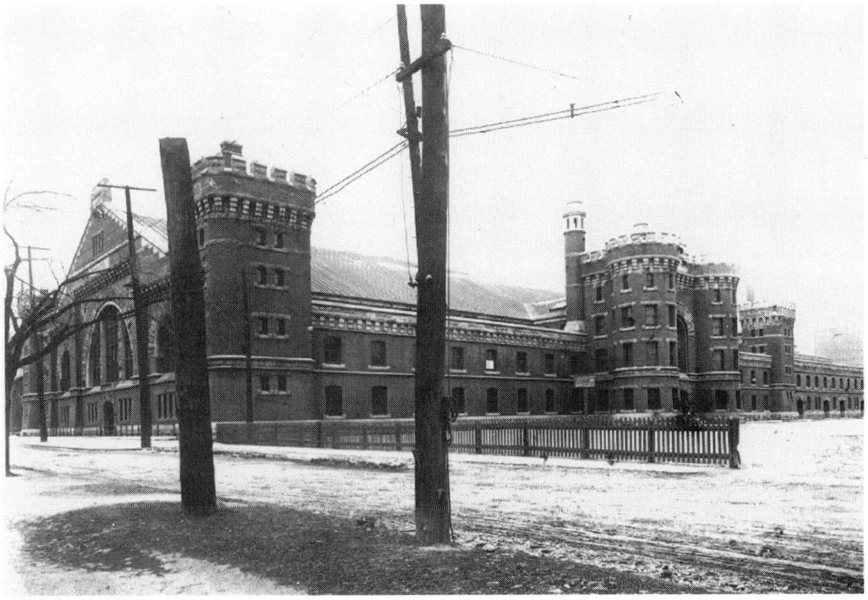

The Militia Armouries, located on the east side of University Avenue. Built in 1891, the building was demolished in 1963 to make room for the present courthouse. Armoury Street commemorates its former presence. NAC/PA48182

A team of architects and decorators set to work to transform the Armouries into a ballroom and a supper room. The decorating was superintended by Ricardo Seaver, the secretary of the Royal Canadian Yacht Club, assisted by an architect, Mr. Darling, and overseen by the Aberdeens' aide-de-camp, David Erskine (the helmetless Viking at the Ottawa ball). The idea of a *"fête champetre"* pink-and-green decorating scheme was suggested by one of Lady Aberdeen's close collaborators, Anne Arthurs, who also took charge of one of the dance sets.

The large drill hall was divided in half to make one room for dancing and another for supper, with a large raised terrace in the centre "like the bridge of an Atlantic liner." The terrace housed both a press gallery and a refreshment area. A temporary kitchen was built outside the building.

An amphitheatre was created in the ballroom section, with tiers of steps covered in green linen rising up on three sides, and galleries for spectators were built above these. "Fairyland" was the term used most often to describe the decorated ballroom. The transformation from the austere iron-girded Armouries to the pink, white and green festooned ballroom redolent with cedar and pine branches was tantamount to magic.

At the northern side of the ballroom was the dais for the vice-regal court. In front of the dais rose three lofty arches formed of pink pillars joined with branches of evergreen and outlined in rose-coloured electric lights. Above the arches on a white ground was the most striking of the decorations: the letters "VR" flanked by "1837" and "1897" spelled out in electric light bulbs of "a striking shade of red."

At the back of the dais hung a borrowed theatre backdrop depicting "a building of a most delicate style of architecture, the colours of which were white and gold, with the faintest shade of blue," boasting a large balcony and many pillars. Steps from the painted building led down to the dais. More than one reporter, zealous to make an imperial connection, identified this fanciful marble pile as a representation of Windsor castle.

At the opposite side of the hall, another pink arch surmounted by a gold crown bore the word "Canada," and on either side were arches similarly labelled "Africa" and "India," all in electric lights. At intervals around the hall behind the steps where the guests sat were more pink faux-stone pillars, between which hung more red electric light bulbs. Each pillar bore an evergreen crown and the shield and name of a British dependency, including Bermuda, New Zealand, Madagascar, Ceylon, and several Canadian provinces.

Even the programme design by Robert Holmes, drawing master of Upper Canada College, carried through the imperial theme. In white and gold on a purple back-

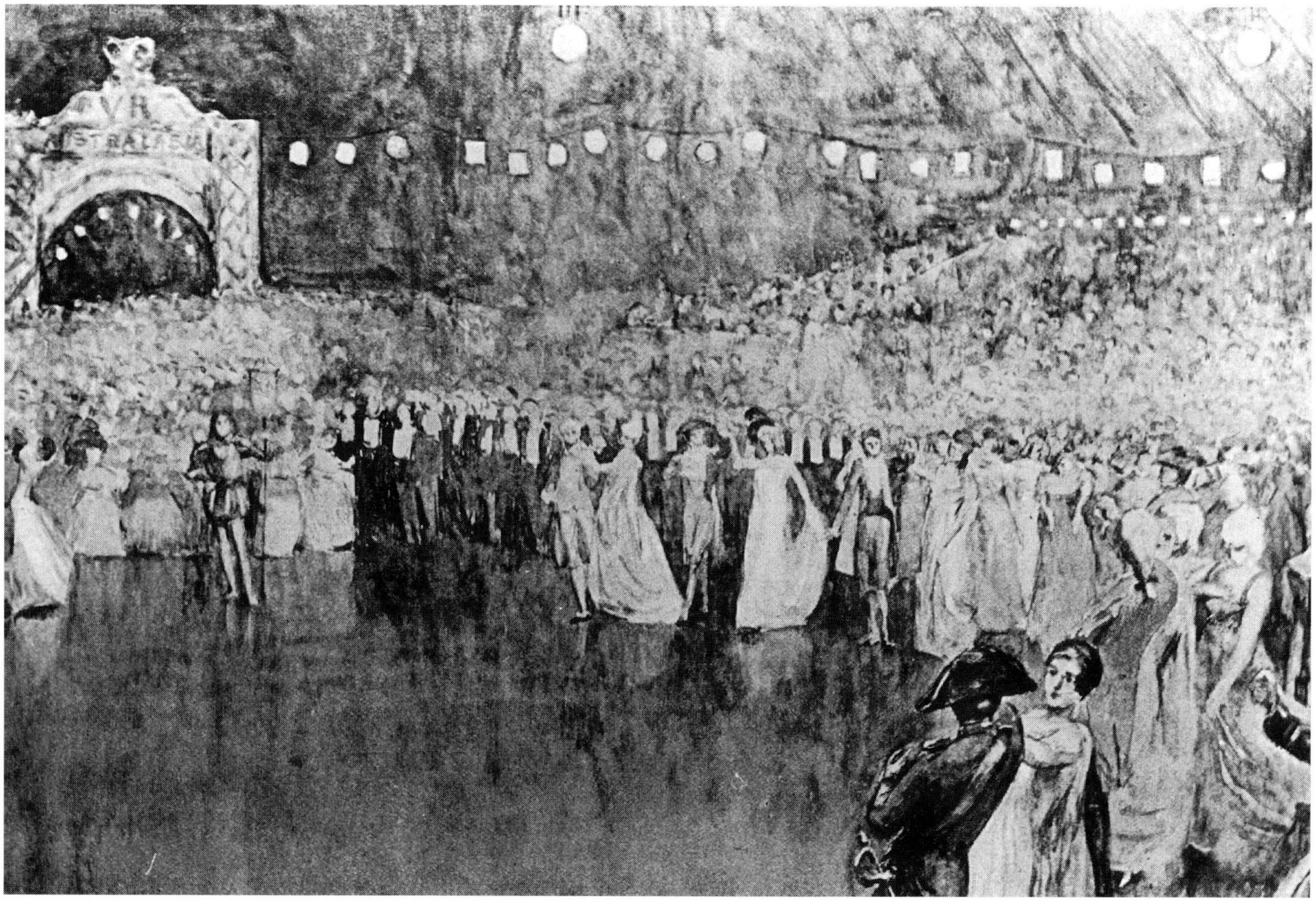

General View of the Ball, by Edmund Wyly Grier. This watercolour conveys the kaleidoscopic sensation which so delighted viewers. The bright lights and the arch inscribed "VR" are also visible. The artist acted as a herald for the Gilbert and Sullivan set. BB

ground, it showed the British Empire as a heart, inscribed "One Queen, One Empire," "sending life and strength into the Imperial tree." The whole was topped off with the imperial crown and and the monogram VRI.

By eight-thirty on the fair, twenty-degree evening of 28 December, carriages filed down the street towards the entrance from both directions. Those who did not have the luxury of carriage transportation could take advantage of the special streetcar service that Aberdeen arranged for the occasion. Twenty-five policemen directed traffic and controlled access to the building. A throng of envious onlookers lined the streets leading to the entrance, and "among them were not wasting strong contrasts to the richly clad throng that poured into the Armouries by the hundreds."

Inside the building, guests rushed off to the dressing rooms improvised in the officers' quarters: one for each group of dancers, with two maids in attendance in each. Following the Master of Ceremonies' bidding, guests leaving the dressing rooms proceeded immediately to the ballroom where they congregated on the newly laid hardwood floor. Wise spectators arrived in plenty of time to get good gallery seats.

Guests admired the "brilliant and kaleidoscopic scene" and the comical incongruities of "A Telephone" asking "A Singhalese Lady" to reserve him a dance, and "Dante" chatting with "The Duchess of Clarence." Guests spent a happy hour or two determining "who was who and what character he or she represented." The *Toronto News* reported:

"This is the greatest event in history," said a Zulu to a Chinese mandarin last night at the Victorian Era Ball. The Zulu was a painted object and wore eye-glasses, the mandarin had vainly endeavoured to conceal a pair of side whiskers which were out of place.[10]

The Four Hundred took their places on the green linen-covered steps as the Master of Ceremonies, Major Septimus Denison, marshalled the sets into their appointed places. Major Denison, aide-de-camp to Lord Aberdeen, was "indefatigable and most cheery and active throughout. He belongs to one of Toronto's bluest United Empire Loyalist Families," wrote Lady Aberdeen. Glionna's Orchestra, stationed under an arch, began the national anthem. The crowd rose to its feet as one as trumpets heralded the arrival of the vice-regal court, "a scene ever to be remembered." The two heralds led the procession, which entered in single file and marched at a slow and stately pace. It included Major Denison; the Lieutenant Governor of Manitoba; the former Premier and recently appointed Lieutenant Governor of Ontario, Sir Oliver Mowat; and his ailing predecessor, Sir George Kirkpatrick, who received a spotaneous burst of applause. Their Excellencies followed, and they bowed to the assemblage when they reached the dais. "Marvellous to relate," wrote a relieved Lady Aberdeen, "this procession went all right, walked slowly and kept together during its progress, so although short looked v. well"; evidently she was concerned about its being otherwise.[11]

The Earl wore full court dress, but he was eclipsed by the regal Lady Aberdeen in "the richest and most beautiful costume ever worn in Toronto, every detail of which was fitting and applicable to the raison d'être of the ball." A blue velvet skirt edged with ermine, a blue velvet bodice, with trim, stomacher and underskirt of white Irish poplin, and court feathers of crimson repeated the colours of the Empire. The heavy gold embroidery on the shoulders, stomacher, and underskirt was based on designs from *The Book of Kells*, and Irish point lace trimmed the sleeves and neckline. (This embroidery was later recycled into another gown, and it may also have been part of a fancy dress worn to the Aberdeens' Irish garden party.) Her red-satin-lined poplin train was borne by six young pages.

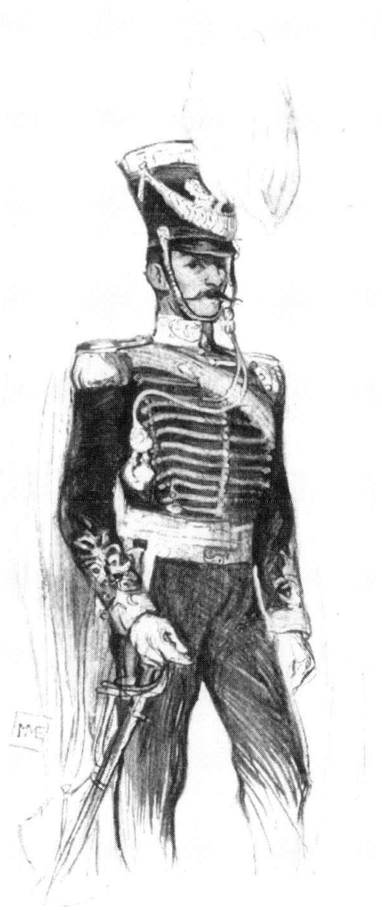

Major Septimus Denison, aide-de-camp to Lord Aberdeen and Master of Ceremonies at the ball, "gorgeous in [the] handsome uniform" of the Governor General's Body Guard. BB, PENCIL DRAWING BY EDMUND M. MORRIS

Once Their Excellencies had taken their seats on the dais, the two heralds called the Empire group into place. From each corner of the hall came one of the four Empire sets – North America, Europe, India and Australia, and Africa, and they converged in the centre in a glittering pageant of Britain's possessions.

To the tune of "Rule Britannia," the group formed a Saint Andrew's cross, much appreciated by the audience, and then did more circling and figure eights, "now in single file, now in companies, and again in a great moving mass of colour." The music changed through other patriotic airs, including "The British Grenadiers" and "The Maple Leaf," with the dancers chiming in when the refrain of "Rule Britannia" returned to the medley. The drill had been choreographed by Professor Davis, who later received a letter of thanks from Their Excellencies. At the end of the march, the sets were presented to the vice-regal court.

The North America set focused mainly on the sources of Canada's wealth. Women personified natural resources such as mines, forests, fishing, and fur – all creatively rendered as emblematic costumes. Their partners dressed as controllers and exploiters of these resources: miners, lumbermen, fishermen, and fur traders. These couples embodied the gender dichotomy of doing versus being. "The abstract, as usual, is feminine and the concrete, masculine," noted an observer. Leading the set were Lady

The Aberdeens as they appeared at the Victorian Era Ball. Her Excellency wore "a royal blue velvet dress, edged with ermine; front of cream Irish poplin, richly embroidered in Celtic designs in gold; bodice trimmed with the same embroidery and Irish point lace; train of cream Irish poplin, with deep border of gold Celtic embroidery, from designs from the famous ancient illuminated manuscript *Book of Kells*; train lined with crimson satin. Ornaments: necklace, tiara and earrings of ancient emeralds, diamonds, rubies, with pearls, and enamel with other Celtic gold ornaments, crimson court plumes and lace veil in hair." The Earl wears his Windsor uniform. (*Toronto Mail and Empire*, 29 Dec. 1897) WJT/NAC/PA27918

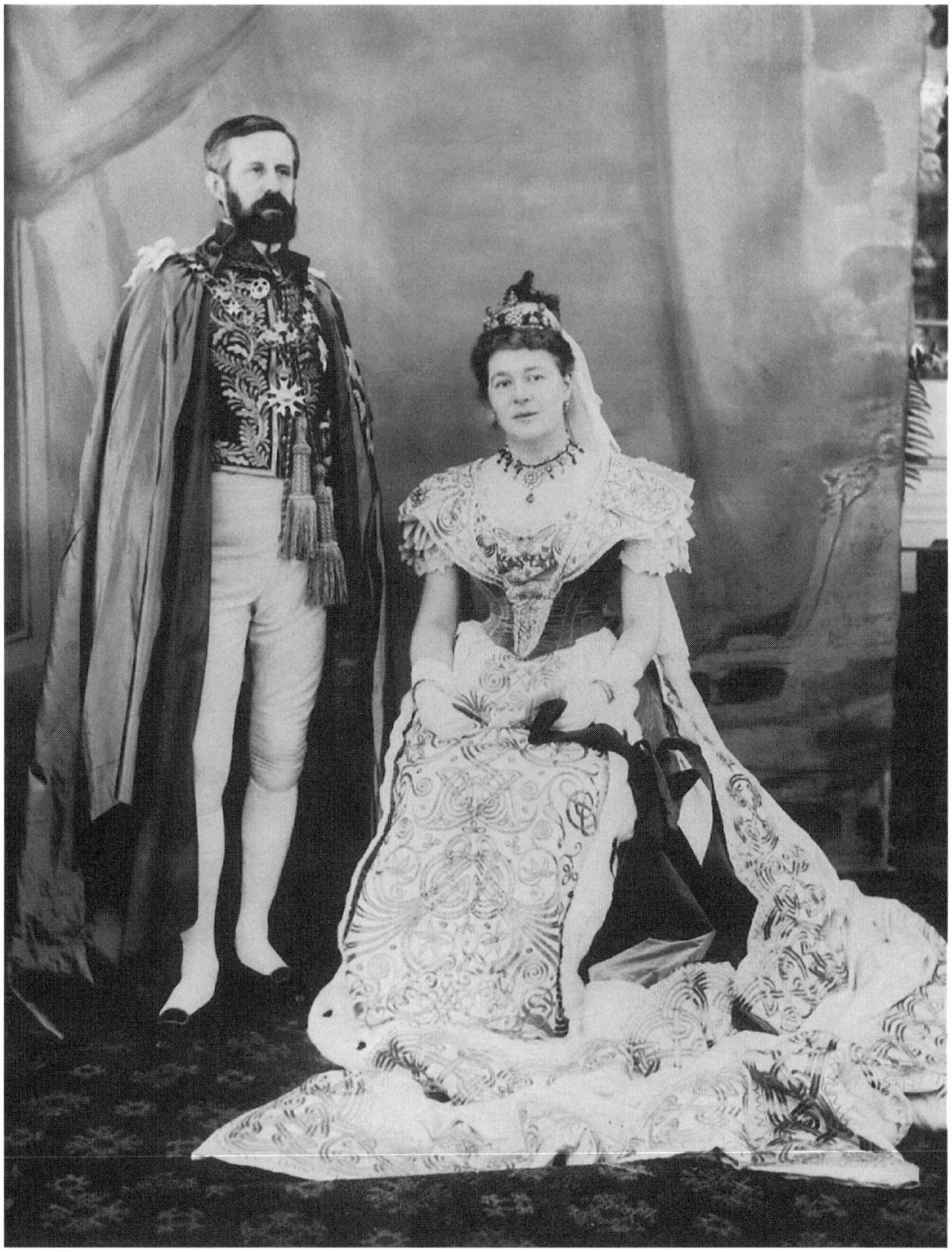

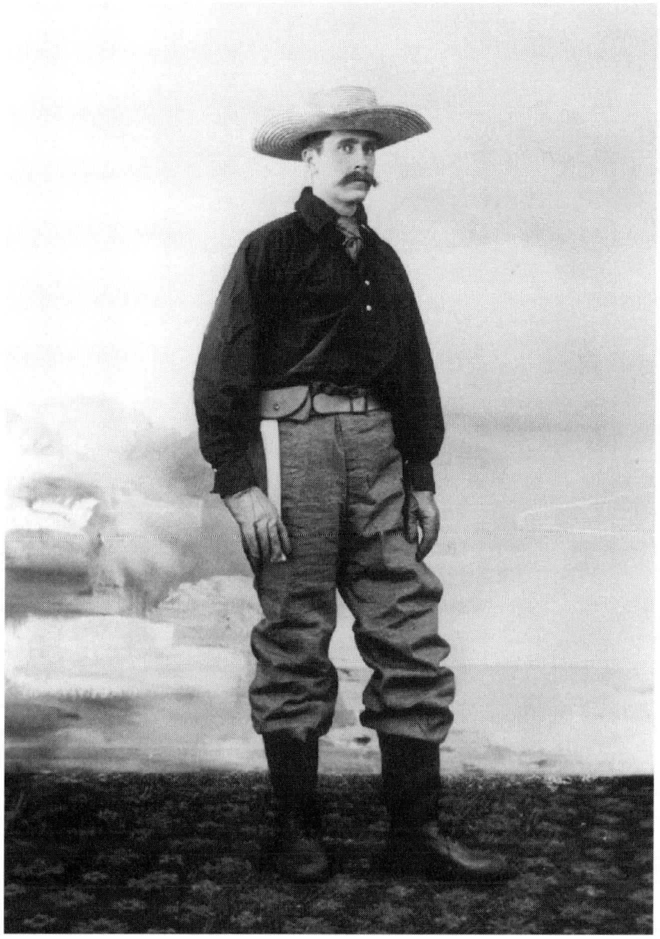

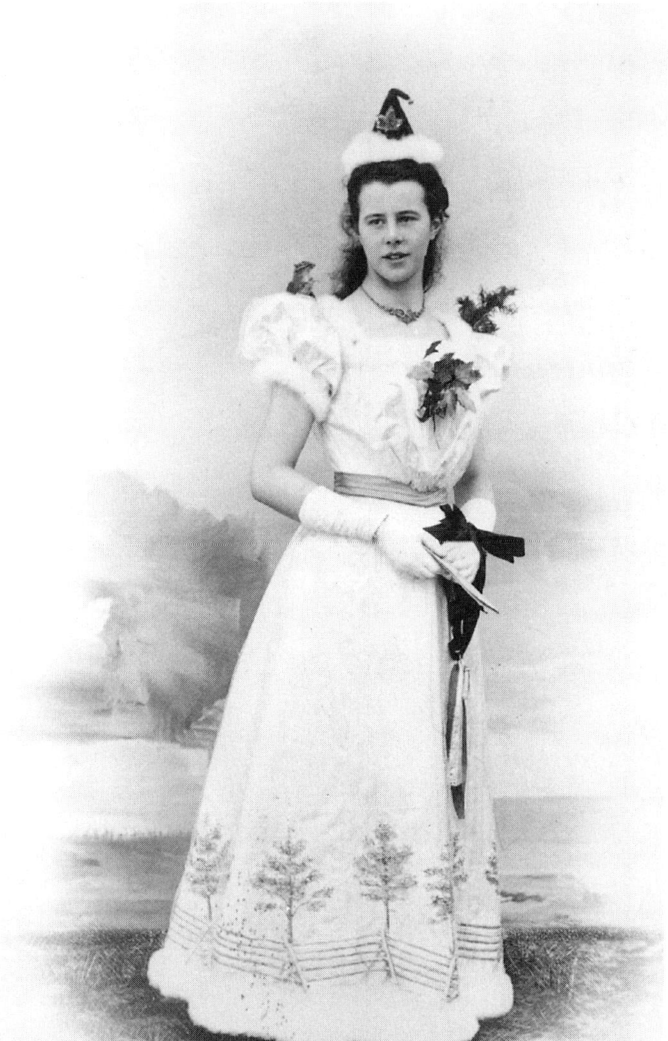

Marjorie Gordon, the Aberdeens' seventeen-year-old daughter, as "Forests of Canada," and David Erskine, the aide-de-camp, as "A Lumberman."

Lady Marjorie wore a white satin dress. White fur edged the hem, and painted snake fences and fir trees circled the lower part of the skirt. A real stuffed chipmunk decorated one shoulder and a miniature fir tree the other, and a corsage of maple leaves adorned the bodice. She completed her costume with a red voyageur-style cap. Reporters gushed over the ensemble and called Lady Marjorie a "charming bit of Canadian girlhood." David Erskine, "in the genuine dress of a lumberman," was much less glamourous, although "perfectly accurate" in blue trousers, with a hatchet and clay pipe.

"Cod" or "Fishing" was incarnated by Miss Augusta Beverley Robinson. The youngest child of the former Ontario Lieutenant Governor, she was a well-known operatic singer who had spent much of the previous year touring Canada and the United States as chief support to the Canadian diva, Madame Albani. In all of her operatic career, however, she probably never impersonated anything as unlikely as "Cod" or "Fishing," with a perfect facsimile of a salmon can label painted on her white satin skirt, a fishing net on her head, and a fish on her shoulder. Her partner, as "A Lower Canadian Fisherman," also had a net on his shoulder to complete "one of the simplest and best worn costumes."

"Mining" wore a "particularly pretty and effective" dress, consisting of a red satin bodice and a gold skirt trimmed with red satin ribbons inscribed "Klondike" and

Above: Lady Marjorie Gordon as "Forests of Canada." The dress of white satin was trimmed with fur, and "in her Canadian gown, all painted around with snake fences and fir trees, and with a perky little chipmunk on one shoulder and a small fir tree on the other, [she] was a compliment to the Vice-regal residence in Canada very highly appreciated by all loyal Canadians." (*Saturday Night*, 1 Jan. 1898) W.J. TOPLEY/ SASKATCHEWAN ARCHIVES BOARD/R-B1146

Above left: David Erskine as "A Lumberman." WJT/PA27920

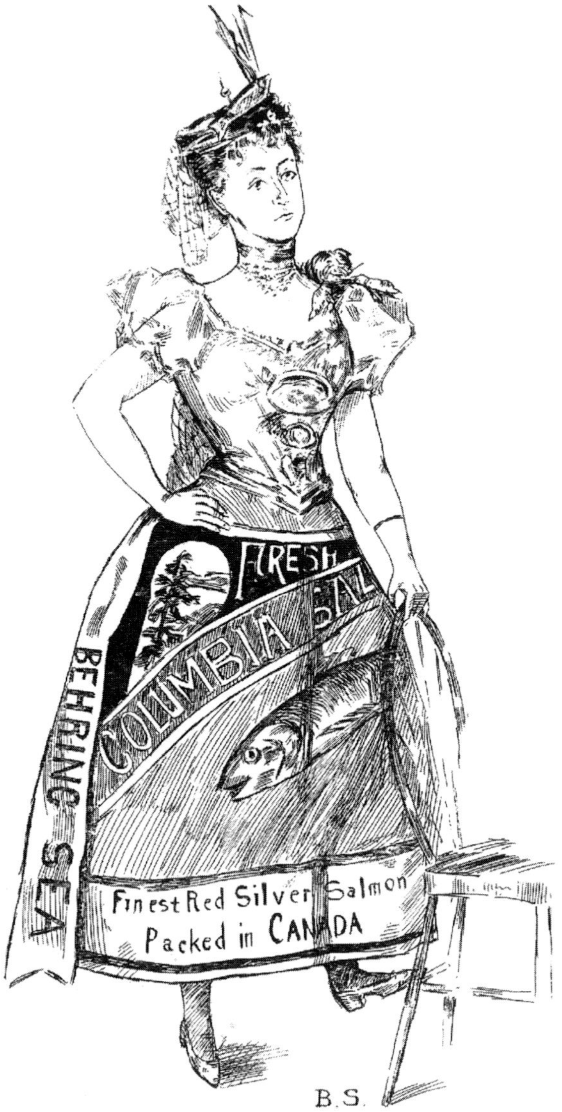

Augusta Beverley Robinson as "Cod," with a salmon can label painted on her short white satin skirt. She wore a piece of fishing net and a toy boat in her hair and more net draped around her "in as artistic a way as possible." The tiny fish on her shoulder could actually wag its tail. BB, PENCIL DRAWING BY BEATRICE SULLIVAN

"Sudbury." Gold nuggets balanced on her shoulder, shovels hung at her waist, and the young lady wielded a pick-axe in her hand. Her miner partner, banker Daniel Wilkie, was far less elegant, wearing a blue shirt, a red scarf and brown pantaloons and carrying miners' tools.

"A Ranchman," Captain Fleming, accompanied "A Dairy Maid," Mrs. Archibald Campbell, Jr., to illustrate Canadian agriculture. Lord Haddo, the Aberdeens' oldest son, "looked just the figure of a harvester" in white muslin shirt and corduroy knickerbockers, accompanying his female counterpart, "Wheat," portrayed by Mrs. Septimus Denison.

Racial and gender stereotypes converged in another pair: Miss Etta Macpherson as "Fur," partnered by "A Halfbreed Fur Trader" wearing a buckskin suit and moccasins and draped in furs. The Native population, much less in evidence here than at the Ottawa ball, was alluded to in the North America set by "A Cree Chief," described as the "one bit of unmerchantable romance." The artist Edmund Morris appeared in a red wool shirt, trimmed with beadwork, ermine and fox, which Chief Sweet Grass had given to his father, Alexander Morris, Lieutenant Governor of Manitoba, at the signing of Treaty Number Six. The costume also appears in a photograph of a ball given by the Lieutenant Governor of Ontario in the early 1880s. Eventually, Edmund Morris donated the shirt and other items he wore to the ball to the Royal Ontario Museum, and he went on to paint many portraits of aboriginal people.

North America would not have been complete without a representation of Canada. Since the appearance of this character at the Dufferin ball, Ardern Holt had published a recommendation for the costume:

> White cloth skirt and jacket bordered with silver cloth, trimmed with puffings of silver tulle and cloth of silver; a blue scarf round hips, edged with silver sleigh bells, and caught up with Canadian blue bird and beaver. The jacket braided and frogged with silver; wreath of maple leaf and rowan berries across bodice. Blue cap after Scotch shape trimmed with swansdown, embroidered with silver; hair powdered; blue satin muff, small bird at side. Chatelaine of snowshoes, toboggans, canoe, and skates. Or, a classic robe of white with a wreath of maple leaves around the bodice and head, hair flowing, or a helmet with maple leaves and effigy of Peace and the beaver. In left hand oval shield representing Union Jack, about two feet high, "Canada" inscribed in centre.[12]

But the nationalistic references in this emblematic costume at the Victorian Era Ball were much more refined and pointed than those prescribed by Holt or seen in the "Dominion of Canada" costume at the Dufferin ball twenty-one years earlier. Edith Mowat, the daughter of Lieutenant Governor Sir Oliver Mowat and the hostess of Government House, came as "Our Lady of the Snows," the title of a controversial

Kipling poem written earlier in 1897 celebrating the preferential tariffs Canada had accorded to Great Britain. In the poem, Kipling portrays Canada as an assertive but ultimately dutiful imperial daughter. He intended the name to be complimentary and even chose "our lady" to please Catholic French Canadians, yet Canadians were galled by the "imputation of arcticity." Among the reasons why this frigid stereotype hit a nerve was a campaign stressing the abundance of rich farmland to attract British immigrants to the West. Coming from the great imperial spokesman, the Bard of Empire, the insult stung all the worse. The matter was even debated in the House of Commons, where it was suggested that Sir Wilfrid Laurier might ask Kipling for a public apology, and that Kipling might give Canada a more appropriate title, such as "Our Lady in whose breast the fire of patriotism glows." Neither occurred, but Kipling was grilled about the poem ten years later when he next visited the country.[13]

Miss Mowat dressed as poetry in motion. Her costume reclaimed the arcticity of the title and was a political retort to Kipling and to anyone who might take his poem at face value. Miss Mowat's white cashmere dress, edged with swansdown, was slashed at the side to reveal a green satin underskirt embroidered with sheaves of wheat. This underskirt alluded to the "fruitful land beneath the snowy covering" which Kipling had omitted. (In her late thirties, she could hardly have been oblivious to the heavy double entendre.) Her white court train was lined with green also, and as jewellery she wore a necklace of icicles. Boldy crossing her bodice was a scarf bearing the most assertive line from the poem, "We be also a people." Another ribbon inscribed with the subservient concluding line, "And I abide by my mother's house," hung from her waist as an afterthought.

The choice of herald for the North America set might also have been interpreted by some as a political statement. A lawyer and Conservative MP, Dalton McCarthy had led the Protestant anti-Catholic and anti-French crusade on dual language rights and the Manitoba Schools Question.

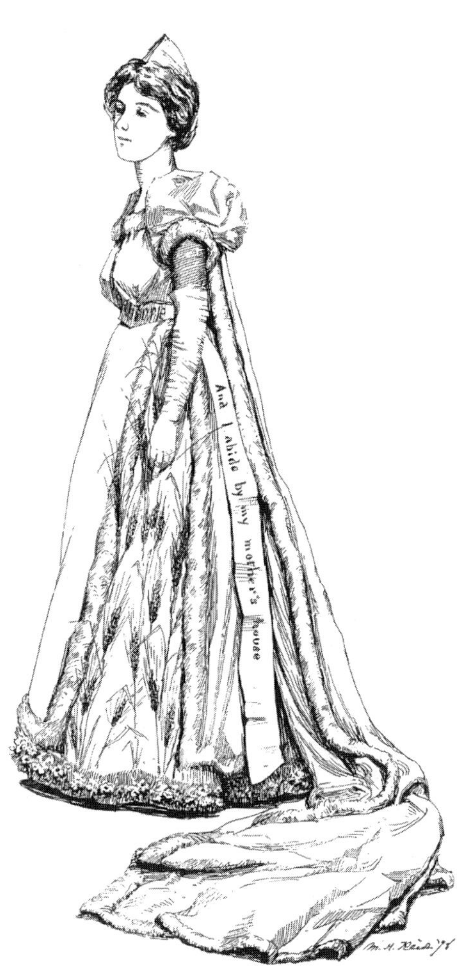

Edith Mowat as "Our Lady of the Snows." This emblematic representation of Canada was intended to contradict Rudyard Kipling's poem. A green underskirt embroidered with wheat under the white fur-trimmed dress expresses Canada's agricultural potential, which Kipling had ignored. The artist muffled Miss Mowat's Statement, however. "We be also a people," the poem's most nationalistic line, was emblazoned across the front of her bodice but here is barely visible, whereas "And I abide by my mother's house," worn more flippantly, is prominent. BB, PEN AND INK DRAWING BY MARY HEISTER REID

The India and Australia set of the Empire March contained but two references to the southernmost countries of the Empire. Archibald Campbell, Jr., as "A Maori Chief of New Zealand" wore a costume with "profuse feather trimmings, Maori blanket, a headdress of wild boars' tusks, and Maori tattooing." The tattooing was no doubt painted on a tight-fitting upper body garment; while expanses of leg might be shown, bare chests were taboo in such a setting. "Australia's" emblematic dress consisted of white satin trimmed with lamb's wool and gold nuggets, with yellow mimosa in her hair.

The rest of the set was composed of various "Burmese," "Singhalese" and "East Indians." Lieutenant-Colonel Gerald Kitson, the herald, had spent considerable time in India with the British military prior to becoming Commandant of Royal Military College in Kingston. The women wore silk skirts with Zouave jackets and scarves. Miss Beatrice Edgar, as "A Maharatta," wore a white skirt trimmed with green, silver and gold, a cerise Zouave jacket, a gold girdle, and a veil and jewels. The women, "brown as berries and beautiful as houris," held their veils over their faces as they danced. Wallace Jones as "A Sikh" wore the uniform of an officer of the Third Bengal Cavalry. As "A Mohammedan," Captain Gerard Tharp, the new Aberdeen ADC, felt that his makeup had been overdone. "I might have done them better justice if the hairdresser had not turned us into *Moors* instead of Indians," he wrote in thanking the lender of his garments; his exotic portrayal had gone a bit too far for his liking.[14]

The third component of the Empire March was the Europe set: representations

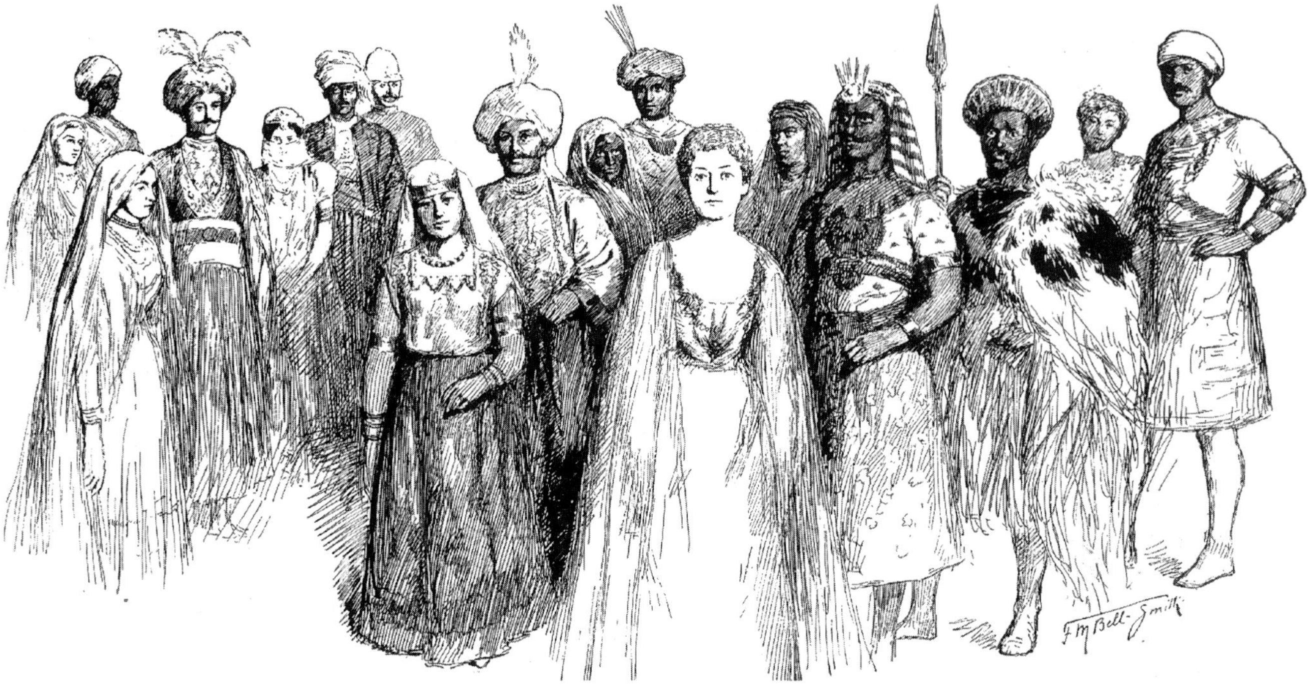

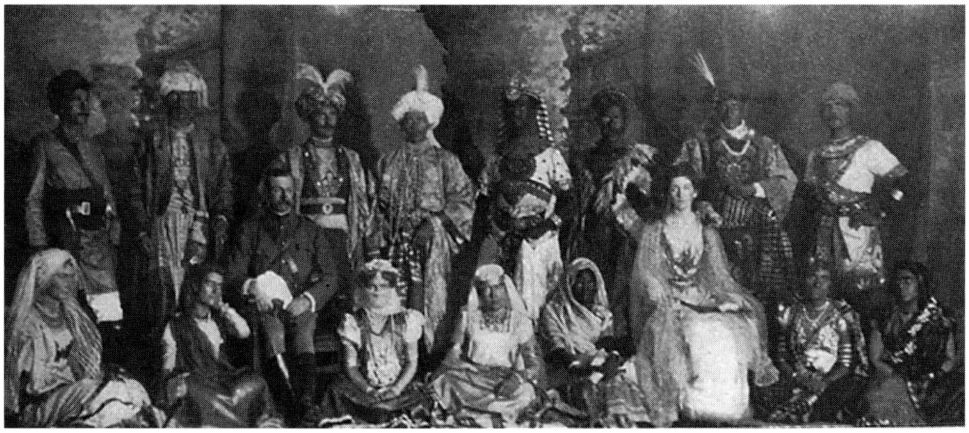

The India and Australia set. In the photorgraph "Australia" sits in a chair on the right with her partner, Archibald Campbell, Jr., as "A Maori Chief of New Zealand," standing just behind her to the left. The other members of the set have not been identified. BB, PENCIL DRAWING BY F.M. BELL-SMITH; PHOTO BY F.W. LYONDE, *LESLIE'S WEEKLY*, 28 JAN. 1898.

of the United Kingdom and other British possessions in Europe. The women completely eclipsed the men, who were barely noticed, and "the costumers of some of the European possessions have had to go deep for a symbolical dress." Most outstanding and conspicuous of all was Edith Nordheimer, who led the set and represented "England, Queen of the Seas." The character was particularly appropriate for Mrs. Nordheimer, the president of the Imperial Order of Daughters of the Empire. (The Nordheimer name was well known outside Toronto society; Samuel Nordheimer was German Consul for Ontario, and pianos made by the family company were sold across the Dominion.) The usual allegorical representation of England was "Britannia" (who had been present at the Earl of Dufferin's ball), but in choosing to dress as "England, Queen of the Seas" instead, Mrs. Nordheimer made some very pointed references to British naval power.

> A petticoat of pale blue satin, with men-of-war and sailing craft painted sailing round it, and softened with a veil of blue tulle. A

train from the shoulders of sea-green satin, lined with shell pink. Rising from the folds of the blue corsage in front is a rising sun, delicately made, and also from the shoulders at the back a sun, carrying out the fact that 'the sun never sets on the English possessions.' On one sleeve the coat-of-arms, and on the other the crossed Union Jacks. A perfect tiny ship on one shoulder of the corsage, and a lovely soft seagull resting in its flight on the other. An Imperial crown worn on the head, and the tripod hanging with seaweed and coral in the hand.

The train was borne by two pages. Steering the regal Mrs. Nordheimer through the March was General Sandham, described simply as "Admiral."[15]

Mrs. Nordheimer's daughters represented "Scotland" and "The Isle of Man." "Scotland" was escorted by "Bonnie Prince Charlie." Also represented were "Wales," in national dress, accompanied by "The Black Prince"; "The Channel Isles"; "Malta"; and Miss Montizambert as a very militant-looking "Gibraltar," with "tiny cannons on [her] shoulders" and on her head "a small fortress with cannons pointing."

The Africa set ended the Empire March. Current imperial attitudes were again embodied in the characters. "An Arab Sheik" heralded the set, led by Mrs. Peter Crerar of Hamilton, another prominent IODE member. She represented the continent itself in a costume inspired by the allegorical representation of Africa in the Albert Memorial in London. The sculptor of that work had avoided a black African exemplar in keeping with Victorian cultural values; an ancient Egyptian figure carried more positive connotations and certainly had more attraction for a ball costume. Marion Crerar wore a "gown of white satin, embroidered in gold, the headdress a golden Isis"; familiar rhetoric inspired her finishing touch: "over all a sheer white chiffon veil, lending the mysterious air that covers the dark continent." Race was not the only issue skirted by the set. The other women came as "Egyptian Ladies of the Upper Classes." The men chose to underscore imperial might in the khaki uniform worn by the South African contingent at Her Majesty's jubilee, which was much like the uniform soon to appear in great numbers in the Boer War.[16]

One small hitch occurred when photographer Frederick Lyonde attempted to take a flash light photograph of the Empire March as these representatives of the four corners of the world formed their St. Andrew's cross. The explosion of his flash set a small fire in some nearby curtains, which the photographer himself rushed to extinguish, burning his hands. A fireman on duty helped to put out the conflagration, but despite their calm efficiency a woman had already fainted. Lyonde and another photographer were later chastised for not exercising more care in choosing where they took their photographs.

After the Empire March came the climax of the evening. The Governor General rose and made a speech:

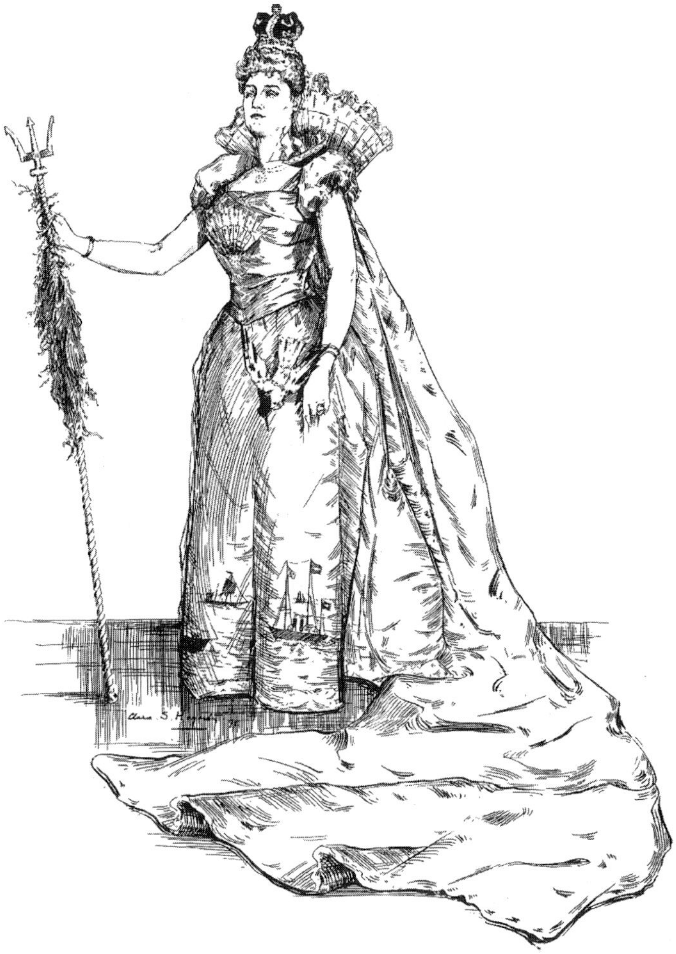

Edith Nordheimer (née Boulton) as "England, Queen of the Seas." This costume refers far more pointedly to British naval power than the usual "Britannia." Painted men-of-war sail around Mrs. Nordheimer's blue satin petticoat, and the suns painted on the front and back of her blue bodice never set. A sea-green satin train lined with shell pink and embroidered with pearls hangs from her shoulders. Other symbols include the ship on her shoulder, the stuffed seagull on her wrist, the coat of arms and Union Jacks on her sleeves, the crown on her head, and Britannia's trident, hanging with seaweed, in her hand.
BB, PEN AND INK DRAWING BY CLARA S. HAGARTY

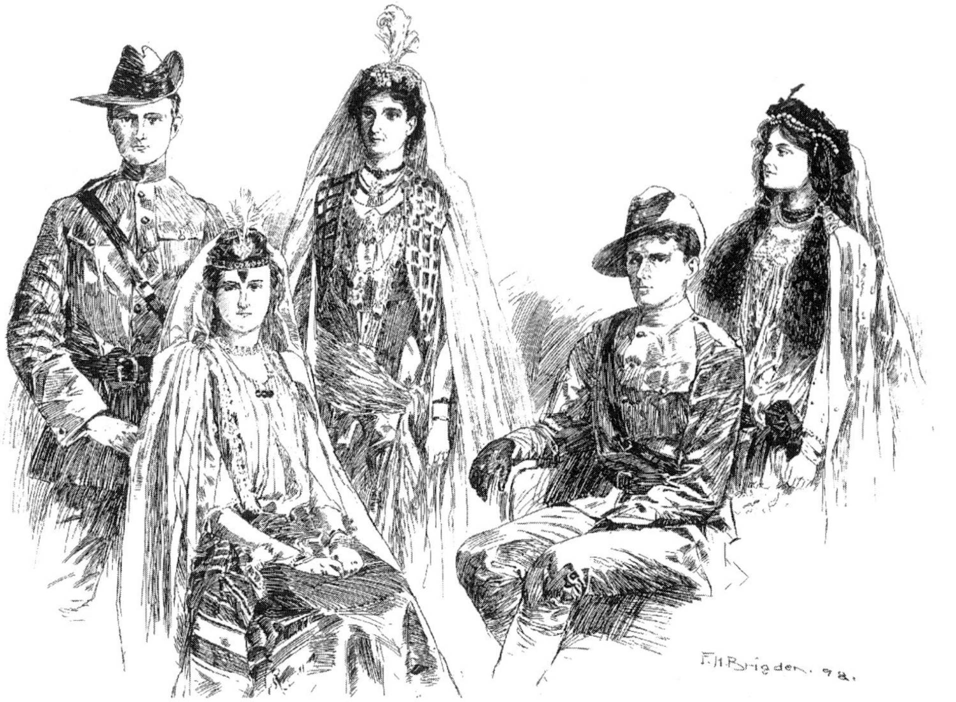

A group from the Africa set, the women dressed as ancient Egyptians of the upper classes and the men in the khaki uniforms of British soldiers. Mrs. Peter Crerar, the leader of the set, wears a sheer white chiffon veil over her entire costume to evince "the mysterious air that covers the dark continent." BB, PEN AND INK DRAWING BY F.H. BRIGDEN

> In presenting to the Queen most loyal good wishes for Christmastide, I submitted to her Majesty some information regarding this Victorian Era Ball, designed to commemorate the diamond jubilee year now about to close. I have this afternoon received in reply a most gracious message from Her Majesty, which we may gladly regard as a token of her Majesty's kindly thought of us all gathered here tonight. "God Save the Queen."

The guests, overcome with emotion, leapt to their feet and broke into "God Save the Queen," finishing the anthem off with three rousing cheers. "It was an impressive moment, as all present felt it to be, and one of those moments which do much to seal a nation's loyalty," wrote Lady Aberdeen.[17]

In fact, the Earl of Aberdeen had made a grave breach of protocol. He had indeed telegraphed the Queen asking for such a message. A reply came only the afternoon of the ball, extending good wishes to the vice-regal couple. Queen Victoria never intended the telegram to be used in this way and, indeed, was not amused. The Earl received a reprimand, but Lady Aberdeen was nonchalant and concluded, "We cannot regret the message being given for the effect was all for the good."[18]

The second group of sets was simply entitled Victorian Costumes and divided chronologically, though specific dates were not given. Their old-fashioned quadrille was danced by each set in turn.

The Victorian Era had lasted so long that costumes from its earlier days had become historic. In the 1887 edition of *Fancy Dresses Described*, Ardern Holt had called coal scuttle bonnets and "short waists below the armpits" "monstrosities." In the 1896 edition, she said about the same styles: "The early portion of this century has found favour at fancy balls of late." The inclusion of this group of sets at the ball and the press's comments on it illustrate the newfound appeal of costume from the early Victorian period to these late Victorians.

Mary Fitzgibbon (née Bernard) as the "Princess von Leinengen," or "Duchess of Kent," Queen Victoria's mother. Her costume, copied from a painting, consisted of a white satin gown with a yellow velvet train trimmed with with sable; on her head she wore a yellow turban with plumes. BB, PENCIL DRAWING BY E. WYLY GRIER; F.W. LYONDE/NAC/PA138846

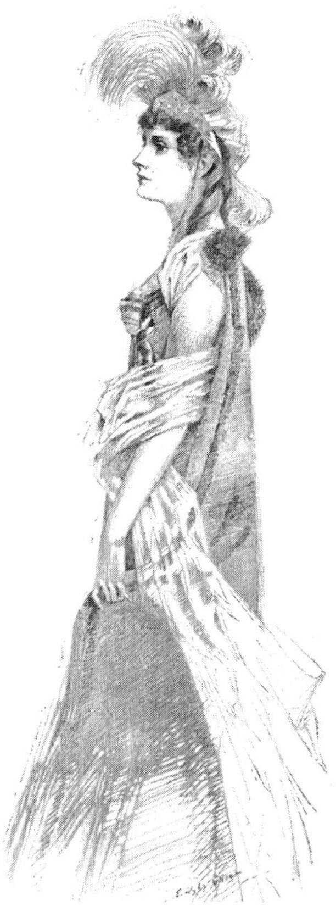

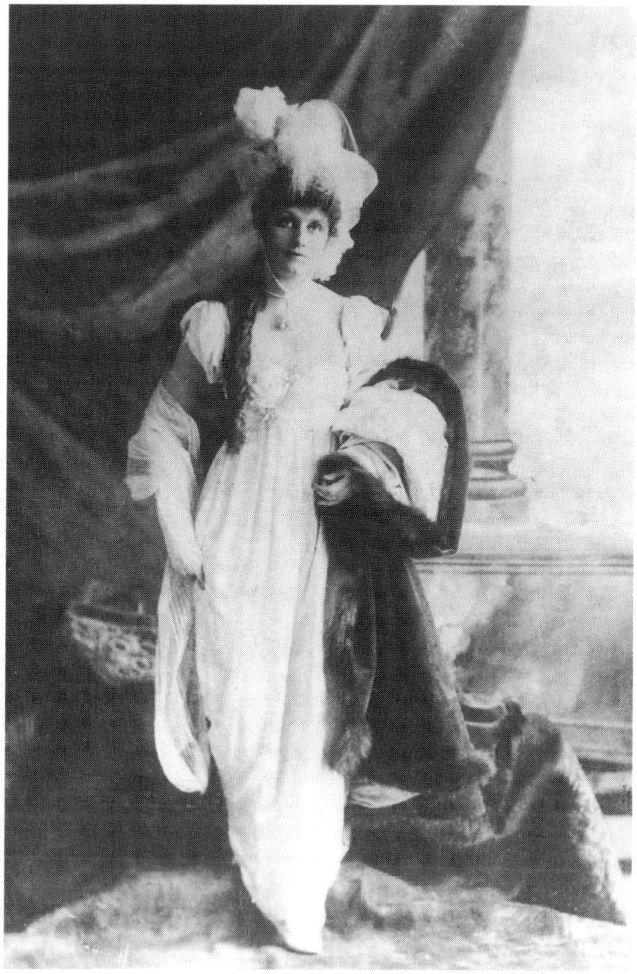

> The greatest call . . . was for early Victorian costumes. Gentlemen with nice, fluffy mutton-chop whiskers, made to order for the occasion, ruffled shirt bosoms, and stocks. Particularly beautiful were the women in wide skirts, with yards of dainty ruffles, quaint fichus and poke bonnets.[19]

Even before the ball, the First Period set, covering costume from roughly 1810 to 1830, had been dubbed the "beauty set," as the organizer had managed to recruit several of the reigning Toronto belles. Lady Kirkpatrick was herself known for her good looks. Before her marriage, as Isabel Macpherson, she had been one of the stars of the Dufferin ball as "Queen of the Gypsies." (Congeniality was not her strong point, however; Lady Aberdeen believed that she was responsible for spreading nasty rumours about herself and the Earl prior to their coming to Toronto.) Each man and woman in the set represented a member of the British aristocracy, including ancestors of Queen Victoria. As usual, the men's costumes were fairly uniform, consisting of "black satin breeches, with black silk stockings . . . dark green coats with brass buttons, short waisted in the style of that of Beau Brummel."[20]

Two of the most striking women at one point actually danced opposite each other, "the eyes of all the vast assembly travelling from one to the other in pleased admiration, unable to accord to either the palm as the most graceful and perfect picture from the days of Queen Victoria's girlhood." Mrs. Eber Ward, as "The Duchess of Clarence," was "a lovely picture" in a "short-waisted frock of white satin, from the shoulders a turquoise blue velvet train . . . and the lovely sunny coiffure decked with waving plumes." But it was Mary Fitzgibbon, as "Princess Von Leinengen," Queen

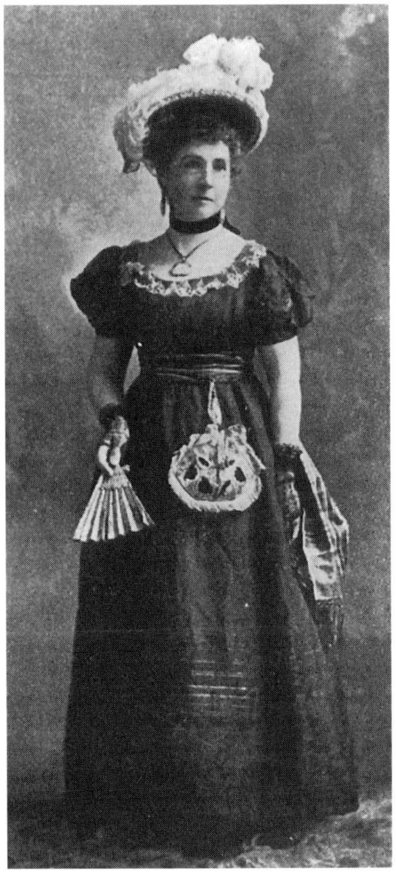

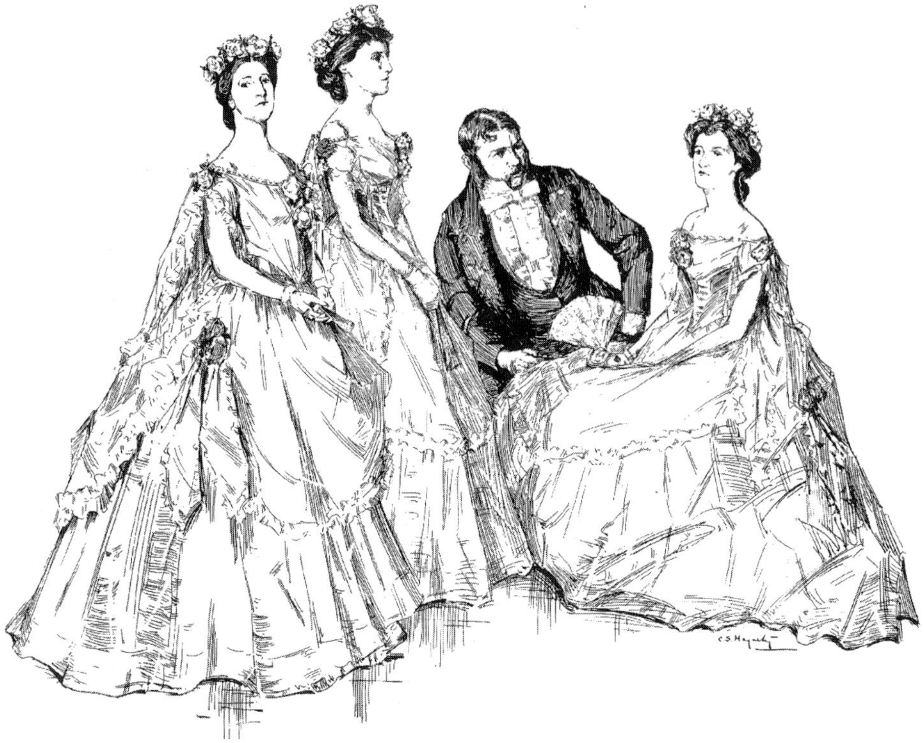

Minnie Forsyth Grant (née Beverley Robinson), of the second Victorian Costumes set, in an heirloom gown from about 1817 – a "beautiful old gown of over 70 years ago, worn by her grandmother, Lady Robinson, cherry red gauze, with gold satin stripe woven in the skirt, short bodice, sash to correspond, early Victorian bonnet in white, with old lace fan and white feathers, tiny bag for kerchief, in old embroidered satin, old inlaid lace, worn at a court ball in Dublin, mitts of Maltese lace; ornaments old cameo earrings, very long and pendant." (*Toronto Globe*, 29 Dec. 1897) BARNES BROTHERS, *TYPES OF CANADIAN WOMEN*

Victoria's mother, who was truly the belle of the ball, and the press paid more attention to her than to anyone else. Copying a portrait by an unidentified German artist, she wore a "white satin frock, with long yellow velvet train, bordered with sable, hung from the shoulders, the lovely head with yellow velvet turban and long velvet plumes" – "the most beautiful woman at the ball" and "every inch a princess." Mrs. Fitzgibbon was talented as well as beautiful; she was well known as a journalist and wrote for the *Toronto Globe* under the pen name Lally Bernard.[21]

Other beauties in the set included Miss Sybil Seymour as "Lady Blessington" in a white gown with a turban of tulle, and Miss Gzowski as "Lady Jersey" in a pink striped gauze dress with hair coiffed "*à la grec*" with broad bands of ribbon. Dr. George Sterling Ryerson was the standard bearer in his grandfather's uniform from 1812.

No named characters danced in the Second Period, which included dress from the 1830s and possibly the 1840s. Again the men looked fairly uniform in their "frilled shirt fronts" and "patch whiskers." The women, however, were irresistible, in their "quaint" poke bonnets and curls. The term "quaint" was applied to nearly everyone. Mrs. Lally McCarthy was the "belle of her pretty set, in a short-waisted white satin frock, white plumed poke, and killing little curls, her straight, prim dignity being most fetching." Another reporter adored her "telling ringlets under her white poke bonnet." Minnie Forsyth Grant, who led the set, was well known for having written a travelogue on Hawaii as well as for her contributions to the local press. She "was a picture" in a heirloom red gauze gown and a plaid scarf from the same period worn as a sash. Mrs. Arthur Hardy, the wife of the new premier, had helped her organize the set.[22]

The Third Period surpassed the other sets with its graceful dancing. The women represented "Bridesmaids of the Princess Royal" from the 1858 painting by George Hayter. The men wore evening dress of 1858: frilled shirts, high collars and large cravats, and coats with quilted satin lapels. Their Dundreary whiskers attracted attention,

Opposite: Miss D'Arcy Boulton, Miss Grace Boulton, and Miss Harmon Brown, with Herbert Mowat, as "Bridesmaids of the Princess Royal," based on a painting by Hayter. The trim on the women's white crinoline dresses and the wreaths on their heads consist of pink roses and white heather. Herbert Mowat sports bushy Dundreary whiskers. BB, PEN AND INK DRAWING BY CLARA S. HAGARTY

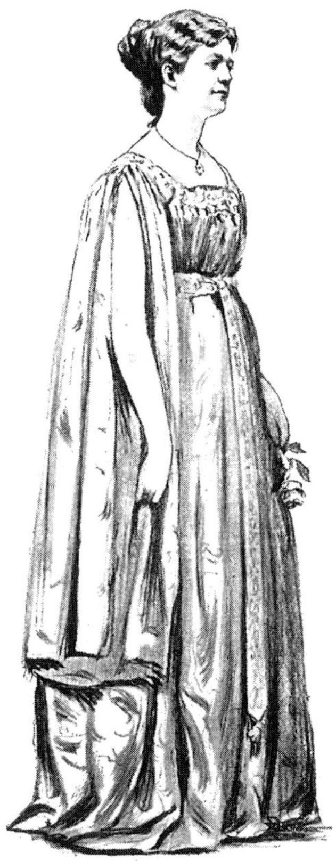

Left: Mary Walker (née Alexander) as "The Lady Ermengilda." Fancy dress instructions tended to make fun of aesthetic dress, but this set treated the theme with respect. Mrs. Byron Edmund Walker's dress is of "Nile green liberty satin, trimming of crepe lisse, embroidered in soft shades of pink and green, jewelled ornaments, in same shades, wing sleeves lined with pink." (*Toronto Globe*, 29 Dec. 1897) BB, PENCIL DRAWING BY GEORGE A. REID

as did their "appropriately solemn and sentimental" demeanour. The women drew many compliments, each wearing a billowy dress of white tulle over white satin, trimmed with pink roses and white heather; onlookers were a bit surprised to find crinoline dresses so graceful. The set was organized by Matilda Edgar, wife of James D. Edgar, the Speaker of the House of Commons, and herself the author of a historical work on the decade between 1805 and 1815 in Upper Canada.

The fourth Victorian Costumes set represented the "Aesthetic Period." Mary Walker, the wife of Edmund Walker, the bank manager with a special interest in art who later helped found the Royal Ontario Museum, was the organizer. The men, including Walker himself, wore evening dress with short velvet coats, wide white Byron collars and elaborate scarves. The women wore "limp gowns" and carried sunflowers or calla lilies. Compliments were sparing for this group portraying a recent and rather loose past, though there were no criticisms. (A Weldon's fancy dress catalogue from this period suggests dressing as "An Aesthetic Maiden," indicating that such characters probably attended other balls, too.) Miss Ethel Ellis as "The Lady Clare" was considered admirably suited to her role, with her fine profile and golden hair. The organizer herself was "The Lady Ermengilda."

The Victorian Costumes group over, a trumpet fanfare announced the third group. "One dance finished and the next came on like clockwork, and between each all the participants were introduced by their real and their assumed names by their respective heralds," wrote Lady Aberdeen. A few guests saluted Their Excellencies in character, including the Indians who made "low salaams" and the early Victorian women who each made a "stately obeisance."[23]

The third and largest group, Literature and Music, danced several sets of lancers and represented characters from the works of Victorian authors. First came the Sir Walter Scott set; Scott's works always provided the most popular inspiration for literary characters at fancy dress balls. The set, headed by Lady Thompson, the widow of the late Prime Minister John Thompson, included three main characters from *Ivanhoe* – "Ivanhoe" himself in chain armour and helmet, the Saxon princess "Rowena" and "The Jewess Rebecca" – "Julian Peveril" from *Peveril of the Peak*, and of course "Di Vernon," of *Rob Roy*, in a green riding habit and plumed cavalier hat.

The next literary set was less traditional but highly appropriate: Rudyard Kipling. The author's Indian characters proved the most popular: "The Burma Girl" from the

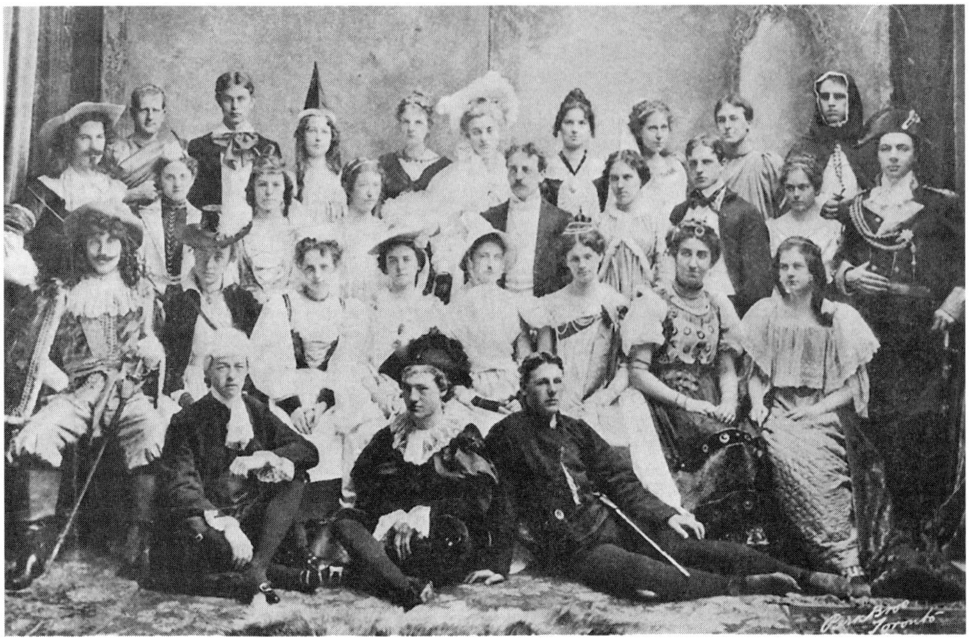

The Literature Set. The characters are from stories by George Eliot and Robert Browning as well as plays by Sheridan Knowles and Alfred, Lord Tennyson. *Front row, seated:* Bingley Benson; Norman Beal as "The Hunchback"; V.E. Henderson as "Robin Hood." *Second row:* James Merrick as "Wentworth, Earl of Stafford"; Miss B. White; Miss Rosalie Jackson as "Tessa"; Miss M. Mason; Miss Clara Benson as "Dinah Morris"; Miss Mina Lynde; Miss Bertha Rosenstadt as "Tedalina"; Miss Amy Morrison. *Third row:* G.H. Black; Miss Marion Lang as "Maid Marion"; Miss Mary Northway; Miss Clara Crane; R.Y. Parry; Miss M.M. Stovel; W.A. Sadler as "Adam Bede"; Miss M.L. Wright; Ogilvie Watson as "Claude Melnotte." *Fourth row:* A.T. Hunter as "Topeas in Calydon"; A.J.G. McDougall; Miss E.E. Preston as "Rosamund de Clifford"; Miss Grace Hunter; Miss Agnes McNally; Miss A. Rosebrugh; Miss Winnifred Hutchison as "Romola"; T.A. Colclough as "Virginius"; F.A. Young as "Savonarola." TORONTO GLOBE, 12 MARCH 1898

poem "Mandalay"; "Sitebhai," "Queen in the 'Naulakha,'" and "Ameera," with their heads swathed in gauzes and brocades; and "Bahadour Khan" and "Gunga Din," in red and white turbans and long coats. Three characters were present from the poem "Pink Domino," which told of a case of mistaken identity at a fancy dress ball. Two young men as "Drums of the Fore and Aft" were found a bit trying to the ears. A second "Our Lady of the Snows" appeared, partnered by "Estreekland Sahib." Her costume, more in keeping with Kipling's winter theme, was less political than Miss Mowat's dress, and not at all subversive. At least two other guests not in any of the organized sets impersonated the same character, with similar wintery symbols. The Kipling set was organized by Miss Kingsmill, daughter of a prominent Toronto judge.

The George Eliot set was the first of two interpreted by the Toronto University Women's Literary Society. Lady Aberdeen's invitation to take charge of the sets had caused much excitement, especially as the members of the society had been given dispensation to choose their own male partners. The set combined characters from Eliot's nineteenth-century stories, as well as several from *Romola*, set in fifteenth-century Florence. "Savonarola" wore the "costume of a Dominican monk." "Tito" in doublet, trunks and hose, "Romola" and "Tessa" were also present. Dress of the English peasantry was perhaps unappealing, so the student portraying "Adam Bede" chose "Adam Bede's Sunday Suit." "Dinah Morris" from the same story wore a nondescript "grey Quaker gown" with a bonnet and apron. Although the students did not have the same resources for their costumes as the society leaders, their garb was nevertheless effective. Biology professor Robert Ramsay Wright was the herald for the set.

The Drama, the second set taken on by the Toronto University Women's Literary Society, included "Robin Hood," in a Lincoln green doublet and a crimson cap with a feather, and "Maid Marion" from Tennyson's *Foresters*, as well as characters in togas from Sheridan Knowles's *Virginius*.

Trinity College undertook the Robert Browning set, featuring "Fra Lippo Lippi" in German dress of the fifteenth century, "The Pied Piper" in a tall pointed hood, and the Italian peasant girl, "Pippa," in a colourful peasant dress. Originally Tennyson, Dickens and Thackeray were also to have sets, but these were abandoned early on in the plans.

Below: Helen Law as "Rowena" from *Ivanhoe*. To highlight her gorgeous garments, Miss Law literally let her hair down. She wears "a Nile green kirtle embroidered with jewels, a scarlet cloak trimmed with blue fox." (*Toronto Globe*, 29 Dec. 1897) BB, PEN AND INK DRAWING BY CLARA S. HAGARTY

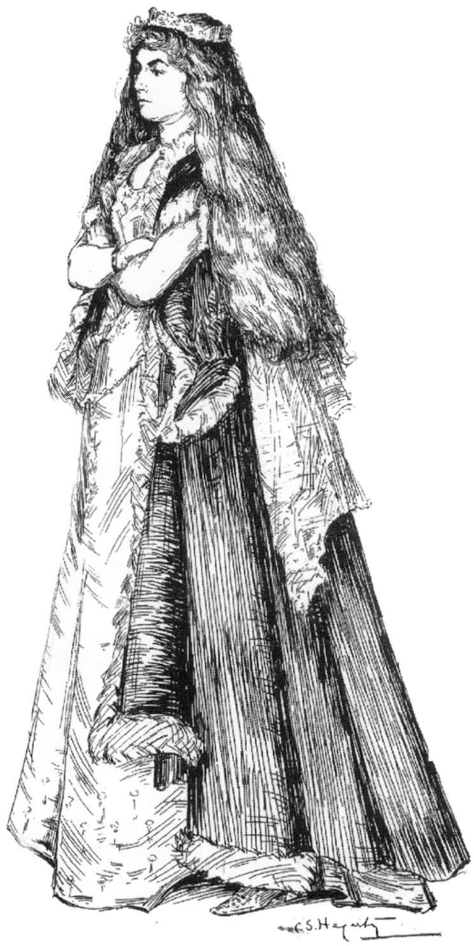

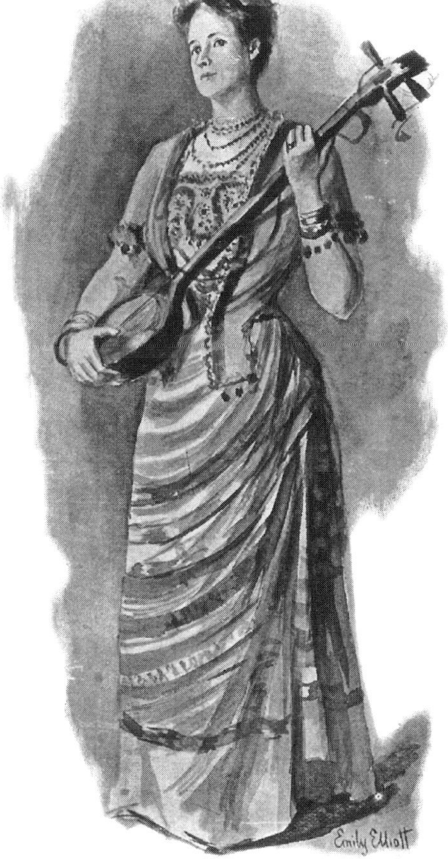

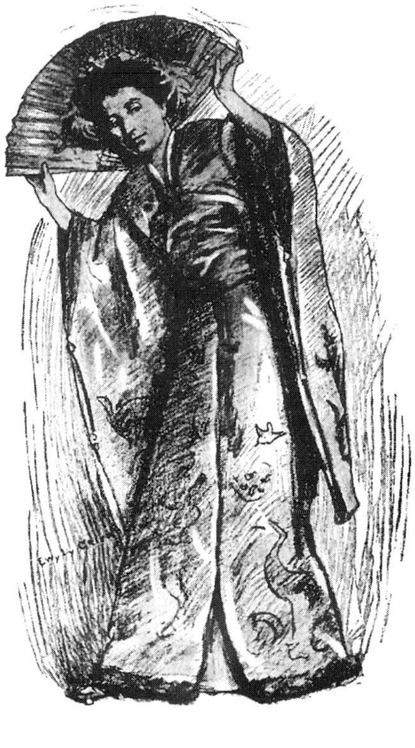

Above: Jessie Ross Robertson as "Pitti-Sing" in the Gilbert and Sullivan set, wearing "a handsome Japanese costume, petticoat of old rose satin, and kimono of white satin, gorgeously embroidered with gold cranes and Japanese designs of all descriptions, brilliantly studded with jewels and faced with gold colored silk, with sash to match. The hair dressed in the ordinary Japanese style, with jewels in it, fan sparkling with jewels to correspond." (*Toronto Globe*, 29 Dec. 1897) BB, PENCIL DRAWING BY E. WYLY GRIER

Centre: Mrs. James Scott as "The Burma Girl," from the poem by Rudyard Kipling. She wears a "striped eastern silk skirt in green, gold, and orange, cream brocaded jacket, edged with jewelled gold lace and deep orange border, jewelled band, green satin cap, embroidered in gold and jewels." (*Toronto Globe*, 29 Dec. 1897) BB, WASH DRAWING BY EMILY ELLIOTT

A bit more splashy was the Gilbert and Sullivan set, with dancing so outstanding that "It made us groan for the lancers one sees in general." The set included "The Pirate King" from *The Pirates of Penzance* and notable characters from the spoof on Oscar Wilde and the aesthetes, *Patience*. "Bunthorne" wore a black velvet suit with knee breeches; a black velvet hat topped flowing yellow curls, and he carried, of course, a lily. From *The Mikado* came "Koko," "Yum-Yum," and a very much remarked "Pitti-Sing" in the person of Mrs. John Ross Robertson. She made a strong impression, just as she had done at the Ottawa ball, in her "perfectly becoming" costume with "yellow and white chrysanthemums worn at either side of the quaint coiffure." Naturally, "Pitti-Sing" carried a fan. The group's herald was artist Edmund Wyly Grier, who produced several sketches of the ball.

After the lengthy Literature and Music group, the fourth group, Science and Invention, provided a refreshing change, with its allusions to technological progress.

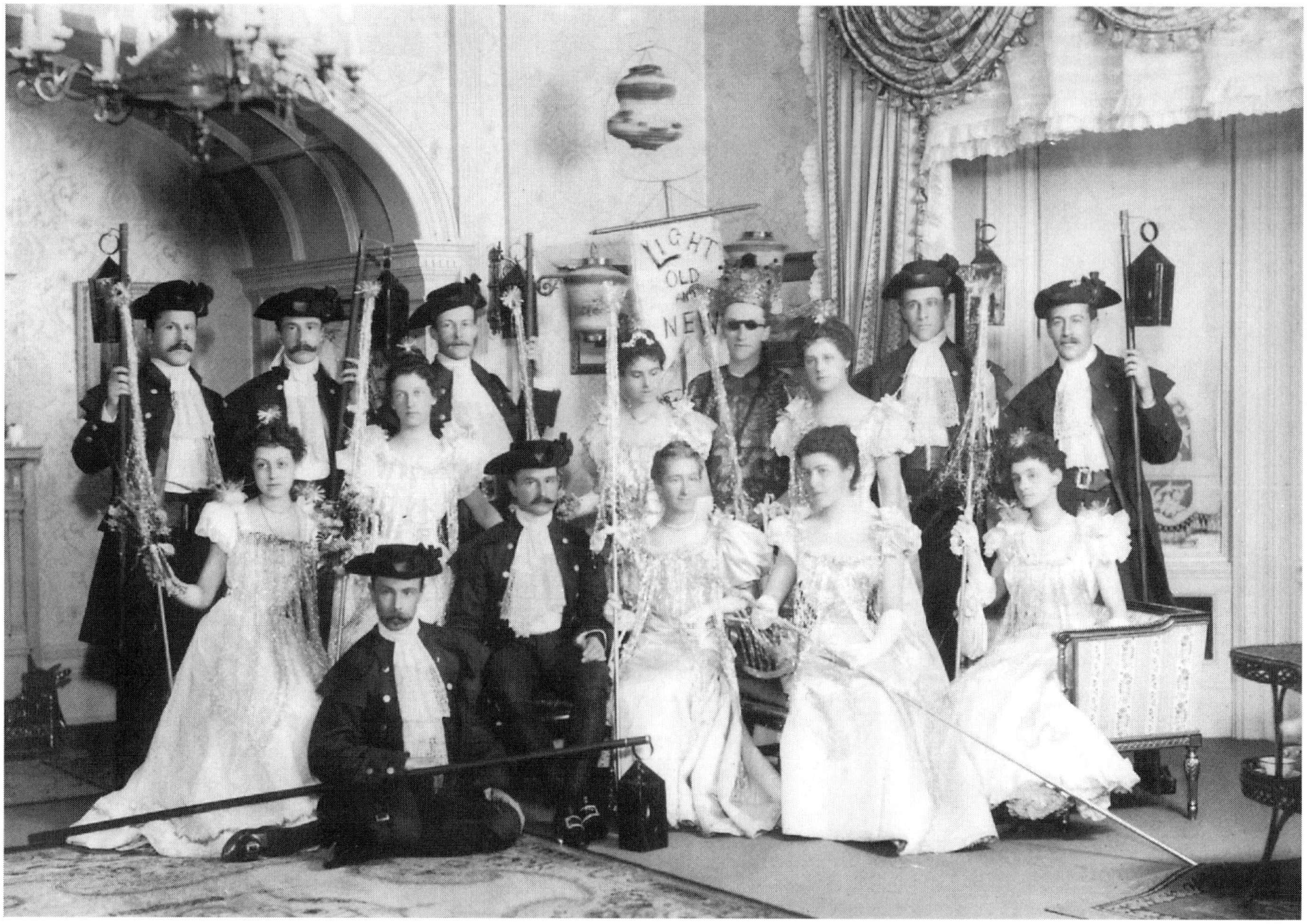

These themes "were a difficult subject to treat and a triumph for the ladies who made the dance of these sets one of the successes of the ball."[24]

First came Electricity, preceded by a herald dressed in Chinese costume bearing a Chinese lantern and a white satin banner inscribed "Light – Old and New." The society lady in charge, Mrs. Lt.-Col. George Sweny, invented the dance, and Roy Sweny played the herald. The eight men in the dance, representing the old light, dressed as eighteenth-century night watchmen in brown velvet coats with double capes, breeches, white lace stocks and three-cornered hats. They carried poles from which swung lanterns with green shades and lighted candles inside. The eight women stole the show. Representing electricity, the new light, they wore high-waisted white gowns veiled in tulle, with silver bouquets attached, and their hair was powdered white. The silver electric lights in their diadems and on the ends of the wands they carried in their hands were powered by small batteries in their chatelaines. The attire was dazzling, but the idea was not entirely original. Alva Vanderbilt wore such a costume to her sister-in-law's New York ball in 1883. Stephen Heward, a member of the set, fondly remembered the many pleasant evenings of rehearsals at Mrs. Sweny's home.[25]

The Postal Progress set was organized by another Miss Kingsmill. The eight men, including barristers Henry Osborne and Hamilton Cassels, dressed as postmen in scarlet coats and caps and white trousers with a scarlet stripe. The women were emblematic representations of postage (or, one reporter thought, carrier pigeons), in

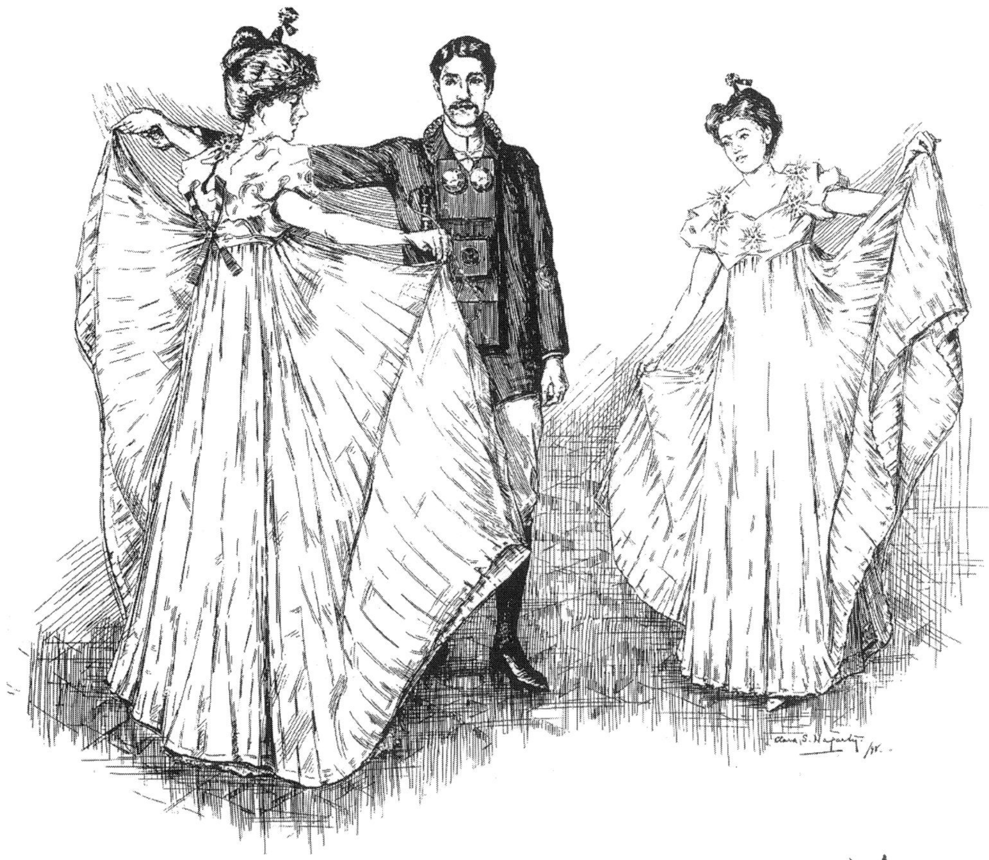

Left: Miss Laidlaw, Adam Creelman, and Miss H. Cattanach in the Inventions dance. Mr. Creelman wears bells and a receiver on his chest to represent a telephone, and the women wear propellors in their hair and at their waists to represent air motors. BB, PEN AND INK DRAWING BY CLARA S. HAGARTY

Below: Miss Osler and Henry Osborne from the Postal Progress set. BB, PEN AND INK DRAWING BY CLARA S. HAGARTY

Opposite: The Old and the New Light. The men, dressed as eighteenth-century watchmen in brown velvet coats, carry lanterns to represent the old light. The women carry batteries in their chatelaines to power electric lights in their hair and on the ends of their wands. In the centre is Roy Sweny, the herald, in Chinese dress. The other men, not in order, are G. Heward, Stephen Heward, A. Kerr, Leighton McCarthy, Harold Montizambert, Col. Otter, and W.F. Sweny. The women are Miss Cassels, Miss Crombie, Miss G. Crombie, Mrs. Cronyn, Miss Small, Mrs. Sweny, and Miss Wilkie. METRO TORONTO REFERENCE LIBRARY

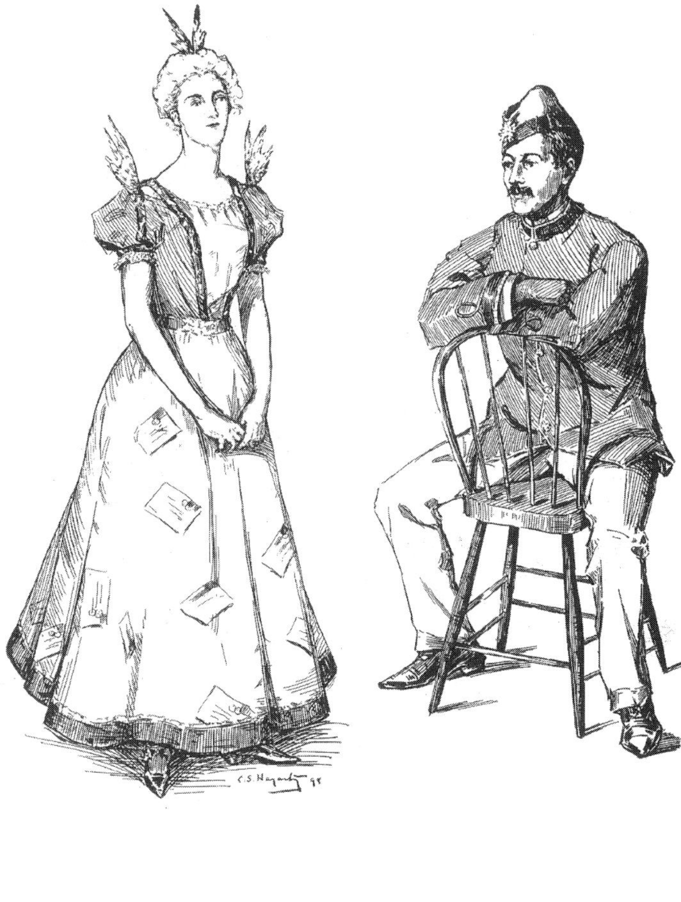

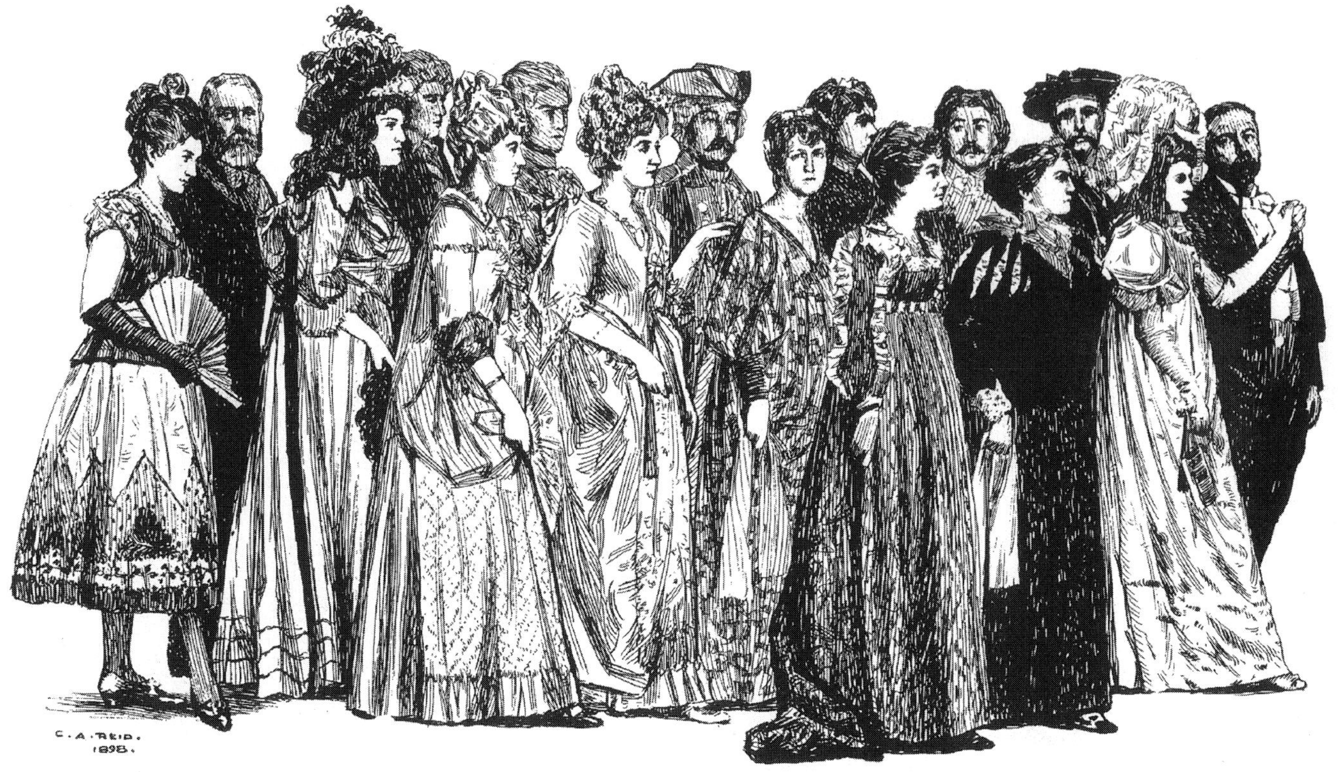

Above and opposite: The March of the Pictures Set, representing paintings by British artists, most of which had been exhibited at the Royal Academy in the previous ten years. *Left to right:* Constance Beardmore as "Carmencita"; three unidentified figures; Mrs. Pelham Edgar; Edmund Bristol; Mr. and Mrs. J.G. Burnham; Mrs. Auguste Bolté; Mr. Johnson; Mrs. Edmund Bristol as "Lucrezia Borgia" and Mr. Bogart as "Cesar Borgia"; Violet Smith and Pelham Edgar as "Hugenots"; Miss Daisy Patteson; Mr. Beardmore; Elizabeth Cawthra; Miss Beardmore; Capt. C. Pearse; Miss McMurrich; Capt. Sydney Pearse; Amy Riordan as "Beatrice" and W.A. Langton as "Dante"; Mabel Cawthra as "Madame Récamier"; Agar Adamson as "Napoleon"; Auguste Bolté and Andrew Dickson Patterson as heralds.

BB, PEN AND INK DRAWING BY GEORGE A. REID

blue dresses trimmed in red and peppered with stamped and addressed envelopes. Gold Mercury wings crowned their powdered heads.

Mrs. Cattanach assumed the Inventions set. Judge Adam Creelman and the other men represented "Telephones," wearing brown jackets, white breeches and red stockings. They carried telephones with jingling bells and receivers on their chests and wore coiled wires around their necks; the sight almost compelled one reporter to cry out "Hello!" The women represented "Air Motors," in empire-style dresses with accordion pleated skirts of white chiffon to represent mill wheels, small windmills on their heads, silver spangles on their bodices, and windmills attached to the backs of their waistlines.

The fifth group, Art, had two sets, Pictures and The Stage, which offered "abundant scope for dress." The group's highly successful minuet to "deliciously sensuous music" was choreographed by A. Roy McDonald. Following the ball, Elizabeth Cawthra, the organizer, wrote, "Our minuet was a great success and everyone enjoyed the ball." Pictures of the Reign included characters from famous paintings produced by artists of the Victorian era. William Quiller Orchardon's works were represented by Ottawa beau Agar Adamson, accompanied by his future wife, Mabel Cawthra. Adamson personified "Napoleon on Board the Bellerophon" (1881) and Miss Cawthra "The Salon of Madame Recamier" (1885). She was "lovely and graceful" in a white satin empire gown embroidered in silver. They originally planned to represent a painting of Napoleon and Josephine, but Miss Cawthra changed her mind when she contemplated posing for a photograph on a sofa.[26]

A young couple represented "A Huguenot on Saint Bartholomew's Day" by John Everett Millais (1852): Pelham Edgar, a lecturer at Victoria University and later an accomplished author and critic, and Miss Violet Smith. W.A. Langton, as "Dante" from the "Meeting of Beatrice and Dante" by Henry Holiday, won much applause as

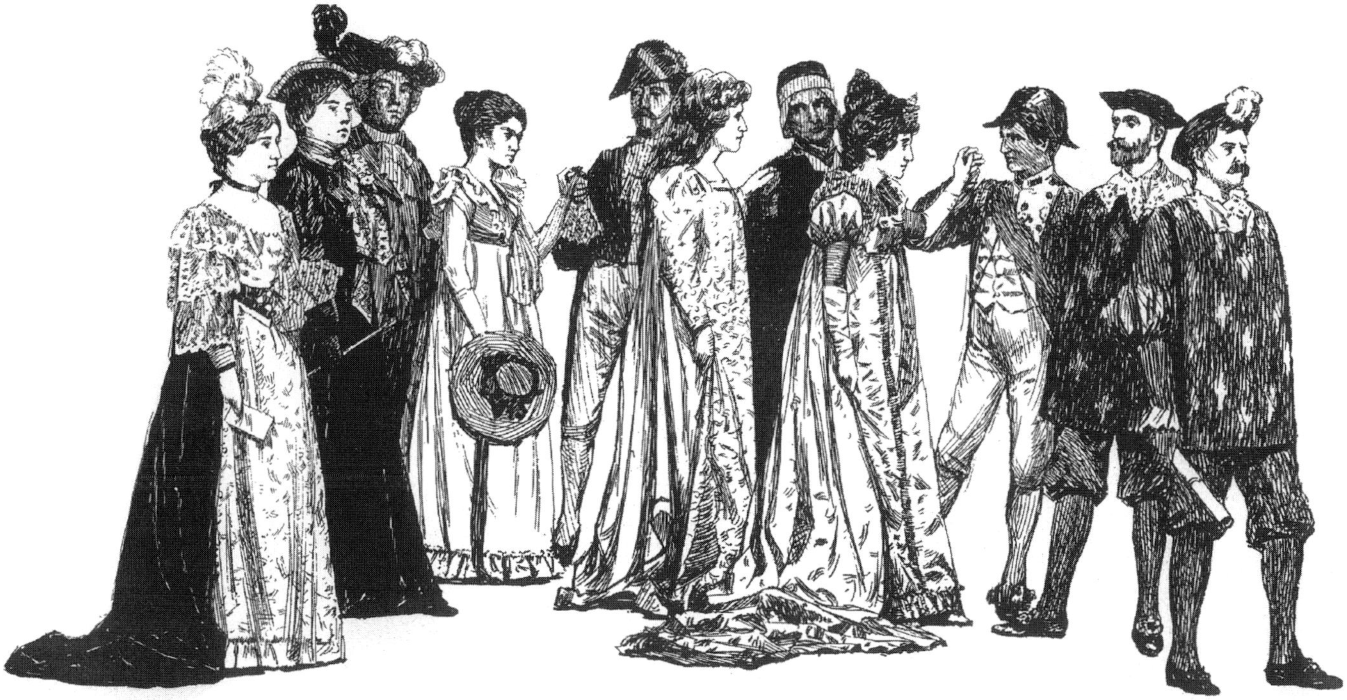

"perfect . . . in every feature" in his "voluminous cloak of red cloth and red velvet cape." Miss Constance Beardmore came as "Carmencita," painted by John Singer Sargent; her yellow satin Spanish dress with black lace was "worn charmingly by the dark-eyed maiden." Three people portrayed "A Glass of Wine with Cesar Borgia," by John Collier, including Mrs. Edmund Bristol as "Lucrezia," in "a perfect gown, perfectly worn." Appropriately, Andrew Dickson Patterson, a well-known Canadian painter, was the standard bearer for the set.

In the Stage set, the ballgoers dressed as popular actors playing dramatic characters. James Ince made "a stunning Doltaire" as portrayed by Sir Herbert Beerbohm Tree in the Canadian play *The Seats of the Mighty*, performed on a London stage earlier that year. His "strikingly handsome get-up" included an apricot velvet coat, knee breeches, and *poudré* hair. His "smooth face" proclaimed that he had ruthlessly sacrificed his cherished moustache for the sake of accuracy. Miss Langmuir represented "Emma Calvé as Carmen." Miss Munzinger was Ada Rehan in her most successful role, "Katharine" in *The Taming of the Shrew*. Mrs. Walter Barwick, the organizer and the wife of a leading barrister, impersonated the French actress Réjane as "Madame Sans-Gêne," one of her most famous roles.

The first set of the sixth and final group, Sports and Amusements, was a bit incongruous. All the same, Harvesting was one of the highlights of the ball. It was organized by the creative and energetic Mrs. Arthurs (whose extensive contributions to the ball Lady Aberdeen later acknowledged with a diamond bracelet). Men represented the modern harvest in blue breeches, red stockings, white smocks, buff jerkins and rustic hats; they carried flower-decked rakes. Women represented the old-fashioned harvest in Dresden-shepherdess-style dresses consisting of blue underskirts, yellow bodices and paniers, black lacing over the stomachers, and Leghorn straw hats decked with poppies and cornflowers; they carried rakes, sickles and poppies.

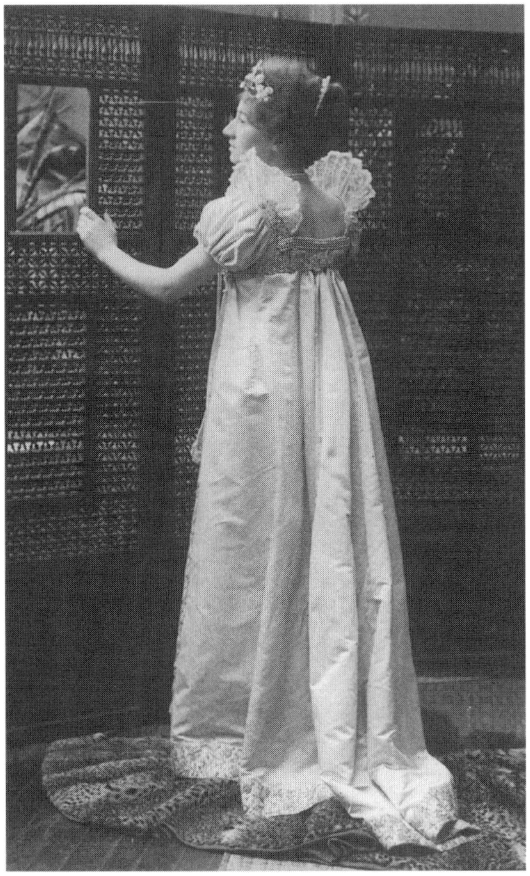

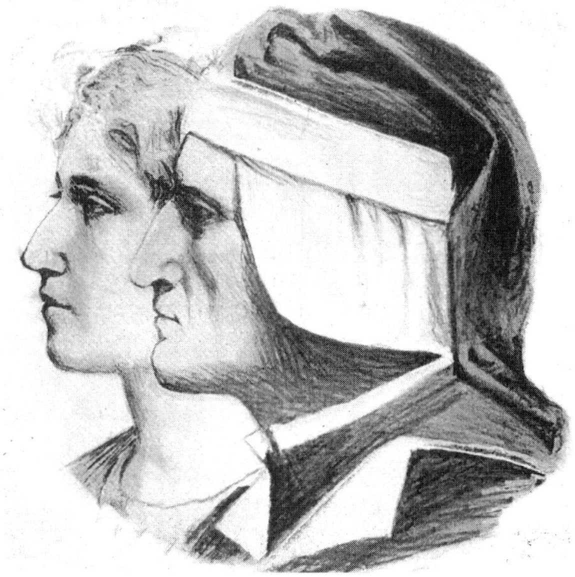

Above: Mabel Cawthra as "The Salon of Madame Recamier," by W.Q. Orchardson. In her white satin empire dress embroidered in silver, her train of white silk faille, and her "many rich jewels," Miss Cawthra was "lovely and graceful." METRO TORONTO REFERENCE LIBRARY

Above right: W.A. Langton and Amy Riordan as "The Meeting of Beatrice and Dante," a particularly successful representation. "Of the many effective pictures, probably Mr. Langton's representation of Dante was the best. The features of the poet and the dress in which he is known to the world were exactly reproduced." Langton dressed in a red cloth cloak and hat, while Miss Riordan wore blue silk brocade with a chiffon veil trailing from her shoulders. (*Toronto News*, 29 Dec. 1897) PENCIL DRAWING BY GEORGE A. REID

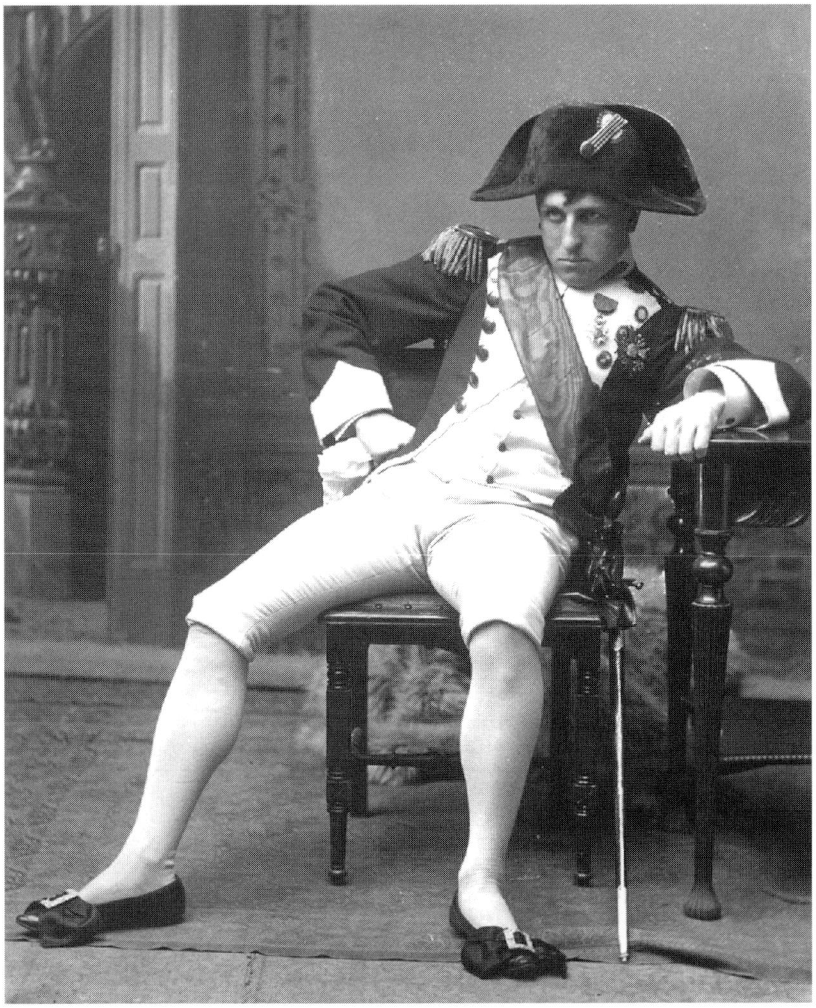

Right: Agar Adamson as "Napoleon on Board the Bellerophon," by W.Q. Orchardson. Adamson actually went on to a brilliant military career. WJT/NAC/PA138384

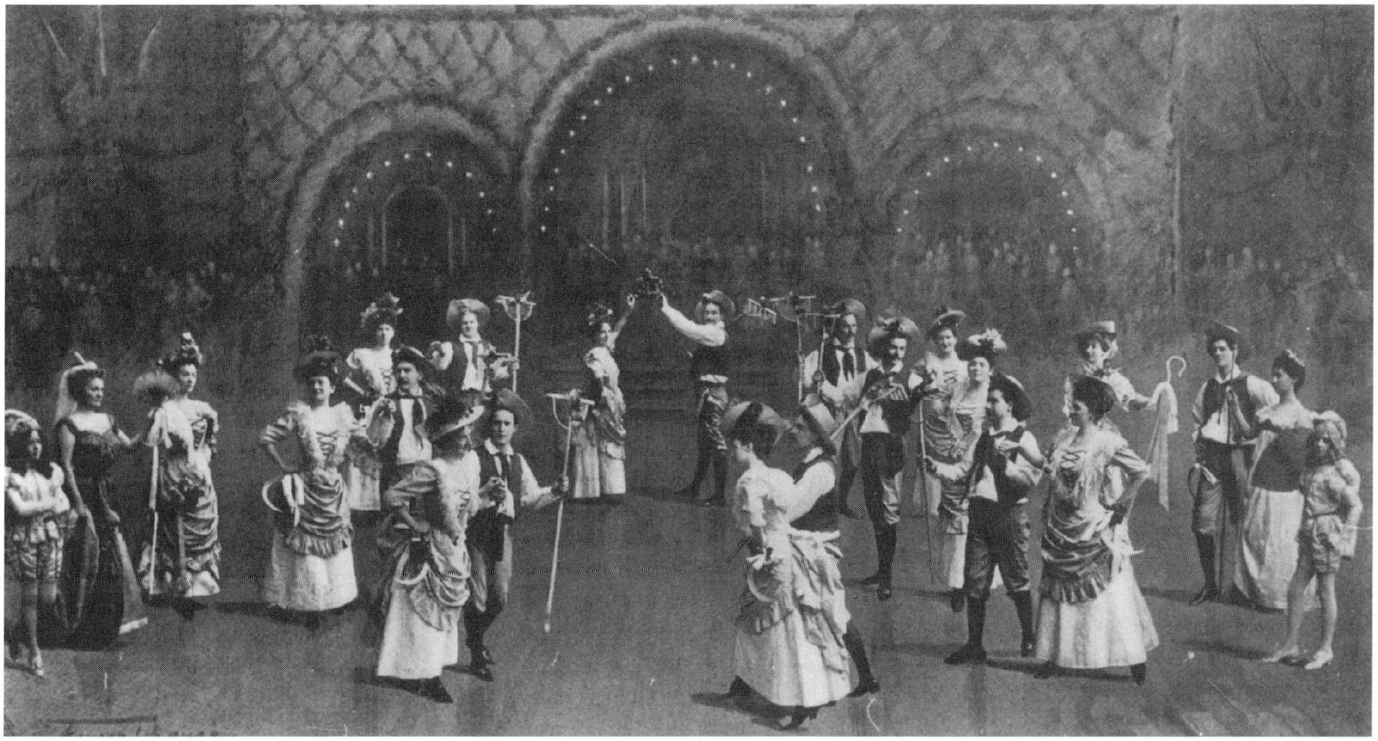

Above: The Harvesting Set. Here they pose in the midst of their Sir Roger de Coverley. The "modern" men wear blue breeches and buff jerkins and carry rakes trimmed with flowers. The "old-fashioned" women wear blue and yellow shepherdess costumes and straw hats, and they carry sickles. On the left is Mrs. Victor Cawthra as "Queen of the Harvest" in yellow satin painted with wheat; on the right is Miss Inez Mitchell as "Manitoba" in a white gown with wheat and leaves in her hair, and carrying a lance and a shield. FRASER BRYCE, *WE TWA*

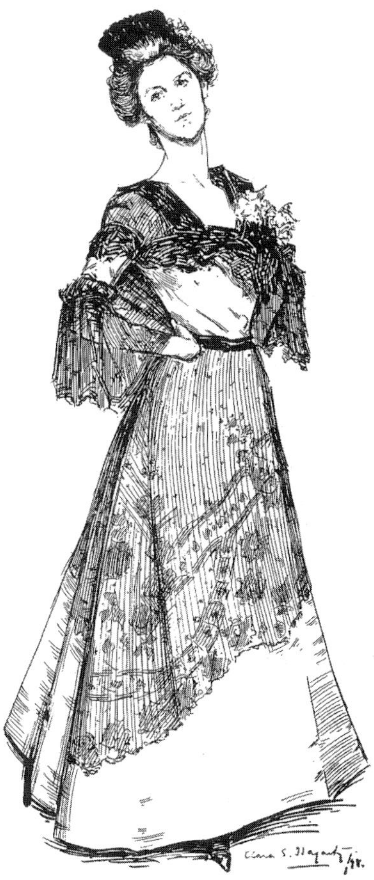

Right: Miss Langmuir as "Emma Calvé as Carmen" in the Stage Set. Her costume is a "yellow satin bodice and skirt, draped with black Spanish lace, caught up with scarlet flowers, Spanish comb and flowers in hair." (*Toronto Globe*, 29 Dec. 1897) BB, PEN AND INK DRAWING BY CLARA S. HAGARTY

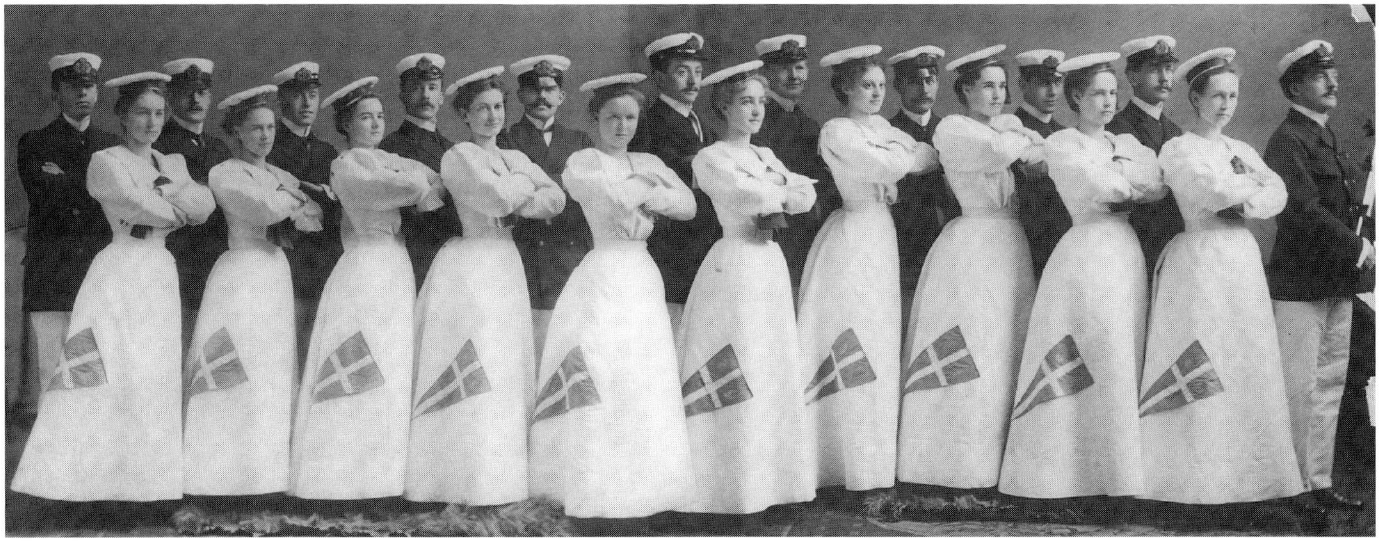

The Yachting Set. Royal Canadian Yacht Club flags decorate the women's white piqué skirts. This photograph is actually printed from two negatives; the division is visible in the centre. Temple McMurrich is second from left, Colin Harbottle is fourth, then Charlie W. Beatty, Louis McMurray and Jack Gilmour; the last two men are Ross Gooderham and Leonard McMurray. The other men, not in order, are Ross Boyd, Mr. Cavanagh, Duncan Coulson and Mr. Higinbotham. The women are: Lillie Tayor, Lillie Phillips, Lillie Lee, Lottie Taylor, Amy Wright, Aileen Gooderham, Blanche Wellington, Violet Gooderham, Mrs. Charlie Beatty and Mrs. James Ross.
FARMER BROS./ROYAL CANADIAN YACHT CLUB

Not only did the public love the rollicking Sir Roger de Coverley, "danced with immense vigour," but the harvesters gave a spectacular performance by pulling in a modern Massey Harris reaper bedecked with wheat, sunflowers, poppies and flags. "Seated in triumph" on the machine was Inez Mitchell representing "Manitoba," surrounded by cornucopias filled with apples, sunflowers, and cereals. Miss Mitchell, a picture of "sweet girlish loveliness," wore a white silk Grecian-style dress with gold trim and golden wheat and leaves in her hair; she carried a lance in her right hand and a shield on her left arm, inscribed "Manitoba." To meet them came "The Queen of the Harvest," Mrs. Arthurs's recently married daughter, Mrs. Victor Cawthra, in a dress of yellow satin painted with sheaves of wheat and a crescent moon on her head; two pages followed her.

The second set, Yachting, was more consistent with the theme of Sports and Amusements. The "trim sailor boys" sported blue serge coats and white duck trousers. The "saucy sailor maids" wore white piqué bodices with wide blue collars and red silk ties. Their short piqué skirts were trimmed with Royal Canadian Yacht Club flags at one side. On their heads they wore round white sailor hats with red streamers – "too fetching for anything." Violet, Aileen and Ross Gooderham, Lillian Beatty and Adelaide Ross, all children of George Gooderham, perhaps the wealthiest man in the province, were part of this set; their father's yacht *Canada* had won an international competition the previous year.

The Games set highlighted popular British sports, such as football, tennis, riding, golf and rowing. Absent were hockey and skating, well-loved by Canadians but abhorred by Lady Aberdeen. "Football," Miss Lucretia Harmon-Brown, wore a white quilted satin skirt and laced white satin bodice over a blue satin sweater. A football for a cap and miniature footballs on the skirt completed the costume. Her partner was simply dressed in "football costume." "Golf," Miss Emily Moss, wore a tailored red jacket – the requisite garment for the sport. She carried a golf club and wore another miniature one on her head. Other sport characters took a more romantic approach to their costumes – "Fencing" wore a cherry-colored eighteenth-century-style dress.

The London Hunt Club represented Hunting – "all hard riders and no figureheads." The women appeared in white satin skirts, pink velvet coats with blue revers, lace jabots, and Gainsborough hats with plumes, and they carried riding stocks. The

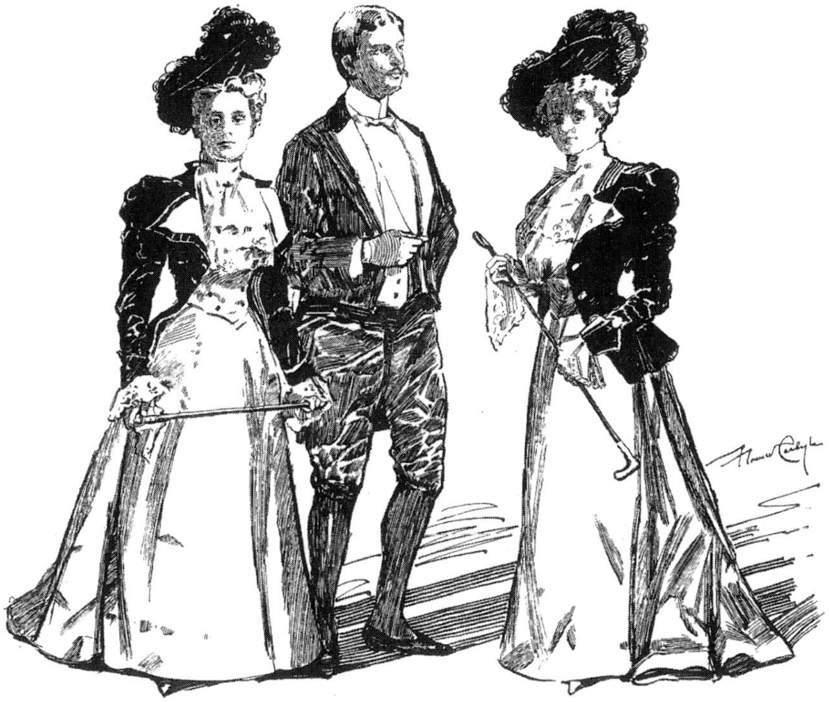

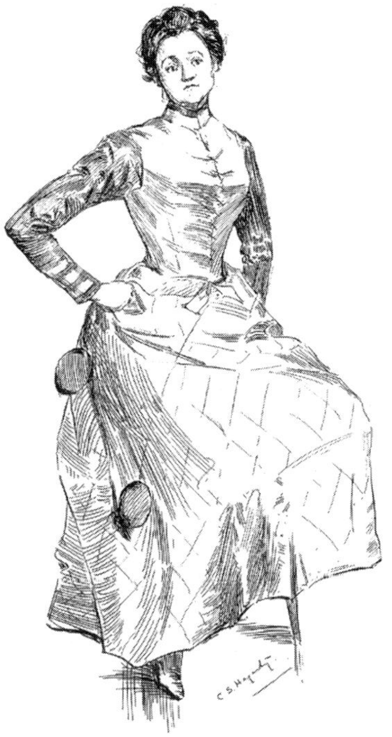

Above: Miss Lucretia Harmon-Brown as "Football" in the Games Set. BB, PEN AND INK DRAWING BY CLARA S. HAGARTY

Above left: Group from the Hunting Set. The London Hunt Club members formed this set and appeared in their pink coats, though the women made their dress more appropriate for a ball with satin skirts and broad-brimmed plumed hats. BB, PEN AND INK DRAWING BY FLORENCE CARLYLE

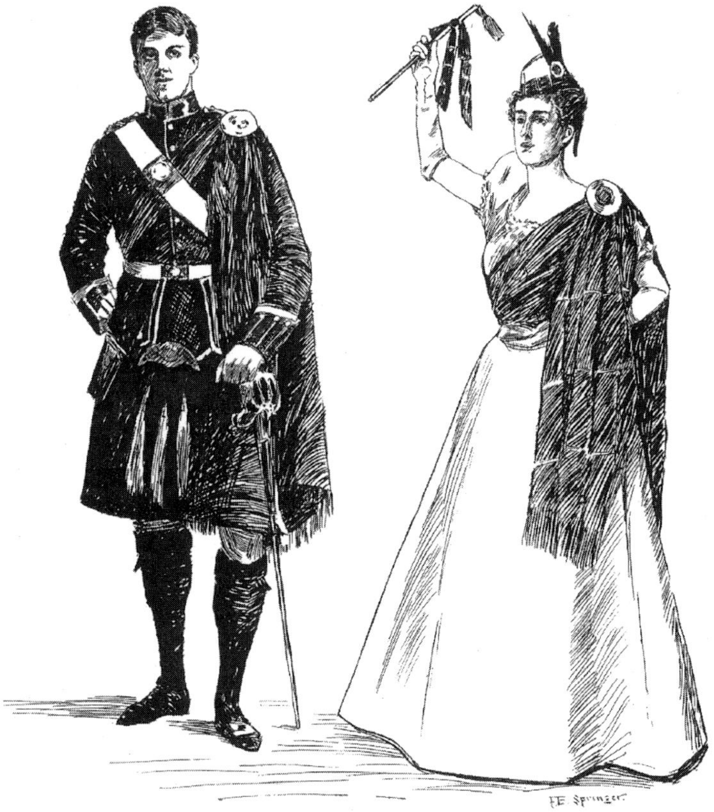

Left: Norman Cosby and Evelyn Cox of the Highland Sports Set. Miss Cox carries a miniature golf club. BB, PEN AND INK DRAWING BY FLORENCE E. SPRINGER

male contingent included Adam Beck and George Gibbons, one of the founders of the club, who were well known in hunting circles.

The character dances drew to a close with Highland Sports. Lord Aberdeen broke into a patriotic smile as the dancers "gaily footed the wily Reel o' Tulloch" to the pipes of the 48th Highlanders. The women wore white satin gowns with plaids of Gordon tartan, a tribute to their hosts, fastened at the shoulder with a Cairngorm, and Glengarry bonnets. Four carried brooms and the other four golf clubs to represent the two Scottish games. His Excellency was enchanted and later danced with Miss Evelyn Cox, one of the young ladies in the set.

Following the dances the vice-regal party was piped into the supper room – the other half of the Armouries – where another flash photograph was taken. The three head tables were adorned with banks of maidenhair ferns and flowers – red roses on the centre table, flanked by pink roses on the right and white hyacinths and violets on the left. All the other tables were decorated with yellow Dorothea roses and gleamed with silver candelabras. The Harry Webb Company provided the dishes, the food and one hundred waiters, all for less than a dollar a head. Their success won them an appointment as caterer to His Excellency following the event.

Four sittings were required to accommodate over two thousand guests. The menu – written in French like the Dufferins' – included a hot soup, *petits salpicons de venaison* (translated by Lady Aberdeen as "hot little beef things"), quail and tomatoes, cold turkey, ham, jellied tongue, and salads. Desserts included *baba à la parisienne*, *charlotte russe*, and *fruits glacés*. Only one accident marred the proceedings – another small fire, this time in a candle shade, which a guest extinguished with a bottle of seltzer water.

In the refreshment room on the terrace, hungry or thirsty guests not part of the first sitting partook of ices, sauterne, claret cup and champagne. They watched the multitude whirl around on the dance floor, mostly in fancy dress. The Aberdeens had issued conflicting instructions about costumes to people not in the organized sets. They were told they would "add to the general effect and success of the evening" by appearing in dress of any of the periods listed on the program, but another statement acknowledged that any who attended in the dress of the present day would complete the celebration of progress throughout the entire era. For many of the characters portrayed at the ball, the extensive research that the Ottawa ball had required was not necessary. The press referred vaguely to the use of costume histories and old pictures, the Aberdeens claimed that a "great deal of reading up" had been done, and certainly for the Literature and Music groups and the Pictures and Stage sets research was a must. The prevalence of fancy dress, researched or not, showed that "Toronto society expected every man that night to do his duty, every woman too. They responded nobly." Press coverage was extensive for the event; only Quebec's French press ignored it completely. Circulars were again in use to encourage both the guests in the sets and those not so distinguished to make a description of their costumes and characters available to the newspapers and magazines before the ball.[27]

A group of guests took inspiration from the press. Mr. Scalfe, as "Mr. Punch at the Races," sported a grey frock coat and field glasses, and he had covered his hat with pages from *Punch*. Miss Frances Harmer was "The Press of 1837" in a "petticoat of old-fashioned wood-cuts, skirt of 1837 newspapers, Garibaldi of white net, with medallions of old pictures, paste pot and scissors." She must have paled in comparison to Emily Cummings (an Indian at the Ottawa historical ball), who came as "The Press of the British Empire, 1897." A journalist known as "Sama" in the society pages of the *Toronto Globe*, she donned a "gown of newspapers from all parts of the British Empire, panel of colored illustrations, sleeves of telegraphic dispatches fastened with ticker tape, necklace of Merganthaler type machine slugs, halftone photogravure plates as buckles."[28]

Among the men, uniforms of all kinds were very popular, from the 34th Ontario Battalion to the Royal Canadian Yacht Club. Academic dress was also well represented, with caps, gowns and hoods signifying degrees from Queen's and McGill universities and Trinity College. The irreverent George Kennedy came as "Dr. Dryasdust" with "spectacles on nose and wearing the scarlet gown and velvet cap of a doctor of the University."

No Canadian guests with their recent fortunes dared to opt for the rugged occupational dress of the working classes. Only Eustace Smith donned his "actual rancher's garb, as requested by Her Excellency." Perhaps Lady Aberdeen had a slightly impure motive – she was actually not at all fond of Mr. Smith. The Aberdeens had attempted to establish her younger brother, Coutts Marjoribanks, on a ranch in Kelowna, BC, and set him on the road to fortune, but Eustace Smith, his footloose companion and foreman, encouraged him to squander plenty of family funds to amuse the two of them. On the other hand, David Erskine, the Aberdeen aide-de-camp, usually had to wear the stiff green and gold uniform of the Scottish Archers, so dressing as a lumberman in the North America set had perhaps been a treat.

For women, the most popular choice was Victorian costume, especially that of the 1830s and 1850s. Emblematic costumes were also fairly common, with several women choosing themes such as "A Daughter of Canada" in "white silk, veiled in tulle, ornamented with green velvet maple leaves." Dr. Augusta Stowe-Gullen represented "Peace" "in the colors of the peace flag, and to symbolize the peace which has been characteristic of the Victorian era; dress of yellow satin . . . white satin ribbons, purple violets on one shoulder, white dove on left shoulder." Miss Shanklin came as "India's Coral Strand" in a black brocade dress, "the corsage almost covered with strands of rare coral, which the fair wearer brought all the way from Capri where it grows in the sea." Of course, also present were the ubiquitous "Night" and "Dawn."[29]

A few women wore academic dress, such as Miss Townsend Sheridan as "Bachelor of Arts" in a "white satin gown, covered with graduating gown and cap of Toronto university." Three women came as nurses, possibly to support Lady Aberdeen's formation of the Victorian Order of Nurses during her stay in Toronto. Their attire was a far cry from evening wear. Faith Fenton, the journalist who had attended the Ottawa ball as a Mennonite and who evidently made her fashion statements by looking plain, wore the "uniform of English jubilee nurses, black dress, holland apron, Queen's medal, and white cap," "far from pretty" one reporter added. Mrs. Welch as "Hospital Sister" wore a "blue serge gown, white linen apron with bib, white cap tying under chin, white collar and cuffs." Another costume that showed support of Lady Aberdeen's endeavours was "National Council of Women," worn by Mrs. George Campbell. The emblematic costume was "light blue silk, trimmed with bow knots of dark and light ribbon (the Council badge), council pins and chiffon."

Another reason for the splendid turnout of all the guests was the fact that Toronto's society was wealthier than Ottawa's, whereas the onerous sartorial demands of vice-regal entertainments were rare. The arrival of the vice-regal couple was expected to give Toronto an economic boost, but it was the announcement of the fancy dress ball which made it a reality. The press liberally extolled the benefits of expenditure for the event. "In the business interests of our city," said *Saturday Night*, "it is to be hoped that all those who have time and money at their disposal will be asked and given a chance to spend both." The *Toronto Globe* discouraged the cheaper option of costume rental and chastised all those who rented costumes rather than helping trade by having one made. The one suggestion that Lady Aberdeen wished guests to keep expenses low was a half-hearted afterthought: "It is in no way the wish of Their Excellencies that any should go to the expense of purchasing rich fabrics or the like."[30]

Fifteen thousand dollars was the estimated cost of the event alone, exclusive of the expense to ballgoers. Many seamstresses, as well as carpenters, electricians, the caterer and the furnace company provided services. "What a godsend it was to [shops] and to trade in general!" the press exulted.[31]

The Toronto "modistes" did well; all Toronto's prominent dressmakers were busy. William Stitt & Co., a Toronto millinery and glove shop which employed its own dressmakers, made Constance Beardmore's "Carmencita" gown. Mrs. McKenna, a widowed theatrical costumier who advertised "fancy costumes to order and for hire," was thought to have been particularly successful.

The Women's Exchange served as an intermediary for many of the costume orders. (It is possible, though not certain, that this organization was the same as the Ladies' Work Depository.) Over the decade, such organizations cropped up in cities across the country to give women in "genteel poverty" a place to market their handiwork. Society women sponsored these associations, which also provided training in needlework. "A lady of considerable experience in matters histrionic, and of excellent taste" placed her ad through the Women's Exchange. Also through the Exchange, Mrs. Antrobus, generally known as a ceramic artist, carried out orders to paint the men-of-war on Edith Nordheimer's satin petticoat, and she impressed many with the embroidery on Jessie Ross Robertson's "remarkably handsome" "Pitti-Sing" costume. The garment was completed by Mrs. Shanley, one of a pair of sisters listed as dressmakers in the city directory, who also worked through the Exchange. Though wearing the most splendid get-ups at the ball, these two prominent women showed that they were not without a sense of social responsibility. And at least one society woman dabbled in design herself: Anne Arthurs, the mastermind behind the decorating scheme and the harvesters' dance, designed and did some of the painting on Lady Marjorie Gordon's "Forests of Canada" dress.

Cosmeticians, tobacconists, and especially hairdressers advertised relentlessly. A hairstylist, Pember, offered "Historical Hair dressing to represent any period from 1837 to 1897," while the upmarket Armand's boasted afterwards that "It goes without saying that the ladies who had their hair so beautifully dressed at Armand's were the prettiest stars of Toronto society at that great ball; they outshined all the rest." One week later, as they encouraged patrons to book for the next ball, Armand's explained their predicament.

> We must also beg to state that the great number of our patrons who were disappointed for not having their hair dressed by us for the great Victorian Era Ball that it was not our fault. We advertised the fact four weeks in advance, and in a few days most all the time was taken up; we were so pressed that we had to dress some ladies' hair the day before the ball. Although we gave preference to our regular patrons and five artists were at work from early morning to late at night it was almost impossible to serve all those who applied.

Armand's set itself apart from the competition by stating in another ad that it had charged $2.00 and $2.50 for hairstyling for the ball, whereas the hairdressers who catered to those Armand's was not able to serve charged a mere seventy-five cents. Regardless, these patrons had returned to Armand's to have their hair dressed for the next ball. "If these ladies were satisfied, why would they prefer to pay $2 and $2.50

instead of seventy-five cents?" The Graham Dermatological Institute recommended specific products for the ball: Liquid Eugenie Enamel, Liquid Rose Bloom, and Princess White Rose Cream. Another advertisement claimed that "the most popular cigar smoked by connoisseurs at the Victorian Era Ball was the celebrated DR. JIM cigar."[32]

The stimulus for expenditure met with opposition, and there is little doubt that it came from the biting tongue of Goldwin Smith. Smith contributed to a variety of newspapers and had become widely read for his controversial opinions, including his championing of annexation to the United States. He was known for his attacks on the office of Governor General, and he may well have written the comment in *The Nation* that the Dufferin ball "was a mistake in both place and time." Earlier in 1897, it had seemed for a while as if Goldwin Smith was relenting. He had held a reception in honour of the Aberdeens which Lady Aberdeen recorded:

> Yes, the Goldwin Smiths! Who would have thought that the day would come when H[is] E[xcellency] and Goldwin Smith would have been seen hobnobbing together, & H.E. drinking his host's health in a silver goblet belonging to the first Governor of Ontario. It is a curious fact that the man who has been preaching annexation of Canada in season & out of season, & who has written contemptuously of the various ceremonials in connection with the Vice-regal Court, should also be the man to receive us in the most absolute royal manner, every point of etiquette being most formally observed – special gate reserved for our carriage alone to enter, band ready to strike up the moment we appeared – red cloth – the Goldwin Smiths themselves on doorsteps & hat in hand – all the time ready to fetch anybody we wanted to speak to. It was all very funny.[33]

Five weeks before the ball, Lady Aberdeen wrote, "Mr. Goldwin Smith is quite interested about our Victorian Era Ball." The breach seemed to be healed, and no doubt these gestures of friendliness earned him a spot as "A Knight of Malta," accompanying "Malta" in the prestigious Empire set. Yet he showed his true colours the day before the ball.

> Editor Star – I have just read the item in this evening's *Star* entitled "A Costly Ball" in which you estimate at $15,000 the expenditure upon the Vice-Regal entertainment to be given in the Armouries on Tuesday next. Have you considered that this amount represents only a fraction of the cost of the great ball? It may be worth the while of a very rich lady like Mrs. Bradley-Martin or the Countess of Aberdeen (often, but improperly styled Her Excellency) to squander upon a night's amusement the endowment of a hospital or a college professorship. Her ladyship, with the resources of Coutts' bank at her command, may desire to float through on champagne her pet scheme for the Victorian Order of Nurses; so that her name may be remembered in Canada as Lady Dufferin's still is in India. But is this a fitting time to ask Toronto people to spend money on a "passing show" far more than they can afford? I know of many who are purchasing costumes for Tuesday night with money which is in fact not their own; money which is due to – and therefore practically

> stolen from – the butcher, the baker, and the candlestick maker. Lord Dufferin's great ball at the old Parliament buildings in the winter of 1873-74 impoverished and demoralized Toronto society for at least a decade afterwards. Is the same thing to be repeated in 1897 without a word of protest? – Bystander.[34]

Back in Ottawa, editors rushed to the Aberdeens' defense but noted that a few tailors had indeed probably not been paid. The *Toronto Star* apologized but suggested snobbishly that tradespeople might avoid hardships and delays if they only knew well enough to deal in cash. The editor also cryptically claimed that Smith's byline, "Bystander," had in this case been assumed by an imposter. In reporting on the matter, the Ottawa papers quoted Smith by name, however. Lady Aberdeen's only public twinge of guilt appears in her preface to the souvenir book, where she states that the entire event was achieved "without lavish display or undue expense."

Not all guests had to spend large sums on their garb, however. A group of anxious men arranged with a Mr. Koehler from New York to send an agent and some costumes to Toronto. The "thoroughly reliable" costumier had supplied fancy dress for the celebrated Bradley-Martin ball in New York earlier the same year. The agent was slated to arrive in the city ten days before the ball, but before that, one of the ballgoers exhibited Koehler's sketches in his home and took orders which he forwarded to New York. Ballgoers could also bring him their own sketches, which he sent on to Koehler. The agent arrived at the Rossin House hotel on 20 December with sixty men's costumes, took further orders for two more days, and then returned to New York. He came back to Toronto two days before the ball with what was required, renting his costumes for $10 each. He received orders from many members of the Pictures set, who represented well-known characters; these may have been the easiest costumes to obtain from a rental firm.

There was no Gordon tartan to be found in Toronto, so the Highland Sports set borrowed all they needed – the secretary of the 48th Highlanders applied to Camp Aberdeen in Cornwall for the loan of its members' plaids and brooches. Also in evidence at the ball were many family heirlooms.

> Historic gowns belonging to U.E. Loyalist ancestors, delicate brocades and laces from the French granddames of the old regime; buckles and jewels that are household heirlooms; swords that have helped win Beaver Dam – a thousand priceless family treasures were worn to do honor to Their Excellencies and the Victorian year.[35]

Heirlooms were most in evidence on the guests who were not part of the sets. Miss Elizabeth Baldwin wore a dress of "yellow brocade [with] crimson petticoat, worn in Toronto over a hundred years ago." Mrs. O'Reilly claimed to be wearing a "pink and white satin gown worn at a ball at Government House in 1837." Mrs. Savigny titled her costume "A Dinner Gown My Auntie Wore." Miss Wright portrayed "The Honorable Harriet Cheshire, Maid of Honour to Queen Charlotte," in her "great, great, great grandmother's wedding dress . . . the dress originally belonged to the sister of the character represented." Miss Vickers, the grand-niece of the author Agnes Strickland, described her costume as:

> a gown of flowered silk, with overjacket of rare old lace, worn by her great aunt; the sleeves were caught at the wrists with large

bracelets of Syrian garnets, jewelled girdle, buckles, brooches en suit, about her neck on a large chain was an ancestral miniature of ivory; her hair was dressed in soft loose curls, held by a high tortoise-shell comb of the same period worn by her grandmother, Susannah Strickland (Mrs. Moodie).[36]

These heirloom costumes outside the organized sets shows a degree of compensation; if one were not selected by the vice-regal hosts and the elite set organizers for the places of prestige, one could always draw attention to a noteworthy family history by flaunting jewels and lace flounces from the past.

A souvenir book to commemorate the ball was entrusted to James Mavor, professor of Political Economy at the University of Toronto, who enlisted seventeen Canadian artists to sketch guests and groups in costume. Among the artists were Royal Canadian Academy members George Agnew Reid, Edmund Wyly Grier and Frederic Marlett Bell-Smith (who had sketched the Dufferin ball), as well as Mary Heister Reid, Sidney Strickland Tully, Edmund Morris (the "Cree Chief"), Florence Carlyle and Clara Hagarty. "The chief interest of the book lies in this: that it contains a sufficient number of really masterly drawings to justify the belief that there is a vigorous artistic movement in Canada," Mavor said in his preface. *The Book of the Victorian Era Ball* contained eighty-seven sketches, fourteen of groups and seventy-three of single figures, and a coloured frontispiece entitled "General View of the Ball," by Wyly Grier. It was seen as a milestone, not only because of the quality of the artwork, but also because of the copper and zinc reproduction process. Except for a few sheets of Japanese paper in each copy and the cloth used for binding, the entire book was made in Canada. Rowsell and Hutchins published two versions: a large-format edition of seventy copies, which sold for six dollars, and a smaller-format edition of 550 copies, which sold for two dollars. Copies were given to all the artists, and two were set aside for Queen Victoria and the Prince of Wales. Profits from the book went to Lady Aberdeen's pet cause, the Victorian Order of Nurses, although it did not sell as well as expected.[37]

Lady Aberdeen's patriotic introduction was reproduced in her own handwriting. "It is with grateful feelings of appreciation that the Governor General and I welcome the memorial of a Ball which may justly be considered historic," she began. Mavor's "Advertisement" explained the concept of the book and the reproduction process. In an introduction, Dr. Parkin, who had proposed the ideas, explained the themes depicted at the ball. When Mavor told him that Lady Aberdeen wanted him to write this introduction, Dr. Parkin replied, "I am no good at things of that sort. But the request has all the force of a command in it, and it must be done, and so I must do the best I can." Parkin's draft contained several paragraphs on the benefits of such an artistic entertainment for pleasure-shunning Anglo-Saxons, which were eliminated in the published text.[38]

All guests in the organized sets and their characters were listed at the end of the book. Below the name of each character in the North America set was a verse from a Canadian poem on a related theme. The press singled out the drawings of the beautiful Mary Fitzgibbon as "Princess von Leinengen" and Pelham Edgar as "A Huguenot" as particularly good likenesses. Goldwin Smith, the ungrateful "Knight of Malta," was not sketched. In her drawing of Edith Mowat, Mary Heister Reid may have obscured the assertive line from "Our Lady of the Snows," "We be also a people," to present a more humble aspect to the Queen. The verse following her character name, however, though patterned on Kipling's poem, was again a retort. It was written by a Mr. Langton, possibly her brother-in-law.

Snow-whitened, frost-knit are my winters,
With healing and blessing fraught,
Bracing the arm for vigorous deed,
And the heart for warmer thought.
Snow-watered are my sunny plains,
Whose radiant plenty flows,
To fill both mine and my mother's house,
Said Our Lady of the Snows.[39]

Some of the artists sketched from photographs. When Lady Aberdeen wrote to Mavor forwarding a photo of Lady Marjorie as "Forests of Canada," she requested that it be reproduced and not sketched, and George Reid drew her with almost photographic realism. Perhaps others posed for the artists; the vocalist Augusta Beverley Robinson, "Cod," wrote to Mavor that she had no plans to be photographed as she found the results never justified the considerable effort. In fact, the extent of the photography done for this event is difficult to gauge, since only a few individual and group photographs have been located. Lady Aberdeen requested pictures from all guests and groups as souvenirs, but no album survives. Nor has the flash photograph of the Empire March taken by Lyonde been found; perhaps his camera was damaged along with the curtains (and his hands) in the fire he started. Lyonde later advertised special prices for all those wishing a sitting, and *Leslie's Weekly* published his photograph of the India and Australia set to accompany an article by Faith Fenton. The Aberdeens and David Erskine were taken by Topley when they returned to Ottawa. The *Toronto Globe* published a large photo of the Literature group three months after the ball.

Naturally, the ballgoers yearned to don their costumes again to revive the ambience of this most glamorous event. The opportunity presented itself only two weeks later, when several of the character dances were repeated for spectators at a benefit evening for the Ladies' Work Depository. Members of the Pictures set cheerfully reordered their costumes from Mr. Koehler in New York.

All the papers touted the Victorian Era Ball as the "greatest social event ever held in Canada," an appropriate commemoration of the diamond jubilee of the "greatest sovereign that has ever sat on the British throne." One report went so far as to draw a comparison with the Duchess of Devonshire's ball, held in London in July, 1897, finding the principal differences in the Victorian Era Ball's smaller scale and its absence of monarchs and peers. Yet the report overlooked the most significant difference of all. Like the Toronto event in Canada, the Devonshire House ball was England's most magnificent fin-de-siècle entertainment, and, like Lady Aberdeen, the Duchess claimed that her ball was a diamond jubilee celebration. However, while she did use a few flags and other decorations in keeping with the theme, a sole "Britannia" costume which appeared at the end was the only blatant allusion to Empire. Of course, Lady Aberdeen was not in a position to muster a coterie of British nobility, but neither was she predisposed to such a subtle approach. The Victorian Era Ball fanned imperialist sentiment well beyond the degree deemed appropriate by the Duchess and her titled guests. Moreover, it took little encouragement for Torontonians – and admirers throughout the country – to appropriate Lady Aberdeen's intent.

The structure of this event and its characters and costumes reveal perceptions and beliefs of late-nineteenth-century Canadians about their own identities, the identity of the country, and their country's role within the Empire. While those in the organized sets did not personally choose the themes and characters they represented, their eagerness to carry off the event and their appreciation of it afterwards show the extent to which they concurred with the underlying message. As Canada prepared for the dawn of a new century and assessed its progress, most of its English Canadian inhabitants willingly embraced the ideals of the British Empire. The Empire set showed the vastness of the territory, and it expressed pride in Canada by placing it first and by recognizing Canada's natural wealth as a key contribution to the Empire. The Victorian Costumes set demonstrated pride in the past, albeit a past more British than Canadian. Literature, Inventions, Art, and Sports and Amusements, by underscoring the progress made in the Queen's reign, highlighted the benefits of the imperial connection to Canada. While the Ottawa historical ball had acknowledged that French history and Native peoples made Canada's past unique, this ball made the statement that the country's present and future lay in its relationship to Britain. No wonder, then, that the element of imperial loyalty left the deepest impression. To quote the *Montreal Star*: "It was first, last, and all the way through a Victorian Era Ball. The crimson and the Royal blue permeated the atmosphere. It beat through color and music until every pulse thrilled for the Empire and every voice sang for the Queen."

Socially, too, the Aberdeens' ploy worked. Just a few days later, Toronto saw them off in grand style. Lady Aberdeen returned from a charitable event to find her drawing room packed with all the society matrons, even Lady Kirkpatrick. Silver-haired Mrs. John Strachan read an address that left the usually stiff-upper-lipped Countess so emotional she could hardly reply. The railway car that took the Aberdeens back to Ottawa the next morning was festooned with roses. And waiting at the station to welcome the returning conquerors back to Ottawa was Sir Wilfrid Laurier, the Mayor, and all the Ministers, "quite an unusual compliment."[40]

CHAPTER 5

The Historical Fancy Dress Ball Montreal, 18 January 1898

For one brief night the phantom glory of New France blazed forth again . . . three lost centuries came fluttering back to us in one bewildering scene.[1]

In the last quarter of the nineteenth century, Montrealers with a bent for preserving local history and collecting historical objects and coins shared their interests through the Antiquarian and Numismatic Society. The society was formed in 1862 and incorporated in 1870, and for the next two decades it met regularly and published a journal. The organization drew together prominent English- and French-speaking citizens, whose common interests transcended cultural differences.

The 1890s witnessed a surge of historical interest throughout Canada, and, with historical societies and museums burgeoning across the country, Montreal's well-established organization entered a new phase of activity. The 250th anniversary of the city in 1892 spawned projects including erecting a monument to Chomedy de Maisonneuve, its founder. In 1895, the society acquired permission to use the historic Château Ramezay as a museum and its headquarters. The stone house, built in 1705 by Governor Claude de Ramezay, had housed many successive English and French governors. Throughout the nineteenth century the building accommodated various academic and municipal functions, but it was threatened with demolition when the City of Montreal and then the Antiquarian and Numismatic Society came to its rescue.

Shortly thereafter, in 1896, a group of historically minded women decided to form their own offshoot of the organization, the Ladies' Branch. Their group aimed to "assist in maintaining the Château de Ramezay, to collect historical relics and encourage the study of Canadian history." Like the main organization, the Ladies' Branch brought together French- and English-speaking women who worked in close collaboration. The members chose Lady Aberdeen to be their first Honorary President. The choice was hardly unexpected – Lord Aberdeen was Patron of the Antiquarian and Numismatic Society, and Lady Aberdeen held similar offices in numerous charitable organizations across the country.[2]

To achieve their organization's goals, the members carefully chose means appropriate to the feminine sphere. In November 1896 they held a tea in the Château where they poured and served in eighteenth-century-style dresses. At that time, they made known their intention to hold a "socially and financially successful ball" in February of the next year. Patterned after Lady Aberdeen's Historical Ball, it would raise funds for improvements to the building.

They were thwarted, however, by the president of the Antiquarian Society, Justice François Georges Baby. When the plan was broached, he withheld his cordial support. The women continued to press the issue, and after what was termed "informal and

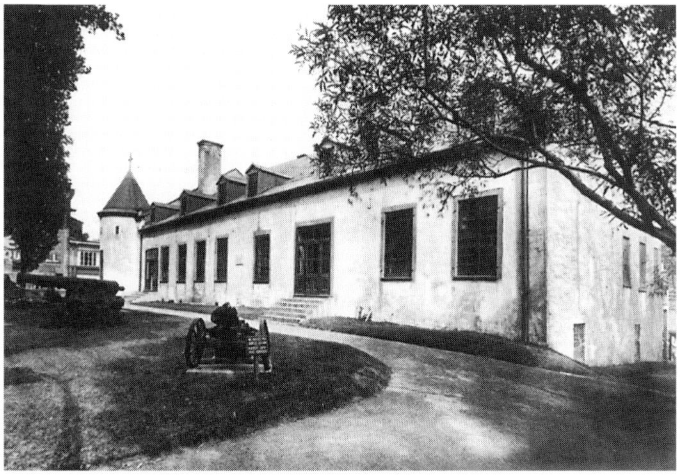

The Château Ramezay. In 1895 this eighteenth-century building became the headquarters for the Antiquarian and Numismatic Society. NAC/C22011

rambling conversation," the Judge formally opposed the plan on two grounds. He feared that the Methodist and Presbyterian administrators of the society were certain to disagree with the idea of a ball, but first and foremost, he harboured a "fear of the deterioration of the tone of the Antiquarian Society, should a ball be held under its auspices." As an alternative, he expounded on the "superior dignity" of historical *tableaux*, perhaps remembering Lady Aberdeen's series of historical scenes in January 1895. Evidently the benefits of the fancy dress balls which followed had not left their mark on everyone.[3]

The Ladies' Branch nevertheless did not modify or abandon the project. In November 1897, about the same time as Lady Aberdeen announced her Victorian Era Ball, they bravely presented the idea again. Judge Baby reluctantly conceded this time, stating that he would not put any obstacles in their way, but that they must bear the entire responsibility themselves. The men of the Antiquarian Society must have been somewhat supportive, however, as they joined, or at least took credit for joining, the many committees.

The Governor General and his wife were easily persuaded to give their support, lending prestige to the event as guests of honour and presiding over it as they had done at their own two balls. Lady Aberdeen's commanding presence in the organization of the event was surely missed, however, as it came off somewhat less polished than the previous two. As if the judge's begrudging approval was not enough to contend with, internal problems handicapped the planning of this ball. By mid-December disagreement had set in, causing the entire Decorating Committee to resign in one fell swoop, quickly followed by several other committees. Though the offense remains unclear, a hasty but sufficiently sincere apology from a guilty member induced everyone to get back on board. Differing ideas on procedure between English and French committee members seem to have been at the heart of the strife. The rumours that followed left "a rather unpleasant impression," which the society attempted to downplay.

By the end of November the printers had churned out some one thousand announcements, six hundred in English and four hundred in French, and in early January the society advertised in the papers. Invitations to the Governor General's balls were sent only to a select group, whereas the goal of this historical ball was to raise funds. Tickets could be purchased by any who could afford the price: five dollars for men, three dollars for women, and three and two dollars for gallery seats. The company remained very select; titled guests, senators and politicians, medical doctors, prominent lawyers, bankers, stockbrokers, and merchants came out in great numbers. The French and English elites mingled easily at the ball, as they did in the Antiquarian and Numismatic Society (except on the Decorating Committee). Though reporters claimed to have seen six hundred people at the event, the final tally by the Ladies' Branch was about four hundred, of which some two hundred and eighty were part of the organized groups. Thus this ball was much smaller than any of the others – only half the size of the Earl of Dufferin's.

The invitation set forth the purpose of the ball:

> The event was designed with a hope of creating in the citizens of Montreal a personal interest in their valuable legacy from the past, the Château de Ramezay, and with a desire to revive for one

> night the château's traditions passed on from the beginning of the eighteenth century to the middle of the nineteenth by a long and illustrious line of French and English governors.[4]

A Costume Committee of three men set the parameters for the dress allowed at the event and published advertisements in the newspapers. These and the invitations left no doubt in anyone's mind as to the choices of costume permitted. All guests were required to appear in fancy dress, and all had to send in descriptions of their proposed costumes in advance of the event. The specific rules applying to *poudré* costume for men showed the organizers' wish to maintain the historical character of the ball, and costumes "approximate to modern" were not allowed. At first, characters had to have been connected with the château from 1705 to 1820, or else be selected from a range of other notable figures in Canadian history from 1534 onwards. When these guidelines proved too stringent, a second newspaper ad appeared, allowing officers in any military uniforms and costume from any nation between 1530 and 1837. Nevertheless, most guests strove to satisfy the earlier set of rules.

The historical groups were not specified initially, and unlike those of Lady Aberdeen's balls, they were drawn up without the assistance of outside scholars or authorities. A much more uneven interpretation ensued, with groups not ordered according to a strict chronology, but rather representing several generations of governors or members of leading families. Within each of the groups, participants were arranged in chronological order for presentations, however. Characters were not described in as much detail in the papers as they had been after the Ottawa or Toronto balls; only names and dates were given. There were some vague references to anxious weeks of research – reading history, consulting records, and examining old paintings – but the relearning of Canadian history was not quite as necessary as it had been when Lady Aberdeen was in charge. In fact, the Costume Committee lightened the burden of research by offering to have sketches made of any costume for a nominal fee. Orders for these "sketches and designs of early Canadian costume" went to the Montreal branch of the Women's Art Association, "so that in every way the work is being facilitated for those wishing to attend the ball."[5]

The Ladies' Branch planned to hold the ball in the château itself, but the lack of sufficient space for the large number of subscribers and the weak floors in the eighteenth-century building were insurmountable obstacles. Instead, they chose the ballroom of the Windsor Hotel. All lamented the lack of historical association in the modern surroundings. "It was only a pity that the handsome walls, modern in the fullest sense of the word, could not have been entirely hidden, but of course that was impossible." Yet the elegant ballroom did offer a few advantages. Its floor "was in excellent condition and glimmered like plate glass." It allowed the costumes to be seen to advantage, a pleasure which the low-ceilinged château with its many small rooms would have denied.[6]

The modern ballroom was transformed with "decorations as historic in character as it was possible to have them." High up on the walls above the windows, blue bunting spangled with fleur-de-lys extended the entire length of the hall, "caught up here and there with striking medallions," oval shields covered with Union Jacks and more fleur-de-lys. From each of the many pillars hung a group of flags, French and British alternately, representing "the old and the new." Above the flags were shields bearing the coats of arms of each of the Governors, French and English, and below the flags were portraits of the Governors, in gold frames, borrowed from the society's portrait gallery for the evening. (These were found "a trifle out of place" on the modern walls of the ballroom.)

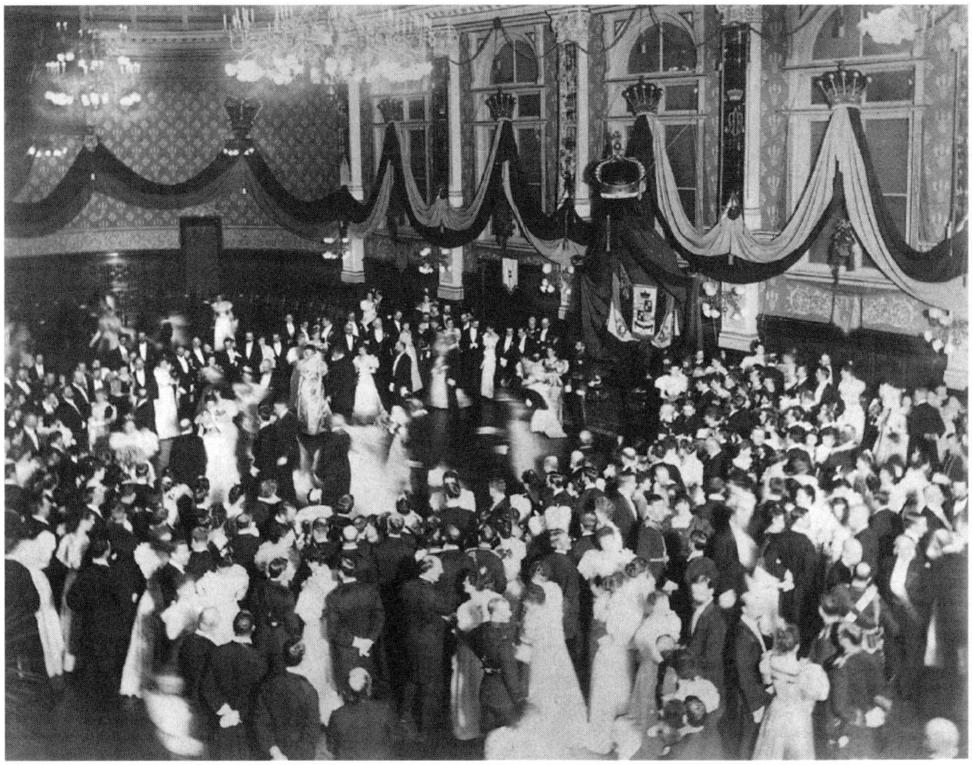

A ball at the Windsor Hotel, 1895, showing the interior of the ballroom. No group photograph was taken at the fancy dress ball; however, this image, with the Aberdeens in the centre, shows how a crowded ball would have looked in the modern setting.
J.C. BENNETT/NAC/PA195507

The low dais was canopied in deep red velvet curtains, edged with gold fringe, falling from a large jewelled "imperial and royal crown." An embroidered royal coat of arms hung at the back, and two pieces of Gobelin tapestry enriched the walls. The empty Louis XV chairs on the fur-carpeted floor awaited the guests of honour, the Earl and Countess of Aberdeen, who breezed into town on the train that evening at six-thirty. The chairs (which, like the tapestries, had been lent by Mme de Bellefeuille-McDonald, the society president and a descendant of the Marquis de Vaudreuil) had originally belonged to the Marquis de Lotbinière, a character represented at the event. The Victoria Rifles Orchestra was stationed opposite the dais on another platform draped in red velvet and strewn with fleur-de-lys.

Anticipation ran high. "Of late nothing else has been talked of in Montreal," Ottawa society columnist Amaryllis wrote. Not long after eight o'clock that evening, a crowd gathered at the entrance to the hotel, anxious to glimpse guests in fancy dress. Police controlled the crowd and kept the street open to traffic. The thermometer hovered near zero Farenheit. The long line of sleighs had formed by nine o'clock, so that by nine-thirty guests filled the hotel corridors before going to the appropriate lettered section in the ballroom. All guests not in historical groups or in *poudré* only were directed to the same section. "The flower-embroidered wide-skirted coats, knee breeches and wigs of the gentlemen, the court trains, high-heeled shoes and powdered hair of the ladies" mingled "in a manner pleasing to the eye." Up in the galleries, lorgnettes wagged as spectators examined the costumes below and awaited the arrival of the vice-regal couple. Lady Marjorie Gordon, escorted by her governess, Miss Wisdom, sat in the gallery this time; she was not part of the pageant and did not dress in costume. Though she had had her first real dances at the Victorian Era Ball and would officially "come out" that summer, doubtless her mother felt that too much party-going was inappropriate for one so young.[7]

Everyone admired the spectacle of seventeenth and eighteenth-century dress:

There was many a fair girl who looked as if she had just stepped from the frame of some old picture, and many a stately dame who seemed to have just dropped from the court of Louis the Fourteenth.[8]

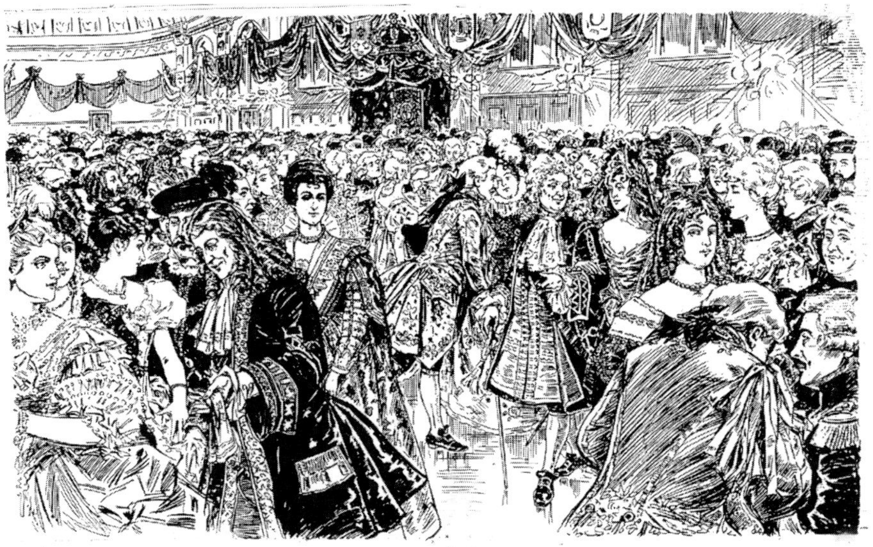

THE HISTORICAL BALL AND LO! IN BRIGHT ARRAY.

"The Historical Ball and Lo! in Bright Array." A sketch from the *Montreal Star*, 19 January 1898.

There were also many historical uniforms on the floor. As at the Ottawa ball, religious characters were tastefully avoided, but at least one reporter noticed the omission: "The sober grey habit of the Recollet, the close black cassock of the Jesuit – had only these been present, there would have been a finished picture of those early illustrious days of La Nouvelle France." No one mentioned a more significant absence. While "Montcalm" was represented, he kept a low profile in civilian dress, and no one portrayed "General Wolfe," although at the historical ball in Ottawa, the two characters had danced side by side in a farandole. Very few French Canadians had been present there, however. In this mixed group, the presence of the two heroes might have made the atmosphere a bit testy. The *Montreal Herald* reporter was most affected by the scene, and as he suspended disbelief he found the historical transformation complete. "It was as if the wine of Canadian history had been drained and gathered in one intoxicating glass. It seemed as if the pages of Parkman had been magically transformed from literature into life." In this historically inebriated state, he was inspired to pen a triolet:

In the days of New France
There were maids fair and courtly,
Who, with air of romance,
In the days of New France,
Stepp'd the stately old dance
With some Governor portly.
Ah those days of New France
When the Maidens were courtly.[9]

About ten o'clock two "richly bedecked" heralds, one in French and the other in English military uniform circa 1755-60, announced the arrival of Their Excellencies with the inaugural bugle call. The guests hurried to their appointed places while a second fanfare signalled the entry of the Earl of Aberdeen, preceded by his aide-de-camp, Captain H.W. Wilberforce. Mr. Quivron lowered his baton and the Victoria Rifles Orchestra "crashed out with the national anthem." As His Excellency made his way through the crowd, "a wave of low curtseys swept down the glittering line of guests." When he had taken his place on his throne chair, the buglers announced the arrival of the rest of the vice-regal party. The heralds led the Countess, followed by the others, to the dais, where the Governor General offered Lady Aberdeen his hand. Making a court bow, she kissed his hand and he then led her to her seat.

The Earl, typically, wore his Windsor uniform. Her Excellency, however, departed

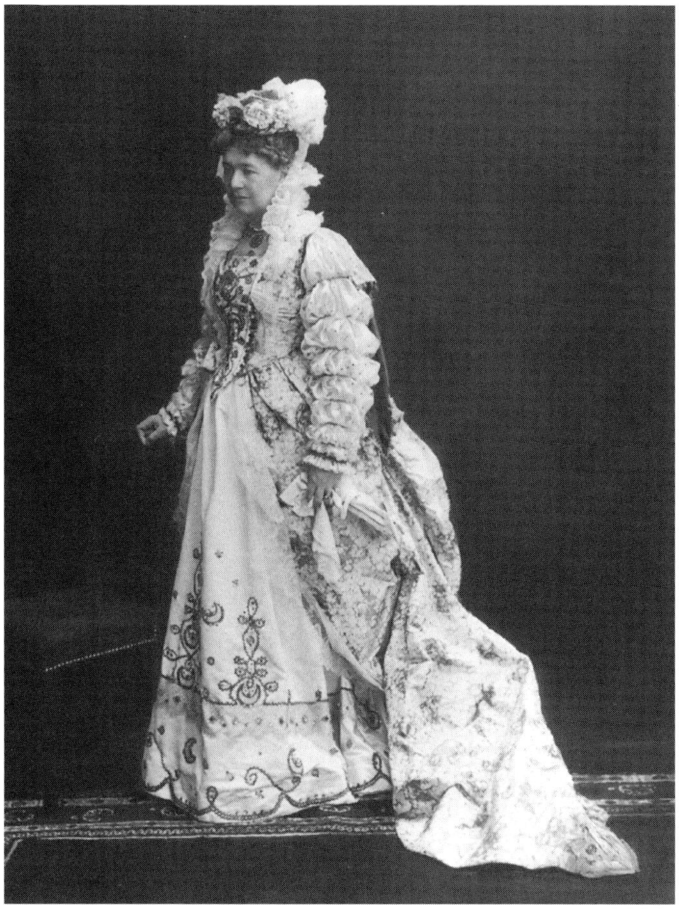

from her usual practice at the balls she had hosted and did not wear court dress. With her love of pageantry and fancy balls, she must have relished the opportunity to choose and wear her own fancy dress costume. Indeed, the enterprising Lady Aberdeen actually designed her dress herself, having it made up by Stitt in Toronto.

The Countess represented the Acadian heroine "Constance de la Tour," the defender of Fort La Tour in 1642 and the wife of Charles de St. Étienne, Sieur de la Tour, Governor of Acadia. She justified her choice by explaining that her maternal grandmother had been a De la Tour, "a descendant of that illustrious line." She had recently requested historians' assistance in ascertaining the nature of her link with the heroine, which had proven to be rather tenuous. Even so, with her experience in conveying political messages through fancy dress balls, Lady Aberdeen knew that her choice of character would be interpreted by English Canada as homage to an aristocratic ancestor and at the same time as "a charming gesture of acknowledgement of French Canadians" by the French press. Beneath a frivolous exterior, Lady Aberdeen once again made a potent political statement. She knew what pleased French Canadians, though she was suprised at her popularity in Quebec and at times found it almost amusing. "These people are so ridiculously pleased at anyone speaking their language," she once wrote after an enthusiastic response to a speech she nervously made in French.[10]

Reporters had a field day describing her costume, though they disagreed over whether it was Louis XIII or Louis XIV in style; in fact, it incorporated elements more in keeping with sixteenth-century costume. That even she would create such a loose interpretation reveals something of late-Victorian attitudes toward authenticity; it seems to have been sufficient that all agreed that the dress was magnificent and that she appeared regal and stately, "being naturally the cynosure of all eyes."

The presentation of all the guests began immediately, as they filed up two by two and were introduced to Their Excellencies by their character names. Bows and curtseys were made with much grace. This procedure took almost an hour, according to one reporter. Another reporter, disgruntled at receiving shabby treatment from the doormen, due, he felt, to his being French Canadian, claimed that this segment of the event was a complete failure. According to him, the groups were not properly organized at their lettered stations, and so the Master of Ceremonies was left standing in confusion holding a long but useless list of names. He added that the presentations were dropped early on. The truth of the matter is impossible to know; however, the statements of the misused reporter should be taken with a grain of salt, since he also claimed that he was not even let in the door. He may have been mistreated, but two other staff members from *La Patrie* were among the guests at the ball.[11]

The first set, as in Ottawa, was a small group of Norsemen. This group did not fit into any segment of the ball's strict time span or geographical area as outlined in the invitation and advertisement. A slip of paper among the minutes of the organizational meetings bears notes for several last minute details including, scribbled and underlined at the top, "4 Norse Men, 4 Norse Maidens." Perhaps it was an after-

Opposite: Lady Aberdeen as "Constance de la Tour," wife of Charles de St. Etienne, Sieur de la Tour, Governor of Acadia. The *Montreal Herald* went wild over Lady Aberdeen's costume. "The bodice and *polonaise*, together with the long train, are of a quaint brocaded taffeta of pale rose pink, with bunches of old fashioned roses and green leaves. The stomacher of white satin, embroidered in a design with gold bullion, sapphire and emerald cabochons, is pointed and bordered with a jewelled band, and also a frill of fine French lace which widens as it approaches the neck, where it forms a great upstanding lace ruffle. The sleeves of white satin striped gauze are cut into a series of puffs by bands of gold, and from the shoulders hang pendant sleeves of the brocade lined with green satin, as is also the train. The handsomest part of this gown, however, is the white satin petticoat *en train*, which is embroidered in front with a panel of jewels of large design, made still richer by a flounce of gold and jewelled lace, while a garland design in gold and jewels forms a deep border on the edge of the skirt. A cap of gold lace, with coronet effect, in the front a twist of green satin, and some pink roses, is decorated at one side, with three waving plumes, while from the back hangs a flounce of lace." (19 Jan. 1898) NPA/MMCH

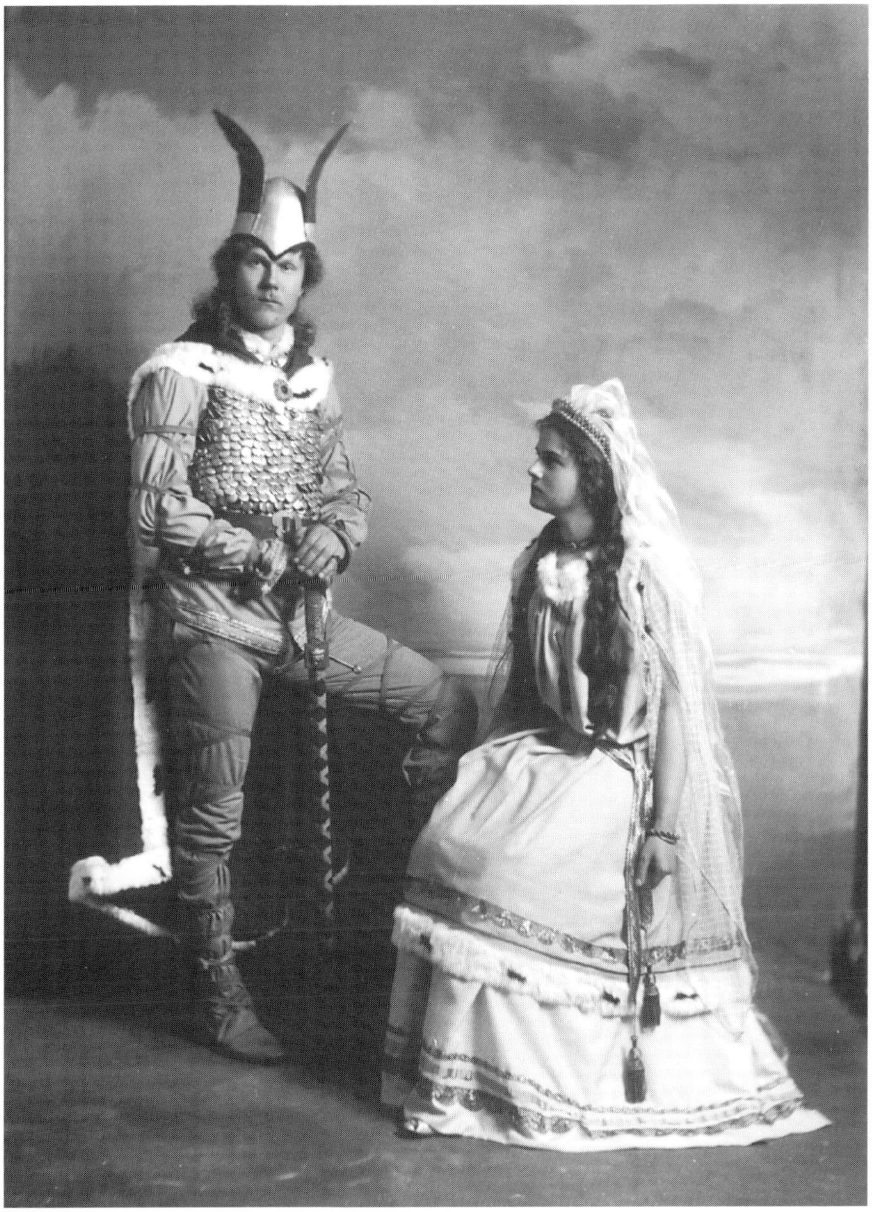

Herbert and Naomi Molson as "Thyrker" and "Freydis." Their costumes are much like those the Vikings had worn in Ottawa two years earlier. NPA/MMCH

thought based on the appeal of the group at the Ottawa event. Among the Vikings were Herbert and Naomi Molson, who belonged to one of Montreal's oldest and wealthiest families. Herbert would become president of Molson's Breweries following the death of his father. The only photographed male member of the group, he wore a costume virtually identical to those worn by the Norsemen in Ottawa, complete with the impromptu coat of mail. A long dark cape trimmed with ermine hung from his shoulders. His sister Naomi dressed like the Ottawa Viking women in a white and pale blue gown with gauze sleeves, an overskirt edged with ermine, and a long gauze veil. She wore her hair in two long thick braids. The entire group of eight was mentioned twice in the papers, once for their "barbaric splendour and crude-looking fittings" and again for their "most becoming" and "quaint" costumes.

Second came the Jacques Cartier group. A.J. Ferguson was "Cartier" himself, in a "brown costume of [the] Middle Ages." His wife, one of the organizers of the set, was "Anne of Austria" in "an exceedingly pretty and becoming gown" of white satin,

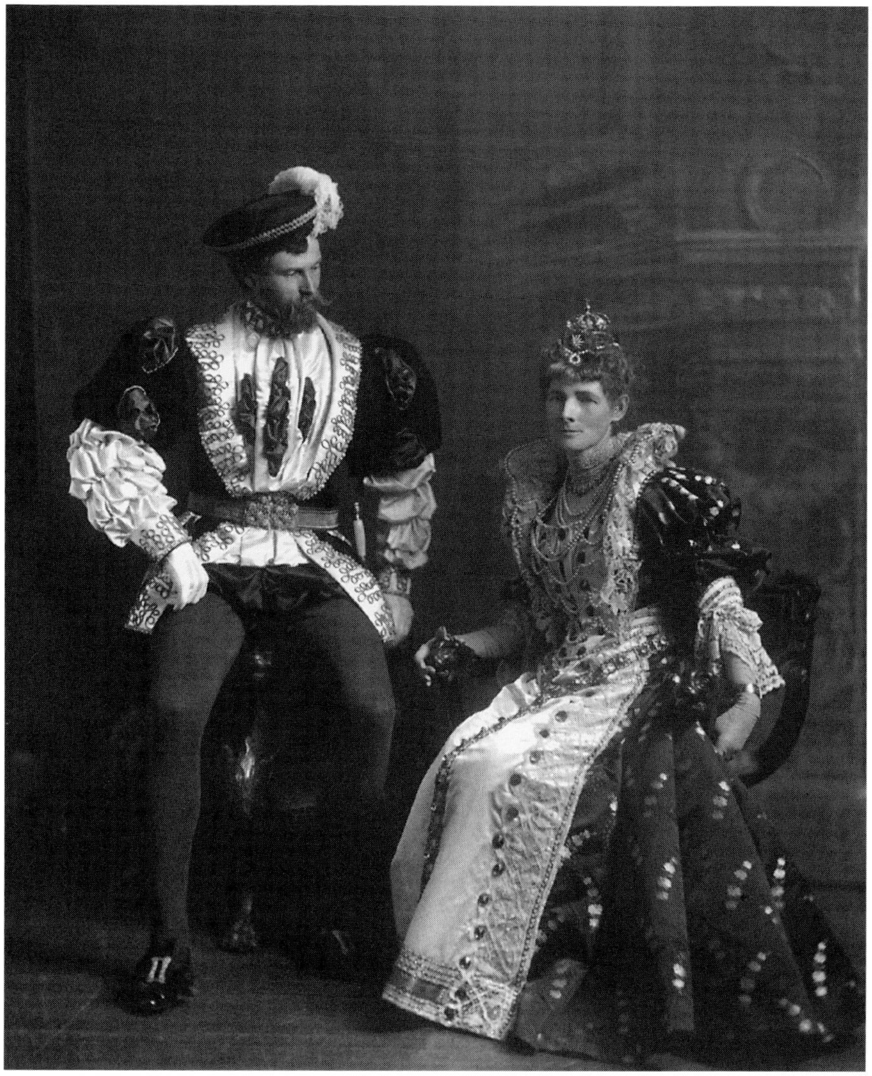

Opposite: Marguerite Thibaudeau (née Lamothe), who organized and led the French Vice-Roys and Governors as the "Marquise de Vaudreuil." Her dress with Watteau back and paniers was in a cream brocade with "Louis XV designs." She wore her hair *poudré* with a diamond star attaching her feather aigrette. NPA/MMCH

Mr. and Mrs. George Marler as "Francis I" and "Marguerite de Valois." Mrs. Marler wore "black and pink brocaded satin, front of pink satin and white lace, Medici collar of lace," a costume she based vaguely on the Marguerite de Valois dress worn by the Princess of Wales at the Duchess of Devonshire's ball. (*Montreal Star*, 19 Jan. 1898) NPA/MMCH

with the front embroidered in amethysts, and a diamond coronet." The much photographed George Marler represented "Francis I," while his wife, the other set organizer, was "Marguerite de Valois." Rather than turning to a representation of her character for her inspiration, Mrs. Marler claimed to be wearing "a copy of the costume worn by the Princess of Wales at the Duchess of Devonshire's ball" just seven months earlier. The costumes bear a few similarities in sleeve design and silhouette and in the ropes of pearls draped across the front, but they were in fact quite different, the Princess of Wales' being white while Mrs. Marler's was black. If Mrs. Marler referred to a newspaper illustration, she may have felt her copy was quite accurate. In any case, the appeal of royalty evidently operated on two levels for her.[12]

Mrs. Arthur Hardy, the wife of the Premier of Ontario, was simply "A Court Lady of 1534," but anachronistically mentioned that her dress was the same one she had just worn to the Victorian Era Ball, where she had been part of the "Victorian Costumes" set – a three-hundred-year difference. Her early nineteenth-century costume was a pink satin Empire gown with a train of crimson brocade.

Nearly eighty people made up the next and largest group, the French Viceroys and Governors, which spanned more than two centuries, from 1542 to 1763. Leading this set was Marguerite Thibaudeau, one of the founders of the Ladies' Branch and the

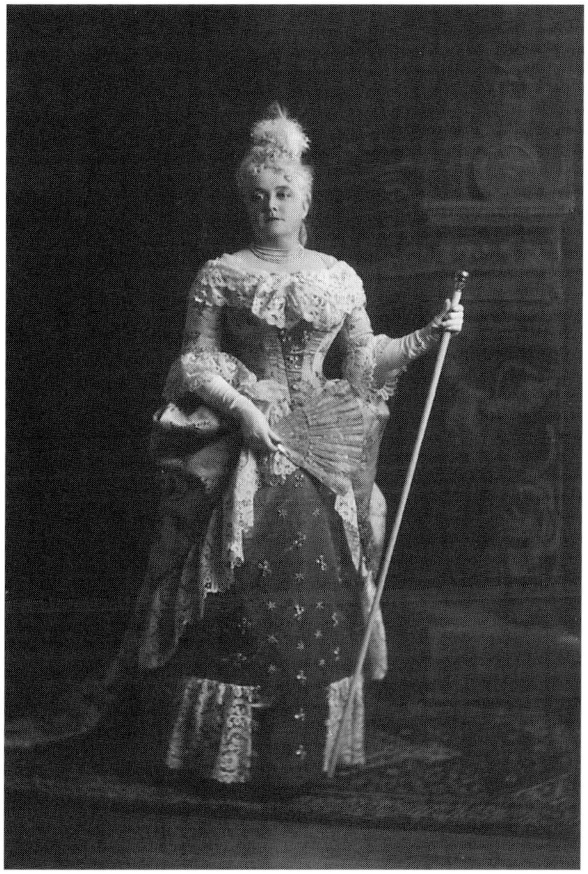

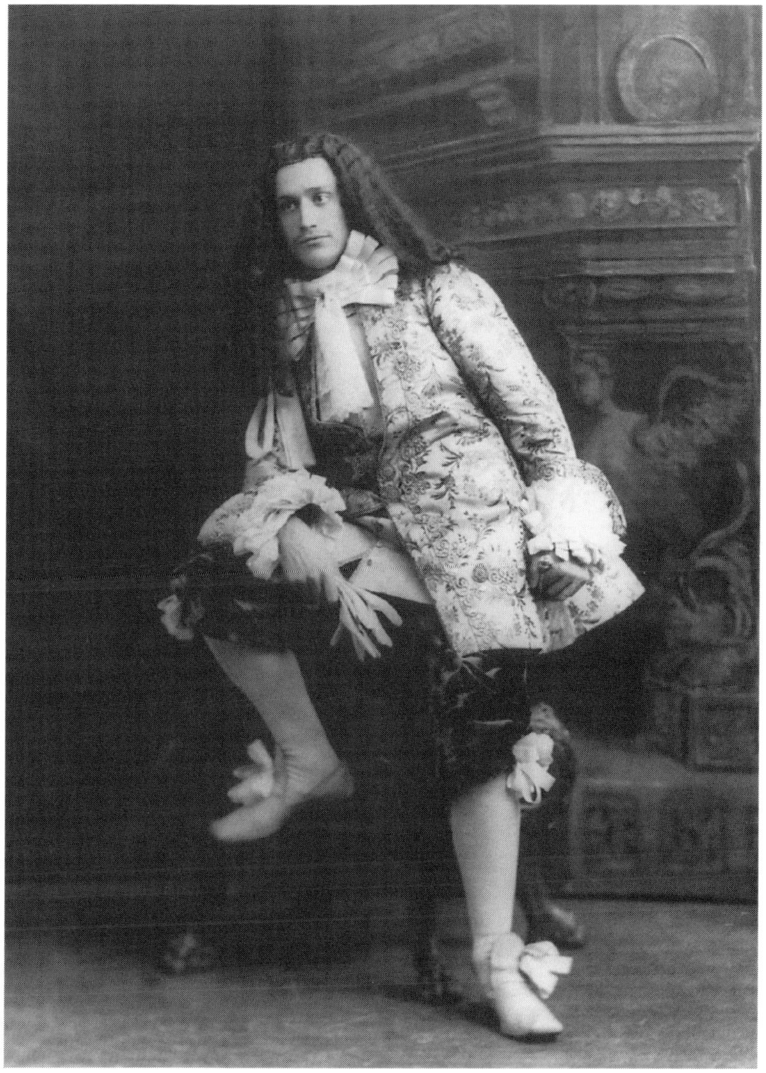

wife of Senator J. Rosaire Thibaudeau. She became well known in Montreal for her contributions to charities such as Notre Dame Hospital, the Women's Historical Society and the Parks and Playgrounds Association, and she supported Lady Aberdeen's pet causes, the National Council of Women and the Victorian Order of Nurses. She is included (among very few women) in *Canadian Men and Women of the Time* (1912), not just as the wife of her husband, but as a philanthropist in her own right. Mme Thibaudeau came as "The Marquise de Vaudreuil, 1710-1725" in cream brocade over a pink satin underskirt. If her fabric appeared particularly magnificent, perhaps it was because her husband was also head of a dry goods firm. He accompanied his wife as "The Marquis de Vaudreuil," in a red velvet eighteenth-century-style suit.

Possibly the most elaborately dressed man in the set was Pierre Beullac as "Jean de Lauzon," wearing a costume created by his father. Raymond Beullac had emigrated to Montreal from France in 1874 and attained distinction as a decorator of churches; then he expanded his business to include decoration of ballrooms and the like and for public and religious festivals, as well as renting fancy dress costumes. These interests led him to start a short-lived Canadian Historical Museum in the early 1890s, featuring wax figures *à la* Madame Tussaud, dressed in appropriate costumes which, of course, he created himself. He was one of the two costumiers summoned to Ottawa by Lady Aberdeen in 1896, and she also hired him to decorate the Senate Chamber for the Historical Fancy Dress Ball. Here on his home turf, he was the costumier of choice for this ball, and he was recommended on the invitation itself.

Pierre Beullac as "Jean de Lauzon," in "a very charming costume of old gold brocade, in blue and gold with yellow satin knee breeches, cravat, collar, and ribbon noeuds d'epaules and wig en peruke." If the young lawyer appears excessively frizzed and beribboned, it is no doubt due to the fact that he was a walking advertisement for his father's costume rental firm. (*Montreal Star*, 19 JAN. 1898) NPA/MMCH

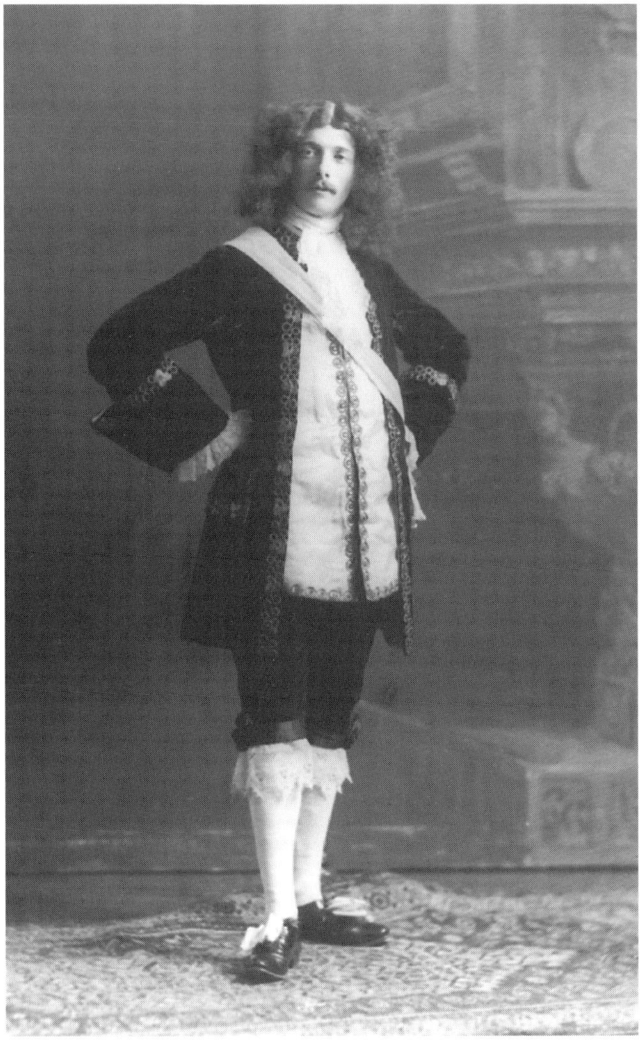 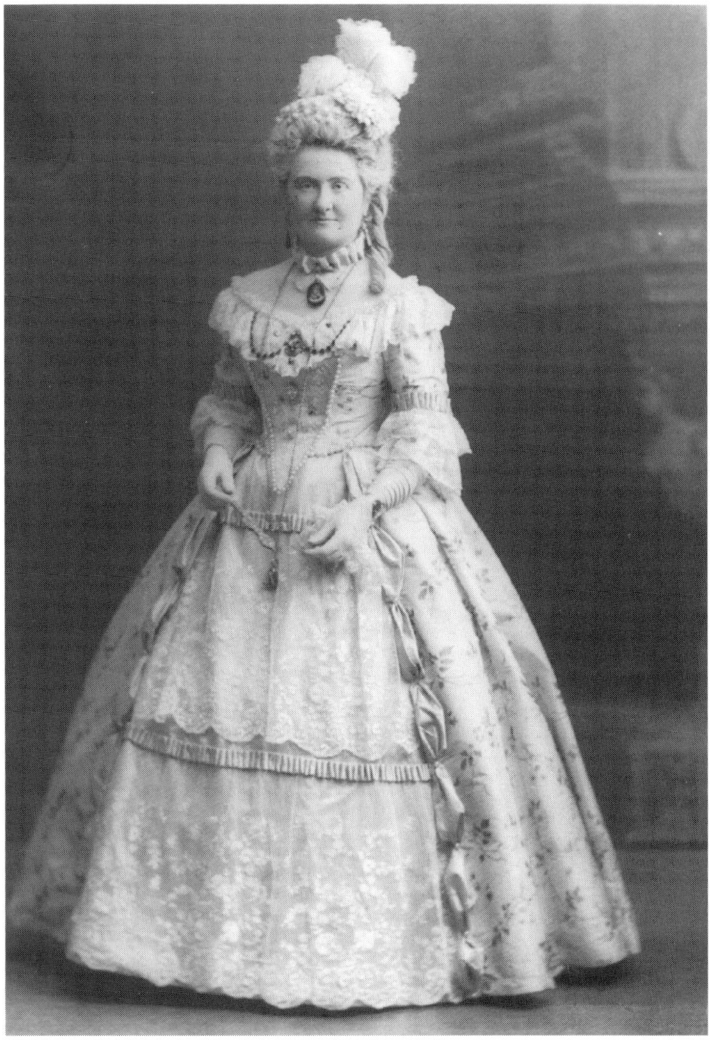

Aimé Geoffrion, as "Daniel Rémy de Courcelles." This son-in-law of Mme Thibaudeau rented his red velvet costume trimmed with gold lace from Beullac. It is the same costume rented to Charles Berkeley Powell in Ottawa two years earlier (*see page 83*). NPA/MMCH

Beullac collaborated with a reporter from *La Presse* to give a sneak preview of the garments he was renting. Several costumes worn two years earlier in Ottawa made their appearance at this ball, some in Pierre Beullac's own set. Another young lawyer, Aimé Geoffrion, as "Daniel Rémy de Courcelles," a seventeenth-century personage, was attired in a red silk velvet costume with gold trimmings, rented from Beullac. A long wig completed his attire, which had been worn with different accessories by Charles Berkeley Powell as the "Marquis of Tracy" in Ottawa.

The women in the group represented governors' wives. Harriet Wheeler portrayed another "Marquise de Vaudreuil" of the Louis XV period. "A woman of strong individuality and wonderful energy," Mrs. Wheeler was well-known for charity work, including raising funds for the Ladies' Benevolent Institution and organizing the Montreal Society of Decorative Art (with objectives much like those of the Women's Exchange in Toronto). Her eighteenth-century costume was thought to be "perfectly correct," though it had a circular hoop skirt rather than paniers. Mme Gélinas as the "Marquise de Guercheville" was also rather anachronistic in a sixteenth-century style dress with a ruff at the neckline, described as a "sumptuous costume from the workroom of Madame Goold," a local dressmaker.

Antique jewellery and accessories were out in full force in this set. "Many an old jewel box had been robbed of its family heirlooms for the occasion. One could catch

Opposite: Harriet Wheeler as a later "Marquise de Vaudreuil," wearing a pink satin hoop skirt trimmed with antique lace flounces and an overdress of pink and white flowered silk. Despite the fact that hoops were a mode of the mid-nineteenth century, not the eighteenth, Mrs. Wheeler's dress was said to be a "a perfectly correct Pompadour costume." Her patches – small pasted-on beauty spots on her face – are typical with an eighteenth-century-style dress and powdered hair. NPA/MMCH.

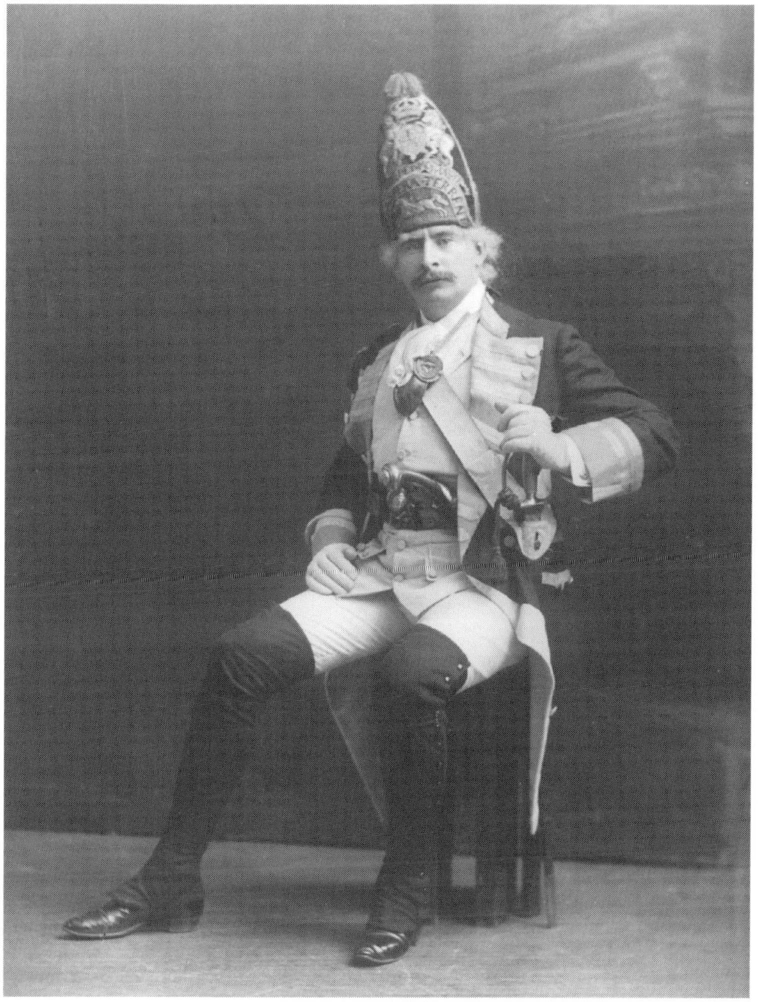

Norman Leslie as "Captain James Leslie," his ancestor, wearing "white silk trousers, black gaiters, scarlet coat, yellow facings, silver epaulettes, white waistcoat, scarlet waist belt, white buckskin gloves. Headdress of the Grenadier guards, sword cross belt and pistols." The rare headdress dates from the 1750s, while the uniform was made by Henry Morgan & Co., no doubt for the ball. NPA/MMCH

sight of dozens of rare old jewels and miniatures and little old fashioned fans," observed the *Montreal Herald*. Miss Louisa Monk, as "Helen de St. Ours," said her costume was inspired by a miniature of her character. She wore two miniatures of eighteenth-century men, one on a ribbon around her neck and the other pinned to her bodice. But there were more than heirloom accessories at the ball:

> A debutante was wearing, strange to say, a gown in which her mother made her debut, and then it was a heirloom. It belonged to a lady whose husband was attached to the court of Louis XV.

The debutante, Maud Terroux, wore one of the two most striking heirlooms of the evening. She portrayed her ancestor, "The Baronne de Beaumouchel," in an eighteenth-century pink silk dress, extant today. Only one other guest's attire might have vied for attention with hers. Norman Leslie represented his ancestor, "Captain James Leslie of the 15th Regiment of Foot," in "exactly the same uniform he wore at the taking of Quebec." Actually, his Grenadier's cap was from this period, while his gorget, shoulder and sword belonged to a more recent ancestor in the early nineteenth century, and his uniform had been made for the ball.[13]

Two young women in the set were particularly attractive, perhaps because their attire differed from the eighteenth-century styles worn by so many of the women. One of the belles of the ball was Eugénie Duhamel, as "A Vivandière of the Royal Roussillon Brigade." She wore a costume with a very military air and a black tricorne over her powdered hair. The ever-popular "vivandière" character had an extensive entry in the 1896 edition of *Fancy Dresses Described*, and by linking the costume to a specific regiment, Mlle Duhamel adapted it to the ball's theme. Mlle de Beaujeu also dressed very differently as "Jeanne Mance," the founder of a seventeenth-century Montreal hospital; though not a nun, she was viewed as a quasi-religious figure. Despite her demure grey velvet gown, white shoulder cape and cap trimmed with guipure lace, she "managed to have no end of partners belonging to worldly pursuits of many kinds." Her plain costume came closer than any other to religious dress.

But the character in this set who stood out among all the others at the ball was

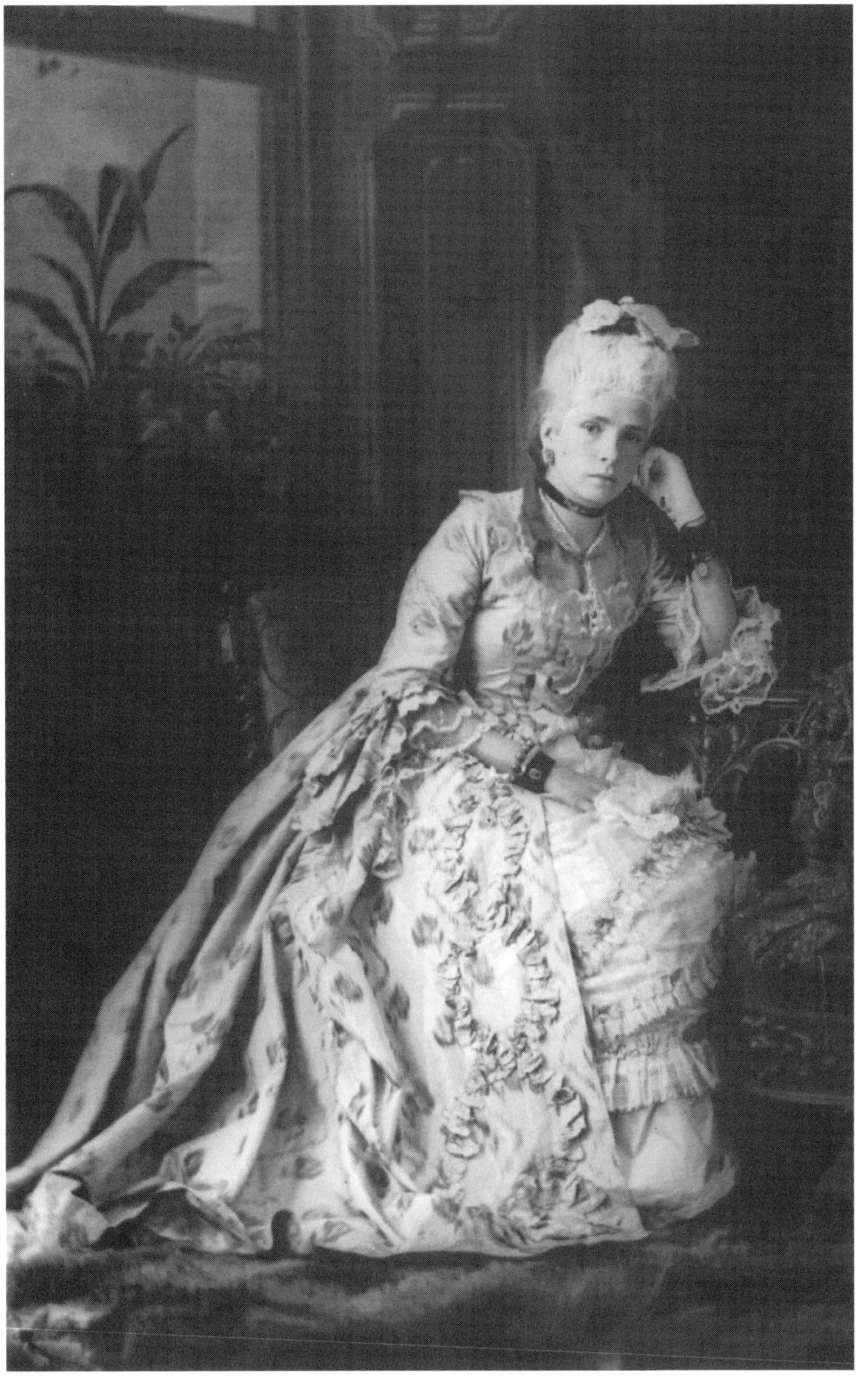

Miss Rolland, the mother of Mlle Terroux, at age sixteen in 1872 or 1873, wearing the same dress as fancy dress. NPA/MMCH

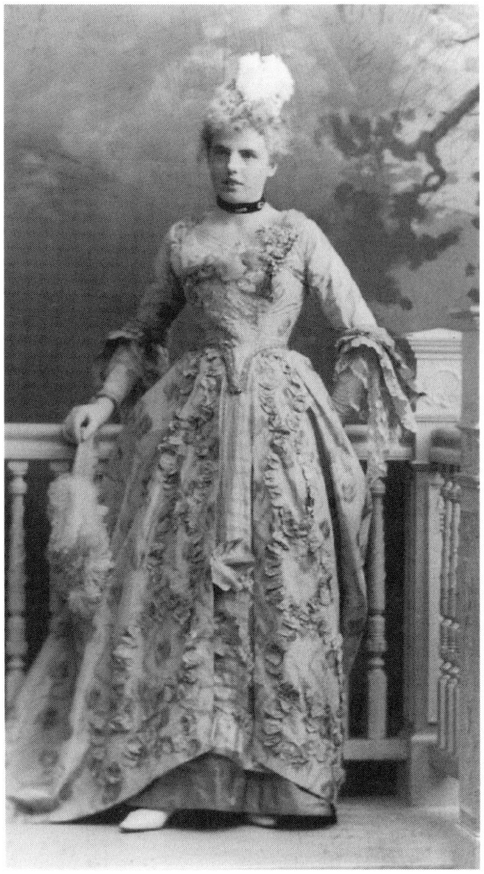

Maud Terroux as the "Baronne de Beaumouchel," her ancestor. She posed for four different photographs in this undescribed dress, whose ill-fitting bodice, uneven hemline, and *chiné* fabric make it unmistakably identifiable as an eighteenth-century garment, albeit one considerably altered. The flowers and puffs of tulle on the bodice, as well as the lace insert, are all additions made to the original for fancy dress purposes, a common practice. The photographs led to the extant garment, dating from the 1770s, in the McCord Museum of Canadian History. NPA/MMCH

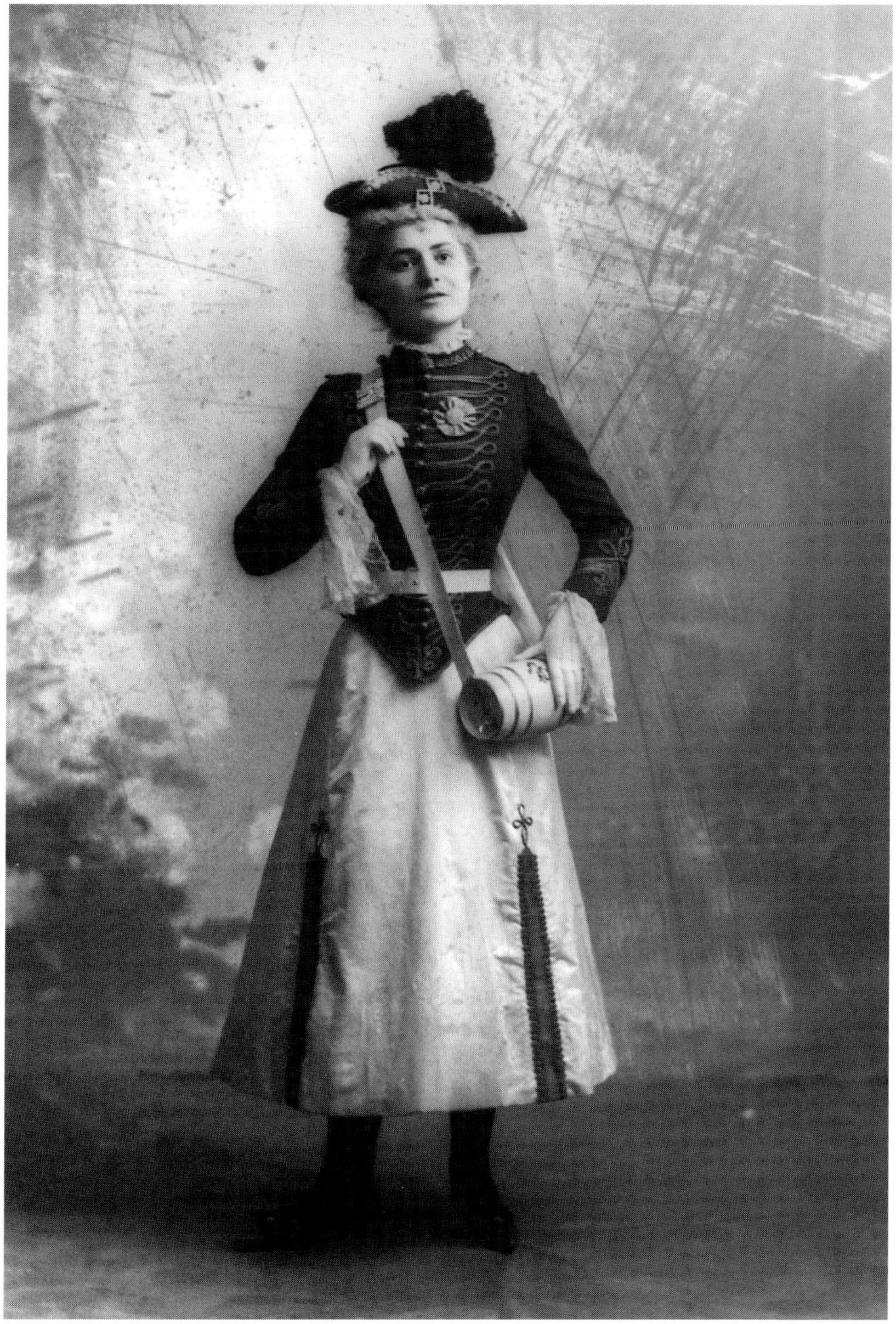

Eugénie Duhamel as "Vivandière of the Royal Roussillon Brigade." She wears a red bodice and white skirt, both trimmed with gold, and a white leather belt, and she carries a small keg. The black tricorne hat adds a masculine touch to the vivandière costume, which probably lay behind its appeal. NPA/MMCH

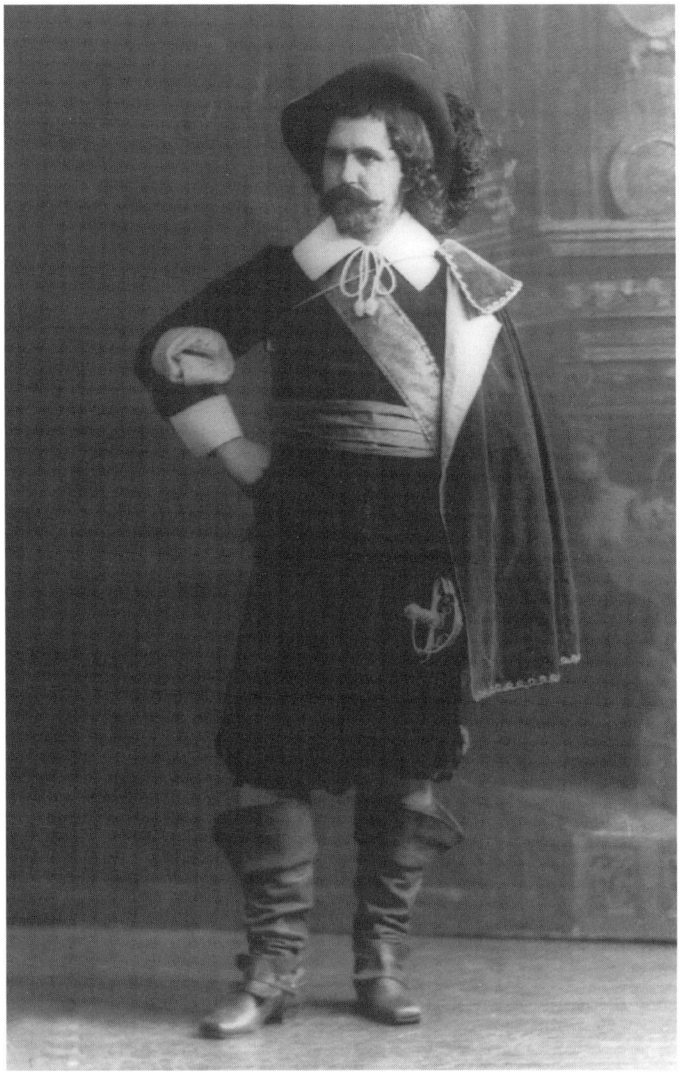

Dr. Robert Wilson as "Samuel de Champlain," "one of the finest characters at the ball. His costume was not only historically perfect down to the smallest detail, he was the living presentment of the first Governor General of Canada. His costume in the style of Louis XIV was of rich dark red velvet, with sleeves *crevé* in old gold satin, short mantle of dark purple velvet, sash and cross belt, boots, all in character, as was also the long wig." (*Montreal Star*, 19 Jan. 1898) NPA/MMCH

Dr. Robert Wilson, a specialist in electrotherapy and radiotherapy, who managed to hit upon the exceptional combination of appropriate character and accurate and becoming costume which was so sought after by those who attended fancy dress balls. As "Samuel de Champlain, 1633," he was singled out as one of the most striking of all the characters. A member of the three-man costume committee, he exemplified accuracy with his "historically perfect" garb. One suspects that it was Dr. Wilson's personality which made the portrayal such a success, for the costume was rented from Beullac.

The next set, Explorers, Discovers and Visitors, was a catch-all for others from the same time span who were not viceroys or governors. It included two women of the Van Horne family, though Sir William Van Horne, president of the Canadian Pacific Railway and perhaps the wealthiest and most famous Montreal resident, was conspicuous by his absence. Mary Van Horne, his sister, made a reference to the family's home town of Joliet, Illinois, by coming as "Madame Jolliet," the wife of explorer Louis Jolliet. She was accompanied by Dr. Herbert Birkett, a laryngologist, as "Henri de Tonti." Both of their costumes survive and bear witness to the local business people who profited from the event. The label of Montreal dressmaker Miss K. Cunningham is in her dress, while that of Henry Morgan & Co., a Montreal department store, is in his blue velvet coat and pink silk waistcoat.

Morgan's department store had advertised profusely before the event. Ads in *La Presse* offer the well-known history of costume by Albert Racinet, in six volumes with "thousands of coloured illustrations," for consultation. Ads in the English papers describe a similar source, though not by title; it may have been part of the same series. "In connection with the Historical Ball . . . we beg to announce having imported a Book containing 500 COLORED DESIGNS OF COSTUMES as worn by men and women in the 14th, 15th, 16th, 17th, and 18th centuries." The volumes were displayed in the men's tailoring department and the ladies' dressmaking department. Morgan's was prepared to make up costumes based on the illustrations "at specially low rates"; Dr. Birkett evidently took advantage of the enticing offer.[14]

Miss Van Horne's sister-in-law, Lady Van Horne, the former Adaline Hurd, came as "A Colonial Dame," another reference to the family's American roots. She wore a "most becoming costume" of grey satin damask with pink stomacher and petticoat. She went further afield for her dress, which bears a Lord and Taylor label from New York. Family history claims that her very white coiffure was a wig. Both of the Van Horne dresses and the Birkett costume are very well-constructed garments showing little sign of wear, which confirms that they were made especially for this event and seldom if ever worn later. The extant garments, along with the newspaper reports, suggest that magnificent costumes were the rule at this ball. Without Lady Aberdeen reminding guests to keep expenditure down, and in a wealthier locale than either Ottawa or Toronto, the pressure to appear worthy of the occasion probably escalated.

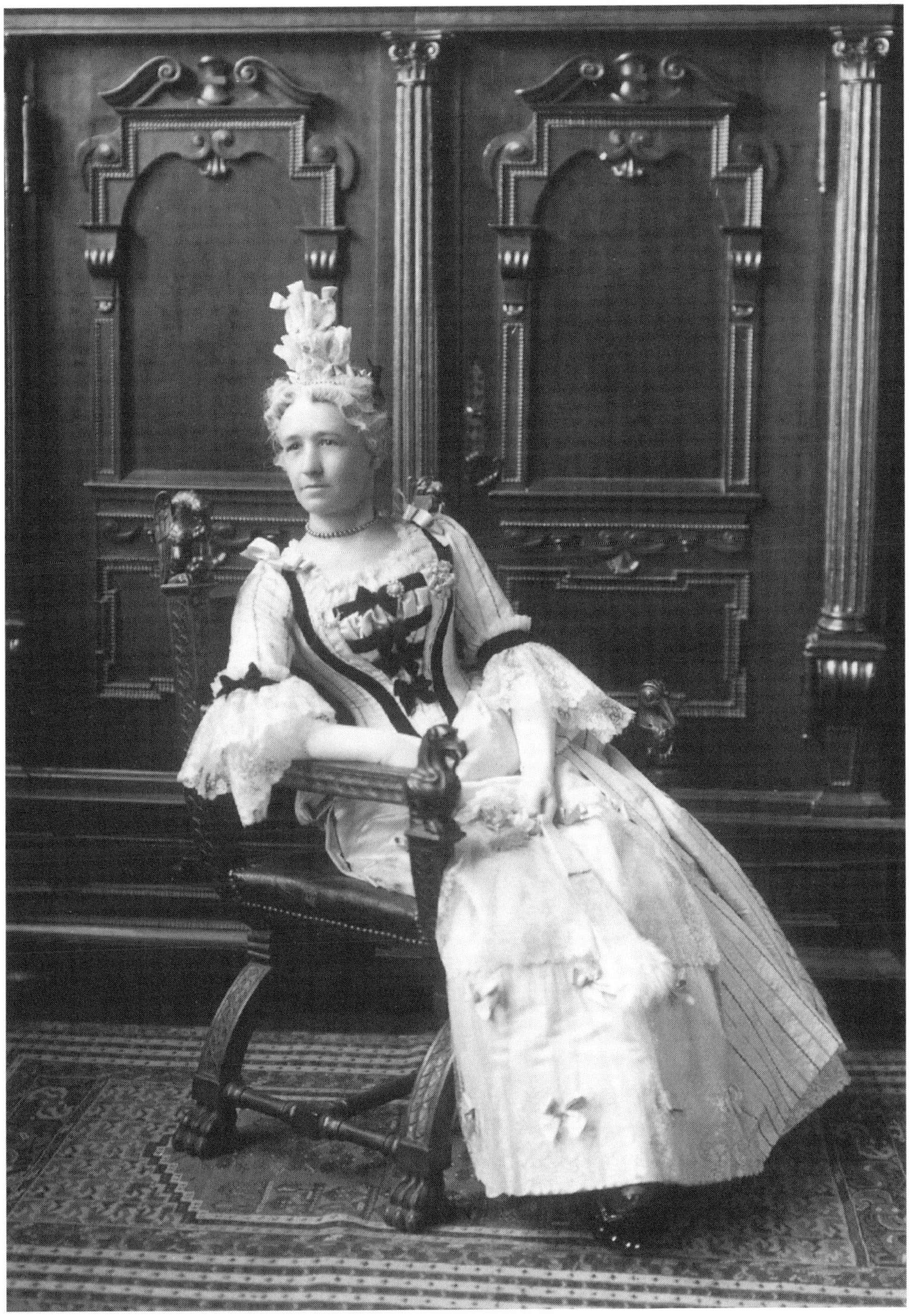

Mary Van Horne as "Mme Jolliet." The sister of railway magnate William Van Horne wears a costume of mauve and white striped brocade over a white satin petticoat trimmed with lace flounces and mauve rosettes. Black velvet bows *à l'échelle* adorn the bodice front. Perched on top of Miss Van Horne's *poudré* hair is a small lace *fontanges*. A silver ribbon rosette pinned to her bodice matches one worn by her partner, Dr. Herbert Birkett, as "Henri de Tonti." His was still pinned to his costume when it was acquired by the Marsil Museum. NPA/MMCH

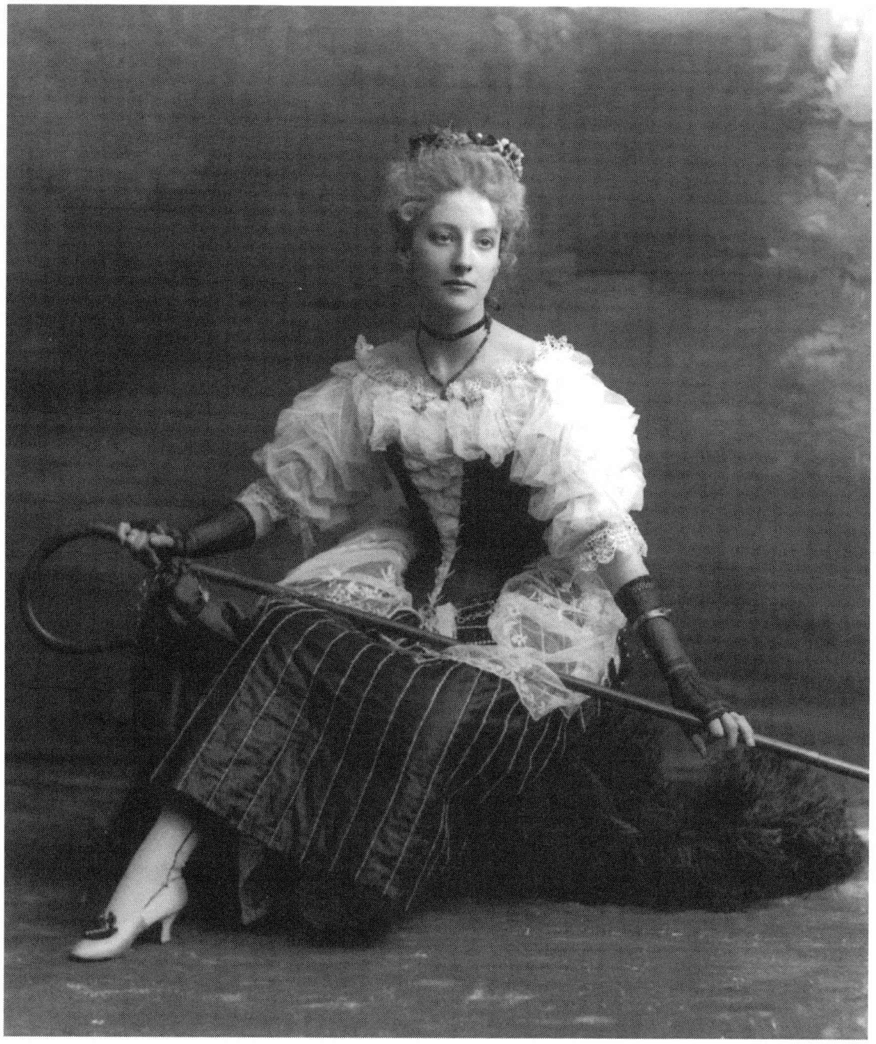

Bearing out this assumption is the fact that there were very few peasant characters at this event. Miss V. McCallum as "Marie Le Gardeur de Répentigny" chose to dress "as a shepherdess in red and silver," with elaborate frilled muslin sleeves. The colour, the satin fabric, and the elaborate style set her miles apart from the more austere Acadian peasants at the Ottawa ball.

The Lemoyne Family of Longueuil set included famous members of one of Canada's most illustrious early families, and among the group were many actual Lemoyne descendants. Characters ranged from seventeenth-century to early nineteenth-century personages. Lady Lacoste (née Marie-Louise Globensky), a director of the Women's Historical Society, had organized the set; she was stunning in a mauve silk panier dress as "Madame Lemoyne." Her husband, Sir Alexander Lacoste, was Chief Justice of the Province of Quebec; he described his very plain garb as "A Judge's Costume." Their sons and daughters and their fiancés made up a large part of the set.

Michael Foley, whose daughter had married into the Lacoste family, dressed as "Charles William Grant, the 4th Baron of Longueuil." Foley noted that the present holder of the title, residing in Scotland, was a relative on his mother's side. His costume included "buckled shoes with bows of crimson satin ribband and red heels," which had indicated noble status in the eighteenth century. Margaret Foley, not to be eclipsed by her husband's claim to noble ancestry, pointed out that she was wearing the family jewels of the Macdougalls, her ancestors. Mr. Foley owned extensive property in Montreal and was founder and proprietor of the *Journal of Commerce*, to which he was extremely devoted.

Miss V. McCallum as "Marie Le Gardeur de Répentigny." Interpreting her character as a shepherdess, she wears a very romantic eighteenth-century-inspired red and silver dress with Watteau pleats at the back and a lace overskirt. Her crook is always a requisite accessory for this type of costume. NPA/MMCH

Other heirlooms appeared in this set; Frances Tessier, the wife of a prominent Quebec City judge, Jules Tessier, represented the seventh Baroness in a white embroidered muslin Empire dress belonging to one of her ancestors. She struck a pose reminiscent of Madame Récamier for one photograph, complete with a shawl draped over her chair. Her sister, Miss Barnard, came in another heirloom dress of yellow silk trimmed with pearls and lace, also from the early nineteenth century. The description of Miss Barnard's dress, matched with her photograph, resulted in the discovery of the extant garment in the McCord Museum of Canadian History.

Dr. Louis de Lotbinière Harwood, a gynecologist, came as his ancestor "The Marquis de Lotbinière"; the Harwood family were the seigneurs of Vaudreuil. He wore "a correspondingly handsome costume of yellow brocade." Mme de Lotbinière Harwood, as the "Marquise de Lotbinière," was admired for her prominent and "very

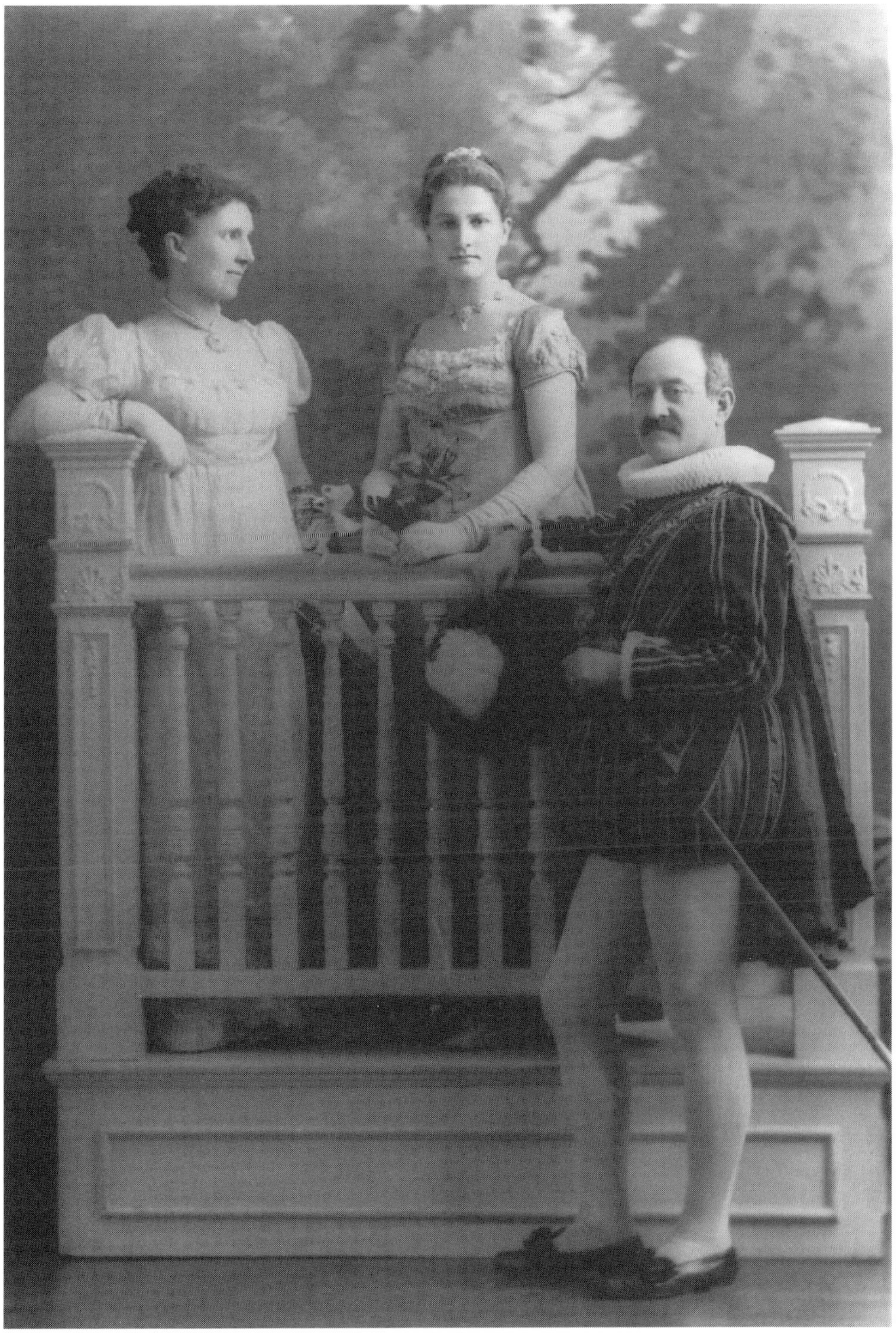

Frances Tessier, Miss Barnard, and M. de St. Phalle. The two sisters appeared in heirloom garments from the early nineteenth century. Miss Barnard, centre, wears "a dress of yellow Levantine silk, trimmed with pearls and English thread lace, antique necklace and ornaments of seed pearls and topaz, which articles are nearly a hundred years old and had been worn by an ancestor, Mrs. Barnard, at the time of the Empire, 1812." M. de St. Phalle wore the shortest breeches of the evening, and in all his photographs he shows the same pride in his appearance. (*Montreal Star*, 19 Jan. 1898) NPA/MMCH

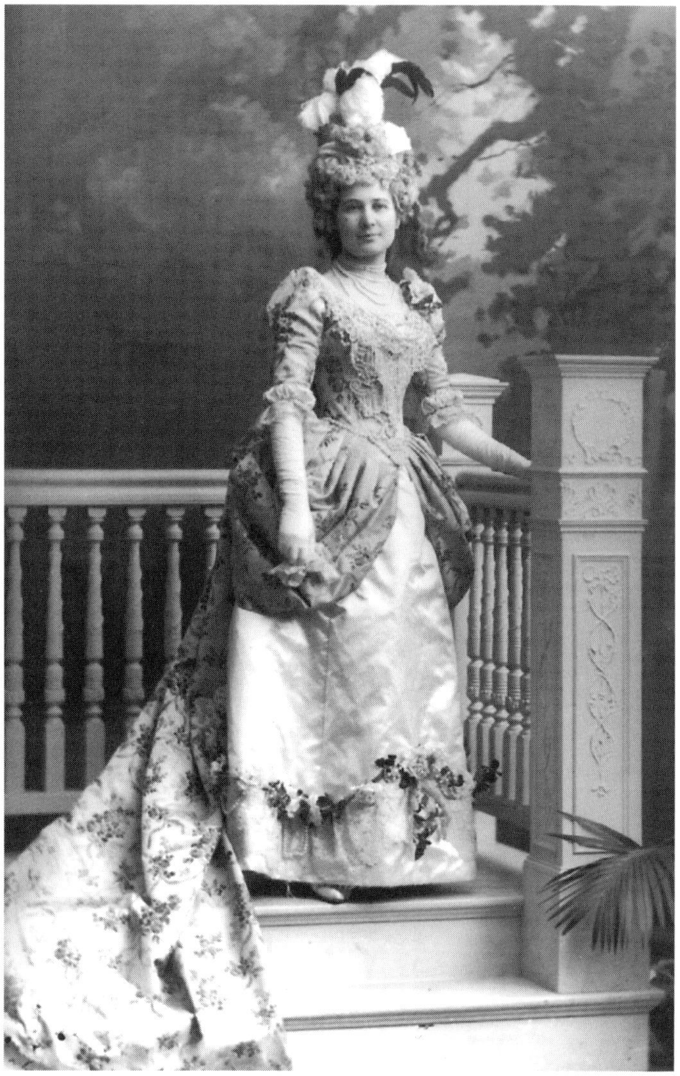

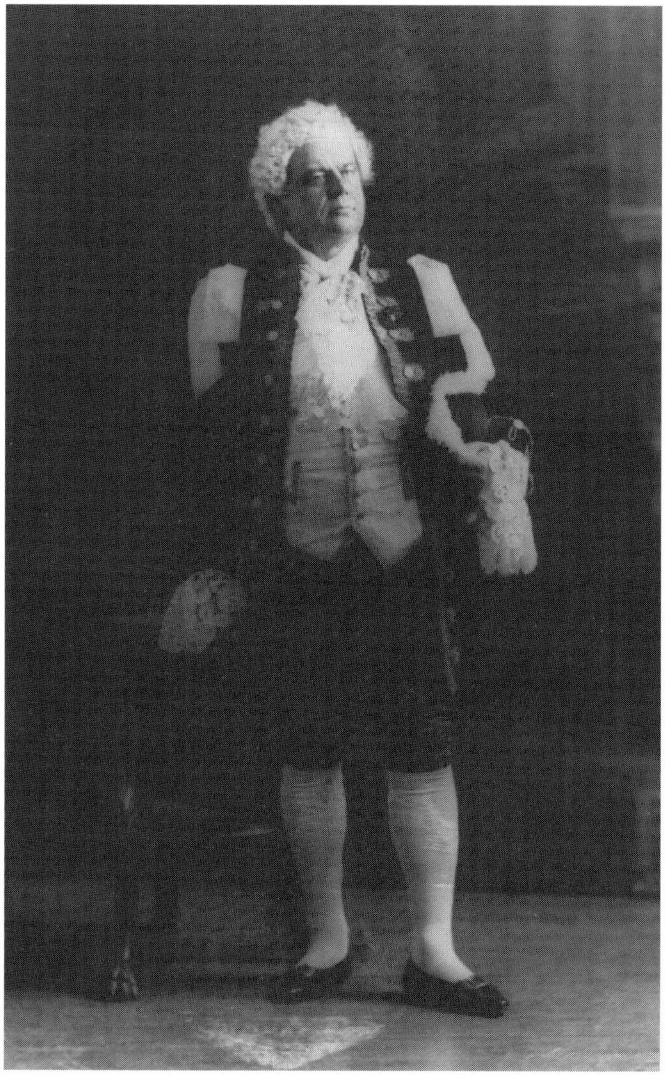

Marie de Lotbinière Harwood (née Masson) as her husband's ancestor, "The Marquise de Lotbinière." Her headdress with its blue, white and black ostrich feathers is imposing and "very effective." Over her white satin skirt she wears a dress of white brocade with a rose motif. The style of the dress and the frayed hemline reveal that it is a remade evening gown. NPA/MMCH

effective" headdress, grandly styled "Louis XV Grande Tenue," crowned with a black aigrette and white and blue ostrich tips. This headdress was the most imposing one in her group, and she was surely one of the most impressive characters of the evening. Although her photograph leaves no doubt that her dress was made over from an evening gown, her overall appearance supports a reporter's claim that "a woman can unearth wonderful odds and ends of evening gowns and reconstruct them into a marvellous facsimile of something historic."[15]

No family connections or heirlooms were needed to highlight the presence of Sir William and Lady Hingston. Senator Hingston, an accomplished surgeon, the organizer of Canada's first board of health and a former mayor of the city, came as "Charles Lemoyne." He "filled the character with courtly grace" in black velvet trimmed with silver, rented from Beullac. Lady Hingston accompanied him as the first "Baroness of Longueuil"; she had shone as part of the vice-regal entourage at the Dufferin ball.

The De Ramezay Family set, representing the kin of the original occupant of the château, included numerous officers of the Antiquarian and Numismatic Society. Rouer Roy, a vice-president, was soon to retire as legal advisor to the City of Montreal. He appeared in the character of "Louis Rouer de Villeray" in "a very fine Louis XV coat and knee breeches of dark red velvet" with a long wig. Mme Rouer Roy, the

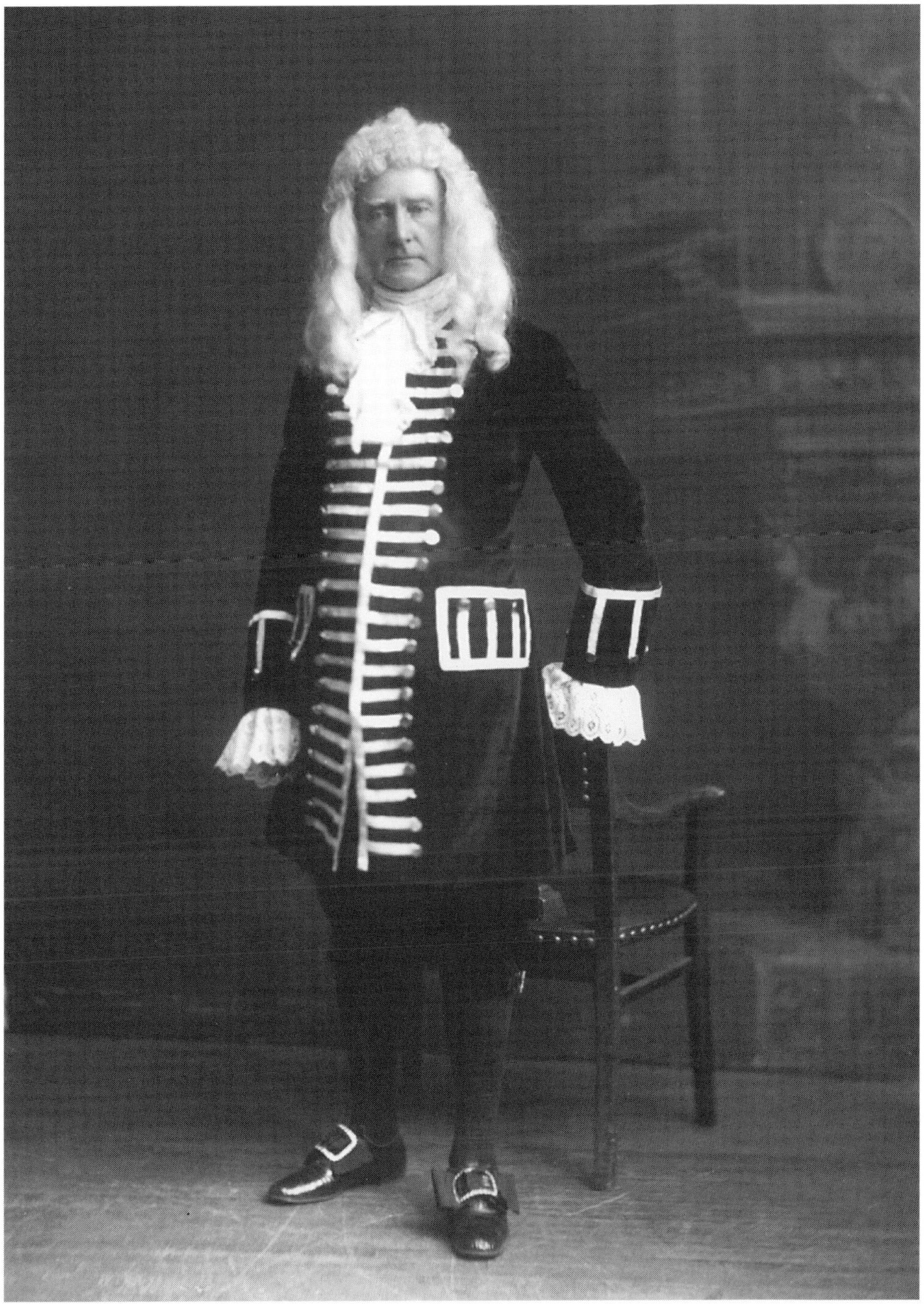

Opposite: Senator Louis Joseph Forget as the "Marquis de Ramezay," wearing a "coat of rich olive silk velvet, trimmed with heavy bullion and gold buttons, olive satin knee breeches, cocked hat with white ostrich feather and bullion trimmings." Forget was president of the Montreal Stock Exchange and the Montreal Street Railway. (*Montreal Star*, 19 Jan. 1898) NPA/MMCH

Left: Sir William Hingston as "Charles Lemoyne." He wears "the evening dress of a gentleman of the reign of Louis XIV, consisting of black velvet surcoat, richly braided in silver, black knee breeches, stockings and shoes, wig of the period." (*Montreal Star*, 19 Jan. 1898) NPA/MMCH organizer and the most outstanding woman in this group, "was indeed a grand dame of the old Regime." The *Montreal Herald* noted how fancy dress could bring out the best in women of her age. "In these old-time costumes a noticeable feature is that the matron of mature years appears to as great advantage as the maiden of eighteen." Another striking member of the set was the Hon. Louis Joseph Forget, a life governor of the society. Forget, a Senator and one of Montreal's leading French businessmen with his own banking and stock brokerage firm, appeared as "The Marquis de Ramezay."

The final group covered a more recent time span and portrayed the succession of English governors since the British conquest. Maria Forget, whose husband was in the previous group, was in charge of this set and represented "Lady Carleton, 1768," in pink and white brocade. Assisting her was Martha Baumgarten, the wife of the president of the St. Lawrence Sugar Refining Co., Alfred Baumgarten. She was outstanding, "perfect in her style as Lady Murray, 1764." Her toilette of magenta silk taffeta was a "very quaint and beautiful costume of the time of George the III."

While the men's costumes were simpler than the previous ones, their scarlet military coats made them stand out. As "Sir George Prévost, 1811," Dr. Robert Ruttan, a professor of practical chemistry in the medicine and science faculties of McGill University, wore a "very handsome and historically correct costume" and was "an exact reproduction of his old portrait now in Quebec." Dr. John Molson, as "Major General Prescott," had more trouble appearing debonaire in his "uniform of 1797"; "Major General Prescott had a very stiff high collar on his coat; it was with difficulty he moved, but this with a short, rather rough wig gave him a historically correct appearance." Edward Clouston, manager of the Bank of Montreal, probably also had trouble moving. His dark blue uniform with gold epaulettes, in which he represented the "Earl of Dalhousie, 1820," appears rather tight in his photograph.[16]

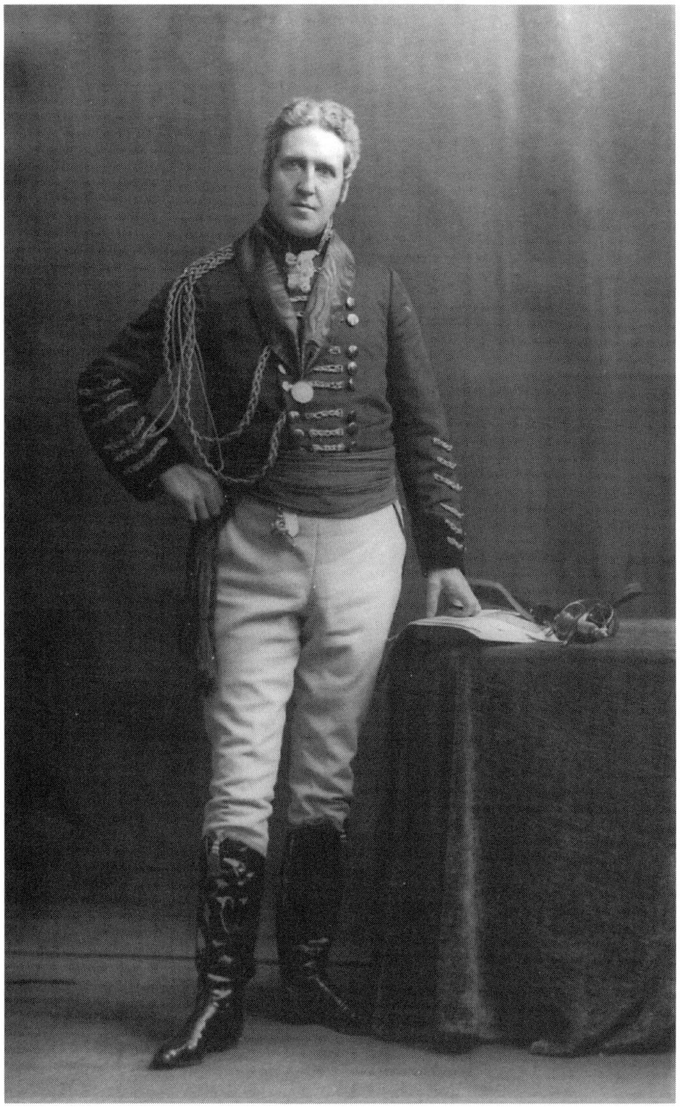

Dr. Robert Ruttan as "Sir George Prévost" is "an exact reproduction of his old portrait" in a scarlet military coat with gold cord trim, a crimson sash, white doeskin trousers, Hessian boots and a sword. (*Montreal Star*, 19 Jan. 1898) NPA/MMCH

Dr. William Henry Drummond, the author of popular poems such as "The Habitant's Jubilee Ode" and "The Wreck of the *Julie Plante*," represented his namesake, "Sir Gordon Drummond, 1815." Other members of the Montreal elite in the set included Andrew Allan, president of the Montreal Ocean Steamship Co., as "General Jeffrey Amherst." His nephew, merchant Hugh Montagu Allan, came as "The Duke of Richmond." Hugh Montagu Allan's wife, Marguerite, was exquisitely garbed in Nile green velvet over a pink and green flowered satin petticoat. Judge and Mrs. Wurtele represented "Seigneur Deguire and His Wife, 1854."

Attached to the various groups were only two Indian characters, and there were no carryings-on as there had been in Ottawa two years earlier. One newspaper recalled "one looking exactly like a native and the other looking exactly like a white man dressed up as an Indian." The latter was almost certainly A.A. McCulloch, who wore no makeup. His costume was identical but for a few added accessories to one he had posed in for a photograph thirty-five years earlier, in 1863. Mr. De Blois Thibaudeau may have been more convincing as the Huron Chief "Kondiaronk." He completed his much-noticed and very successful costume with paint on his face.[17]

Guests not part of the groups also wore fancy dress. Colin Campbell attended as "The Seigneur de Rouville," circa 1760, in whose house he had actually been born. Mrs. Colin Campbell was "most becomingly gowned" in a "smart encroiable costume" consisting of a striped red and yellow skirt, a short black velvet coat and a three-cornered hat, and *poudré* hair. "The Incroyable" was a popular character mentioned in many nineteenth-century publications on fancy dress; originally the term referred to a male dandy of the very early nineteenth century, but for fancy dress the costume was always feminized with a skirt. A "stray oriental" was spotted in the gallery; no doubt this was A. Amos in the Turkish costume he had brought back from his travels.

After the presentations, at eleven o'clock, the court group and some of the organizers and distinguished guests, eleven couples in all, danced the opening set of lancers. The group included members of the Aberdeen camp, such as their personal physician Dr. Shirres, and Mme Hector Prévost, wife of the Montreal aide-de-camp. It also took in prominent guests, such as Senators William Hingston and Rosaire Thibaudeau; organizers, including Mme Rouer Roy; and the outstanding beauties Mrs. Hugh Montagu Allan and Mrs. Thomas Tait.

Then followed dances by the historical groups – but only two performed. The intention had apparently been otherwise; at the previous balls these dances had been the highlight of the evening, and no self-respecting set leader would have dared to default on her obligation. For reasons unstated, however, only two groups prepared dances, both taught by the same Professor Frank Norman who had been congratulated for his work at the Ottawa ball. Indeed, they were exactly the same as two of the dances he had arranged for that event. Nevertheless, they were appreciated. "The greatest credit must be given all the ladies and gentlemen taking part in the two dances, and also to Professor Norman, who has proved himself an eminently capable instructor."[18]

Twelve couples from the English Governors group danced an old-fashioned quadrille, "most artistically performed." The dancers formed in two lines across the hall, and as a finale the men held their swords at the salute while the women made the "deep court curtsey" in front of the dais. The quadrille was quite similar to the modern lancers, "with grace and stateliness added." The Toronto press made much of its own Mrs. Thomas Tait, who "wore one of the loveliest costumes at the Historical Ball," made, like Lady Aberdeen's gown, by the dressmaker Stitt. She and Fred Meredith as "Lord and Lady Sherbrooke" were particularly striking in the dance. Her ostensibly Empire-style dress (with no defined waistline) was of sumptuous cream and silver brocade, embroidered with jewels. A front panel made from yellow satin was veiled in silver embroidered tulle. A train of cream satin brocade was lined with scarlet moiré velour, which added a vivid if intermittent touch of colour, and its corners were embroidered in a medieval design in gold and silver. What charmed observers the most, however, was Mrs. Tait's "priceless drapery," a *pointe à l'aiguille* lace shawl, which one reporter thought many would remember from her mother's early married days. The lace was "most artistically arranged about the shoulders," being held on one side with a large diamond crescent. "A coronet of five diamond stars shone in the sunny locks, which were coiffed *à l'Empire*."[19]

Then ten men and ten women of the De Ramezay family group performed the minuet, "with a stately grace and studied manner that was charming to witness," making it "one of the chief features of the ball." Very effective was the "tunnel figure" in which the men formed an arch with their swords, beneath which the women passed. The ladies "managed their trains and fans with the greatest dexterity," and in fact did a better job than the men, who were a bit stiff. The climax was the salute to Their Excellencies: they all dropped into a low bow and curtsey in front of the dais. The dancers included Frederick Walton, Dean of Law at McGill, Leigh Gregor, a German literature professor, and Hartland MacDougall, a stockbroker, as well as Miss Gault, daughter of the "Cotton King of Canada," and two Miss Refords, daughters of shipping magnate Robert Reford.

Dancing became general as the orchestra executed a program of lancers and waltzes and finally played "Aurore," a two-step. At midnight, nearly all the guests entered the Windsor Hotel dining room, the scene of a "most elaborate supper." Since only about four hundred guests attended the ball, they could all sit down to supper at once. The architectural features of the otherwise undecorated room created a "rich setting that showed off to advantage the elaborate costumes of gorgeous colouring and costly textures" worn by the seated guests. The menu played on the historical theme, offering such delicacies as *consommé en tasse à la Frontenac*, *filet de boeuf à la Montgomery*, and *pâté de gibier à l'Aberdeen*. No doubt stern Sir Alexander Lacoste cast a disapproving eye at those imbibing too freely; he was known to be very outspoken about the "abominable vice of intemperance."

After the supper, dancing recommenced with a polka and carried on with waltzes and two-steps, occasionally interspersed with a lancers. The Victoria Rifles Orchestra "never played in better spirit." Dancing continued until early in the morning and the floor was constantly crowded.

Although the ball had been on a somewhat smaller scale than those which had preceded it, it had still created ample business for Montreal tradespeople. Dry goods merchants referred to it affectionately as *la grande affaire*. John Martin, Sons, & Co., Military and General Outfitters, advertised in the business-oriented *Gazette* that they would make costumes to order for the ball. Both John Martin and Henry Morgan & Co. advertised a scant ten days to two weeks before the event; clearly they could have costumes made up very quickly. Hairdressers also reaped a golden harvest. Even a week before the ball, the only appointments open for the day of the ball were at seven in the morning; unfortunate ladies with these appointments would have to spend the entire day in powder and patches. Women could have their hair styled and powdered by Palmers, at 1745 Notre Dame Street, which made an attractive offer two weeks before the event:

> Fashionable Hair Dressing. Make your arrangements for the great ball on the evening of January 18th. On Thursday Jan. 13, all the young ladies in our five handsomely appointed dressing parlors will have their hair powdered and dressed in the prevailing fashions, Louis XIV, Louis XV, Madame La Pompadour and Marie Antoinette. This will give the public an intelligent idea in the correct decoration of the head.[20]

Even wax flowers for buttonholes were advertised specifically for the event.

Like ball guests in Ottawa and Toronto, the Montreal ballgoers ensured that their event would be commemorated. The William Notman studio had been interviewed about photographs in late December, and a discreet note appeared in one newspaper in early January.

Messrs. W. Notman and Son have generously offered to photograph the members of groups individually or in small groups in order to the preparation [sic] of a souvenir album to be presented to the Château. Members of groups are therefore requested to call at Messr. Notman's studio in costumes in order to give them the necessary number of sittings.[21]

From the day of the ball through to the end of June, sitters filed into the studio almost daily, posing for some two hundred photographs. Members of some of the more prominent families such as the Van Hornes and the Allans were photographed in their homes. Who footed the bill for the photography is not known. Notman presented a large leather-bound album, containing a photograph of each guest, to the Antiquarian Society, which they used as inspiration for fund-raising costume balls in the twentieth century. Marguerite Thibaudeau compiled her own small photograph album. One guest even had his portrait painted in costume. John Try-Davies, a Supper Committee member, posed in January or February 1898 for artist Robert Harris, wearing his eighteenth-century costume and contemplating a miniature held in his hand. There was no attempt to publish a souvenir album, however.

While the photographer, hairdressers, tailors and merchants got their share of the miniature business boom, the missing historical dances and the possibly disorganized presentations betray the fact that this ball was not carried off with quite the same finesse as the two held by Lady Aberdeen. The organizing committee, however, had a great deal of resistance to contend with right from the start. "After much hard work, and it may be suggested, weariness of flesh and spirit," wrote one reporter in the know, "the ball became an actuality." For the fledgling Ladies' Branch of the Antiquarian and Numismatic Society, whose efforts had been met with such heel-dragging by their male counterparts, the event can only have been a coup. Their efforts raised $375, used to restore and decorate two period rooms at the château, the Louis XV Room and the Habitant Room. "The success of the ball, both financially and as a very beautiful sight, must have fully repaid all those who had worked so hard for it beforehand," said the *Toronto Globe*.[22]

Press coverage of this ball was less extensive than the coverage of the balls organized by the Aberdeens. Robertine Barry, alias the journalist "Françoise," who attended the ball as "Marie Magdaleine Lemoyne" in the Lemoyne Family set, provided one of the most interesting accounts in her article in *La Patrie*. Well known for her witty writing, she would later found her own paper, *Le Journal de Françoise*. Like her good friend, poet Emile Nelligan, she was of mixed Irish and French-Canadian parentage but staunchly identified with the latter. "Françoise" had all the more reason to be proud because the ball had been organized by a group of women, and because French-Canadian women had played a leading part. She congratulated Maria Forget, president of the Ladies' Ball Committee, who had assumed a large part of the responsibility, as well as vice-president Marguerite Thibaudeau, Lady Lacoste, and Mme Rouer Roy.

Unlike the fancy dress balls in Ottawa and Toronto, this one may not have been the most magnificent entertainment ever seen in Montreal, though it must rank among the best, and its social impact was similar: "an event in the social history of Canada that will not soon be forgotten." Its patriotic character was not emphasized quite as strongly as that of the Ottawa ball but was nevertheless mentioned. "It was a Canadian jubilee in miniature. The Canadian who did not feel the stirring, thrilling sense of loyalty and patriotism running through it all must have known little of the history of his country," said the *Montreal Herald*. The *Montreal Star* claimed:

> It had spread the love of historical studies and research, which was in the main, the object of the undertaking. . . . That these historical balls will, besides all else, make us realize and appreciate the fact that Canada has a history full of stirring deeds of brave men and women, which it behooves her sons and daughters to remember with pride, is also a matter of consequence beyond the enjoyment of the hour.[23]

La Presse summarized how this ball related to the others.

> Lady Aberdeen's historical ball held at the National capital a few years ago was the first of a series of such events, which we hope will continue, since these representations contribute more to the learning and enjoyment of Canadian history than schoolbooks . . . which otherwise must alone be responsible for teaching students the history of our national glories.[24]

The series was not to continue; the Montreal Historical Fancy Dress Ball was the last. With the passing of another decade, the approach to creating a living history lesson burgeoned beyond anything the late Victorian mindset could have countenanced.

In November 1898, the Aberdeens brought their term to an end and departed for England. Rumours of their being recalled abounded, and they themselves believed that they were expected to stay for another year; they felt that they had cut their term short. They did not leave without regrets. Towards the end, Lady Aberdeen had a change of heart about Ottawa. "I must own to beginning to feel a sneaking fondness for the place itself, in spite of its shabby old Government House put away amongst its clump of bushes," she confided. The reasons they invoked for their departure were purely personal, financial matters being foremost. "The expenses of our regime had been very heavy. Our plan of residing at the different centres, in addition to Ottawa, and entertaining at each, while being desirable in itself, had added largely to our burdens," she wrote. While securing popularity and respect for their hosts, these magnificent entertainments had exacted a heavy toll.[25]

The Aberdeens were succeeded that same year by Gilbert John Elliot, 4th Earl of Minto (1854-1914), and his wife Mary. This couple, who had frequented the exalted and racy Marlborough House set in England, attending rounds of country house parties which pandered to the Prince of Wales, brought a more detached approach to the social role of the Governor General. Even before leaving England, they felt the public reaction to the Aberdeen regime. Queen Victoria warned Lady Minto not to get "mixed up in any new venture which might be criticized." Minto wrote to his brother about Lady Aberdeen, "She had a great many people by the ears. She went in for absolutely everything she cd. think of and invented other things to go in for. . . . They absolutely upset society."[26]

The Mintos ushered in a decade of change. Habitual repression and restraint were gradually disappearing towards the end of Victoria's reign. Though the Edwardians held fast to decorum, the new spirit was far more ebullient and extravagant. Balls and parties at Rideau Hall took on a gay new atmosphere, though fewer attended. The Mintos were far more zealous about excluding those not entitled to official recognition from their entertainments, and in their letters home they repeated complaints heard around the city about the formerly large numbers of regular Rideau Hall guests completely unworthy of such honour.

Politically, Canada entered an optimistic period of propsperity and expansion, under the guidance of Prime Minister Sir Wilfrid Laurier. The highlight of the Mintos' Canadian career was the 1901 visit of the Duke and Duchess of York, later to become King George V and Queen Mary. The couple toured the country and gave citizens a new fervour for royalty; a royal visit could always be counted on to foster the imperial cause, and enthusiasm for imperial unity grew rapidly.

The Mintos' successor, Albert Edward, 4th Earl Grey (1851-1917), bolstered this enthusiasm. Canada's most ardent imperialist held the longest vice-regal term to date, from 1904 to 1911. An excellent – though sometimes long-winded – orator, Grey toured tirelessly, everywhere extolling and promoting Canada. He schemed constantly for improvements and put forward an unprecedented number of projects. Grey's work led to the appointment of the Arts Advisory Council, which assumed responsibility for the National Gallery. He enjoyed theatricals and set up the Grey Drama Festivals, a series of annual competitions for musical and dramatic trophies. Sports retained an important priority – he donated the Grey Cup for football and established a trophy for golf.

But perhaps the single most memorable event of Lord Grey's career was his version of a costumed entertainment. In 1908, a full decade after the last major fancy dress ball, he instigated a massive pageant in Quebec City, larger and more expensive and flamboyant – and fraught with more political controversy – than any of the events held by either the Dufferins or the Aberdeens.

As early as 1906 he began organizing the Quebec Tercentenary with the twin purposes of promoting imperial unity and "harmonizing and unifying the two great races which together make the Nation of Canada." Initially the tercentenary had been primarily of interest to French Canadians and was being organized by the Société St-Jean Baptiste. To their annoyance, Grey took over the project to celebrate the birth of Quebec and French Canada and turned it into a glorification of the Conquest and Great Britain's imperial grandeur. In the face of considerable opposition from French-Canadian anti-imperialists, he set up an Empire-wide fund to purchase the Plains of Abraham and establish the site as a national park. Then he appointed the Battlefields Commission to administer the site.[27]

The event itself was on an epic scale. The crowning glory was the week-long presence of Prince George, a surefire means of making sure the excitement about the event centred on its imperial character. Descendents of Montcalm, Lévis and Murray arrived as guests of the government. Quebec was besieged with an estimated 150,000 visitors, including tourists from the United States and Europe.

All these visitors came to a ten-day event, whose highlight was a series of historical pageants held on the Plains of Abraham from 23 to 30 July. Each day, a different scene in the history of Canada was acted out on the plains. Forty-five hundred costumed actors took part in the eight pageants. The scenes themselves were limited to the history of the French regime, a demand which the citizens of Quebec had made, refusing to act in a show that would glorify the Conquest. One hundred Algonquins were brought in courtesy of the Canadian Pacific Railway; the organizer had declared he wanted the largest possible number of "savages." The Natives acted out stereotyped "Indian" roles scripted by the organizer, wielding bows and arrows and posing for many photographs within their encampment of teepees.

The eight great scenes illustrated by the reenactments began with the arrival of Jacques Cartier and continued with the heroic achievements of Champlain, the

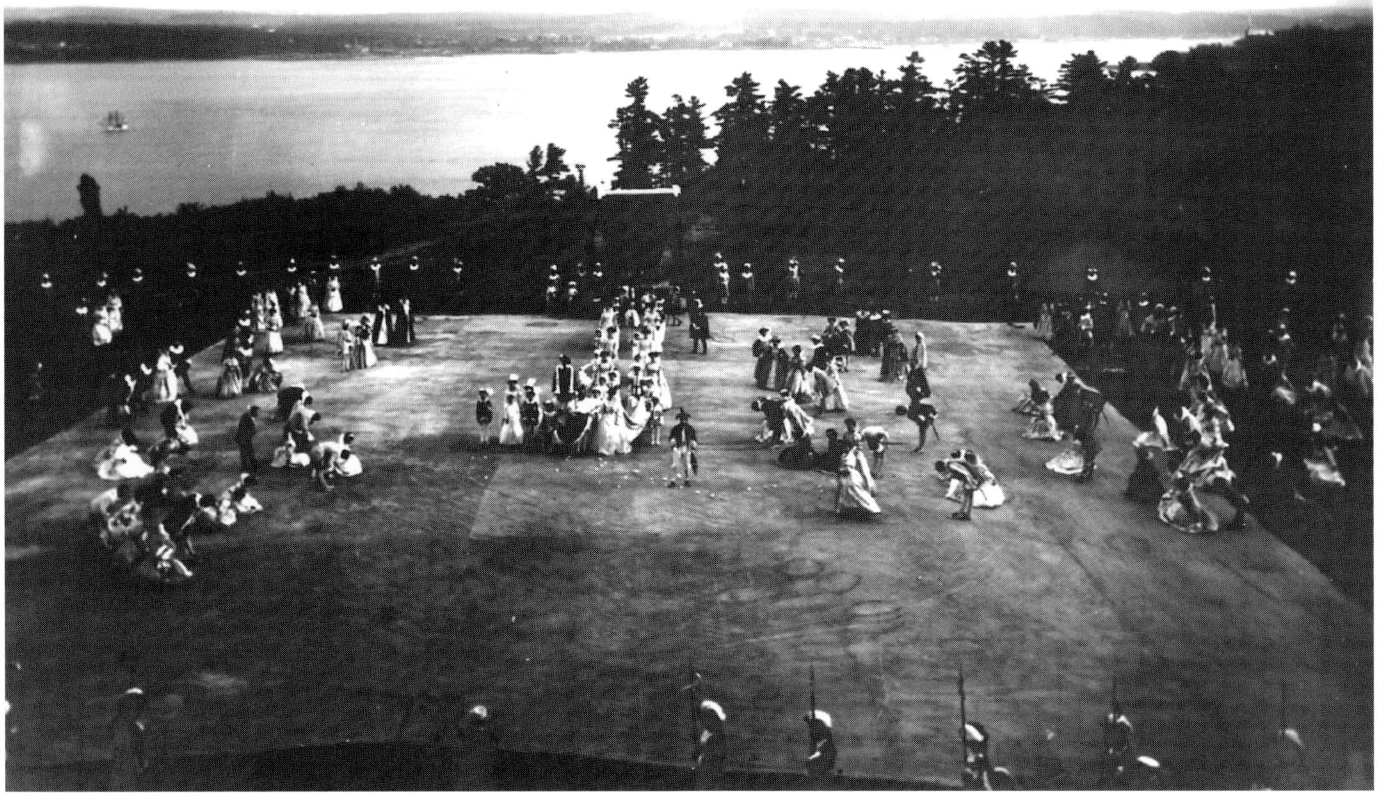

The opening of Scene I of the Second Pageant, acted out on the Plains of Abraham on the fourth day of the Quebec Tercentenary, 24 July 1908. In this scene, set at the Louvre in 1608, Henry IV grants Champlain a commission to set out for New France. To the strains of minstrels, the ladies and gentlemen of his court, dressed in farthingales and ruffs, troop in behind the ermine-clad sovereign and his wife, amid a bowing throng. A dialogue with Champlain follows, and then forty couples dance a pavane.

J.E. LIVERNOIS/NAC/PA24139

Ursulines, Dollard des Ormeaux, the Marquis de Tracy, Daumont de Saint-Lusson, and the representatives of the fourteen First Nations pledging their fidelity to the King of France. The final pageant was to illustrate the fall of the French Regime, with a confrontation between Wolfe and Montcalm. The two heros and their contingents arrived together, however; as one participant wrote, "so as not to annoy the French people, there was no fight, only reconciliation." The scene ended with the singing of "O Canada" and "God Save the King." It was suggested that the British flags appeared a bit more flamboyant than the French ones.[28]

Aside from the pageants themselves, there were complementary activities including parades, military and naval reviews, a state ball and a vice-regal garden party. An historical fancy dress ball capping off the last evening of pageants could hardly compete for notice. Britain, the United States and France each sent battleships, and the Prince of Wales reviewed a military gathering of 12,000 troops. All this did not come without a price tag – a budget of $350,000 was spent for the event. An organizer, Frank Lascelles, had been employed to bring the event together; artist Charles Huot had been commissioned to design costumes; Professor Frank Norman, the dancing instructor at the Aberdeen balls, took charge of choreography. Lascelles enlisted many other people to assist with the management of the pageants, as well as to participate.

There was no doubt that the event was designed mainly to foster pride in the imperial connection and to celebrate French-Canadian history secondarily, if at all. The messages behind the fancy dress balls of the 1890s had remained sufficiently ambiguous for French and English Canadians to interpret them in their own ways. The intent of the Quebec tercentenary was far more blatant and so the event stirred up much more controversy. Grey wrote proudly to British Prime Minister Lord Chamberlain,

"We are justified in hoping that a new imperialism will blossom in Quebec." Popular French-Canadian politician Henri Bourassa had a different opinion. He wrote to his friend Goldwin Smith, who always had a ready ear for a grumble against the misguided excesses of a Governor General:

> In my soul, there is not a shadow of a doubt . . . that [Lord Grey] decided, from the beginning, to transform the celebration of the birth of Quebec and of French Canada into a grand historic reminder of the Conquest in order to show his imperialist friends in London that the new imperial religion has made progress among French Canadians. His second objective consists of affecting the spirit of French Canadians by rubbing their noses in the notion of imperial grandeur.[29]

Grey's appropriation of the Quebec Tercentenary bears witness to his zealous brand of vice-regal leadership, driven to define and foster Canadian historical consciousness and nationalism in a way in which none of his predecessors – not even Lady Aberdeen – would have dared. Political messages notwithstanding, the pageant's immensity and logistics place the event on a separate scale from the previous Governor Generals' Canadian fancy dress balls. Yet the 1908 event represents the extreme to which this type of entertainment could be taken, in a more permissive Edwardian society and at the pinnacle of imperial enthusiasm in Canada. The Victorian culture which had shaped the Dufferins' and the Aberdeens' fancy dress balls had itself become historic.

Notes

INTRODUCTION

1. Lily Dougall, "Home and Social Life," in *Women of Canada: Their Life and Work*, comp. National Council of Women (n.p. 1900, reprint 1975), 19.

2. John Buchan, *Lord Minto, A Memoir* (London: Nelson, 1924), 180.

3. Journal of Lady Monck, quoted in Elizabeth Batt, *Monck: Governor General, 1861-1868, A Biography* (Toronto: McClelland and Stewart, 1976), 78.

4. J.D. Edgar, *Canada and Its Capital* (Toronto: Morang, 1898), 113; J.E. Collins, *Canada Under the Administration of Lord Lorne* (Toronto: Rose, 1884), 310.

CHAPTER 1

My analysis of the fancy dress phenomenon is rooted in the numerous primary source accounts and images of these balls, as well as the books and articles providing recommendations for fancy dress. Several of these are referenced here; some others which have served in my study include: Cermer Mada (alias G. Mercer Adam), "What to Wear at Fancy Dress Balls," *Saturday Night*, 5 Jan. 1889; *Fancy Dress: A Short Chronological Series of Costumes* (London: Liberty, n.d.); *Male Character Costumes: A Guide to Gentlemen's Costume*, 2d ed. (London: Samuel Miller, [1895]); *Travestissements*, 3 vols. (Paris: Abel Goubaud, [1880-1890]); and Weldon's Limited, *Weldon's Fancy Dress for Ladies*, First Series and Second Series (London: Weldons, [1895-1900]).

1. *Masquerade and Carnival: Their Customs and Costumes* (n.p., Butterick, [1897]), 7.

2. Anthea Jarvis and Patricia Raine, *Fancy Dress* (Aylesbury: Shire, 1984); Anthea Jarvis, "'There was a young man from Bengal . . .': The Vogue for Fancy Dress, 1830-1950," *Costume* 16(1982): 33-46; Sara Stevenson and Helen Bennet, *Van Dyck in Check Trousers: Fancy Dress in Art and Life, 1700-1900* (Scotland: Scottish National Portrait Gallery, 1978).

3. Alicia Finkel, "'*Le Bal Costumé*': History and Spectacle in the Court of Queen Victoria," *Dress* 10 (1984): 64-72; *Illustrated London News*, 14 May 1842, 7 June 1845, 21 June 1851.

4. Karen Halttunen, *Confidence Men and Painted Women* (New Haven: Yale University Press, 1982), 174-182; Leonore Davidoff, *The Best Circles: Society, Etiquette, and the Season* (London: Croom Helm, 1973), 51.

5. *Illustrated London News*, 25 Jul., 1, 8 Aug. 1874.

6. Sophia Murphy, *The Duchess of Devonshire's Ball* (London: Sidgwick and Jackson, 1984); *London Times*, 8 July 1897.

7. Beverly Gordon, "Dressing the Colonial Past: Nineteenth Century New Englanders Look Back," in *Dress and American Culture*, ed. Patricia A. Cunningham and Susan Voso-Lab (Bowling Green: Bowling Green Popular Press, 1994), 109-139.

8. *New York Times*, 27 Mar. 1883.

9. *New York Times*, 31 Jan. to 14 Feb. 1897; E.F. Johanet, "Un bal costumé: tribulations d'une millionaire américaine," *La Revue canadienne*, 34(1898): 123-129.

10. Alden G. Meredith, *Mary's Rosedale, or Gossip of Little York* (Ottawa: Graphic, 1928), 155-164; Fanny Jarvis Meredith memoirs, C.P. Meredith Papers, National Archives of Canada; *Montreal Herald*, 25 Feb. 1865; Lillian Scott Desbarats, *Recollections* (Ottawa: privately printed, 1957), 32, 74.

11. *Montreal Gazette, Montreal Herald, Montreal Star, Montreal Witness* 2 March and *passim*, 25 Feb. to 13 May 1870; Reverend Ashton Oxenden, *My First Year in Canada* (Montreal: Dawson, 1871), 59.

12. Ardern Holt, *Gentlemen's Fancy Dress: How to Choose It*, 2nd ed. (London: Wyman, 1882), 3.

13. *Toronto Daily Mail*, 24 Feb. 1876.

14. Ardern Holt, *Fancy Dresses Described, or What to Wear at Fancy Balls*, 6th ed. (London: Debenham and Freebody, 1896), vii.

15. Mrs. Aria, *Costume: Fanciful, Historical, Theatrical* (London: Macmillan, 1906), 179; Holt, *Fancy Dresses Described*, 279.

16. *Canadian Illustrated News*, 18 Mar. 1876; Mrs. Aria, 189.

17. Gladys Beattie Crozier, "The Art of Choosing Fancy Dress," *Everywoman's Encyclopedia* [1906]: 1057; Holt, *Fancy Dresses Described*, xiii.

18. Crozier, 1507; Holt, *Gentlemen's Fancy Dress*, 3.

19. *Toronto News*, 29 Dec. 1897.

20. Holt, *Gentlemen's Fancy Dress*, 4; *Toronto Sunday World*, 2 Jan. 1898.

21. *The Nation*, 3 Mar. 1876; *New York Times*, 9 Feb. 1897; *Toronto Sunday World*, 2 Jan. 1898.

22. Allen Churchill, *The Splendor Seekers* (New York: Grosset and Dunlap, 1974), 67; *Montreal Herald*, 24 Feb. 1876; *Ottawa Evening Journal*, 18 Feb. 1896.

23. Mrs. Aria, 185.

24. Feo Monck, 2 Mar. 1865, *Monck Letters and Journals, 1863-1868*, ed. W.L. Morton (Toronto: McClelland and Stewart, 1971), 241.

25. *Ottawa Free Press*, 19 Feb. 1896; *Saturday Night*, 8 Jan. 1898; Allen Churchill, *The Upper Crust* (Englewood Cliffs NJ: Prentice Hall, 1970), 38.

26. *Ottawa Evening Journal*, 2 Feb. 1889; Marquis and Marchioness of Aberdeen and Temair, *We Twa: Reminiscences of Lord and Lady Aberdeen*, (London: W. Collins, 1925), vol. II, 51.

27. Jean-Philippe Worth, *A Century of Fashion*, trans. Ruth Scott Miller (Boston: Little Brown, 1928), 131-2; *The Nation*, 3 Mar. 1876.

28. Marchioness of Dufferin and Ava, *Our Viceregal Life in India: Selections from My Journal, 1884-1888* (London: John Murray, 1890), vol. 2, 40; *St. John Daily News*, 24 Feb. 1876.

29. *Saturday Night*, 11 Dec. 1987, 13; *Toronto Sunday World*, 2 Jan. 1898; *Godey's Lady's Book*, January 1850, 81.

30. *Montreal Star*, 3 Mar. 1870.

31. Holt, *Fancy Dresses Described*, 180; *Eastern Chronicle*, 27 Feb. 1896; Crozier, 1058.

CHAPTER 2

The story of the ball is principally drawn from the detailed accounts published in the *Ottawa Daily Citizen*, *Ottawa Free Press*, *Ottawa Times*, *Toronto Daily Mail*, *Toronto Globe*, *Montreal Gazette*, *Montreal Herald*, *Montreal Star*, and *La Minerve*, all on the day following the ball, 24 February 1876. The *Canadian Illustrated News* also published a lengthy account accompanied by sketches on 18 March 1876.

The period leading up to the ball has been pieced together through advertisements and editorial material in the *Ottawa Daily Citizen* (22 Jan. through 20 March 1876), the *Ottawa Free Press* (13 Jan. through 28 Feb. 1876), and the *Ottawa Times* (21 Jan. through 28 Feb. 1876). The ball was also mentioned in the days following it in the *Montreal Star*, *Toronto Globe*, *Nation*, *St. John Daily News*, *Canadian Home Journal*, *New York Daily Graphic*, and *New York Times*.

Lady Dufferin's preparations for the event are chronicled in *My Canadian Journal, 1872-1878* (1891; reprint, Toronto: Coles, 1971), the published selection of her letters home from Canada. Biographical information on the Dufferins is taken from the sources detailing Dufferin's political accomplishments, including John Cowan, *Canada's Governors General, 1867-1952* (Toronto: York, 1952); William Leggo, *The History of the Administration of the Right Honourable Frederick Temple, Earl of Dufferin* (Montreal: Lovell, 1878); George Stewart Jr., *Canada Under the Administration of the Earl of Dufferin* (Toronto: Rose-Belford, 1878); Sir Alfred Lyall, *The Life of the Marquis of Dufferin and Ava* (London: John Murray, 1905); and R.H. Hubbard, *Rideau Hall: An Illustrated History of Government House, Ottawa* (Ottawa: Queen's Printer, 1967) and "Viceregal influences on Canadian Society," in *The Shield of Achilles: Aspects of Canada in the Victorian Age*, ed. W.L. Morton (Toronto: McClelland and Stewart, 1968), 256-274. Lady Dufferin's nature has been interpreted by Marian Fowler, *The Embroidered Tent: Five Gentlewomen in Early Canada* (Toronto: Anansi, 1982), and by her nephew, Harold Nicolson, *Helen's Tower* (London: Constable, 1937).

Biographical information on the ball guests is gleaned from *Representative Canadians: A Cyclopaedia of Canadian Biography*, ed. George Maclean Rose (Toronto: Rose, 1888), and Henry Morgan, *Types of Canadian Women and Women Who Are or Have Been Connected with Canada* (Toronto: Briggs, 1903). The *Ottawa Directory 1875 and Dominion Guide* (Ottawa, n.p., 1875; CIHM 46777) provides a social profile of the ballgoers and further information on Ottawa merchants. Personal impressions are found in the E.A. Meredith Diary and Fanny Jarvis Meredith Memoirs and in the Janet Hall Diary, all at the National Archives of Canada.

Images of this ball are in the Topley collection in the National Archives of Canada. Topley's carefully kept sitter logbook provides a record of the photographs taken; many of his glass negatives are intact. Lady Dufferin's photo album contains photographs of the family and a few select guests.

1. *Ottawa Times*, 24 Feb. 1876.
2. Lyall, *The Life of the Marquis of Dufferin and Ava*, 215; Dufferin, *My Canadian Journal*, 4-5.
3. Dufferin, 25-26, 61.
4. Nicolson, 145.
5. Stewart, *Canada Under the Administration of the Earl of Dufferin*, 51; Nicolson, 160.
6. Dufferin, 213; Nels Juleus, "Lady Dufferin's Amateur Theatricals," *Canadian Drama* 11:1(1985): 245-250.
7. Dufferin, 123, 62.
8. *The Nation*, 3 Mar. 1876.
9. Fanny Meredith Memoirs, Meredith Papers.
10. Janet Hall diary, 23 Feb. 1876.
11. *Toronto Globe*, 24 Feb. 1876.
12. *Canadian Illustrated News*, 18 Mar. 1876; Dufferin, 223.
13. E.A. Meredith diary, 24 Feb. 1876, Meredith papers; Meredith's life sets the tone for Sandra Gwyn's account of life in official Ottawa, *The Private Capital: Ambition and Love in the Age of Macdonald and Laurier* (Toronto: McClelland and Stewart, 1985).
14. *St. John Daily News*, 24 Feb. 1876.
15. Dufferin, 221.
16. *Toronto Globe*, 24 Feb. 1876.
17. *Ottawa Free Press*, 7 Feb. 1876.
18. *Ottawa Free Press*, 5 Feb., 23 Feb. 1876.
19. Meredith diary, 24 Feb. 1876.
20. *Canadian Illustrated News*, 18 Mar. 1876.
21. Holt, *Gentlemen's Fancy Dress*, 4.
22. Dufferin, 223.
23. *Ottawa Daily Citizen*, 24 Feb. 1876.

24. *Ottawa Free Press*, 23 Feb. 1876; *Ottawa Evening Journal*, 14 Nov. 1931.

25. *Montreal Star*, 25 Feb. 1876; *The Nation*, 3 Mar. 1876.

26. *Ottawa Times*, 24 Feb. 1876; *Toronto Daily Mail*, 24 Feb. 1876.

27. Nicolson, 155; *Ottawa Free Press*, 24 Feb. 1876.

28. Meredith diary, 24 Feb. 1876; *Canadian Home Journal*, 25 Feb. 1876.

29. *Ottawa Free Press*, 24 Feb. 1876; Dufferin, 223; *New York Daily Graphic*, 4 Mar. 1876.

30. Leggo, *The History of the Administration of the Right Honourable Frederick Temple, Earl of Dufferin*, 429; *Canadian Illustrated News*, 18 Mar. 1876; *New York Daily Graphic*, 22 Feb. 1876.

31. *Ottawa Free Press*, 30 Dec. 1897; *Toronto World*, 29 Dec. 1897.

CHAPTER 3

The story of this ball is taken from the souvenir album, *Illustrations of the Historical Ball Given by Their Excellencies the Earl and Countess of Aberdeen: Ottawa, 1896*, introduced by Sir John George Bourinot (Ottawa: Durie, 1896), as well as the extensive accounts which appeared in the *Ottawa Daily Citizen*, *Ottawa Evening Journal*, *Ottawa Free Press*, *Toronto Globe*, *Toronto Mail and Empire*, *Toronto World*, *Montreal Herald* and *Montreal Star* on the day following the ball, 18 Feb. 1896. Editorials on the ball's educational effects appeared on 17 Feb. in the *Ottawa Daily Citizen* and the *Ottawa Free Press*, on 18 Feb. in the *Free Press* and the *Ottawa Evening Journal*, and on 19 Feb. in the *Toronto Globe*, the *Montreal Herald*, and the French paper *La Presse*. *The Lounger*, a short-lived Ottawa magazine, published an article and photographs in its first issue, July 1896, and the *Canadian Home Journal*, whose editor, Faith Fenton, attended the ball, carried an illustrated story in March 1896.

Lady Aberdeen's journal, both the published version, *The Canadian Journal of Lady Aberdeen, 1893-1898*, ed. John T. Saywell (Toronto: Champlain Society, 1960) and the manuscript in the National Archives of Canada, provide her perspective on the event; the manuscript contains material which was edited out of the published version. The Aberdeens tell the story of their Canadian entertainments in their memoirs, *We Twa: Reminiscences of Lord and Lady Aberdeen*, 2 vols. (London: Collins, 1925). The Aberdeens' carefully kept scrapbooks of press clippings, held by the National Archives of Canada, bring together a great deal of press coverage. All three Ottawa papers published advertising for the ball and mentions in social notes from early January through May of 1896.

Biographical information on the Aberdeens comes from Saywell's introduction to the published *Journal*; Doris French, *Ishbel and the Empire: A Biography of Lady Aberdeen* (Toronto: Dundurn, 1988); and Marjorie Pentland, *A Bonnie Fechter: The Life of Ishbel Marjoribanks, Marchioness of Aberdeen and Temair* (London: Batsford, 1952). Biographical information about ballgoers is drawn from two books by Henry Morgan: *Types of Canadian Women and Women Who Are or Have Been Connected with Canada* (Toronto: Briggs, 1903), and *The Canadian Men and Women of the Time: A Handbook of Canadian Biography* (Toronto: Briggs, 1898 and 1912). The *Ottawa City Directory, 1896-97* (Ottawa: Might Directory Company of Toronto, 1896; CIHM 46972) provides further information on Ottawa citizens and merchants.

Topley took some two hundred photographs, recorded all the names of sitters and dates in a log book, and pasted a print of each image taken into a sitter album, with the number of the glass negative recorded carefully underneath. The logbook, the album, and many of the negatives are held by the National Archives of Canada.

The extant costume worn to this ball consists primarily of items worn by those who came as Indians. Hayter Reed's shirt, headdress, and mocassins, his son's shirt and staff, the dresses worn by Miss Bloomfield and Miss Laura Smith, as well as a beaded bag worn by the latter are in the Ethnology collection of the McCord Museum of Canadian History. Prior to being identified through the photographs in this book, they were not known to have been worn as fancy dress. Pasquaw's garments, worn by Mr. Critchley, and a dress that may have been worn by Mrs. Atkinson are in the Ethnographic Collection of the University of Alberta. Mrs. McLeod Stewart's dress, remade from her 1876 costume, is in a private collection.

1. Bourinot, *Illustrations from the Historical Ball*, 7.

2. Saywell, Introduction to *The Canadian Journal of Lady Aberdeen 1893-1898*, xxxii.

3. Aberdeen, *Journal*, 5, 194.

4. Hilary O'Kelly, "Reconstructing Irishness: Dress in the Celtic Revival, 1880-1920," in *Chic Thrills: A Fashion Reader*, ed. Juliet Ash and Elizabeth Wilson (London: Pandora, 1992), 75-83.

5. Aberdeen, *Journal*, 94, 361; Pentland, *A Bonnie Fechter*, 125.

6. Aberdeen, *Journal*, 186.

7. Aberdeen, *Journal*, 446.

8. Aberdeen, *Journal*, 317.

9. Bourinot, 21.

10. Bourinot, 20.

11. *Montreal Herald*, 19 Feb. 1896.

12. Aberdeen, *Journal*, 318; *Ottawa Daily Citizen*, 15 Feb. 1896.

13. *Ottawa Evening Journal*, 25 Jan. 1896; *The Lounger*, July 1896.

14. *The Lounger*, July 1896.

15. Aberdeen, *Journal*, 8.

16. *Ottawa Free Press*, 18 Feb. 1896.

17. *Toronto Mail and Empire*, 18 Feb. 1896.

18. Aberdeen, *Journal*, 322.

19. *Canadian Home Journal*, Mar. 1896; Aberdeen, *Journal*, 322.

20. *Toronto Globe*, 19 Feb. 1896.

21. *Ottawa Evening Journal*, 18 Feb. 1896.

22. *Ottawa Daily Citizen*, 19 Feb. 1896.

23. *Ottawa Evening Journal*, 18 Feb. 1896; *Ottawa Free Press*, 18 Feb. 1896.

24. *Ottawa Free Press*, 18 Feb. 1896.

25. Aberdeen journal, 25 Feb. 1896.

26. *Ottawa Free Press*, 18 Feb. 1896.

27. Aberdeen, *Journal*, 336; House of Commons, *Debates*, 14 Apr. 1896, 6319-6325; *Ottawa Evening Journal*, 16 Apr. 1896.

28. Aberdeen journal, 22 Feb. 1896.

29. *The Lounger*, July 1896.

30. *Toronto Globe*, 19 Feb. 1896.

31. *Ottawa Free Press*, 18 Feb. 1896.

32. *Montreal Star*, 14 Mar. 1896

33. *Ottawa Evening Journal*, 14 Mar. 1896.

34. Aberdeen journal, 22 Feb. 1896.

35. *Toronto World*, 18 Feb.1896

36. *Toronto Globe*, 19 Feb. 1896.

37. *La Presse* (Montreal), 19 Feb. 1896, my translation.

38. *Toronto Sunday World*, 23 Feb. 1896; *Ottawa Evening Journal*, 18

CHAPTER 4

Book of the Victorian Era Ball Given at Toronto On the Twenty Eighth of December MDCCCXCVII (Toronto: Rowsell and Hutchins, 1898) is one of the principal sources of information about guests and their characters. Further information comes from accounts in the *Toronto Globe*, *Toronto Mail and Empire*, *Toronto News*, *Toronto Star*, *Toronto Telegram*, *Toronto World*, *Ottawa Evening Journal*, and *Montreal Star* on 29 Dec. 1897, and in *Saturday Night* on 1 Jan. 1898. The *Globe*, the *Mail and Empire*, and *Saturday Night* all began mentioning the event in late November and continued to discuss it well into January 1898.

The Aberdeens' journals, memoirs and press scrapbooks provide information on their own perceptions of the event; the diary of Elizabeth Cawthra, in the Baldwin Room of the Metropolitan Toronto Reference Library, also chronicles the preparations. The James Mavor papers in the Fisher Library at the University of Toronto contain correspondence concerning the souvenir book.

Biographical information on the guests was taken from the same sources listed for Chapter 3. The *Toronto City Directory for 1897* (Toronto: R.L. Polk, 1897; CIHM A01091) gives further information on those who attended and provided services for the ball.

Photographs of this event proved difficult to find. In Ottawa, Topley photographed the Aberdeens, Lady Marjorie Gordon as "Forests of Canada," David Erskine as "A Lumberman," and Agar Adamson as "Napoleon." The Harvesting Set's photograph was published in the Aberdeen memoirs, *We Twa*. Mary Fitzgibbon and Minnie Forsyth Grant's pictures were published in Henry Morgan's *Types of Canadian Women*. Mabel Cawthra's photograph was found in the Cawthra papers. The Yachting Set's picture was located in the Archives of the Royal Canadian Yacht Club. The sources for the other photographs are given with the captions.

Very few costumes have been found. Four items are in the Royal Ontario Museum: Minnie Forsyth Grant's red heirloom dress, a herald's costume worn by a member of the Walker family in the Aesthetic Dress Set, and an eighteenth-century dress worn by Elizabeth Baldwin are in the costume collection; Edmund Morris's beaded and fur-trimmed red wool shirt, his leggings, and all his accessories worn as "A Cree Chief" are in the ethnology collection.

1. *Toronto World*, 29 Dec, 1987.

2. Aberdeen, *Journal*, 409.

3. Aberdeen, *Journal*, 441.

4. Aberdeen, *Journal*, 441.

5. Elizabeth Cawthra diary, 13 Nov. 1987, Cawthra Papers; Aberdeen, *Journal*, 446.

6. *Book of the Victorian Era Ball*, vi.

7. *Book of the Victorian Era Ball*, vi.

8. Aberdeen, *Journal*, 447.

9. *Toronto Star*, 29 Dec. 1897.

10. *Toronto News*, 29 Dec. 1897.

11. Aberdeen, *Journal*, 442, 448.

12. Holt, 1896, 36.

13. Angus Wilson, *The Strange Ride of Rudyard Kipling: His Life and Works*, (London: Sinclair and Warburg, 1977), 253-254; House of Commons, *Debates*, 30 April 1897, 1546-1550.

14. Letter from Captain Tharp to Elizabeth Cawthra, n.d., Cawthra Papers.

15. *Toronto Globe*, 29 Dec. 1897.

16. *Toronto Mail and Empire*, 29 Dec. 1897; Stephen Bayley, *The Albert Memorial: The Monument in Its Social and Architectural Context* (London: Scolar, 1981), 55, 103, 107.

17. *Toronto Mail and Empire*, 29 Dec. 1897; Aberdeen, *Journal*, 449.

18. Aberdeen, *Journal*, 449.

19. Holt, *Fancy Dresses Described*, 5th ed., 81; 6th ed., 270; *Toronto News*, 29 Dec. 1897.

20. *Toronto Globe*, 29 Dec. 1897.

21. *Saturday Night*, 1 Jan. 1898; *Toronto Mail and Empire*, 29 Dec. 1897.

22. *Saturday Night*, 1 Jan. 1898.

23. Aberdeen, *Journal*, 449.

24. *Toronto Globe*, 28 May 1898.

25. Stephen A. Heward, *For My Children* (Toronto: n.p., 1946), 10-11.

26. Cawthra diary, 29 Dec. 1897, Cawthra Papers; Anthony Adamson, *Wasps in the Attic* (Toronto: privately printed, 1987), 141-146.

27. *Toronto World*, 2 Jan. 1898.

28. *Toronto Globe*, 29 Dec. 1897.

29. *Toronto Globe*, 29 Dec. 1897; *Toronto Sunday World*, 2 Jan. 1898.

30. *Saturday Night*, 11 Dec. 1897; *Toronto Globe*, 16 Dec. 1897.

31. *Toronto World*, 2 Jan. 1898.

32. *Saturday Night*, 1, 8 Jan., 12 Feb. 1898.

33. Aberdeen, *Journal*, 408.

34. Aberdeen journal, 24 Nov. 1897; *Toronto Star*, 27 Dec. 1897.

35. *Montreal Star*, 29 Dec. 1897.

36. *Toronto Globe*, 29 Dec. 1897.

37. *Book of the Ball*, v.

38. *Book of the Ball*, iii; Parkin to Mavor, 20 Jan. 1898, Mavor Papers.

39. *Book of the Ball*, 52.

40. Aberdeen, *Journal*, 450.

CHAPTER 5

The Archives of the Women's Branch at the Château Ramezay Museum provides newspaper clippings, notices and invitations, and minutes of meetings concerning the ball. Accounts of the event were published in the *Montreal Gazette*, *Montreal Herald*, *La Patrie*, *La Presse*, *Montreal Star*, *Montreal Witness* and *Toronto Globe* on 19 Jan. 1898. The *Canadian Antiquarian and Numismatic Journal* (Montreal: Alphonse R. Pelletier, 1898) also carried an account of the event. Shorter accounts were published in the *Toronto Mail and Empire* and *Saturday Night*. The Montreal papers began discussing the ball in late December 1897.

The Aberdeen press scrapbooks contain some material about the ball; however, the journals do not mention it. Biographical information on the ballgoers comes from the same sources as for the previous two chapters. *Lovell's Montreal Directory for 1897-98* (Montreal: Lovell, 1898. CIHM 37072) contains information on dressmakers and merchants.

The Notman studio in Montreal recorded this event with some two hundred images pasted into a sitter album, which can now be viewed on microfilm at the McCord Museum of Canadian History. Most of the glass negatives are intact. Two albums, one made by Notman himself and another put together by an organizer, Marguerite Thibaudeau, are in the collection of the Château Ramezay Museum. The Robert Harris painting of John Try-Davies belongs to the collection of the Montreal General Hospital.

This is the ball for which the most costumes have been located. Lady Van Horne and Mary Van Horne's dresses at the McCord Museum of Canadian History had always been identified as fancy dress. Maud Terroux's and Miss Barnard's heirloom dresses had not previously been known to have had this use and were identified by means of their photographs. A photograph of the dress worn by Miss Barnard can be found in Jacqueline Beaudoin-Ross, *Form and Fashion* (McCord Museum of Canadian History, 1992), 19. Part of the mystery behind Colin Campbell's garment was solved when it was matched to his fancy dress photograph. At the Château Ramezay, two more costumes were located, although the individuals wearing them did not stand out at the ball. Dr. Herbert Birkett's costume is in the collection of the Marsil Museum. The story of the assemblage of items worn by Norman Leslie is told in Bernard Pothier and Roderick Grant, *The Leslie Collection*, National Museum of Man Mercury Series, Canadian War Museum No. 5 (Ottawa: National Museums of Canada, 1975). The cap can be viewed at the Canadian War Museum in Ottawa, while the rest of the costume belongs to Fort Henry, Kingston.

1. *Montreal Herald*, 19 Jan. 1898.

2. *Women of Canada*, 395.

3. Letter, 21 Dec. 1896, Ladies' Branch Papers.

4. Invitation, Ladies' Branch Papers.

5. *Montreal Star*, 21 Dec. 1897.

6. *Montreal Gazette*, *Montreal Herald*, 19 Jan. 1898.

7. *Ottawa Free Press*, *Montreal Witness*, 19 Jan. 1898.

8. *Montreal Herald*, 19 Jan. 1898.

9. *Montreal Herald*, 19 Jan. 1898.

10. *La Patrie*, 24 Jan. 1898, my translation; Aberdeen, *Journal*, 329.

11. *La Patrie*, 19 Jan. 1898.

12. *Montreal Herald*, 19 Jan. 1898.

13. *Montreal Herald*, *Montreal Star*, 19 Jan. 1898; Bernard Pothier and Roderick Grant, *The Leslie Collection*, National Museum of Man Mercury Series, Canadian War Museum No. 5 (Ottawa: National Museums of Canada, 1975).

14. *Montreal Star*, 8 Jan. 1898.

15. *Toronto Sunday World*, 2 Jan. 1898.

16. *Montreal Herald*, 19 Jan. 1898.

17. *Toronto Globe*, 19 Jan. 1898.

18. *Montreal Gazette*, 19 Jan. 1898.

19. *Saturday Night*, 22 Jan. 1898.

20. *Montreal Herald*, 6 Jan. 1898.

21. *Montreal Herald*, 8 Jan. 1898.

22. *Montreal Star, Toronto Globe*, 19 Jan. 1898.

23. *Montreal Gazette, Montreal Herald*, 19 Jan. 1898; *Montreal Star*, 22 Feb. 1898.

24. *La Presse*, 17 Jan. 1898, my translation.

25. Aberdeen, *Journal*, 478; Aberdeen, *We Twa*, vol. II, 137.

26. Lady Minto, in Countess of Oxford and Asquith, *Myself When Young by Famous Women of Today* (London, 1938), 234; Minto to Arthur Elliot, 25 Dec. 1898, Minto Papers, National Archives of Canada.

27. Grey to Laurier, 19 Dec. 1906, Grey Papers, National Archives of Canada, quoted in Hubbard, *Rideau Hall*, 119.

28. Ethel Chadwick diary, Chadwick Papers, National Archives of Canada, quoted in Sandra Gwyn, *Tapestry of War* (Toronto: Harper Collins, 1992), 31.

29. Quoted in Jacques Mathieu, *Plains of Abraham: The Search for the Ideal* (Quebec: Éditions du Septentrion, 1993), 247, 256.

Bibliography

Aberdeen, Countess of (Ishbel Maria Marjoribanks Gordon). *The Canadian Journal of Lady Aberdeen 1893-1898*. ed. John T. Saywell. Toronto: Champlain Society, 1960.

Aberdeen & Temair, Marquis and Marchioness of. *We Twa: Reminiscences of Lord and Lady Aberdeen*. 2 vols. London: Collins Sons, 1925.

Antiquarian and Numismatic Society of Montreal, Women's Branch. *Château Ramezay*. Montreal, 1984.

Aria, Mrs., comp. *Costume: Fanciful, Historical, and Theatrical*. London: Macmillan, 1906.

Bara, Jana. "Photography Personified." *History of Photography*, 13:3 (1989), 241.

Batt, Elizabeth. *Monck: Governor General, 1861-1868, A Biography*. Toronto: McClelland and Stewart, 1976.

Beaudoin-Ross, Jacqueline. *Form and Fashion: Nineteenth-Century Montreal Dress*. Montreal: McCord Museum of Canadian History, 1992.

Berger, Carl. *The Sense of Power: Studies in the Ideas of Canadian Imperialism 1867-1914*. Toronto: University of Toronto Press, 1971.

Book of the Victorian Era Ball Given at Toronto On the Twenty Eighth of December MDCCCXCVII. Toronto: Rowsell and Hutchins, 1898.

Buchan, John. *Lord Minto: A Memoir*. London: Nelson, 1924.

Careless, J.M.S. *The History of Canadian Cities: Toronto to 1918*. Toronto: National Museum of Man, 1984.

Carrel, Frank and Louis Feiczwiez, eds. *The Quebec Tercentenary Commemorative History*. Quebec: Daily Telegraph, 1908.

Churchill, Allen. *The Splendor Seekers*. New York: Grosset and Dunlap, 1974.

__________. *The Upper Crust*. Englewood Cliffs NJ: Prentice Hall, 1970.

Collard, Edgar Andrew. *Montreal Yesterdays*. Toronto: Longmans Canada, 1962.

Collins, Joseph Edmund. *Canada Under the Administration of Lord Lorne*. Toronto: Rose, 1884.

Cooper, Cynthia. "Toronto's Victorian Era Ball: Fancy Dress for the Diamond Jubilee." In *Victorian: The Style of Empire*. Ed. Howard Creel Collinson, 121-140. Toronto: Decorative Arts Institute, 1996.

Cooper, Cynthia, and Linda Welters. "Brilliant and Instructive Spectacles: Canada's Fancy Dress Balls, 1976-1898," *Dress* 22 (1995), 3-21.

Cowan, John. *Canada's Governors General, 1867-1952*. Toronto: York, 1952.

Crozier, Gladys Beattie. "The Art of Choosing Fancy Dress." *Everywoman's Encyclopedia*. U.K.: n.p., [1906-1912].

Davidoff, Leonore. *The Best Circles: Society, Etiquette, and the Season*. London: Croom Helm, 1973.

deMarly, Diana. *Worth: Father of Haute Couture.* New York: Holmes and Meier, 1990.

Downie, Jill. *A Passionate Pen: The Life and Times of Faith Fenton*. Toronto: HarperCollins, 1996.

Dufferin & Ava, Marchioness of. *My Canadian Journal 1872-1878*. 1891. Reprint, Toronto: Coles, 1971.

__________. *Our Viceregal Life in India: Selections from My Journal, 1884-1888*. 2 vols. London: John Murray, 1890.

Edgar, J.D. *Canada and Its Capital*. Toronto: Morang, 1898.

Finkel, Alicia. "*Le Bal Costumé*: History and Spectacle in the Court of Queen Victoria." *Dress* 10 (1984): 64-72.

Fowler, Marian. *The Embroidered Tent: Five Gentlewomen in Early Canada*. Toronto: Anansi, 1982.

__________. *In a Gilded Cage: From Heiress to Duchess*. Toronto: Vintage, 1994.

Fox, Celina, and Aileen Ribeiro. *Masquerade*. London: Museum of London, 1983.

Francis, Daniel. *The Imaginary Indian: The Image of the Indian in Canadian Culture*. Vancouver: Arsenal Pulp, 1992.

French, Doris. *Ishbel and the Empire: A Biography of Lady Aberdeen*. Toronto: Dundurn, 1988.

Gordon, Beverly. "Dress and Dress-up at the Fundraising Fair." *Dress* 12 (1986): 61-72.

__________. "The Ninteenth Century Looks Back: Costuming the Colonial Past." In *Dress and American Culture*. Ed. Patricia A. Cunningham and Susan Voso-Lab, 109-139. Bowling Green: Bowling Green Popular Press, 1993.

Gwyn, Sandra. *The Private Capital: Ambition and Love in the Age of Macdonald and Laurier*. Toronto: McClelland and Stewart, 1985.

Halttunen, Karen. *Confidence Men and Painted Women: A Study of Middle Class Culture in America, 1830-1870*. New Haven: Yale University Press, 1982.

Hollander, Anne. *Seeing Through Clothes*. New York: Avon, 1975.

Holt, Ardern. *Fancy Dresses Described, or What to Wear at Fancy Balls*. 5th ed. London: Debenham and Freebody, 1887. 6th ed., 1896.

__________. *Gentlemen's Fancy Dress*. London: Wyman, 1882.

Hubbard, R.H. *Rideau Hall: An Illustrated History of Government House, Ottawa*. Ottawa: Queen's Printer, 1967.

__________. "Viceregal Influences on Canadian Society." In *The Shield of Achilles: Aspects of Canada in the Victorian Age*. Ed. W.L. Morton, 256-274. Toronto: McClelland and Stewart, 1968.

Illustrations of the Historical Ball Given by Their Excellencies the Earl and Countess of Aberdeen - Ottawa, 1896. With Introduction by Sir John George Bourinot. Ottawa: Durie, 1896.

Jarvis, Anthea. "'There was a young man from Bengal . . .': The Vogue for Fancy Dress, 1830-1950." *Costume* 16 (1982): 33-46.

Jarvis, Anthea, and Patricia Raine. *Fancy Dress*. Aylesbury: Shire, 1984.

Joseph, Nathan. "Costumes." In *Uniforms and Nonuniforms: Communication Through Clothing*. 183-202. New York: Greenwood, 1986.

Juleus, Nels. "Lady Dufferin's Amateur Theatricals," *Canadian Drama* 11:1 (1985): 245-250.

Kiewet, C.W. and F.H. Underhill, eds. *Dufferin-Carnarvon Correspondence, 1874-1878*. Toronto: Champlain Society, 1955.

Laver, James. *Memorable Balls*. London: Derkek Verschoyle, 1954.

Leggo, William. *The History of the Administration of the Right Honourable Frederick Temple, Earl of Dufferin*. Montreal: Lovell, 1878.

Lyall, Sir Alfred. *The Life of the Marquis of Dufferin and Ava*. London: John Murray, 1905.

MacKay, Donald. *The Square Mile: Merchant Princes of Montreal*. Vancouver: Douglas and McIntyre, 1987.

MacNutt, W. Stewart. *Days of Lorne*. Fredericton: Brunswick, 1955.

Male Character Costumes: A Guide to Gentlemen's Costume. 2d ed. London: Samuel Miller, [1895].

Martyn, Lucy Booth. *The Face of Early Toronto*. Toronto: Paget, 1982.

Masquerade and Carnival: Their Customs and Costumes. n.p., Butterick, [1897].

Mathieu, Jacques, and Eugen Kedl. *The Plains of Abraham: The Search for the Ideal*. Trans., Kathë Roth. Quebec: Éditions du Septentrion, 1993.

Maynard, Margaret. "'A Dream of Fair Women': Revival Dress and the Formation of Late Victorian Images of Femininity." *Art History* 12.3 (Sept. 1989): 322-341.

Meredith, Alden G. *Mary's Rosedale, or Gossip of Little York*. Ottawa: Graphic, 1928.

Morgan, Henry James, ed. *The Canadian Men and Women of the Time: A Handbook of Canadian Biography*. Toronto: Briggs, 1898. 2nd ed. 1912.

__________. *Types of Canadian Women and Women Who Are or Have Been Connected with Canada*. Toronto: Briggs, 1903.

Morton, W.L., ed. *Monck Letters and Journals, 1863-1868*. Toronto: McClelland and Stewart, 1971.

__________. "Victorian Canada." In *The Shield of Achilles: Aspects of Canada in the Victorian Age*. Ed. W.L. Morton, 311-334. Toronto: McClelland and Stewart, 1968.

Moyles, R.G., and Doug Owram. *Imperial Dreams and Colonial Realities: British Views of Canada 1880-1914*. Toronto: University of Toronto Press, 1988.

Murphy, Sophia. *The Duchess of Devonshire's Ball*. London: Sidgwick and Jackson, 1984.

Nathan, Archie. *Costumes by Nathan*. London: Newnes, 1960.

Nicolson, Harold. *Helen's Tower*. London: Constable, 1937.

Noonan, James. "Theatre and Spectacle under the Aberdeens." *Canadian Drama*. 16.2 (1990): 147-172.

O'Kelly, Hilary. "Recontructing Irishness: Dress in the Celtic Revival, 1880-1920." In *Chic Thrills: A Fashion Reader*. Ed. Juliet Ash and Elizabeth Wilson, 75-83. London: Pandora, 1992.

O'Leary, Thomas. *Château de Ramezay Museum and Portrait Gallery Catalogue*. Montreal: n.p., 1907.

Pentland, Marjorie. *A Bonnie Fechter: The Life of Ishbel Marjoribanks, Marchioness of Aberdeen and Temair*. London: Batsford, 1952.

Pothier, Bernard, and Roderick Grant. *The Leslie Collection*. National Museum of Man Mercury Series, Canadian War Museum No. 5. Ottawa: National Museums of Canada, 1975.

Rieger, Jennifer and Mary Williamson. *Toronto Dancing Then and Now*. Toronto: Metropolitan Toronto Reference Library, 1995.

Rose, George Maclean, ed. *Representative Canadians: A Cyclopaedia of Canadian Biography*. Toronto: Rose, 1888.

Rowat, Teresa. *Aperçu: Dressing Up*. Ottawa: National Archives of Canada, 1986.

Rudyard Kipling's Verse: Definitive Edition. 1940. Reprint, London: Hodder and Stoughton, 1960.

Rutherford, Paul. *A Victorian Authority: The Daily Press in Late Nineteenth-Century Canada*. Toronto: University of Toronto Press, 1982.

Stasz, Clarice. *The Vanderbilt Women: Dynasty of Wealth, Glamour and Tragedy*. New York: St. Martin's, 1991.

Steele, Valerie. *Fashion and Eroticism: Ideals of Feminine Beauty from the Victorian Era to the Jazz Age*. New York: Oxford University Press, 1985.

Stevenson, Sara and Helen Bennet. *Van Dyck in Check Trousers: Fancy Dress in Art and Life, 1700-1900*. Scotland: Scottish National Portrait Gallery, 1978.

Stewart, George, Jr. *Canada Under the Administration of the Earl of Dufferin*. Toronto: Rose-Belford, 1878.

Sutherland, Fraser. *The Monthly Epic: A History of Canadian Magazines, 1789-1989*. Markham: Fitzhenry and Whiteside, 1989.

Travestissements. 3 vols. Paris: Abel Goubaud, [1880-1890].

Triggs, Stanley. *William Notman: The Stamp of a Studio*. Toronto: Art Gallery of Ontario, 1985.

__________. *The Composite Photographs of William Notman*. Montreal: McCord Museum of Canadian History, 1994.

Waite, Peter B. *Canada, 1874-1896: Arduous Destiny*. Toronto: McClelland and Stewart, 1971.

Wason, Janet. "The Victorian Era Ball and Its Role in Toronto Society," *Canadian Dance Studies* 1 (1994), 27-42.

Wecter, Dixon. *The Saga of American Society: A Record of Social Aspiration, 1607-1937*. New York: Scribners, 1937.

Weldon's Limited. *Weldon's Fancy Dress for Ladies*. First Series and Second Series. London: Weldon's, [1895-1900].

Westley, Margaret. *Remembrance of Grandeur: The Anglo-Protestant Elite of Montreal*. Montreal: Libre Expression, 1990.

Women of Canada: Their Life and Work. Comp. National Council of Women, for distribution at the Paris International Exhibition. n.p. 1900. Reprint, n.p., 1975.

Worth, Jean-Philippe. *A Century of Fashion*. Trans. Ruth Scott Miller. Boston: Little Brown, 1928.

Index

C

N

O

P

Y

This publication was designed and typeset by Julie Scriver
of Goose Lane Editions in Fredericton.
Printing and binding furnished by Tri-Graphic Printing of Ottawa.

The text face is Venetian 301 issued in
digital format by Adobe Systems.
The paper is 200M Jenson Satin.

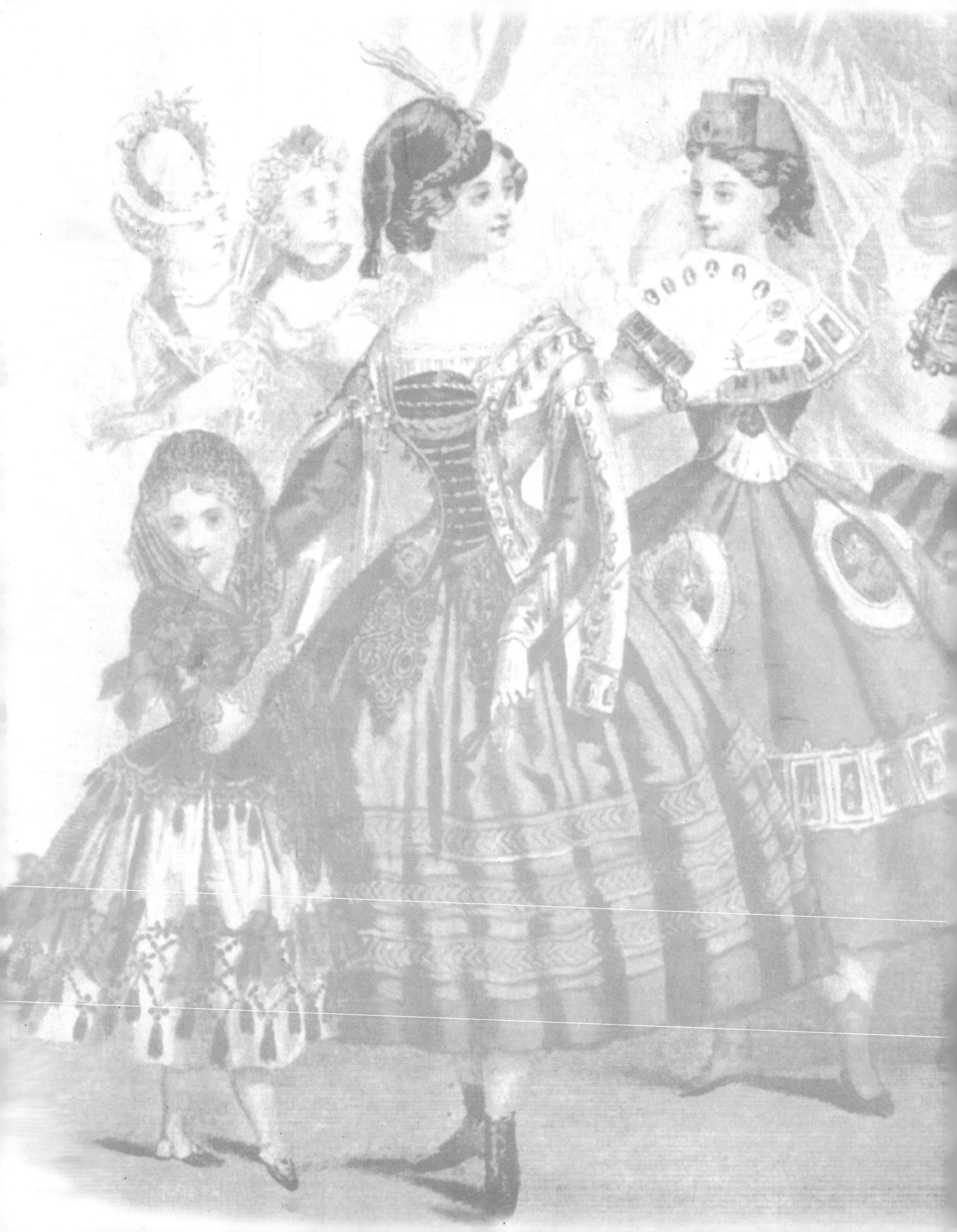